Herbs

Herbs

An Illustrated Encyclopedia

A Complete Culinary, Cosmetic, Medicinal, and Ornamental Guide

Kathi Keville

Illustrations by Roman Szolkowski

Friedman/Fairfax

PUBLISHERS

A special thanks to Sal Gilbertie, The Wells Sweep Herb Farm,
and Gardens of the Blue Ridge.

A FRIEDMAN/FAIRFAX BOOK

© 1994 by Michael Friedman Publishing Group, Inc.

ISBN 1-56799-065-7

Editor: Sharyn Rosart
Art Director: Jeff Batzli
Photography Editor: Christopher C. Bain
Production Director: Karen Matsu Greenberg

Typeset by Classic Type, Inc.
Printed and bound in China by Leefung-Asco Printers Ltd.

For bulk purchases and special sales, please contact:
Friedman/Fairfax Publishers
15 West 26 Street
New York, NY 10010
212/685-6610 FAX 212/685-1307

DEDICATION

This herbal encyclopedia is dedicated to herbalists—
those known and unknown—who have bequeathed
their knowledge to us, and to my herbal friends and
colleagues who have been responsible for a renaissance
of herbalism in the twentieth century, and especially to
those beginning to study hers: may you carry on the
tradition to future generations.

ACKNOWLEDGMENTS

Thank you Christopher Hobbs, David Winston, and Dr. James Duke, who
read selected parts of the manuscript, and also to Christopher for letting me
loose in his wonderful library. Thanks, too, Robert Brucia (and his library),
who helped fill in many gaps of information and kept me laughing
at the same time. Thank you David Hoffmann for information, advice, and
especially for reminding me to breathe. Thank you Joan DeFato for your
assistance in the Los Angeles Arboretum Library.

Thank you Mark and Margie Wheeler, Louis and Virginia Saso, Steven
Foster, and Tim Blakely for adding your experience in cultivating herbs, and
for your encouragement. And thanks to all my herbalist friends—a part of
each one of you makes up this book.

A special thank you to Ron Bertolucci for the emotional support that sus-
tained my spirit through long hours of research and writing, and for making
all those delicious dinners while I kept working. Thank you Dr. Joel Alter for
caring about my health, and about me. Thank you Marian Wyckoff for many
wonderful neck rubs and for your enthusiasm.

My very sincere appreciation to editors Sharyn Rosart and Al Moak, and
to designer Jeff Batzli for their patience, thoughtfulness, and direction and for
all of their extra work in producing this encyclopedia. A warm thank you
to Roman Szolkowski for capturing the soul of the plants in his beautiful
paintings.

And finally, thank you God for this wonderful earth with its multitude of
useful plants. May we help to sustain it for future generations.

TABLE OF CONTENTS

THE HERBS
21

INTRODUCTION

My fascination with herbs began in my own herb garden. I was intrigued by the multitude of colors, shapes, and fragrances they offered. Each time I would begin reading about one herb, yet another one would catch my eye and I would try to acquire the plant for my garden. They slowly took over realms previously claimed by vegetables until over fifty different herbs were in residence. Herbs began enhancing every culinary creation that came from my kitchen, and curiosity about other ways to use them even led me to learn how to make herbal cosmetics and natural dyes. Soon my kitchen was filled with jars and bottles of herbal concoctions and bunches of hanging herbs. I began to read of their colorful and lively history. Then one day I got sick. Nothing major or dramatic—just a flu with a fever that sent me to bed. I realized an entire herbal pharmacy was planted outside my door, and I indulged in some bitter-tasting brews. The herbs effectively eased my symptoms—indeed, they worked so well I could hardly believe it. Encouraged by these first results, I continued the experiments on both family and pets. That was over twenty years ago, and I haven't been to a doctor for a minor illness yet.

That first herb garden was only a small one, which necessitated much pruning back to make room enough for people as well. I was constantly experimenting with all the trimmings I felt obliged to use. I dreamed of a garden large enough to let the herbs ramble, and my dreams eventually culminated in an acre-and-a-half (.6 hectare) garden filled with five hundred different herbs.

The garden itself has been my best source of herb knowledge. It taught me more than I can express in words. Perhaps some credit goes to the borage, an herb described by the sixteenth-century herbalist Gerard as being "for the comfort of the heart" and to "make the mind glad." Perhaps the fragrance of lavender helped, since as the study of aromatherapy tells us, it raises one's spirits. All I know is that the herbs in my garden have fostered within me an appreciation for the beauty of nature and for their creator. With the incredible diversity of herbs in this world, it can be no accident that anywhere we go in the world we are provided with a complete botanical pharmacy. Years ago I found a garden sign that now sits among the flowering thymes. It reads: One Is Closer to God in the Garden than Anywhere Else in the World.

The encyclopedia in your hands is designed to lead you down an herbal garden path. It is a potpourri of herbal history, science, and practical use. These are my favorite herbs to grow and use. Some were chosen because they have an incredible fragrance; others have flowers or leaves that transform the garden with their patterns and colors; and many are included because of their special tastes or medicinal qualities. I hope that as you read you will be encouraged to plant your own herb garden and to discover the delights it will unfold to you. May you find such an avocation fulfilling, interesting, and, most of all, fun.

CHAPTER 1

THE HISTORY OF HERBS

North Wind Picture Archives

We can't be sure what early experimenter first chewed a medicinal leaf and applied the soothing pulp to a wound. Nor do we know who first added some tasty herb seeds to enhance the flavor of dinner, or who discovered that certain plants can color cloth, perfume the air, and even improve the complexion. What we can assume is that herbs have been a part of civilization since our ancestors first walked the earth. For thousands of years, herbs have filled medicine bags, cosmetic bowls, culinary spice jars, perfume vials, and dye pots.

Since very early times, the healing arts, and with them medicinal herbs, were considered a gift from the gods. Herbal healing usually involved purification rites and prayer. In most early cultures throughout the world, it was the priests and priestesses, the shamans, and the wise women who knew how to use medicinal plants. These ancient herbalists built the foundations of herbal history and passed on their knowledge through song, chant, and story. Their wisdom still fills modern herb books today. Although we have no records of the earliest herbal musings, a Sumerian tablet from around 2500 B.C. lists the popular herbs of the era. We have it today because someone thoughtfully made a copy in the seventh century B.C. Legend relates that Emperor Shen Nung, who the Chinese say was the first to discover medicinal herbs and to till the soil, composed the *Pen-ts'ao Ching,* or *The Classic Herbal,* around 2700 B.C. Modern scholars think this text dealing with over one hundred

herbs was actually transcribed in the first century A.D., but was based on information from a much earlier tradition. Around this time, China's "Yellow Emperor" is said to have composed the medicinal text the *Nei-Ching.* Written accounts of herbal lore from the third and fourth centuries B.C. contain Indian and Persian influences. Most of the Egyptian remedies recorded in the *Ebers Papyrus* around 1550 B.C. are herbal. The sacred Hindu book *Rig Veda,* which dates from around 1000 B.C., also includes medicinal herbs.

Early in history, herbs and spices played an important role in establishing trade routes. In 1485 B.C., Egypt's Queen Hatshepsut sent sailing vessels along the Nile River to collect East African myrrh trees for a garden terrace. Trade throughout Arabia, Egypt, and the entire Middle East advanced greatly around 1000 B.C. when the donkey was replaced by the camel, which could carry as much as 500 pounds (225 kg). For centuries, the Arabs maintained a monopoly on the treasured Oriental spices through cunning and by telling bizarre tales of dangerous animals. An "incense route" was established between south Arabia and the markets of Syria and Egypt, and it was later followed by the "amber route" from the Black Sea to the Baltic Sea.

King Merodach-baladan II of Babylonia (721–710 B.C.) wrote perhaps the world's first treatise about horticulture, which included

The herb garden and storeroom of the 16th century.

details on cultivating coriander, garlic, thyme, and other herbs. Tablets from the library of King Ashurbanipal, who ruled Assyria between 668 and 626 B.C., describe 250 herbs, including anise, cumin, coriander, dill, and thyme. We can assume that many of these were grown in his royal gardens.

Aesculapias, a healer who lived in Greece probably around 1250 B.C., did not leave an herbal but did leave a reputation that eventually won him a position in the Greek pantheon of Gods. Both Aesculapias and the deity Thoth of Egypt (who was believed to preside over herbal prescriptions) were portrayed holding a staff with a snake entwined. The caduceus remains the symbol of modern medicine. The great Greek healer Hippocrates (460–377 B.C.), who christened his school on the Greek Isle of Cos "The Aesculapian," was heavily influenced by Egyptian as well as Greek medicine. Theophrastus of Eresus (circa 372–286 B.C.), wrote two treatises, *Historia Plantarum* and *De Causis Plantarum,* or *Inquiry into Plants* and *Growth of Plants,* listing around five hundred medicinal herbs based upon his travels and upon the writings and the extensive medicinal herb garden of his teacher, the philosopher Aristotle. The fourth-century B.C. Alexandrian school of medicine drew many foreign scholars, who contributed even more to herbal knowledge in Greece.

Meanwhile, in India, *mushkakadigana,* or herbal medicine, was included in the medical writings of India's Susruta the Older (circa fourth century B.C.), Charaka (first century A.D.), and Susruta (second century A.D.). Around the same time, trade on the "silk route" (which was also a spice route) began between China and the Mediterranean countries through Kashgar (now Shufu, in western China) and the Pamir Mountains to Seleucia (now Iraq) and then to the Mediterranean. Rome was also active in trade with India, as evidenced in the recipes of Apicius, a first-century Roman gourmet who spent his fortune on exotic foods. His ten cookbooks were compiled several centuries later into *De Re Coquinaria.* The best known of a number of Greek herbals was written by Dioscorides, a physician for the Roman army in the first century A.D. His travels helped him incorporate knowledge about six hundred herbs into what became the primary European text for fifteen hundred years. It was also translated in the great cultural centers of Baghdad, Damascus, and Cairo.

The fall of the Greek and Roman empires led to the Dark Ages in Europe (the period from about A.D. 641—the fall of the city of Alexandria—to the twelfth century). Herbal knowledge was preserved in the kitchens, gardens, and fields of wise women and healers. These women, whose names are not recorded, passed their knowledge down from mother to daughter. They called herbs "simples" because they were so attainable and easy to use. Herbs were also grown and used within the cloistered walls of the monasteries. Charlemagne, king of the Franks, ordered anise, fennel, fenugreek, and other herbs planted in his imperial gardens in Germany in 812, and the monastery at St. Gall in Switzerland had sixteen herb beds in the year 830. The monks were also busy hand-copying the earlier texts. The earliest verbal traditions that conveyed herbal information were thus transcribed.

While Europe slept, the Muslims spread a wealth of medicinal knowledge into northern Africa and Spain. The prophet Mohammed (570–632) himself was once a spice merchant who led camel caravans. As his empire expanded, so did the use of spices for food and medicine and the sharing of knowledge. In 635, the Muslims captured Syria, Persia, and Basra, which was mentioned in the *Arabian Nights* as a thriving spice port trading with India, Arabia, Turkey, and Persia. Constantinople, located where Istanbul is today, was another thriving spice trade port from 330 until 1453. Avicenna (980–1037), who is said to have founded an Arabic medical school that incorporated Greek studies, wrote the *Canon Medicine.* Later translated into Latin, it became a standard European university textbook used into the seventeenth century. Large, cultivated herbal plantations of the *maharaji* of the East Indian archipelago are described in the tenth-century historian Ali al-Masudi's *Mead-*

King Ashurbanipal of Assyria and his queen dined on herbs from their royal gardens in the 6th century B.C. His famous library described 250 different herbs. (From a marble tablet.)

The beak-nosed Egyptian god Thoth was said to be responsible for recording herbal prescriptions.

Inside the walls of the monastery were the gardens that provided the monks with their food, medicine, and condiments.

ows of the Gold. The Persian Al-Samarqandi (d. 1222), who wrote an impressive herbal in the thirteenth century, was influenced by Indian, Babylonian, Arabic, and Greek herbal medicine.

China, too, was going through its own dark ages, at least in the fields of philosophy and medicine, from about 960 to 1120, but the Chinese did manage to invent a printing press during this period. This invention opened up a faster, far more efficient method of spreading information. The Chinese Li Shih Chen compiled the *Pen Ts'ao Kang Mu* in 1596. It documented the use of two thousand natural drugs and included eight hundred prescriptions.

Greek medicine, supplemented with Arabic thought, was finally revived by eleventh- and twelfth-century European scholars who translated texts from Arabic into French and then into Latin, the universal scholastic language—although centuries of copying had begun to take its toll on accuracy. A few new texts were also written. Hildegard of Bingen (1098–1179), a Christian mystic from Germany, wrote *Physica*, a Latin herbal blending mysticism, visions, and practical experience. Many of her remedies are applied externally and work through the skin. Although well accepted at the time it was written, the work later fell into obscurity. While the monks were busy copying old texts, they became inspired to try their hand at making some of the Arabic syrups and elixirs. In the process, they came up with liqueurs, such as Chartreuse and Benedictine, which are still popular today.

Then, in the eleventh and twelfth centuries, Greek, Latin, Saracen, and Arabic cultures blended together at the *Schola Salernitana* in Salerno, Italy, which drew scholars from all over Europe. The Medical School of Salernum, Italy, has its origins in the ninth century. Its *Regimen Sanitatis Salernitanum* was considered the medical "Bible" for Western Europe for the next few centuries. The school itself was active well into the fifteenth century. The graduates, by the way, were crowned with bay leaf wreaths.

In 1492, Columbus, inspired by the high prices of spices and thinking he had found a back door to India, stumbled upon the New World, a new land filled with a repertoire of herbs. Cayenne and allspice were the first of many spices to be introduced to the Europeans. In 1545, the University of Padua, Italy, established the first "physic" garden for studying medicinal herbs since the days of Hippocrates. Other Italian and European schools followed suit, and the University at Pisa also prepared an herbarium of pressed plants. Botany and medicine began developing separately for the first time and finally became individual disciplines. Herbals, such as Hieronymus Tragus's *Kreuterbuch*, published in Germany in 1539, provided the first accurate herbal illustrations—which were presented for identification, not mere decoration. In 1554, Flemish physician R. Dodoens departed from the standard alphabetical listing to group herbs according to their properties in his *Cruydboek*. Although his next herbal, *Pemptades* (1583), is not well known today, fourteen years later it formed the basis of John Gerard's now famous *Herball, or Generall Historie of Plantes* (1597), for which Gerard failed to give Dodoens credit. Not that Gerard didn't know his stuff. Personal gardener to Lord Burleigh, he was probably the most famous herbalist in Elizabethan England. His London herb garden contained herbs from all over the world. The most valuable edition of his treatise was expanded by Thomas Johnson in 1633. Today, his herbal is quoted more than any other.

Seventeenth-century herbalists William Coles, who wrote *The Art of Simpling* (1656), and Nicholas Culpeper (1616–1654),

Monks spent hours in the scriptorium, carefully hand-copying books containing the descriptions and uses of hundreds of herbs.

A druggist in an apothecary of the Middle Ages prepares his herbal remedies.

who wrote *Culpeper's Herbal,* were both influenced by Paracelsus, the Swiss-born alchemist and physician who had practiced in the previous century, and promoted his doctrine of signatures in their works. This theory held that plants resembled the organs that they healed. Thus, lungwort was assumed to be good for the lungs and walnuts beneficial for the brain. Culpeper became a focus of controversy because he wrote his herbal in everyday English instead of Latin, making it accessible to the common people. The spread of this once closely guarded knowledge greatly upset the medical doctors, who had tried to protect their practices by keeping the information on common herbs in Latin.

Meanwhile, the country herb women and midwives, as they had done for centuries, were treating the majority of Europe's population—the poor. The discovery of digitalis (see *Digitalis purpurea,* foxglove) is the story of one of these healing women. They maintained an herbal tradition outside the boundaries of established medicine. Many of the unfortunate witch trials were directed at these outcasts who included poisonous plants such as foxglove in their practices, and who were considered suspiciously secretive about their skills.

The eighteenth century saw Carl von Linne, better known as Linnaeus, establish a botanical classification of plants with Latin names. The gradual worldwide acceptance of this system provided a universal language of identification for plants. By the nineteenth century, scientific knowledge was advancing at a rapid pace, and as the practice of medicine became more specialized, herbal healing methods received less attention. Around the turn of the century, a group of doctors and pharmacists known as the Eclectics collected medical information from many sources (as their name implies), including herbal texts. The Eclectics, including Dr. John King, Finley Ellingwood, Harvey Felter, and the Lloyd brothers, played a role in giving herbs more validity in the scientific world of that time. Their medical herb books remain important references in many modern herbalists' libraries.

As synthetic drug alternatives became cheaper, more and more emphasis was placed on developing the "magic bullet"—drugs and pills that contain specific active constituents to target the primary symptoms of an illness. Herbs still played a role but were considered less significant of themselves, merely providing the chemical models and sometimes the raw ingredients on which to build the new drugs. Of course, even on the threshold of the scientific age, there were early twentieth century herbalists—such as Jethro Kloss, who wrote *Back to Eden* in 1939—who still used herbs in their natural state. Kloss and, later, the well-known Dr. John Christopher, author of *School of Natural Healing,* were greatly influenced by Thomsonian Herbalism, founded in the late eighteenth century by Samuel Thomson, who emphasized cleansing the body of toxins. Other schools of herbal thought also persisted, including that of the women herbalists such as the "yarb women" of the back hills of rural America. Today, modern medicinal herbalism comes from a rich variety of heritages.

It is my hope that the future will see an integration of modern medicine and traditional medicine based on herbs, with an emphasis on prevention. Today, a new interest has been kindled in those attracted to herbs' fascinating lore, the simple but effective medicines they offer, the natural cosmetics and fragrances they provide, and, of course, the spectrum of flavors they bring to the dinner table.

Christopher Columbus stumbled upon America while in search of a short cut to East Indian spices.

The Swedish botanist Carl von Linne (or Carolus Linnaeus) initiated the system of plant classification used today.

CHAPTER 2

THE CHEMISTRY OF HERBS

The chemistry of herbs can be as fascinating as their history. Herbs contain compounds that work with the body to promote healing. They work together synergistically to produce a wide variety of results. When chemists look at an herb, they see this complex array of compounds fitting together like parts of a puzzle. Often one herb contains the same piece of the puzzle found in another herb. For instance, horehound and hyssop are helpful to the lungs, partially because of the substance *marrubiin,* which is common to both. Anise and fennel contain *anethole,* as a component of their essential oils, giving them both the taste and smell of licorice. The constituents *citronellol* and *citrol* give the multitude of lemon-scented herbs a common fragrance. The same constituent may occur in different herbs—but under different names to designate from which herb it comes.

Medical scientists can't always tell us how the individual compounds in an herb work, and often aren't even aware of them all, but herbalists prefer to use the whole plant so that all of the compounds can work together. Herbalists call it "wholistic" and, indeed, many whole herbs have been found to be more effective than their isolated active ingredient. Ginkgo, for example, works better to increase brain functions and circulation than its isolated flavonoids. Researchers pinpointed the tranquilizing valeric acid found in valerian, then discovered that the herb contains highly sedative *valepotriates* as well; recently, evidence has been found of an additional sedative compound in valerian. Milk thistle contains the active compound *silymarin,* which is used as a drug to encourage liver regeneration, yet researchers now think that another compound in the herb called *betaine hydrochloride* may be equally important. Thus, while the main constituents of each herb are listed in this encyclopedia, keep in mind that other components may in the future be found to be equally important.

Herbal medicine represents a particular approach to healing, one that differs somewhat from modern medicine. Instead of relieving a single symptom with a single active ingredient, a holistic herbal therapy strives to heal the entire system. Headaches are one example. Herbs are chosen not only to ease the pain but also to eliminate the underlying condition responsible for the headache.

Herbalism also emphasizes preventive medicine, to attempt to keep people from getting sick in the first place. This is not a new concept. Herbs have played this role through the ages. In ancient China, herbal doctors were paid only if they kept people well. Using medicinal herbs does not mean turning our backs on modern medicine, but it can provide a simple, inexpensive way of maintaining health that avoids the side effects so common with many drugs. Sometimes the herbs take longer, but a deep and long-lasting healing results. Not that there aren't poisonous herbs to avoid. Foxglove and belladonna may be beautiful growing in the garden, but are too strong to use as common medicines.

The key to using herbs is discretion. Most of the herbs in this encyclopedia are what I call "over-the-counter" herbs—ones you can use for illnesses you would treat yourself anyway, such as a simple sore throat or a fever. Herbs can also be used as part of the therapy for serious diseases, but you should also seek an accurate diagnosis and the advice of a qualified health practitioner. No amount of herbs will help if you are treating the wrong disease. The fact that a tradition or a scientific study indicates that an herb is effective in treating chronic diseases, such as diabetes or a heart condition, doesn't mean it is time to toss out your insulin or digitalis! Instead, consider that regular use of the appropriate herbs may eventually make it possible to reduce dependency on drugs. As far as safety goes, herbs have a good track record that goes back hundreds of years—compared to an estimate by the Environmental Protection Agency that 125,000 Americans die each year because they incorrectly took prescribed medicines.

In China, traditional medicine (including herbs) is integrated into the nation's health-care system along with Western medicine. Natural remedies are estimated to be used in about forty percent of the cases treated. The World Health Organization says traditional medicine is well suited for the Third World; it is less expensive than Western medicine, is often equally as effective, and is well accepted by many cultures. The WHO estimates that eighty percent of the people in developing nations still rely on herbal treatments. In Germany, herbal preparations are considered an alternative therapy but are sold alongside drugs in the pharmacy. The United States lags behind in accepting the medicinal validity of herbalism, but interest is growing rapidly.

Much scientific study has been done on herbs. In describing the findings, I've intentionally focused on clinical studies performed on people. They show how people who took feverfew, for instance, experienced less severe headaches, or how hawthorn improved cardiovascular action. As far as I'm concerned, these human experiences provide more accurate information about how herbs affect us than do animal studies with mice or dogs. One of the *many* herbs that has a different effect on people and animals is catnip. While this herb is a sedative to people, it is an exciting stimulant to the cat. Additionally, I personally have a difficult time rationalizing the often callous treatment and extremely painful procedures to which test animals are subjected. This doesn't strike me as a positive approach to healing. Fortunately, consumer pressure is leading to alternative testing methods using computers, laboratory-produced tissues, and volunteers, and researchers are finding that these often provide more precise information than animal tests. Better communication among scientists is also cutting down on the needless duplication of many tests.

HARVESTING, DRYING, AND USING HERBS

Although the herb was originally defined, in the strict botanical sense, as a plant without woody, persistent stems above ground, now any useful plant may be referred to as an herb. The realm of herbalism includes the entire spectrum of the botanical world. Herbs lend themselves to be used in many different contexts.

Harvesting Herbs

While cultivation considerations vary with individual herbs, you can follow some general guidelines for harvesting. (The few exceptions are indicated in the text.) Ideally, each part of the plant is picked when it is in its prime.

LEAVES A plant's foliage is almost always strongest just before and during flowering. If appropriate, buds or flowers can be harvested along with the leaves. The plant should usually be cut back about one-third to one-half, leaving enough for its continued growth. If only a few leaves are needed, they can be taken from different parts of the plant.

FLOWERS An herb's flowers are harvested when they are in their prime, either in bud stage or when just coming into full bloom, depending upon their intended use.

SEEDS The herb's seeds are harvested when mature. If the seeds tend to fall as soon as they are ripe (as with dill, for example), tie a paper bag over the seed head to catch them. When harvesting, the stem can be bent over so the seeds fall to the bottom of the bag. Then dry the seed right in the bag.

ROOTS, RHIZOMES, AND BULBS The underground parts of an herb are harvested after the plant's leaves die down. For most herbs, this will be in late summer or fall (for some herbs, such as garlic, it will be earlier.) You should try to pick the time during which the nutrients and other properties are concentrated in the underground portion for winter storage. They may also be collected early in the spring, just as the very first leaves are emerging. After that, useful constituents are rapidly used up for the plant's spring growth spurt. In the case of biennials, collect underground portions in either their first fall or their second spring. After that, they become woody and usually useless. Almost all useful roots, rhizomes, and bulbs come from biennial or perennial plants.

Drying Herbs

Dry herbs in a warm place, but not in too hot a location, away from sunlight. A place with well-circulated air will speed drying. During drying, herbs lose some of their properties, especially their essential oils, so the faster they can be dried, the better. If you have the space, the easiest method is to tie the herbs into small bunches and hang them upside down. They can also be placed in a thin layer on screens. In humid climates, where drying is slow, the bundles should be quite small and the herbs on screens should be stirred a couple of times daily.

The gardener at work harvesting from his 16th century herb garden. (By Hans Weiditz, 1542.)

Culinary Uses

Culinary herbs can be used either dry from the spice rack or fresh, right out of the garden. Use a proportion of approximately twice as much fresh to dried herb. Although dried herbs have lost some oils, they are more concentrated. A true gourmet, however, does not follow any recipe strictly. Recipes include the suggestion to "taste and adjust the flavorings accordingly" to perfect the flavor. Feel free to use the recipes in this encyclopedia as guidelines for your own experiments. Within the recipes are metric conversions. Cups are converted in milliliters, while dry ounces are converted in grams.

The familiar aroma of basil, the pungent taste of cayenne, and the sweetness of anise all derive from easily evaporated essential oils. Ideally, herbs should be ground with a mortar and pestle or electric coffee mill just before using them so they keep their flavor. I store my own culinary herbs whole in airtight containers, away from sunlight and heat. You can combine your favorite dried herbs into spice blends, which can be sprinkled into foods as a last-minute touch. These make tasty salt substitutes for those striving to eat a healthier diet. Herbs can also be incorporated into delicious vinegars, oils, and mustards or combined with honey and other condiments to replace any recipe's ho-hum, plain ingredients.

In earlier eras, bitter herbs such as rue and wormwood were used in cooking to provide contrasting flavors. Although they are no longer popular spices, they are still used to flavor alcoholic drinks and, occasionally, to season food. Gentian is found in Angostura bitters, and every modern beer uses hops. Many Greek and Italian cooks still enjoy bitter herbs not as seasonings but as foods in themselves. A dish of dandelion or chicory greens, for example, may be served as an afterdinner salad, and it gives the added benefit of improving digestion.

There is a fine line between most culinary and medicinal herbs; indeed, there's a lot of crossover. You may not have realized that every time you enjoy pasta or a pizza laden with basil and oregano, eat a spicy curry dish, or even sprinkle parsley flakes on a potato, you are treating yourself with medicinal herbs. In fact, cooking with herbs is one of the easiest, as well as most delicious, ways to use herbal medicines. Most herbs enhance digestion, helping you digest the very foods they flavor! The Chinese are known for their distinctive cooking that incorporates medicinal herbs into their regular diet.

Medicinal Uses

While our ancestors may have been content with chewing a bitter root to soothe a digestive upset or rubbing a broken leaf on a sting, today we extract herbs into water to make tea, into alcohol for extracts, and into oil for the base of skin preparations. The following list describes the forms in which herbs may be used for medicinal purposes.

Herbal Teas

The standard tea formula is 1 teaspoon (5 ml) of herb for every cup (240 ml) of water. Chop herbs finely so their properties and flavor are released. Tea can be refrigerated for a few days. Herbal ice cubes provide handy long-term storage. Make a tea concentrate using 1 tablespoon (15 ml) of herbs for every cup (240 ml) of water, pour the mixture into an ice-cube tray, and freeze. To use, pop an ice cube into a glass of water, and it will melt into an instant tea.

Infusions

Leaves and flowers of herbs can be "steeped" by pouring boiling water over them and letting them stand, covered, about ten minutes. Strain the herbs, and the tea is ready. Use a teapot or pan or place a tea strainer right in the teacup.

Decoctions

Roots and barks are thick, so they require five to twenty minutes of low simmering to draw out their properties. Sassafras, valerian, and other aromatic herb roots and barks should be covered and heated below simmering to extract their essential oils.

Cold Infusions

Soak, or infuse, the herbs for eight hours in cold water, then strain.

Sun Teas

Place the herbs and water in a glass jar in a warm place, or in the direct sunlight if you wish, for a few hours, then strain.

Extracts

Most herbal extracts, or tinctures, are extracted in a combination of alcohol and water (or sometimes vinegar). The alcohol content averages around fifty percent. A few herbs, such as goldenseal and black cohosh, contain some constituents that can be extracted only in alcohol, making an extract more useful than a tea. Thirty drops of an extract (about half a standard dropperful from a 1-ounce

A mortar and pestle; basic tools of the herbalist's trade.

Garlic: reputed to keep away colds and vampires!

[60-ml] bottle) is roughly equivalent to one cup of tea. Added to a cup of water or juice, these extracts become instant teas. Many herbalists suggest diluting extracts in this way to improve assimilation. There are only about fifteen drops of alcohol per cup—this can be evaporated off, if necessary, by placing the extract in a cup and pouring boiling water over it. Tinctures can also be used directly on the skin. When extracts were commonly used by doc-

tors as medicines, they were standardized in the pharmacist's *U.S Pharmacopoeia,* and certain herbs were recognized as "official" medicines. Today, herb companies may not follow these standards, and the strengths of their products can vary.

By the way, don't confuse herbal tinctures with the homeopathic remedies or flower essences that are sold in the same type of dropper bottles and preserved with alcohol but are used differently. These "energized" products are so diluted that no trace of the original herb is found in the bottle. Homeopaths do use full-strength herbal extracts of arnica, calendula, and Saint-John's-wort externally.

Syrups

Syrups are concentrated teas, sweetened and preserved with approximately fifty percent honey and/or thirty percent glycerine (an edible sweet, sticky substance that is a by-product of soap making). Most syrups are designed to ease sore throats, but any herbal remedy can be made into a syrup to improve its taste. Kept refrigerated, syrups store for weeks. Herbal cough drops, designed for sore throats, are syrups made into hard candies.

Compresses and Poultices

Compresses are prepared by soaking a folded, soft cloth in a very strong tea (1 tablespoon [15 ml] of herb per cup [240 ml] of water) that is used hot or cold, depending upon the situation. The compress is placed over an injury or on the forehead to ease a fever or headache. Poultices are chopped herbs that are lightly cooked in water and mashed or blended into a pulplike consistency. They are placed directly on the skin or, for a less messy alternative, inside several layers of cheesecloth.

Herbal Oils

Salves, liniments, and other herbal remedies for the skin are made from herbal oils thickened with beeswax, lanolin, or cocoa butter. Herbs are extracted directly into a vegetable oil base. Liniments contain heating herbs that relieve muscle pain.

Cosmetic Uses

Herbs are becoming more and more popular in cosmetics. Even the most expensive brands proudly proclaim a list of natural herbs. Herbs are found in facial creams, hand lotions, deodorants, shampoos, and hair rinses. Facial, or "toilet," waters were once the rage among fashionable beauties. Elder, rose, and rosemary were some of the reputed "antiaging" herbs used in these distilled waters. The waters were also used for medicine, to flavor food (especially rose water), and for the properties of their scents. Today, they are sold as aromatherapy products.

Aromatherapy Uses

Ever since incense was first used in healing practices, fragrance has played a role in healing both the mind and body. Modern scientific investigations are turning up fascinating information about the way different fragrances affect our sense of well-being and can influence our physical health. Lavender and orange aromas are said to be

uplifting, and some believe that simply by smelling rosemary and bay one may improve the memory. Aromatherapy does not restrict itself to simply smelling the fragrance. Essential oils can be incorporated into salves and creams and are sometimes diluted for internal use. A few drops placed in a vaporizer or dropped in a pan of simmering water make an herbal steam to clear congested lungs and sinuses.

Essential oils are made by steam distilling, by pressing, or sometimes with solvents (which are later removed). It takes significant quantities of an herb to produce just a small vial of essential oil. Since they are so concentrated, many harmless herbs become potentially dangerous as essential oils and must be used with care. In terms of measurements, one drop of an essential oil equals an entire cup of tea. Because the essential oil is a component in the herb, the suggested uses for aromatherapy are often identical to those of standard herbalism. For instance, peppermint, which owes most of its medicinal properties to its essential oil, is used as an aid to digestion as an herb tea and/or as a drop of peppermint essential oil placed on a lozenge. Other herbs, such as comfrey, aren't suitable for aromatherapy because they contain almost no essential oil and owe their properties to other constituents.

Other Herbal Uses

Many herbs can be used for natural dyes, stains, and inks. Different mordants (chemicals that fix dyes) in each herb vary the colors it can produce. Herbs with flexible stems and branches have been used to weave baskets, and elder stems have even been used to make small flutes. Still other herbs, like garlic and pennyroyal, are insect repellents. Lavender and rose are just a couple of the herbs used to make fragrant potpourris. In fact, many herbs have multiple uses.

Orange geranium offers one of the thousands of scents found in an herb garden.

The *Illustrated Herb Encyclopedia* is divided into subject headings for easy access. The herbs were selected on the basis of practical use and may be found growing in herb gardens in North America, Europe, and Australasia. All the herbs included are available through regular or specialty herb nurseries. Mail-order sources are provided in the appendix.

Name

Most herbs have many common names. Indeed, often exactly the same name will be used for more than one plant. To prevent confusion, herbalists also designate herbs by scientific names, according to the system designed by Swedish botanist Carolus Linnaeus. In this system, plants have Latin names that group them into a genus (the first name, which is always capitalized) and then designate them individually as species (the second name, which is lowercased here in adherence to guidelines in the international system of nomenclature). There may also be divisions under a given species (such as varieties or man-made cultivars). The herbs within are alphabetized by Latin name, followed by common name.

Family

The largest scientific grouping is the family, which contains various genera. The family is not usually indicated in the botanical name. Often, the Latin names derive from one of the plant's earlier names; sometimes, a plant is named for an outstanding characteristic; or the name may be intended to honor an individual. Botanists sometimes change plant designations as they study them, so genus, species, and sometimes even family names can be changed. These name changes are indicated in the text as "previously," so if you refer to another source that uses an outdated name, you'll recognize it. The names used here are those used by the 1976 *Hortus*

Third, with species names not capitalized, in accordance with botanical classification ordinances.

Description

The plant descriptions here are also based on *Hortus Third*, along with personal observations made in my herb garden. Nature is filled with wonderful variations, so you may find plants taller or shorter, or you may observe other differences from the descriptions here in different climates and under different growing conditions. The time of blooming also varies according to region.

Habitat

We cannot always be certain of the exact location of an herb's origin, so most habitat descriptions cover a large area. Consideration of an herb's native habitat can tell us a great deal about its ideal growing conditions. Its homeland is the area to which it is adapted, and the conditions found there represent the very best ones for that herb.

Cultivation

Annuals have a growing cycle of one year; biennials take two years (usually flowering in the second year); and perennials last for years. Many perennial herbs will inhabit your garden for at least ten years, and in that time they may multiply by self-seeding or spreading. It is usually easier and faster to propagate established perennials by dividing their roots than by taking cuttings, which need time to develop a root system. (Cuttings are made from fresh, woody growth. All but the topmost leaves are removed, and the end is

Essential oil distillation from fresh herbs in the Middle Ages to produce aromatic medicines and perfumes.

placed in wet sand or other medium to sprout.) Perennial seeds tend to be more difficult to germinate and much slower growing than those of annuals, which have only one season to live.

ZONE The zone number represents the most severe climate a particular herb can tolerate, although many factors can influence such toleration. A zone chart is located on page 215.

GERMINATION Most herbs can be grown from seed. This is the only way to propagate many annuals. The average time the seeds need to germinate is indicated under this heading. Some seeds need either light (plant these shallowly) or dark (these can be covered with plastic) conditions to germinate. Some seeds must be stratified by placing them in a small amount of water in the refrigerator to duplicate winter's freeze. In areas where freezing is natural, the seeds can be planted outside in the autumn.

SPACE Use the guidelines under this heading to space herbs in the garden. The design of your garden may dictate spacing that is somewhat different. While annuals reach their full size rapidly, perennials generally take a few years to achieve full growth. You may wish to interplant perennials with temporary annuals or plant them close for the first year, then replant them as they grow.

SOIL TEMPERATURE The right soil temperature often initiates germination. Use a soil thermometer to determine optimum temperatures. Commercial growers often run heat cables under their plant flats or closely regulate cold frames and greenhouses.

SOIL Optimum soil conditions provide maximum growth and healthiest herbs, although most herbs are very flexible in their requirements. Most herbs are not very far removed from their wild cousins. Too rich a soil and too much water can make them lush, but not very potent. A very poor soil, on the other hand, often produces a weak, poor-quality plant. A pH testing kit (available at most garden centres) isn't necessary but will help you determine the herbs your garden will best produce. In each entry, pH information is given when available.

SUN The majority of herb plants thrive in the sun. However, a few herbs prefer shade, and some will settle for either.

PROPAGATION Under this heading details are provided for propagating (reproducing) the specific herb. Preferred techniques are recommended. Special harvesting methods are also listed here.

Garden Design

Herb garden design can spark your creativity as much or more than the design of any other type of garden. Specific suggestions are given, but you should feel free to experiment—after all, that's what creativity is all about. As you garden, you will continually get more ideas about which plants look best next to each other. Keep in mind that even after you plant a herb, it can be moved later as your garden plan changes or enlarges.

Constituents

Each herb contains an integrated puzzle of different chemicals. These are responsible for its taste, fragrance, medicinal properties, and uses. Under this heading are listed the most important constituents as far as has been determined by current science.

Related Species

Many herbs have a number of surprising relatives in their genus or family. Sometimes, these "cousins" have similar uses or histories.

There is also much confusion concerning proper identification among related and unrelated plants. This heading clears up much of that confusion. Varieties are also listed here.

History

Herbal history is rich with many tales and exciting herbal adventures that will both amuse and enlighten.

Culinary

Herbs are important elements in the culinary arts. Here is information on their uses, both past and present, in cooking, in alcoholic drinks, and as wild edibles. Historical recipes offer a glimpse at the ancestry of many of our modern recipes. I've updated them so you can try them out in your own kitchen. I've also offered a few hints for the culinary use of each herb.

Medicinal

Herbs have a very long history of medicinal use. Under this heading you will find a combination of historic medical folklore, traditional uses of the herb in many cultures, current herbal practice, and scientific studies, mostly from clinical work with human patients. All of these offer a valid look at medicinal herbalism. Together, they provide a comprehensive medicinal perspective on each herb. While herbs have an almost amazing ability to heal the body, this information is not offered as a replacement to seeking a qualified medical practitioner for serious problems. If is especially important to obtain an accurate diagnosis of any disease before deciding if self-treatment is appropriate.

Aromatherapy

Essential oils are important herbal constituents. There is a wide range of possible uses for these oils. Included among these possibilities are healing and perfumery functions and, most fascinating, the purported role of essential oils in influencing the emotions.

Cosmetic

The original cosmetics were based on herbs. Today, herbs are still used to give modern products fragrance and are once again appreciated for the ability to improve skin complexion and hair condition and appearance.

Considerations

While most herbs provide a safe method for flavoring foods and healing the body, a few are downright poisonous. Others are safe when used with discretion, although large amounts can irritate. What is a "large amount"? It depends upon many factors, but more than eight cups of a tea in a given day, or the equivalent amount of extract, should be considered overdoing a potentially good thing. Essential oils are so concentrated that overdosing is easy. Use them internally only with great care—no more than a couple of drops at a time (roughly equivalent to two to four cups of tea). Essential oils are usually not placed directly on the skin but are diluted in oil or alcohol so that they won't cause blistering.

Other

Under this heading are listed such uses of herbs as insect repellents, dye plants, and handicrafts, such as basketmaking.

THE
HERBS

Achillea millefolium • Yarrow

FAMILY: Compositae.

DESCRIPTION: Low-growing leaves, with straight flower stalks. Height: To 3 feet (90 cm). Width: To 1 foot (30 cm). Flowers: Tight groups of tiny, 1/4-inch (6-mm) white flowers, clustered in 3- to 4-inch- (7.5- to 10-cm-) umbels on stiff, upright stems. Leaves: Very finely divided and feathery on stems to 8 inches (20 cm) long, becoming smaller toward the top of the plant. Blooms: June to August.

HABITAT: Europe and western Asia; naturalized in North America, Australia, and New Zealand.

CULTIVATION: Perennial. Zone: 2. Germination: 10 to 14 days. Needs light to germinate. Space: 8 to 14 inches (20 to 35 cm). Soil Temperature: 78° to 80° F (25° to 26° C). Soil: Well drained, fairly dry; will tolerate poor soil; very drought resistant. pH: 4.2 to 7. Sun: Full sun, will become straggly in shade. Propagation: Occasionally from seed or by cuttings, but most often by root division. Once established, yarrow spreads by root division—often rampantly. It will bloom the second year. The center of the bed dies back after about 5 years and will need replanting with fresh root divisions.

GARDEN DESIGN: All the various yarrows provide a colorful, long-lasting display in the garden. They are best used in informal clumps.

CONSTITUENTS: Essential oils (to 1.4%) includes azulene (to 51%), and—not found in all species—borneol, camphor, cineole, terpineol, eugenol, trace of thujone; lactones, flavonoids, tannins, coumarins, saponins, sterols, glycoalkaloid (achilleine), salicylic acid, sugars.

RELATED SPECIES: Herb books tend to list white yarrow as the only medicinal species, but other species have been used in folk medicine in their native regions. 'Coronation gold' *(A. filipendulina)*, has its 3-foot (90-cm) flower stalks. The species is originally from Asia Minor and the Caucasus. The short, woolly yarrow *(A. tomentosa)*, with silver leaves, is often grown in rock gardens. It hails from Eurasia. Sneezewort *(A. ptarmica)*, meaning "produces sneezing," has white, pearllike flowers and is also from Eurasia. The similar mace yarrow *(A. decolorans)*, with cream-colored flowers, has toothed leaves. Variations on white yarrow include 'Cerise Queen' *(A. millefolium* 'Kelwayi')*, pink yarrow ('Rosea'), and the short, 2-foot (60-cm) yellow yarrow *(A. millefolium* 'Moonshine')* with silver-gray foliage.

HISTORY: The Anglo-Saxons named yarrow *gaeruwe,* from *gearwian,* meaning "to prepare" or "to treat," referring most likely to its curative properties. Other names, which generally describe yarrow's ability to stop bleeding, include soldier's woundwort, knight's milfoil, and *herba militaris.* It is said that the hero Achilles used yarrow to heal the wounds of Greek troops during the Trojan War in 1200 B.C. In Medieval times, yarrow leaves were rolled and put up the nose to stop bleeding. Its finely divided leaves were the reason for another name, milfoil meaning "many leaves." Druids used yarrow stalks to divine seasonal weather, while the Chinese cast the *I Ching* oracle with them to determine the future.

CULINARY: Even though they are extremely bitter, yarrow leaves were added to 17th-century salads. The Swedes, calling it "field hop," made their beer with it—a beer Linnaeus reported to have been even more intoxicating than hops beer.

MEDICINAL: Thanks to the flavonoids they contain, yarrow flowers encourage circulation, lower blood pressure, and help stop bleeding anywhere in the body. A couple of cups of hot yarrow, peppermint, and elder flower tea is an old remedy for reducing fevers and treating colds, measles, and eruptive diseases. It also helps relieve urinary tract infections and stones. In China, yarrow is used in poultices and to ease stomach ulcers. It is said to stop excessive blood flow especially well in the pelvic region, so is used to decrease excessive menstruation, postpartum bleeding, and hemorrhoids. Chewing the fresh leaves relieves toothache.

COSMETIC: Yarrow preparations are used to counter oily skin.

CONSIDERATIONS: There are reports that large doses cause headaches, dizziness, and even light sensitivity in some people, although this is not well documented. Yarrow has a tendency to cause allergic skin reactions or sneezing in people sensitive to the aster family.

OTHER: All of the species dry well and are often used in dried herb and flower arrangements, although the color of the reds and pinks will gradually fade. Biodynamic gardeners use small amounts of yarrow leaf preparations to speed compost decomposition. A substance exuded by the roots is said to increase the disease resistance of nearby plants. It is an insect repellent, although it also inhibits seed germination in the soil. Yarrow has been mixed with tobacco and snuff for flavoring.

© Derek Fell

Achillea millefolium. **Yarrow has made itself at home in many parts of the world. Wherever it grows, it has been used as a "fever herb." The white European yarrow is most often used medicinally, but other species offer varying shades of pinks, mauves, and yellows.**

Achillea millefolium
YARROW

Acorus americanus • Calamus
(Previously *A. calamus*)

FAMILY: Araceae.

DESCRIPTION: Rushlike, grows in grassy clumps. Height: 2 to 6 feet (60 to 180 cm). Width: 1 foot (30 cm). Flowers: Yellow-green, very small, jut out at a 45° angle part way up stem. Only flowers in water. Leaves: Lance-shaped, 3/4 inch (2 cm) wide, with a prominent midrib, light green, with a musky, cinnamonlike fragrance. Rhizome: Spongy, stout, red-brown peel, white inside, small roots underneath. Very aromatic. Blooms: May to August.

HABITAT: Central Asia, perhaps eastern Europe, now found distributed throughout the Northern Hemisphere, in marshes and slow-moving creeks.

CULTIVATION: Perennial. Zone: 3. Space: 1 foot (30 cm). Soil: Rich, moist, boggy. pH: 5 to 7.5. Sun: Partial shade (or sun if roots are in water). Propagation: By division—plant crown with about 2 inches (5 cm) of rhizome attached. The root shrinks as much as 75% when dried. They should be 2 to 3 years old before harvesting. When grown in water, it forms raftlike masses of interwoven roots. Don't peel, since the oil glands containing the essential oil are on the outer surface.

GARDEN DESIGN: Calamus is limited in design possibilities, but makes an interesting conversation piece and will grow in marshlike conditions not suited to many other herbs.

CONSTITUENTS: Essential oils include linalool, eugenol, azulene, pinene, cineole, camphor; sesquiterpenes, acoric acid.

RELATED SPECIES: *A. calamus* 'Variegatus' has striped leaves. *A. gramineus* is a dwarf with narrow leaves. Indian calamus *(A. calamus* var. *angustifolius Schott)* has similar properties but a slightly different chemistry.

HISTORY: Calamus, also known as sweet flag, has been an item of commerce for at least 4,000 years. The Roman *calamus,* the Greek *kalamos,* and the Sanskrit *kalamas* all describe the reed. Dioscorides called it *acoron,* from *coreon,* meaning "the pupil of the eye," in reference to one disease it treated. The Turks carried the rhizome with them to counter infections, and the Orientals considered it an aphrodisiac. The calamus mentioned in the Bible was probably another aromatic, grasslike herb. The Mongolian Tartars are thought to have brought calamus to Russia in the 11th century. It was not well known in most of Europe until 1574, when the Viennese botanist Clusius obtained it from Asia Minor and later distributed rhizomes to botanists in surrounding countries. The lemony leaves were thrown on floors for their sweet smell—in the 19th century, England's Norwich Cathedral was still being strewn with calamus on holy days.

CULINARY: The roots have long been candied and were chewed to relieve indigestion. The spicy flavor has made calamus a substitute for cinnamon, nutmeg, and ginger in cooking. Calamus, with angelica, flavored 17th-century broths, Benedictine and Chartreuse liqueurs, as well as some beers and gin. The young leaf buds are eaten in salads. Where calamus grows wild, the flowers have been eaten—Dutch children enjoyed the rhizomes as chewing gum.

MEDICINAL: Calamus rhizome is a bitter tonic that stimulates the digestive juices and is combined with gentian in the tonic Stockton bitters. It counters overacidity, heartburn, and intestinal gas. Herbalists report it useful to help reduce severe loss of appetite due

Acorus americanus
Calamus

to cancer or other illness or the eating disorder anorexia nervosa. Traditional Islamic medicine employs calamus for stomach and liver inflammation and rheumatism, as well as a calamus–rose oil–vinegar mix to treat burns. Chinese studies show that calamus extracts kill bacteria, lower blood pressure by dilating the blood vessels, stop coughing, and eliminate lung congestion.[1] Traditional Chinese medicine uses it to treat deafness, dizziness, and epilepsy. The Regional Research Institute in India found that calamus reduces epileptic fits and even eases some emotional problems. It is also used in India to treat asthma. The Native Americans of the

Great Plains chewed it when they had a fever, cough, cold, or toothache. The American species is especially sedative to the central nervous system and stops muscle spasms.[2]

AROMATHERAPY: Calamus is used in perfumery and is similar to orris root. Egyptians say the fragrance is an aphrodisiac.

CONSIDERATIONS: In 1978, the Food and Drug Administration (FDA) banned the use of calamus root, oil, and extracts, as well as preparations containing the suspected carcinogen *B*-asarone, after experiments showed Indian calamus had carcinogenic effects on rats. They also produced liver and heart abnormalities and depressed growth. So far, problems with European and American rhizomes, which do not contain *B*-asarone, are rare and animal tests with the oil show low toxicity.[3]

OTHER: Calamus has been used like orris root powder in tooth powders, hair powders, and dry shampoos. It was once also used as a snuff powder for both people and horses. The Omaha Indians baited fish with it and fed it to their watchdogs to make them fierce. In India, calamus dust is used to kill white ants and fleas. It sterilizes male grain weevils so they can't reproduce.[4]

Agastache foeniculum • Anise Hyssop
(Previously *A. anethiodora, Lophanthus anisatus*)

FAMILY: Labiatae.

DESCRIPTION: An obvious member of the mint family, with upright, square stems. Height: 3 feet (90 cm). Width: 2 feet (60 cm). Flowers: Vivid blue-purple, rise in 2- to 6-inch (5- to 15-cm) spires. Leaves: Opposite each other, oval at the base, coming to a point at the tip. Roughly textured, toothed edges, with the largest ones at the base, about 2 inches (5 cm) wide and 3 inches (7.5 cm) long. Strongly licorice scented. Blooms: July to September.

HABITAT: A North American native from the midwestern United States, it now grows wild in surrounding areas.

CULTIVATION: Perennial. Zone: 4. Germination: 1 to 2 weeks. Space: 1 to 1¹/₂ feet (30 to 45 cm). Soil Temperature: 70° to 85° F (21° to 29° C). Soil: Well-drained, semirich, sandy loam. Sun: Prefers full sun but adapts to partial shade. Propagation: Seed, cuttings, root division. The seeds germinate so easily that you can soon have a garden full of anise hyssop from self-seeding. The seed and plant may be difficult to obtain, but it's well worth the effort.

GARDEN DESIGN: If you have room for more than one anise hyssop, plant this extremely ornamental herb as a tall border or in a grouping set back to stand out among shorter plants.

RELATED SPECIES: A tea of Korean mint *(A. rugosa)* is used to ease angina heart pains. It acquired the name after being introduced by a seedsman who brought it back from the Korean War.

HISTORY: Neither an anise nor a hyssop, this herb belongs to a genus of plants commonly called giant hyssop and tastes like anise.

CULINARY: A delightful licorice-mint taste makes anise hyssop leaf tea pleasing either hot or iced. Your guests will think it is a tea blend and will be surprised to discover it is only one herb. The Plains Indians of North America found it a tasty food sweetener. To replace anise in a recipe, make a strong anise hyssop tea (using 1 teaspoon in ¹/₂ cup, or 5 ml in 120 ml) and replace half of the recipe's liquid with it.

MEDICINAL: The root of anise hyssop was an ingredient in North American Chippewa Indian lung formulas, and the Cree sometimes carried the flowers in their medicine bundles.

OTHER: It is an excellent bee plant that produces nectar all day and is commercially grown for its delicious honey. Hummingbirds also love it.

Agastache foeniculum
ANISE HYSSOP

Agrimonia eupatoria
Agrimony

Agrimonia eupatoria • Agrimony

FAMILY: Rosaceae.

DESCRIPTION: An upright herb with square, reddish stems. Height: To 5 feet (150 cm). Width: 1½ feet (45 cm). Flowers: Numerous, yellow, with 5 petals, ½ inch (1 cm) wide, at the top of long, slender spikes. Leaves: Soft, hairy, with silver-gray undersides and deep green tops. Grouped together with 7 to 13 on a stem, in various sizes, with the longest ones reaching 3 inches (7.5 cm). Slightly aromatic with an astringent taste. Fruit: Prickly seed burrs with hooked bristles. Blooms: June to July.

HABITAT: Agrimony is found in western Asia, Europe, and North Africa, where it grows in weedlike fashion along roadsides and in hedges.

CULTIVATION: Perennial. Zone: 3. Germination: 14 to 24 days. Space: 12 inches (30 cm). Soil Temperature: 70° to 85° F (21° to 29° C). Soil: Average, well drained, fairly dry. Sun: Full sun. Propagation: Plant seed or divide in the spring, or transplant root division in the autumn.

GARDEN DESIGN: Agrimony isn't a showy plant, but its scalloped leaves and small flowers provide an interesting contrast to lighter green or gray herbs. The seeds spread easily throughout the garden, so consider cutting the stalks before the seeds begin to drop.

CONSTITUENTS: Polysaccharides (20%), tannins (to 8%), flavonoids (luteolin, apigenin, quercin), essential oils, coumarins, silica.

HISTORY: The tall flowering stalks of agrimony catch the eye and have given this herb the nickname "church steeples." It was also christened *Philanthropos*, or "beneficial," possibly in tribute to its medicinal virtues, although some historians think the name refers to the generous way agrimony seeds catch the clothing of anyone who rubs against them. The Greek historian and geographer Strabo (63 B.C. to A.D. 21) discussed agrimony along with wormwood and betony. Both the Anglo-Saxons and the early Greeks, who named it after *argemon*, meaning, "a speck in the eye," regarded agrimony as a beneficial wash for eyes and wounds. The Saxon Leechbooks mention *agremoman* in 1,000 A.D. In the Middle Ages, agrimony was thought to produce such heavy sleep that an Old English manuscript informs:

> If It is leyd under mann's head,
> He shal sleepyn as he were dead;
> He shal never drede ne wakyn
> Till fro under his head it be taken.

In the fourteenth century, Chaucer mentioned *egrimoyne* in *The Yeoman's Prologue*. It was an ingredient in the famous 16th-century antiseptic wash "Arquebusade Water." This lyrical name is not a dance step, but refers to a musketlike handgun called the arquebus or harquebus. The weapon is now outdated, but the French continue to apply *Eau de Arquebusade* to sprains and bruises.

MEDICINAL: True to its reputation, the agrimony leaf is an astringent that stops bleeding. It is also used as a mouthwash or gargle to reduce inflamed gums or throat. In fact, studies in China report that agrimony can increase blood coagulation up to 50%[1], and traditional Chinese medicine uses the tea to stop profuse menstruation. European herbalists suggest a few cups of agrimony tea daily to heal peptic ulcers and colitis, to gently control diarrhea, to tone the digestive tract lining, and to improve food assimilation. Gerard, in his 16th-century *Herball*, recommended the tea "for those that have naughty livers"—including sufferers from jaundice, cirrhosis, and gallbladder stones, as well as skin eruptions resulting from liver dysfunction. One glycoside it contains has been shown to reduce excessive bile production in the gallbladder.[2]

OTHER: The entire top of the plant also produces a yellow dye.

EAU DE ARQUEBUSADE

½ ounce (14 g) each:
dried tops of agrimony
calamint
fennel
hyssop
lemon balm
marjoram
peppermint
rosemary
sage
savory
thyme
wormwood
A few fresh leaves of angelica and basil, plus fresh lavender flowers.

Chop plants and combine with 1 quart (1 l) 190 proof grain alcohol. Let stand for 14 days, then strain. The original version was then distilled.

Agrimonia eupatoria. **The flowers of agrimony are small and not very showy, but its attractive foliage makes it an ornamental, as well as a useful, garden herb. Agrimony's yellow flowers turn to seed-filled burrs famous for attaching themselves to passersby.**

Alchemilla vulgaris
LADY'S MANTLE

Alchemilla vulgaris • Lady's-Mantle

FAMILY: Rosaceae.

DESCRIPTION: Short, creeping herb. Height: To 1¹/₂ feet (45 cm). Width: 1 foot (30 cm). Flowers: Small, delicate, yellow, supported on thin stems like lacy clouds. Leaves: Round, slightly lobed, sharply toothed around the edges, 2 to 8 inches (5 to 20 cm) in diameter, with folds making them slightly cupped. Covered with soft, downy hairs. Blooms: June to August.

HABITAT: Found from Europe to the Arctic Circle, in Greenland, Labrador, and parts of Asia.

CULTIVATION: Perennial. Zone: 3. Germination: Very slow, increased by stratification. Space: 6 to 8 inches (15 to 20 cm). Soil Temperature: 60° to 70° F (15° to 20° C). Soil: Average, well drained. pH: 6.5 to 7. Sun: Shade, or partial shade if well watered in cool climate. Propagation: From seed, or divide by carefully separating eyes. Has deep spreading roots, so keep weeds down.

GARDEN DESIGN: Well suited to grow in rocky, protected areas or in hanging baskets.

CONSTITUENTS: Probably tannins.

RELATED SPECIES: There are many similar subspecies. Parsley *(A. arvensis)* is used for urinary tract problems.

HISTORY: The ancients named this herb, which they believed to have magical properties, after alchemy, the Arabic *alkemelych.* We can see why when we consider how dew collects in the cup-shaped leaves and sparkles in early morning sunlight. The plant was said to impart properties into the dew that promoted quiet sleep when it was sprinkled on the pillow. Jerome Bock (known as Tragus) first mentioned the name "lady's mantle," or *Frauenmantle,* in German, and described it as resembling a woman's cloak in his 1532 *History of Plants.*

MEDICINAL: The name "lady's mantle" probably also refers to the herb's use in treating many female health problems. Europeans, especially Swedes, find it useful to reduce heavy menstruation and prevent menstrual and even intestinal cramping. They also recommend it when a woman's body is adjusting hormone levels, such as after childbirth and during menopause. It makes an astringent douche for vaginal infections and is usually combined with antiseptic herbs. The fresh root has been used at least since medieval days to stop the bleeding of a cut and as an eyewash. The tea also controls diarrhea.

COSMETIC: Creams and lotions incorporate lady's mantle to soften dry, rough skin; lighten freckles and birthmarks; clean the pores; and clear the complexion of acne.

OTHER: The flowers can be dried for arrangements and wreaths. The leaves produce a green dye for wool.

Allium sativum • Garlic

FAMILY: Liliaceae.

DESCRIPTION: Grows in grasslike clumps. Height: 1 foot (30 cm). Width: 6 inches (15 cm). Flowers: Small, rose-white or green-white, clustered in 3- to 4-inch (7.5- to 10-cm) globes, on tall stems rising from the underground bulb. Leaves: Thin, narrow, flat, gray-green, straight, pointed. Fruit: Small black seeds, although small bulbs may also develop, and can be planted. Bulbs: Globe-like, containing 8 to 20 individual cloves, surrounded by a white, sometimes pink, paperlike covering. Blooms: June to July.

HABITAT: Asia, but introduced into warm climates worldwide.

CULTIVATION: Annual. Germination: 1 to 3 weeks. Space: 6 to 10 inches (15 to 25 cm). Soil Temperature: 65° to 75° F (18° to 21° C). Soil: Rich. pH: 4.5 to 8.5. Sun: Full sun. Heat develops the best flavor. Propagation: Plant seed in the fall. Plant individual cloves with pointed ends up, in early spring or fall in areas where the ground does not freeze. Outer cloves produce the best quality. Planted in March, they will be ready to harvest in July or August. Harvest after the blooms die down, then sun-dry for a day. Garlic braids hanging on the wall are an attractive and handy way to store them. Soak the long stems in water for a few hours, then tightly braid a few bunches together. Flowers that hold their shape when they dry, such as annual statice, can be braided in, too.

GARDEN DESIGN: Garlic's slender silhouette can be slipped in here and there about the garden. This sparse plant looks better grouped or in a row than in its own plot.

CONSTITUENTS: Essential oil (0.3% to 0.4%—alliin, which converts to allicin when cloves are cut, which is further converted to diallydisulphide, the antibacterial sulfur compound), enzyme (alliinase), vitamins (A, B₁, B₂, C, thiamin, niacin, riboflavin), minerals (magnesium phosphorus, potassium).

RELATED SPECIES: Wild garlic (*Allium* species) is found growing wild in the United States.

HISTORY: Garlic's common name describes its leaves and use, from the Anglo-Saxon *gar* (lance) and *leac* (leek, or pot-herb). Grown in the Mediterranean and central Asia for centuries, garlic was widely used as medicine by the ancients. It was found in King Tut's tomb (circa 1358 B.C.) and, according to Greek historian Herodotus, was eaten for endurance by the slaves who constructed the great Cheops pyramid. King Ashurbanipal of Assyria (668–633 B.C.) wrote about it on a cuneiform scroll. The East Indian herbalist

Allium sativum
GARLIC

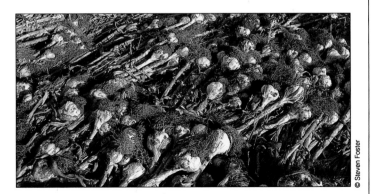

Allium sativum. The pungency of garlic has found its way into cuisines around the world. That same pungent quality is responsible for its antiseptic properties.

Charaka said in the first century A.D. that garlic would be worth its weight in gold, if it weren't for its smell.

Obviously a versatile herb, garlic has been used by rich and poor alike through the years to keep away disease, evil spirits, moles—even racing competitors! It was a main ingredient in the "Four Thieves Vinegar" used by 4 Marseilles thieves who confessed that "garlek" protected them while they robbed plague victims' bodies. In the early 18th century, it was used by French priests to protect themselves from a highly contagious fever in London's poor section, while their English counterparts, who did not use it, were not so lucky. European doctors in World War I and World War II applied sterilized swabs of sphagnum moss and garlic to dress wounds and prevent gangrene. A somewhat surreal history can be found in *The Book of Garlic: Lovers of the Stinking Rose* by Lloyd J. Harris (Panjandrum/Aris Books).

CULINARY: One of the most popular flavoring herbs in the world, garlic is incorporated into butters, vinegars, salts, dried seasonings, salad dressings, soups, and main dishes. The Chinese even prepare a honeyed garlic. Fresh cloves have the best flavor. When you want to soften cloves so they are easier to crush, sprinkle on a little salt. Avoid powdered garlic, which has rancid undertones. When you cook with garlic, the amount of medicinal properties left corresponds to how strong it tastes. If you find the odor unacceptable, it is not necessary to abstain, despite the advice given by Bottom in Shakespeare's *A Midsummer Night's Dream:* "And, most dear actors, eat no onions nor garlick, for we are to utter sweet breath. . ."—simply chew parsley to sweeten the breath.

MEDICINAL: Garlic discourages the growth of many bacteria and viruses including candida, trichomonas, staph, and *E. coli,* as well as intestinal worms. As an oil or vinegar, it can be used to treat ear and mouth infections. In Chinese clinical studies, garlic cured 67% of a group of patients with intestinal bacterial infections and 88% who had amoebic dysentery. Their blood cholesterol and fat (lipid) levels were also significantly lowered. Researchers noted some success in treating deep fungal infections, whooping cough, lead poisoning, and some carcinomas. Even appendicitis was improved in a number of studies.[1] Low concentrations, approximately one small clove a day, have been found to improve intestinal digestion, while larger quantities slow it down. Studies of factory workers found that garlic not only detoxified harmful levels of lead from the blood, it seemed to prevent its accumulation in the first place.[2] Subjects who ate garlic for six months found that their "bad" LDL cholesterol and triglyceride levels went down, while their "good" HDL cholesterol levels increased.[3] Garlic also helps normalize systolic blood pressure levels and can sustain them up to 24 hours. Many cultures turn to garlic to control mild diabetes. Conflicting clinical studies show it both lowers and raises blood sugar, suggesting that it may regulate insulin.[4]

The natural killer cells (NK) of the immune system are dramatically activated by garlic. Many studies point to garlic's antitumor effects. For example, residents in one region in China who don't eat garlic have about 1,000 times higher rates of stomach cancer than those in a neighboring garlic-eating region. Detailed studies can be found in 2 scientific reviews.[5] Some of garlic's other claims to fame include treating retina conditions, hepatitis, and almost every lung condition. The fresher the garlic, the better it works. Garlic oil capsules work better than dried garlic powder.

CONSIDERATIONS: Large doses occasionally cause indigestion, and some reports claim they make the eye more sensitive to light. Garlic can also irritate very sensitive skin.

OTHER: Research from David Greenstock of the Henry Doubleday Research Association in England shows that garlic sprays kill cabbage white and ermine moth (98%), onion fly larvae (95%), mole crickets (91%), pea weevils (87%), and field slugs (82%), and deter aphids and Japanese beetles.

GREENSTOCK'S BUG FORMULA

3   *ounces (85 g) garlic, chopped*
2   *teaspoons (10 ml) mineral oil*
1   *pint (500 ml) water*
1/4 *ounce (7 g) oil-based hand soap*
    Water to dilute

Soak garlic in oil for 1 week. Then dissolve soap into water and mix in the garlic oil. Strain out garlic. When ready to use, dilute 1 part in 20 parts water and spray on plants. (Note: The soap can be replaced with 1/2 ounce (14 g) of liquid all-purpose, biodegradable soap.)

FOUR THIEVES VINEGAR OR MARSEILLES VINEGAR

This recipe was still used until the late 19th century, although without the camphor (a good idea, considering it can be toxic when taken internally) and rue. Some versions even eliminated the garlic! Herbs can be used dried or fresh.

4   *ounces (113 g) each:*
    rosemary tops
    sage flowers
    garlic, sliced
2   *ounces (56 g) lavender flowers*
1 1/2 *ounces (42 g) rue flowers (if available)*
1   *ounce (28 g) camphor*
1   *teaspoon (15 ml) cloves, ground*
1   *gallon (4 l) wine vinegar*

Combine all ingredients in a bottle and let stand 7 days, occasionally giving it a good shake. Strain out the solid.

HONEYED GARLIC

1/2 *cup (112 g) garlic cloves, whole*
1/2 *cup (120 ml) honey*

Peel the cloves and place in a very clean, wide-mouthed jar. Heat the honey until it liquefies, and pour it over the garlic. Stir with a chopstick to eliminate any air bubbles. Let cool and seal with a loosely fitting lid or cork. Let stand for about 4 weeks, then both the garlic and the garlic-flavored honey can be used.

GARLIC SPREAD

3/4 *cup (180 ml) olive oil*
6 or 7 *garlic cloves*
1   *tablespoon (15 ml) onion powder*
2   *tablespoons (30 ml) parsley, chopped*
1/4 *teaspoon (1.25 ml) salt*

Blend ingredients until smooth. Bake in oven on low for 15 minutes. Serve as a side dish, or spread on bread.

> *The Garlic, in Spanish it's "ajo,"*
> *Is better than any placebo.*
> *Most important to mention*
> *It checks hypertension,*
> *Better than most herbs I know.*
> — *"GARLIC," JAMES DUKE (b. 1929), AMERICAN*

A field of garlic, destined to become vinegar, garlic bread, or bug spray.

Allium schoenoprasum • Chives

FAMILY: Liliaceae.

DESCRIPTION: Dense, grasslike clumps growing out of small bulbs. Height: To 2 feet (60 cm). Width: To 12 inches (30 cm). Flowers: Pink to purple compact spheres composed of many small flowers. Leaves: Straight, hollow with sharp points. Blooms: April to May.

HABITAT: Thought to have originated in Siberia and spread from there into America, where *A. sibiricum* is found from Alaska to Maine.

CULTIVATION: Perennial. Zone: 3. Germination: 10 to 14 days. Space: Set clumps 8 inches (20 cm) apart. Soil Temperature: 60° to 70° F (15° to 21° C). Soil: Well-drained, average garden type, slightly acid, and well watered. pH: 6 to 8. Sun: Full sun or partial shade, although the latter produces stragglier plants and fewer flowers. Propagation: From seed, or divide roots of larger plants. Sow in late summer for an indoor winter crop, or if your ground doesn't freeze, dig up chives in the late winter and bring indoors to force an early start. Chives grow best if cut down to 4 inches (10 cm) 2 to 3 times during the summer. If the cut, brown edges bother you, snip off a few close to the bottom rather than giving the whole bunch a haircut.

GARDEN DESIGN: Chives supply a burst of spring color. They make an attractive low-growing garden edging. Unlike many other herbs, they are easy to contain.

CONSTITUENTS: Essential oils, vitamins (A, C, thiamine, and niacin), minerals (iron, calcium, magnesium, phosphorus, potassium).

RELATED SPECIES: Garlic chives or Chinese chives, (*A. tuberosum*, previously *A. odorum*), called *nire* in Japan, have flat leaves and a garliclike taste and smell.

HISTORY: At first only the Siberians enjoyed their native chives. The story is told that when they heard of the approach of Alexander the Great (356–323 B.C.) when he was still a few thousand miles away, they appealed to him with the only treasure they had— chives—in honor of his upcoming marriage to Princess Roxana. The gift was deemed especially appropriate since the herb was reputed to be an aphrodisiac. The next time you ponder a pile of chopped chives on a potato, consider that they retained this reputation right into the 19th century. Our name for them comes from the French *cive*, derived from the Latin name for onion, *cepa*.

CULINARY: Chives taste so much better fresh than dried, it is fortunate that they have a long growing season. They are tasty in cheese, egg, or potato dishes or with any food that does not overpower their delicate onionlike flavor. Be aware that their taste does increase in strength when they are stored in an uncooked dish overnight. Chives lend their flavor to the French *fines herbes*. The flowers make an attractive and flavorful vinegar.

MEDICINAL: Suggested in the Orient as a cold, flu, and lung congestion remedy. From Marcus Valerius Martialis, circa A.D. 100, came this warning: "He who bears chives on his breath/Is safe from being kissed to death."

CHIVE BLOSSOM VINEGAR

1   **pint (500 ml) fresh chive blossoms**
1   **quart (1 l) white vinegar or wine vinegar**

Allium schoenoprasum
CHIVES

Place the blossoms in a clean wide-mouthed jar. Pour vinegar over them and stir to release any air bubbles. Store on a shelf at room temperature for 2 weeks. Then strain out the blossoms (a kitchen strainer will do) so no particles remain. Bottle and store at room temperature. This vinegar is best made every year since its pale purple color eventually fades.

FINES HERBES

Equal parts fresh:
   chervil
   chives
   parsley
   tarragon

Mince together with a sharp knife, and add to food at the last minute.

Aloe barbadensis
ALOE VERA

Aloe barbadensis • Aloe Vera
(Previously *A. vera* and *A. perfoliata*)

FAMILY: Liliaceae.

DESCRIPTION: A squat succulent. Height: 1 to 5 feet (30 to 150 cm). Width: 1 to 3 feet (30 to 90 cm). Flowers: Orange or red, grouped on top of tall, erect stems; hanging down like tiers of small, 1-inch (2.5-cm) cigars. Leaves: Fleshy, very succulent blades rise 1 to 2 feet (30 to 60 cm) from a rosette center. They are pale green and mottled with paler spots, prickly along the edges. Blooms: Midsummer when planted in the ground. Aloe takes 2 to 3 years to flower.

HABITAT: East African native, naturalized in North Africa, Spain, Indonesia, and the Caribbean, where it is cultivated commercially.

CULTIVATION: Perennial. Zone: 3. Germination: Sometimes months. Space: 3 feet (90 cm). Soil Temperature: 60° F (15° C). Soil: Sandy loam that is very well drained. Infrequent, deep watering so the roots don't get soggy. pH: 5 to 7.5. Sun: Potted plants need filtered sun or complete shade. They turn brown when fully exposed to the sun. Plants in large pots or in the ground can be adapted to full sun by gradual introduction. Propagation: Easiest by rooting young, outer suckers.

GARDEN DESIGN: In gardens that experience frost, locate potted plant in a shady location. In warmer locations, plant aloe in the ground.

CONSTITUENTS: Glycoside (anthraquinone, also called aloe-emodin and aloin, to 25%), polysaccharides, saponins, essential oil, steroids, enzymes, antibiotic, minerals, cinnamic and salicylic acids. The fresh leaf contains about 96% water.

RELATED SPECIES: Aloe is sometimes confused with the genus *Agave* and other succulents, some of which are soothing but do not have the same medicinal and cosmetic properties. It is also *not* related to the aloe of the Bible. Aloewood or agalwood *(Aquillaria agallocha)*, from the Greek *agallochon*, is a resinous, soft, and very aromatic wood from India that yields aggur oil for incense and perfume.

HISTORY: An important herb for over 3,000 years, the Egyptian *Papyrus ebers* and temple walls describe the use of aloe vera to treat burns, skin ulcers, and parasites. Aloe is thought to be the secret ingredient Cleopatra added to her beauty cream. The name goes back to the Arabic *alloeh* or the Hebrew *halal*, meaning "bitter, shiny substance"—describing the medicinal inner leaf of the plant. The Arabs first record using this bitter substance as a laxative in the 6th century B.C. In the 1st century A.D., the herbalist Dioscorides recommended aloe vera for digestive tract, kidney, mouth, and skin diseases. The east African island of Socotra was the only place aloe was cultivated in the 4th century B.C., so Aristotle reportedly asked Alexander the Great to conquer the island to assure a constant supply. Socotra remained the only source of aloe vera until 1673 when English druggists began importing it from Barbados—giving it the species name barbadenis. An early herbal import, it had first reached England much earlier and was said to have helped the frail health of the west Saxon king, Alfred the Great (849–899).

MEDICINAL: Commercial aloe juice is made from the inner leaf, which is blended and strained, with a preservative added. To make aloe "gel," the juice is thickened with seaweed to mimic the leaf's original thick consistency. The crystalline part called aloin—a brownish gel found alongside the leaf blade—is powdered and used in some commercial laxatives. It is so strong that it must be combined with other herbs to prevent intestinal griping. The commercial juice and gel remove this part of the leaf, so both the juice and the gel are soothing to digestive tract irritations, such as peptic ulcers and colitis. In one study, the stomach lesions of twelve peptic ulcer patients were all completely healed.[1] A popular ingredient in commercial drug store products, aloe is commonly used to soothe burns, including sunburn and radiation burns. Aloe is also applied to wounds, eczema, ringworm, and poison oak and poison ivy rashes. There is evidence that it effectively regenerates injured nerves. One study reports aloe to be successful in healing leg ulcerations and severe acne and even finds that it promotes hair growth![2] When 56 frostbite patients were treated with a product containing 70% aloe, only 7% developed infections, compared to 98 frostbitten patients not treated with aloe, 33 of whom eventually needed amputation.[3] It has also proved helpful in treating periodontosis (diseases of the gums and bones holding the teeth). One study injected aloe extracts into the diseased areas of 128 patients with varying degrees of gum disease. Within a week, the development of symptoms stopped, pain decreased, and "marked" improvement followed in all patients.[4]

Aloe is widely used in folk medicine, both as a liniment and as a drink, to reduce the swelling and pain of arthritis and rheumatism. Diabetics in the Arabian peninsula eat aloe to control their blood sugar levels. A clinical study did find that when volunteers who were not insulin dependent took half a teaspoon daily for 4 to 14 weeks, their fasting blood sugar levels were reduced by half, with no change in body weight.[5] Research information can be found in *Aloe Vera: Quotations from Medical Journals on Aloe Research (1935 to 1977)* by Max B. Skousen (Aloe Vera Research Institute, 1979), *Aloe Vera: New Scientific Discoveries* by Max B. Skousen (Aloe Vera Research Institute, 1982), and *Aloe Vera* by Diane Gage (Healing Arts Press, 1988).

COSMETIC: Aloe is a popular base for many cosmetics. It is a soothing emollient for the skin that works wonders for complexion care, soothes sunburn, and also prevents scarring. The aloin it contains is a sunscreen that blocks 20% to 30% of the sun's ultraviolet rays. Aloe's natural pH is about 4.3, ideally suited for skin, which is between pH 4 and 6.

CONSIDERATIONS: Excessive use of aloe (containing aloin), or any strong laxative, encourages hemorrhoids. This part of the plant should not be taken internally during pregnancy, since it can stimulate contractions, or while nursing, since it passes through breast milk.

OTHER: African hunters still rub aloe on their bodies to reduce perspiration and their scent.

HOMEMADE ALOE GEL

Remove the outer leaves from the plant (the inner, new growth must remain) and carefully peel off their thin skin. Apply the gel as is or process the leaves in the blender to make a more uniform consistency. Stir in 500 units vitamin C powder per cup, and store in the refrigerator. For internal use, remove the dark area just under the leaf surface.

Aloysia triphylla
LEMON VERBENA

Aloysia triphylla • Lemon Verbena

(Previously *A. citriodora, Lippia citriodora, Verbena citriodora,
V. triphylla*)

FAMILY: Verbenaceae.

DESCRIPTION: Tall shrub. Height: 5 to 10 feet (1.5 m to 3 m).
Width: 3 to 5 feet (.9 to 1.5 m). Flowers: Small white to pale purple,
on short spikes. Leaves: Yellow-green, narrow, and sharply pointed,
to 3 inches (7.5 cm), in whorls of 3 to 4, with a strong lemon scent.
Blooms: July to September.

HABITAT: Argentina, Chile, Peru, and cultivated in tropical
countries.

CULTIVATION: Perennial. Zone: 7 to 8. Germination: 4 to 6
weeks, or longer. Space: 3 to 4 feet (.9 to 1.2 m). Soil Temperature:
90° F (32° C). Soil: Well drained. Sun: Grow in a greenhouse at
about 55° F (13° C). Propagation: It isn't easy, but it is possible to
grow lemon verbena from seed. Herbalist Louis Saso of Saso Herb
Gardens in Saratoga, California, has been successful by maintaining
a very high soil temperature. Even cuttings are tricky. Choose green
stems (only the tips) in midsummer, with a 65° F (18° C) soil temperature to root them. I've seen mature, well-mulched lemon
verbenas survive snowy, 25° F (–4° C) winters, where the ground
didn't freeze. Herbalist Steven Foster reports that even in Maine,
they can be severely cut back, dug up, and buried in moist sand
inside for the winter. (Water them every few weeks to keep the sand
moist.) Deciduous in the winter. They are subject to spider mites,
which can be deterred with a garlic spray.

GARDEN DESIGN: A potted lemon verbena (that is brought
inside for the winter) presents an artistic show of this graceful herb.
In warmer regions, it becomes a large bush.

CONSTITUENTS: Essential oil (citral).

RELATED SPECIES: Not closely related to vervain *(Verbena
officinalis),* also called verbena.

HISTORY: Brought to Europe by the Spanish, lemon verbena
was christened Herb Louisa after Maria Louisa, wife of King Charles
IV of Spain, and later the botanical name was designated Aloysia in
her honor. It became stylish to place a few leaves in finger bowls at
Victorian banquets.

CULINARY: Lemon verbena is found in preserves, stuffings,
wines, and desserts; it makes a delicious tea. It is used sometimes
in cooking and as a liqueur flavor, especially in its native South
America.

MEDICINAL: Lemon verbena has not been studied much, but
is known to assist digestion and kill bacterial infections such as the
intestinal *E. coli,* tuberculosis, and staph infection. Historically, like
most lemon-scented herbs, it has treated colds, sinus congestion,
indigestion, and diarrhea. A hot tea will lower a fever. In South
America, the tea is also given to asthmatics.

COSMETIC: Soaps and cosmetics scented with lemon verbena
have a clean, fresh lemon and fresh herblike fragrance.

OTHER: Lemon verbena is a popular addition to lemon-scented
potpourri both for its scent and for the interesting shape of its dried
leaves. It acts as an insecticide against mites *(Tetranychus telarius)*
and aphids.

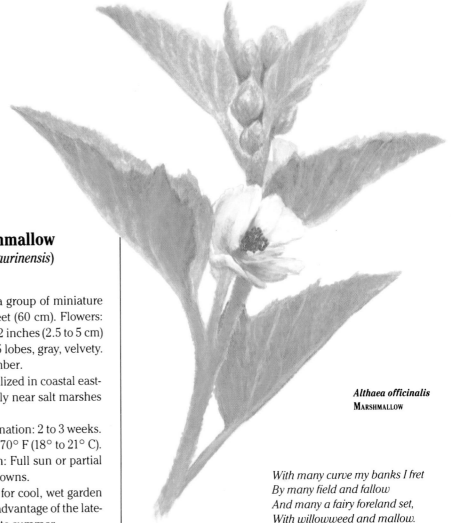

Althaea officinalis
MARSHMALLOW

Althaea officinalis • Marshmallow
(Previously *A. kragujevacensis, A. taurinensis*)

FAMILY: Malvaceae.

DESCRIPTION: Erect stalks, resembling a group of miniature hollyhocks. Height: 4 feet (1.2 m). Width: 2 feet (60 cm). Flowers: Single or clustered, pale blue to rose pink, 1 to 2 inches (2.5 to 5 cm) across. Leaves: Broad ovals, usually with 3 to 5 lobes, gray, velvety. Root: Long, narrow. Blooms: August to September.

HABITAT: Europe, Norway to Spain, naturalized in coastal eastern United States, Asia Minor, Australia, usually near salt marshes or the ocean.

CULTIVATION: Perennial. Zone: 5. Germination: 2 to 3 weeks. Space: 2 feet (60 cm). Soil Temperature: 65° to 70° F (18° to 21° C). Soil: Fairly rich, cool, moist, slightly salty. Sun: Full sun or partial shade. Propagation: By seed, root, or divide crowns.

GARDEN DESIGN: Marshmallow is ideal for cool, wet garden spots not suitable for many other plants. Take advantage of the late-blooming flowers to perk up a wet corner in late summer.

CONSTITUENTS: Mucilage, asparagin, flavonoids, tannins.

RELATED SPECIES: Related to the common hollyhock *(Althaea rosea)* which was used medicinally to decrease inflammation. Cultivars of the related rose of sharon *(Hibiscus syriacus)* are often listed as 'Althaea.'

HISTORY: In the 4th century B.C., Greek Theophrastus suggested althaea root in sweet wine to stop coughing. In the 9th century, Emperor Charlemagne ordered marshmallow cultivated in his monasteries. The modern name comes from the Anglo-Saxon *merscmealwe (merse* means "marsh," and *mealwe* is "mallow").

CULINARY: The original *pâte de guimauve* was a soothing paste of powdered marshmallow root and became a confectionery called marshmallows—although our current version contains none of the original herb. The Romans considered marshmallow a delicious vegetable. The Fellahs in Syria, the Greeks, and the Armenians have all eaten it and found it valuable during famines. The roots can be boiled, then fried in butter. The young spring tops are added to salads.

MEDICINAL: Marshmallow is soothing and healing to stomach and intestinal inflammations such as ulcers. It is a specific treatment for tight, hard coughs, urinary tract infections, and prostate problems. It has been found to increase immunity by stimulating

With many curve my banks I fret
By many field and fallow
And many a fairy foreland set,
With willowweed and mallow.
—ALFRED, LORD TENNYSON (1809–1892), ENGLISH

white blood cells.[1] The tea can be made by soaking the root in cold water for a few hours to extract the mucilage rather than the starch.

COSMETIC: The pulverized roots make a soothing and drawing poultice and are occasionally blended in ointments and creams to soothe chapped hands.

MALLOW SYRUP

This recipe comes from the *Paris Pharmacopoeia*.

4   ounces (113 g) dried marshmallow roots
2   ounces (56 g) raisins
7   pints (4 l) water
15   drops orange-flower water

Boil the mallow, raisins, and water down to 5 pints (3 l) and strain through cheesecloth or coarse strainer (the mixture will be very thick). Add orange water.

Anethum graveolens • Dill
(Previously *Peucedanum graveolens*)

FAMILY: Umbelliferae.

DESCRIPTION: Aromatic, feathery herb with smooth, ribbed stems and a slightly bluish cast, especially when seen at a distance. Height: 2 to 3 feet (60 to 90 cm). Width: 1 foot (30 cm). Flowers: Small, numerous, and yellow, on umbels. Leaves: Thin, feathery, yellow-green. Fruit: Flat, 1/8 inch (3 mm), with ribs. Blooms: June to July.

HABITAT: Native to southwestern Asia and the Mediterranean and naturalized extensively throughout Europe and North America.

CULTIVATION: Annual. Germination: 21 to 25 days. Needs light to germinate. Space: 10 to 12 inches (25 to 30 cm). Soil Temperature: 60° to 70° F (15° to 21° C). Soil: Moderately rich. pH: 5 to 7. Sun: Full sun. Propagation: It does not like transplanting so sow directly into garden. The herb will produce seeds 2 months after planting. It will self-sow.

GARDEN DESIGN: Dill is tall enough to go toward the middle of the bed, or wispy enough to be set forward.

CONSTITUENTS: Essential oils include carone, limonene, phellandrine; coumarins, glycoside in seeds; leaves contain vitamin C, minerals (magnesium, iron, calcium, potassium, phosphorus).

HISTORY: Dill was valued as much as money by the ancients. Greeks who could afford it flaunted their wealth by burning dill-scented oil. One industrious 4th-century Greek, Andradacus, became wealthy when he bought all the available dill oil, withheld it from the market for three years, then sold it for an extremely high profit.

> Stretching out a bony hand,
> the old man pleaded,
> Pay me with Dill Seed rare,
> so my cupboard will not be bare.
> —ROME, CIRCA SECOND CENTURY B.C.

The ancient Romans knew dill as *anethum,* which was later shortened to "anet" and "anise." The Bible mentions anise, meaning dill, as one of the tithes paid (Matthew 23). Later, it was called *dille,* from *dilla,* the Norse word "to lull," probably because for centuries it was considered a soothing herb, capable of producing sleep and easing digestive woes. Charlemagne (circa 742 to 814), a lavish gourmet, insisted that crystal vials of "Dille Oil" be placed at banquets to stop the disquieting hiccups of guests who ate or drank too much. In the 17th century, Nicolas Culpeper listed dill as a "tonic that strengthens the braine." It was already renowned as a diet herb in the 19th century when Dr. Felix Pouchet recommended in *Medical Botany,* "To prevent obesity, boil Dill in water to make a thick broth & drink some each day." The Puritans were known to place dill seeds in their Bibles to discreetly chew so that their stomachs would not rumble during the long church services. But perhaps one of the real secrets of dill's popularity through the centuries was summed up in 1608 in *The Englishman's Doctor:*

> One quality therof yet blame I must,
> It makes men chaste and women filled with lust.

CULINARY: Dill is best known in the United States as a pickling spice, especially for dill pickles. The seeds and leaves also flavor soups, sauces, egg dishes, dips, carrots, cucumbers, potato salad, breads, and occasionally pastries. Otherwise, dill is more popular in northern Europe, especially in Poland, Russia, and Hungary, where it almost always accompanies sauerkraut and potatoes. The seeds were once roasted and made into a coffeelike beverage. The taste closely resembles caraway, which has a similar chemistry.

MEDICINAL: Dill seed improves digestion and appetite and sweetens the breath. The oil kills bacteria and relieves flatulence.[1] Greek Hippocrates's solution in the 4th century B.C. was to "Clean the teeth with a ball of Wool dipped in Honey; rinse with 1 teaspoon (5 ml) of Dill Seed boiled in 1/2-cup [120 ml] of White Wine." Europeans gave their colicky babies "Gripe Water," composed of dill with fennel or anise and mixed with baking soda (sodium bicarbonate) and syrup. Lebanese mothers still use dill for the same purpose. It is frequently used in India's Ayurvedic and Unani medicines for indigestion, fevers, ulcers, uterine pains, and kidney and eye problems. Ethiopians chew the leaves along with fennel to treat headaches and gonorrhea.

AROMATHERAPY: Little "dilly" pillows were placed in European cradles so the fragrance could lull babies to sleep. Dill also scents perfume and soap.

DILL PICKLES

Homemade dill pickles are very easy to make and taste so much better than canned ones from the grocery store. The difference is obvious, even when they are added to potato salad or sandwiches.

1 1/2 pounds (670 g) cucumbers, sliced
1   cup (240 ml) vinegar
1   cup (240 ml) water
2   tablespoons (30 ml) salt
4   garlic cloves, peeled
2   teaspoons (10 ml) dill seeds
1   sprig dill weed (if available)
1   bay leaf

Combine ingredients and bring to a boil. Pour into a very clean jar, and let stand in the refrigerator for 2 weeks. Also, try the same recipe, replacing the cucumbers with lightly cooked green beans.

Anethum graveolens. **Dill, a popular culinary seasoning, is best known for contributing to the distinctive taste of the well-known dill pickle.**

Anethum graveolens
DILL

QUICK PICKS

If you can't wait, delicious dilled cucumbers can be ready in a few hours to add to salads and sandwiches or to eat as a side dish. My mother used to make these for me on hot summer days.

2   **medium-size cucumbers**
     Salt
$^1/_2$ **cup (120 ml) vinegar**
2   **tablespoons (30 ml) water**
$^1/_4$ **teaspoon (1.25 ml) freshly ground black pepper**
1   **teaspoon (5 ml) dill seed**
1   **tablespoon (15 ml) fresh dill weed (optional)**
1   **teaspoon (5 ml) fresh mint leaves, chopped (optional)**

Peel cucumbers, or score lengthwise with fork tines to soften the peel. Cut into very thin slices. Sprinkle lightly with salt and let stand 2 hours. Rinse off salt and combine cucumber slices with remaining ingredients. Marinate at least 1 hour. Refrigerate and serve.

BERNSES OBERLAND DILL POTATO SOUP

Here is a classic dish from the Oberland region of the Swiss Alps. The Swiss serve it with muscat wine and Swiss cheese.

1   **tablespoon (15 ml) butter**
1   **medium onion, minced**
3   **tablespoons (45 ml) flour**
4   **large potatoes, cubed**
2   **teaspoons (10 ml) parsley, minced**
1   **leek, minced**
6   **cups (1.4 liters) water**
$^1/_2$ **teaspoon (2.5 ml) dill seed**
1   **small sprig fresh dill**
1   **stalk celery, minced**
1   **teaspoon (5 ml) salt**
$^1/_8$ **teaspoon (.6 ml) white pepper**
     Paprika to taste

Melt butter in a large saucepan, add onion, and brown lightly for 3 minutes, stirring constantly. Stir in flour and continue stirring 5 minutes, or until brown. Add all other ingredients, except paprika, and cover. Simmer gently about 35 minutes. Remove dill sprig and lower flame. Blend into a creamy puree. Add paprika. Serve piping hot in preheated bowls.

Angelica archangelica • Angelica
(Previously *A. officinalis*)

FAMILY: Umbelliferae.

DESCRIPTION: Tall and stately when in flower. The whole plant has a distinct aromatic fragrance and taste. Height: 5 to 6 feet (1.5 to 1.8 m), occasionally as much as 7 feet (2.1 m). Width: 3 feet (.9 m). Flowers: The large heads are spheres of small, light yellow, almost green flowers. Leaves: Few, deeply dented and large palm-like on hollow, fluted stems. Fruit: Green, oblong fruits $1/6$ to $1/4$ inch (4 to 6 mm) long. Root: Hard, fibrous, containing a thick, yellowish juice. Blooms: June to July.

HABITAT: Angelica may have originated in Syria, then spread to Europe. It now grows abundantly in Lapland and Iceland.

CULTIVATION: Biennial, but may live up to 3 years before flowering. Zone: 4. Germination: 21 to 28 days. Stratify by placing in refrigerator 6 to 8 weeks. Space: $2^1/2$ to 3 feet (75 to 90 cm). Soil Temperature: 60° to 70° F (15° to 21° F). Soil: Rich, moist loam, slightly acid. pH: 5 to 7. Sun: Full sun but prefers semishade. Propagation: By seed or sometimes by division. The seeds stay viable only about 6 months, unless stored in refrigerator. Bugs are very attracted to them, so if you do store them, keep them in a sealed container. Angelica prefers a cool climate and grows well by a creek or stream. Growing stinging nettle plants nearby is said to increase angelica seed's oil content by 80%. Dig the roots in the first fall or second spring, and harvest the stalks any time during the summer.

GARDEN DESIGN: It is not only people who find angelica attractive—fruit flies and blackflies flock to it. Keep this in mind when planting angelica, locating it in a remote location from the house and patio, such as in the center of an herb bed, where its stately figure will hold court above the other herbs.

CONSTITUENTS: Essential oils (1%) include phellandrene, pinene, limonene, caryophyllene, linalool; coumarins (umbelliferone, bergapten, xanthotoxol), acids, resins, sugar, sterols.

RELATED SPECIES: Most of the approximately 50 angelica species are medicinal, although their chemistries are not identical. Identify them carefully! They have been occasionally confused with poisonous members of the Umbelliferae family. Traditional Chinese medicine considers don quai *(A. sinensis)* superior for building blood and regulating the body. It is well known in the United States as a women's tonic to adjust menstrual irregularities. In a Chinese study, don quai improved impaired liver functions of 60% of the patients with chronic hepatitis or cirrhosis of the liver. Many of them also experienced an improved blood count.[1]

HISTORY: Angelica's sweet stems and seeds have been used for European candies and other confections since the Vikings brought the herb to central Europe in the 10th century. It is first mentioned medicinally by European herbalists in the 15th century. The name is reported to have been given it by a monk when the Archangel Raphael descended and announced it was a cure for the plague. Its reputation as a health-restorer has followed it through the centuries. In 1974, French newspapers reported that Annibal Camoux of Marseilles had lived to 120 years old because she had chewed angelica root daily.

CULINARY: Candied angelica stems are served by themselves or made into a colorful jelly. They were originally the green candies in fruitcakes. Considered a vegetable in northern countries like Iceland, Siberia, and especially Lapland, the raw stems are eaten with butter. Chances are you will find these dishes a little tart, but try angelica cooked with rhubarb, which will sweeten the vegetable's sour taste. Laplanders take advantage of angelica's broad leaves and antimicrobial properties to wrap and preserve their fish on long journeys—a biodegradable alternative to plastic wrap. In Norway, the powdered roots flavor bread. As a legacy of the Benedictine monks of the Middle Ages who added the root to wines and elixirs, angelica remains an ingredient in vermouth; it is combined with juniper berries in gin; and it is used in Chartreuse, the herbal liqueur first made by the monks at La Grande Chartreuse near Grenoble, France.

Angelica archangelica
ANGELICA

Angelica archangelica. **The stately, towering flowers of angelica make it stand out in any garden. The candied stalks were once a popular sweet.**

MEDICINAL: Medieval monks used angelica root elixirs as digestive and lung medicines—even to treat the plague. Angelica has proved itself useful to relieve muscle spasms of asthma and bronchitis. Herbalists also use it to regulate a women's menstrual cycle, especially after extended use of the birth control pill or an intrauterine device.

CONSIDERATIONS: Very large amounts act too strongly on the central nervous system. Some people experience dermatitis from repeatedly touching the fresh leaves.

OTHER: The root's fragrance attracts deer and fish—it was widely used by early European and North American hunters.

CANDIED, OR CRYSTALLIZED, ANGELICA STALKS

2 cups (480 g) angelica roots and young stems
¹/₂ cup (120 g) salt
2 cups (500 ml) boiling water
2 cups (500 ml) sugar
2 cups (500 ml) water
1 tablespoon (15 ml) lemon juice

Place angelica in a bowl and cover with the salt and boiling water. Let sit about 24 hours. Drain, peel, and wash in cold water.

Cook the sugar in the water to 238° F (114° C). Add angelica and lemon juice, and cook 20 minutes. Drain angelica and put syrup aside.

Place angelica on a rack in a cool, dark place for 4 days and refrigerate the syrup. Then combine the syrup and roots and cook to 238° F (114° C) 20 minutes, or until candied. Drain on a rack until thoroughly dry. Store in a tightly covered container.

Anthriscus cerefolium
CHERVIL

Anthriscus cerefolium • Chervil

FAMILY: Umbelliferae.

DESCRIPTION: Small, rounded herb. Height: 2 feet (60 cm). Flowers: White, in flat umbels, ¹/₁₀ inches (.25 cm). Leaves: Pale, green, delicate, fernlike. Blooms: June to July.

HABITAT: Native to Russia and western Asia.

CULTIVATION: Annual, sometimes biennial. Germination: 7 to 14 days. Space: 8 to 12 inches (20 to 30 cm). Soil Temperature: 60° to 70° F (15° to 21° C). Soil: Rich, well drained, with light, consistent moisture. pH: 7 to 8. Sun: Partial shade or sun, cool, wet climate. Propagation: The germination rate rapidly declines as the seeds age. The leaves will be ready in 6 to 8 weeks after sowing. The French say it is extremely easy to grow, although other gardeners don't always agree. A very hardy herb, it can survive mild winters to sprout again in the spring and does well in a pot or windowbox.

GARDEN DESIGN: Filtered shade highlights chervil's glossy leaves as the sun strikes them. A large patch is needed to bring out its licoricelike scent into the garden. Medieval gardeners planted chervil toward the back of the bed, among the angelicas and behind the parsley.

CONSTITUENTS: Essential oil.

HISTORY: Chervil reached the Mediterranean long before the Christian era. The Romans called it *cerefolium.* Referring to the herb as *khairephyllon,* or "leaf of joy," Greek nobles carried a sprig to wave blessings to friends. In the 18th century, Englishman John Wesley was still declaring that "cerfille is cheering to the spirits." The English botanist John Gerard wrote in 1597 that chervil, "eaten in salad when they are green, with oil and vinegar, by the agreeableness of their taste, are better than other salads through the sweetness of their aroma, and nothing is healthier for weak stomachs."

CULINARY: The taste of chervil's leaves resembles parsley with a licorice overtone. The leaves can flavor cheese and egg dishes or garnish a dish instead of parsley. It's a good thing the French find chervil so easy to grow. With tarragon, it seasons ravigote, vinaigrette sauces, and the famous béarnaise, a mainstay of French cuisine since its inception in 1835. Chervil is one of the *fines herbes* and is the fresh *pluches de cereuille* used in many French stew and soup recipes, such as the renowned "Mélange de Potage au Cerfeuil" from Roubaix. Chervil, or *perifolio,* can also be found in Spanish soups and sauces. Cooking diminishes the flavor, so add it at the last minute or preserve it as an herb vinegar. It can be a substitute for tarragon. For centuries, the Arabs produced a chervil- *(rig-el-ghurab)* and-cherry-flavored liqueur that was copied by 14th-century Europeans by soaking the ingredients in brandy for a few weeks and then straining them.

MEDICINAL: Chervil is mostly regarded as a culinary herb, but does have medicinal properties. Poultices of chervil leaves have been laid on boils, bruises, and other skin afflictions by the ancient Arabians, Greeks, Romans, and Europeans. It was boiled in wine for urinary disorders and for use as a speedy diuretic.

COSMETIC: The famous French beauty Ninon de L'Enclos (circa 1616 to 1709) complained, "If God had to give women wrinkles, He might at least have put them on the soles of her feet." She washed her face twice daily in chervil to prevent wrinkles and drank fresh chervil juice to maintain her slender figure.

NINON'S COMPLEXION FORMULA

1   pint (500 ml) fresh milk
2   cups (470 ml) fresh chervil leaves
1/2 cup (120 ml) brandy

Boil milk gently with 1 cup (240 ml) chervil leaves. Allow to cool, strain out the leaves, and keep refrigerated. Gently heat 1 cup (240 ml) chervil leaves in brandy. Let sit overnight to cool. Strain and bottle. Store at room temperature. Every morning, splash the chervil milk on the face, then rinse with spring water. Every evening, splash on the brandy mixture.

SAUCE BÉARNAISE

1/2 cup (120 ml) white or red wine
2   tablespoons (30 ml) tarragon vinegar (see Artemisia dranunculus var. sativa)
1   tablespoon (15 ml) shallots, finely chopped
2   peppercorns, crushed
2   sprigs tarragon, chopped
1   sprig chervil, finely chopped
3   egg yolks
1/4 cup (6 ml) melted butter

Combine wine, vinegar, shallots, peppercorns, and herbs in a double boiler. Cook over direct heat until reduced to half its volume, then allow to cool. In a double boiler, lightly heat, while stirring briskly until very well blended. Slowly stir in yolks and butter. Use to flavor main dish.

MÉLANGE DE POTAGE AU CERFEUIL

1   cup (240 ml) chervil leaves, minced
1   leek, minced
1/2 onion, minced
1/2 stick butter
1/4 cup (60 ml) cream
1/2 cup (120 ml) white wine
4   cups (960 ml) hot potato soup
    Fresh sprigs chervil (for garnish)

Sauté the chervil, leek, and onion in the butter, stirring constantly. When the onion begins to turn clear, add cream and wine. Carefully add the mixture to the soup. Serve topped with a fresh sprig of chervil.

Aralia racemosa • Spikenard

FAMILY: Araliaceae.

DESCRIPTION: An oversize herb, with stems coming from one main stalk. Height: To 6 feet (1.8 m). Width: 3 feet (90 cm). Flowers: Clusters consisting of 10 to 25 small, greenish blooms. Leaves: Few, large, to 2 1/2 feet (75 cm) long, composed of oval leaflets with sharp points. Berries: Almost round, hard, red-brown berries that turn dark purple. Root: Thick, with heavy bark, pungent smell and taste. Blooms: July to August.

HABITAT: Canada to North Carolina, west to Utah and Arizona.

CULTIVATION: Perennial. Zone: 4. Germination: 2 to 3 weeks. Use fresh seed, stratify 40 days. Space: 3 feet (90 cm). Soil Temperature: 60° to 65° F (15° to 18° C). Soil: Fairly rich, moist. Sun: Semishade. Propagation: Easiest by seed; also by root cutting. Well adapted to cultivation and city life.

GARDEN DESIGN: The large leaves give a dramatic, subtropical effect that can draw attention to the back of the shade garden.

CONSTITUENTS: Essential oil, resin.

RELATED SPECIES: North American and Asian species have similar properties. This is not the fragrant spikenard (*Nardostachys jatamansi*) of the Bible.

HISTORY: This herb is usually referred to as American spikenard to differentiate it. J. Carver reported in his 1778 travelog that "the plant appears to be exactly the same as the Asiatic spikenard, so much valued by the ancients. Its berries are of such a balsamic nature, that when infused in spirits, they make a most palatable and reviving cordial." All of the spikenards were popular in American medicine. In his 1828 *Medical Flora*, C. S. Rafinesque mentioned "it is often called Sarsaparilla, the root being similar to [*Smilax officinalis* of Mexico] and having similar properties...." It was the main ingredient in the 19th-century "Compound of Spikenard." In the same family as ginseng, the various American species *do* look like giant ginsengs. They are all called "manroot," although spikenard's root is much larger and less inclined to have ginseng's distinct, humanlike form.

CULINARY: Native Americans ate the root, and one of their favorite recipes combined it with wild onion, gooseberry, and honey. They also relished the young tips in soup. The roots were once made into a tonic herbal beer, and the berries flavored other beers and were turned into a wine similar to elderberry wine.

MEDICINAL: Considered tonic, like sarsaparilla, spikenard's roots have treated a long list of complaints, including indigestion, dysentery, blood diseases, syphilis, various skin conditions (including ringworm), as well as gout, rheumatism, local pains, and some heart problems. It was an important blood purifying tea, particularly during pregnancy. Herbalists still use it to balance women's cycles, including helping with premenstrual syndrome. Its actions are similar to those attributed to sarsaparilla's progesteronelike constituents, although hormonal activity in spikenard has not been proven. A pleasant-tasting syrup was made with spikenard and elecampane for lung conditions like whooping cough, asthma, and general coughs. A root poultice was chewed and applied to wounds, and a solution mixed with wild ginger was placed on fractured limbs. The berry juice was dropped into the ear canal to ease earache.

Aralia racemosa
Spikenard

© Derek Fell

Arctium lappa. **Nature's version of Velcro, burdock is best known for its adhesive qualities—its fruit is a sphere of gray-brown burrs with hundreds of tiny hooks that attach themselves to clothing, fur, and hair when even minimal contact is made with them.**

Arctium lappa • Burdock

FAMILY: Compositae.

DESCRIPTION: A large herb, with tall stalk and huge leaves. Height: To 10 feet (3.1 m). Width: 3 feet (90 cm). Flowers: Round heads of purple on a 3- to 4-foot (.9- to 1.2-m) stalk. Leaves: Large, wavy, dull green top with fine, gray, downy underside, to 20 inches (50 cm) long. Supported on stout stems that rise from a central location. Fruit: Sphere of brown-gray burrs. Root: Long taproot, up to 3 feet (90 cm) long. Blooms: August to September.

HABITAT: Eurasia. Via animals, people, and anything it could cling to, burdock has distributed itself throughout Europe and the United States in slightly damp areas.

CULTIVATION: Biennial. Zone: 3. Germination: 6 to 10 days. Space: 2 to 3 feet (60 to 90 cm). Soil Temperature: 70° F (21° C). Soil: Dry, medium rich, well drained. pH: 5 to 8. Sun: Full sun. Propagation: Sown directly into the garden.

CONSTITUENTS: Inulin, essential oil, resin, antibiotic substance, polyacetylenes, organic acids; seeds contain fixed oils (15% to 30%), glycoside (arctiin), chorogenic acid; leaves harbor arctiol, fukinone, taraxasterol.

RELATED SPECIES: A smaller version *(A. minus)* is used similarly.

HISTORY: Burdock's species name, *lappa,* is probably derived from the Latin *lappa,* meaning burr, and the Greek "to seize," owing to burdock seed heads that cling to one's hair and clothing. Shakespeare already knew: "They are Burrs, I can tell you, they'll stick where they are thrown," he wrote in *Troilus and Cressida.* The modern world can thank burdock for inspiring Swiss inventor George de Mestral, who developed the self-adhesive fastener, Velcro.™ One day when George and his dog came back from the country covered with burrs, he observed the seed's hundreds of tiny hooks through his magnifying glass. It got him thinking, and eventually, he developed a way to imitate them with plastic.

CULINARY: Burdock may not seem like typical table fare, but the flower stalks, cut before the flowers bloom, can be boiled as a vegetable or eaten raw after being sprinkled with oil and vinegar. (Watch out, the stalks are slightly laxative!) The Japanese are fond of eating *gobo,* their name for burdock. They collect young roots, about 2 feet (60 cm) long, and add them finely sliced to stir-fries, soups, and stews or eat it raw. Japanese produce shops and some natural food stores sell these fresh roots. They are also roasted to make "coffee" and can be pounded and added to pancakes or prepared like potatoes. I enjoy the taste and use them in some recipes instead of carrots, although they are definitely not as sweet. A burdock-and-yellow-dock spread was once eaten for its medicinal properties. The Russians season fish and game by wrapping them in burdock leaves and cooking the bundle in a pit that has previously been heated with a fire.

MEDICINAL: For centuries, burdock root has been considered one of the most important "blood-purifying" herbs to help the liver and kidneys detoxify the body. It is also used to cleanse the body of uric acid and other residues that accumulate from rheumatism, arthritis, and gout. I've seen it do wonders as both a tea and skin wash to clear up eczema and psoriasis. The roots are most commonly used, but Chinese and some Western herbalists also employ the seeds, especially for skin problems. Tests confirm that it kills both bacterial and fungal infections.[1] The Chinese also find burdock useful for colds, flus, measles, and constipation. French herbalists suggest the fresh root to lower blood sugar levels in diabetics and because it contains the easily digestible starch inulin. To date, no clinical studies on humans have been done to verify animal studies showing the ability of the seeds to lower blood sugar. It is also believed, but is not proven, that the root regenerates liver cells and stimulates the gallbladder. Burdock is used in many parts of the world in herbal cancer treatments.[2] The shredded leaves have also been folded into egg whites and applied as a skin dressing to accelerate healing.

CONSIDERATIONS: Burdock has a clean track record for safety, except for an isolated report in a 1978 issue of the *Journal of American Medicine,* in which poisoning from burdock tea was reported. However, the tea was probably contaminated with belladonna, since atropinelike symptoms were recorded.

BURDOCK SPREAD

¹/₂   **cup (120 ml) burdock root, finely cut**
¹/₈   **cup (30 ml) yellow dock root, finely cut**
1   **cup (240 ml) apple cider vinegar**
¹/₂   **cup (120 ml) sour cream or yogurt**

Simmer roots in the vinegar for about 5 minutes. Process in a blender, then add the cream or yogurt. Serve on potatoes or other vegetable dishes.

> *Mother went rambling, and came back with a burdock on her shawl, so we know that the snow has perished from the earth.*
> —LETTERS OF EMILY DICKINSON, EMILY DICKINSON (1830–1886), AMERICAN

Armoracia rusticana • Horseradish
(Previously *Cochlearia armoracia, Nasturtium a., Radicula a.,* and *Rorippa a.*)

FAMILY: Cruciferae

DESCRIPTION: Height: To 5 feet (1.5 m). Width: 2 feet (60 cm). Flowers: White clusters, held erect. Leaves: Wavy, broad, tapering towards the bottom, upright on short stems 15 inches (38 cm) wide, 1 to 3 feet (30 to 90 cm) tall. They reduce in size as they progress up the flower stalk. Root: Fleshy taproot, yellow-white, to 2 feet (60 cm). Blooms: June.

HABITAT: Southeastern Europe, in damp soils. Naturalized in North America.

CULTIVATION: Perennial. Zone: 2. Space: 10 to 15 inches (25–38 cm). Soil: Loose, rich soil, at least 18 inches (45 cm) deep. pH: 6 to 8. Sun: Full sun or partial shade. Propagation: From root cuttings in spring. Take off rootlets from the main tap root. Seeds are not viable. Harvest the roots in early autumn, before they get too pithy and bitter. They can be stored for months in dry sand to keep them fresh.

GARDEN DESIGN: Horseradish may not be the most attractive herb in the garden, but it is certainly interesting. Be forewarned that once established, it will always be there.

Armoracia rusticana
HORSERADISH

CONSTITUENTS: Fresh root: glycoside decomposes to the enzyme myrosin to produce mustard oil, vitamins B and C, and minerals (calcium, phosphorus, iron); antibiotic, asparagin.

HISTORY: No early distinctions were made between the table radish and the horse—or "corse"—radish. It is thought to be one of the traditional bitter Passover herbs, with coriander, horehound, and lettuce. Horseradish was eaten by the Germans and Scandinavians instead of mustard, but was not very popular with other Europeans until the mid-17th century, when the French began to use *moutarde des Allemands,* or German mustard, on their food. The French still eat horseradish, slicing the whole root at the table and salting it. It is mostly used in fish or meat dishes or in sauces, following Chaucer's observation "Woe to the cook whose sauce has no sting." Placing the fresh root in distilled vinegar prevents discoloration.

CULINARY: Grate horseradish root into lemon juice, vinegar, or directly into a sauce just before using. Its mustard oil zing is produced only when the root is exposed to air and it rapidly loses its punch after that. It also increases in bitterness as it ages, so it is best used before 3 months. When using the dried root, reconstitute it at least 30 minutes before serving. Horseradish is the main ingredient in Dresden Sauce.

MEDICINAL: Horseradish stimulates digestion and is traditionally eaten with fatty foods to help digest them. It is mixed with glycerine to make a syrup for treating bronchitis, lung and sinus congestion, and whooping cough although simply eating a meal with a horseradish paste condiment will likely have the same effect. The proven antibiotic action hinders both respiratory and urinary tract infections.[1] It is also taken to kill worms, as a diuretic, and to relieve rheumatism and gout. A poultice of the sliced root can be applied directly on boils.

COSMETIC: In earlier centuries, horseradish was infused in milk and slapped on the face to stimulate circulation and make the complexion rosy. It was also mixed with vinegar and applied to remove freckles.

CONSIDERATIONS: Large doses can produce inflammation in the digestive tract and may burn sensitive skin. It can also be emetic.

OTHER: Studies at the Massachusetts Institute of Technology show that horseradish derivatives may be useful to replace current microbial treatments that remove toxic pollutants (amines, phenols, and the like) from water and make them insoluble.

DRESDEN SAUCE

1   cup (240 ml) sour cream or yogurt
¹/₂   teaspoon (2.5 ml) prepared mustard
¹/₂   teaspoon (2.5 ml) horseradish, fresh if possible
¹/₄   teaspoon (1.2 ml) salt

Combine ingredients and serve with main course.

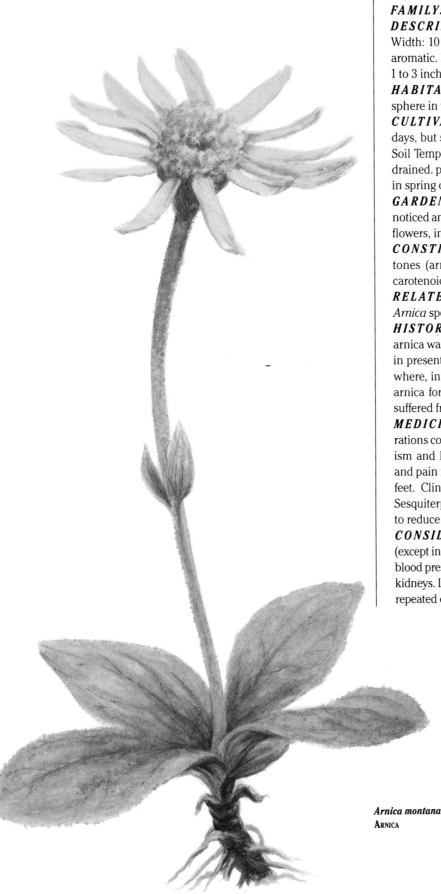

Arnica montana • **Arnica**

FAMILY: Compositae.

DESCRIPTION: Perennial. Height: 1 to 2 feet (30 to 60 cm). Width: 10 inches (25 cm). Flowers: Golden yellow, daisylike, and aromatic. Leaves: 4 to 8 downy leaves that spring up from a rosette 1 to 3 inches (2.5 to 7.5 cm) long. Blooms: May to June.

HABITAT: Central Europe in higher areas of the Northern Hemisphere in woods and open meadows. Protected in parts of Europe.

CULTIVATION: Perennial. Zone: 6. Germination: 25 to 30 days, but sometimes 2 years. Space: 12 to 15 inches (30 to 37 cm). Soil Temperature: 55° F (13° C). Soil: Moist, sandy, and very well drained. pH: 5.5 to 7.5. Sun: Full sun. Propagation: Divide the roots in spring or grow from seed.

GARDEN DESIGN: Plant arnica where its flower will be noticed and highlighted. It is best displayed in groups, among other flowers, in woodsy settings or rock gardens.

CONSTITUENTS: Essential oil (thymol), sesquiterpene lactones (arnicin, helenalin), flavonoids, polysaccharides, inulin, carotenoids, tannins.

RELATED SPECIES: Arnica can be replaced by a number of *Arnica* species found in the United States.

HISTORY: In 1751, Briton John Hill, in his *Herbal,* lamented that arnica was "greatly recommended by ancients but much neglected in present-day practice." It was, however, well known in Germany where, in the 18th century, Johann Wolfgang von Goethe credited arnica for saving his life when it relieved the anginal attacks he suffered from hardening of the arteries.

MEDICINAL: In Germany, more than 100 different drug preparations contain arnica flowers and sometimes the leaf. Both herbalism and homeopathy use arnica extract to reduce inflammation and pain from bruises, sprains, tendons, dislocations, and swollen feet. Clinical studies support its ability to enhance circulation. Sesquiterpene lactones, the active principles in arnica, are known to reduce inflammation, decrease pain, and kill germs.[1]

CONSIDERATIONS: Arnica is usually not used internally (except in homeopathic dosages). It initially lowers the heartbeat and blood pressure, then raises it and also irritates the digestive tract and kidneys. Large doses may cause dizziness and tremors. Occasionally, repeated external application produces skin irritations.

Arnica montana
ARNICA

Artemisia abrotanum • Southernwood
(Previously *A. procera*)

FAMILY: Compositae.
DESCRIPTION: Many-branched with individual branches resembling miniature trees. Height: 3 to 5 feet (.9 to 1.5 m). Width: 1 foot (30 cm). Flowers: Yellow-white, small. Leaves: Green, feathery, aromatic, with a bitter lemon scent. Blooms: Late autumn.
HABITAT: Throughout southern Europe.
CULTIVATION: Perennial. Zone: 5. Space: 2 feet (60 cm). Soil: Well drained. pH: 5.5 to 7.5. Sun: Full sun. Propagation: Rarely flowers and doesn't produce viable seed when it does, so propagate by root division, cuttings, or layering. The branches readily sprout where they lie on the ground. Pruning, especially where there is a long growing season, keeps the plant from getting too straggly.

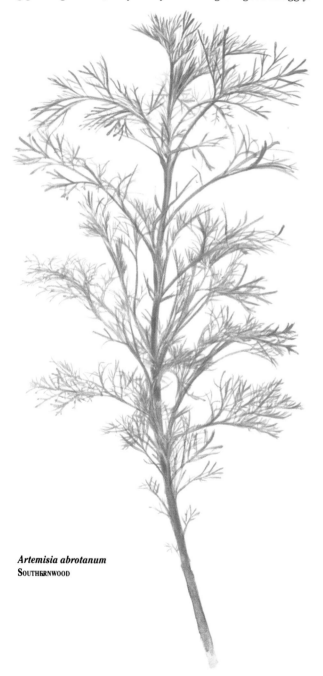

Artemisia abrotanum
SOUTHERNWOOD

GARDEN DESIGN: The feathery leaves provide textures that contrast well with darker herbs and can provide a break from borders of green, bushy herbs. It is particularly noticeable in the autumn when they turn shades of orange and brown. Southernwood has a tendency to flop on its neighbors, but can be pruned back early in the autumn or spring or tied back.
CONSTITUENTS: Essential oil (absinthol).
RELATED SPECIES: There are two varieties, tangerine southernwood and camphor southernwood.
HISTORY: When it arrived in 1548, the English called it *suthernewude*, or "a woody plant from the south," and immediately put it to use to cover their dirt floors. The French named it *garde robe* because they placed it among their woolens to deter moths. Southernwood ashes were mixed with olive oil to promote hair growth, giving rise to both the common names, young lad's love and old man's beard. Perhaps owing to these virile associations, the leaves were included in bouquets given to women being courted. St. Francis de Sales wrote, "To love in the midst of sweets, little children could do that, but to love in the bitterness of Wormwood is a sure sign of our affectionate fidelity." Women also carried southernwood nosegays, with lemon balm, to church so they wouldn't feel drowsy. Judges, too, took advantage of southernwood nosegays, with rue and rosemary, to protect themselves from "gaol fever" (typhoid) in the courtroom.
CULINARY: Although quite bitter, southernwood is used in some European cooking.
MEDICINAL: Southernwood encourages menstruation, is antiseptic, and kills intestinal worms. It was used to treat liver, spleen, and stomach problems. It is seldom used medicinally today, except in Germany, where poultices are placed on wounds, splinters, and skin conditions and it is employed occasionally to treat frostbite. Its constituents have been shown to stimulate the gallbladder and bile, which improves digestion and liver functions.[1]
AROMATHERAPY: Southernwood leaves are mixed with other herbs in aromatic baths. The scent has been said since ancient times to counter sleepiness.
OTHER: It is an insect repellent—even bees don't care for it! The stems yield yellow dye, and the foliage is used in fresh and dried flower decorations.

Mrs. Todd was an ardent lover of herbs, both wild and tame, and the sea breeze blew into the low end-window of the house laden not only with sweet-brier and sweet-mary, but balm and sage, borage and mint, wormwood, and southernwood. If Mrs. Todd had occasion to step into the far corner of her herb plot, she trod heavily upon thyme and made its fragrant presence known with all the rest.
—COUNTRY OF THE POINTED FIRS, SARA ORNE JEWETT (1849–1909), AMERICAN

*The garden border where I stood
Was sweet with pinks and southernwood.*
—"REFLECTIONS," JEAN INGELOW (1820–1897), ENGLISH

Artemisia absinthium • Wormwood

FAMILY: Compositae.

DESCRIPTION: Bushy, coarse herbal shrub. Height: 4 feet (1.2 m). Width: 2 feet (60 cm). Flowers: Small, ¹/₈ inch (3 mm) across, tinted yellow. Leaves: Slightly hairy, gray, divided to give an almost lacy effect. Blooms: August to September.

HABITAT: Europe, naturalized in parts of northeastern United States and Canada.

CULTIVATION: Perennial. Zone: 4. Germination: 10 to 24 days. Needs light to germinate, so plant at shallow depth. Space: 3 feet (90 cm). Soil Temperature: 60° to 70° F (15° to 21° C). Soil: Dry, fairly poor, some clay. pH: 5.5 to 7.5. Sun: Full sun preferred, but tolerates partial shade. Propagation: By seed, cuttings, or root division on larger plants. The leaves and probably the roots exude a substance that restricts growth of neighboring plants. Strong herbs like yarrow and rue seem to not mind, but thymes, mints, and other culinary herbs would prefer not growing next to wormwood! Herbalist Steven Foster reports that during his informal experiments, mints and oreganos growing next to wormwood were stunted, with a height of about 6 inches (15 cm), compared to the 2-foot (60-cm) relatives growing outside a 3-foot (90-cm) perimeter.

GARDEN DESIGN: The leaves of all the various wormwoods add texture and depth to garden design. Since they have a tendency to sprawl, use them as a background or central attraction in a bed.

CONSTITUENTS: Essential oil includes thujone, to 35%, bitters (absinthum), sesquiterpene lactones (absinthin, etc.), flavonoids, azulenes.

RELATED SPECIES: Related to mugwort *(A. vulgaris)*, southernwood *(A. abrotanum)*, tarragon *(A. dracunculus)*, and the sagebrushes of American desert country. Roman wormwood *(A. pontica)* and old woman *(A. maritima)* are attractive garden additions. A sesquiterpene lactone in sweet wormwood *(A. annua)* called *quighaosu* has successfully cured thousands of Chinese with malaria.[1]

HISTORY: The Romans called it *absinthium*, after *absinthial*, their word for "bitter." The bitterness (probably of *A. herba-alba* or *A. judaica)* is described in the Bible (Proverbs 5). The ancient Greeks dedicated wormwood to the goddess Artemisia and claimed that it counteracted the poisons of hemlock, mushrooms, and even sea dragons. Several species were used to eliminate intestinal parasites by the Greek herbalist Dioscorides, although the name really comes from the Anglo-Saxon *wermode,* which means "waremood," or "mind preserver."

CULINARY: Wormwood provides the bitter taste for vermouth, or *wermuth* (along with *A. pontica* and other wormwoods), for the Italian wine Cinzano, and in martinis. Until it was banned in France and the United States in 1915 and in Germany in 1923, it also flavored absinthe. This popular 19-century aperitif, considered one of the most dangerous alcoholic drinks, caused absinthism, or wormwood poisoning. It was enjoyed by many 19-century French artists, like Toulouse-Lautrec, Eugène Henri Gauguin, and Charles Pierre Baudelaire. Dr. Wilfrid N. Arnold of the University of Kansas City has theorized that addiction to absinthe, as well as to camphor and turpentine, caused Vincent van Gogh to suffer hallucinations and seizures, which contributed to his eventual suicide. Wormwood was also added to hops to make beer more heady. By the way, wormwood is a traditional stuffing for goose.

Artemisia absinthium
WORMWOOD

MEDICINAL: Wormwood leaves' primary use is to stimulate the gallbladder, help prevent, and release, stones, and to adjust resulting digestive problems. Clinical studies with volunteers proved that wormwood does effectively increase bile.[2] It expels roundworms and threadworms, probably due to its sesquiterpene lactones. It is also a muscle relaxer that is occasionally added to liniments, especially for rheumatism. Members of the Bedouin African tribe, who sell wormwood in the Cairo market, place the antiseptic leaves inside their nostrils as a decongestant and drink it for coughs. The leaves are burned around their newborns to ensure their health.

CONSIDERATIONS: Large amounts of wormwood can be toxic to people, as well as worms. The thujone it contains is addictive and can damage the central nervous system. The United States FDA classifies it as "dangerous." It is thought to interact with the same brain receptors as does marijuana *(Cannabis sativa).*[3] Products that are flavored with wormwood must contain thujone-free extracts. Absinthe can cause insomnia, nightmares, convulsions, and vomiting.[4] Don't use wormwood at all if pregnant.

OTHER: Wormwood is a moth and flea repellent and is occasionally used in potpourri. It makes a beautiful foundation for dried wreaths, although it is brittle and best formed while still fresh.

While Wormwood hath seed get a handful or twaine
To save against march, to make flea to feraine:
Wherre chamber is sweeped and Wormwood is strowne,
No flea for his life dare abide to be known
What saver is better (if physick be true)
For places infected than Wormwood and Rue?
It is a comfort for hart and the braine,
And therefore to have it its not in vaine.
—"JULY'S HUSBANDRY," *TUSSER'S HUSBANDRY,* THOMAS TUSSER (1527–1580), ENGLISH

Artemisia dracunculus var. *sativa* • Tarragon

FAMILY: Compositae.

DESCRIPTION: Sparse, leafy herb. Height: 2 to 3 feet (60 to 90 cm). Width: 1 foot (30 cm). Leaves: Narrow, rounded at first, then pointed; shiny, smooth, deep green; distinct aniselike flavor.

HABITAT: Possibly southern Europe, perhaps also the steppes of Asia. Cultivated commercially on a small scale in Europe, particularly in France and Yugoslavia, and in the United States, especially in California.

CULTIVATION: Perennial. Zone: 4 to 5. Space: 1 foot (30 cm). Soil: Very well drained, fairly rich. pH: 5.5 to 7. Sun: Full sun. Propagation: Easiest by root division. Tarragon demands patience. It doesn't produce seed, and cuttings can take 2 months to root. Protect when temperatures fall below 10° F (–12° C). Not suitable for a winter houseplant. It is best to renew the patch every 3 to 4 years. Tarragon needs a winter dormancy period, so is easier to cultivate in a cool climate. It is next to impossible to obtain fresh tarragon in the winter, although it can be grown in cold months as an annual, by starting plants late and tricking them with grow lights and warmth. You might want to stake your plants to keep the sprawling leaves off the ground.

GARDEN DESIGN: Tarragon has a weedy habit and is not planted for its design qualities! Nevertheless, it is certainly an important addition to any kitchen herb garden.

CONSTITUENTS: Essential oil (estragole, to 70%), flavonoids (rutin, quercertin).

RELATED SPECIES: Russian tarragon *(A. dracunculus,* previously *A. redowski)* is easier to grow and does produce seed but is far inferior in flavor to true tarragon, lacking the distinctive aniselike taste.

HISTORY: Historians think French tarragon really originated in Asia and invading Mongols brought it to Spain in the mid-1100s. It was called *taragoncia,* from the Arabic *tarkhun.* Tarragon was hardly mentioned, except by the Muslim herbalist Avicenna, until the 13th century, and then only briefly by Ibn-al-Baytar, an Arabian herbalist in Spain, as a vegetable seasoning and breath freshener that also happened to induce sleep. He said it was well known in Syria (where it is still eaten) but was rare in Egypt. French tarragon seems to have finally reached France in the 14th century, when St. Catherine visited Pope Clement VI, carrying herbs from her native Siena—one of the few Italian regions where tarragon is commonly grown today.

Tarragon began its rise to fame in Europe in the 16th century. The 17th-century herbalist John Evelyn proclaimed it beneficial for "head, heart, and liver." Catherine the Great (1684–1724) introduced Russia to French-style tarragon. French Queen Marie Antoinette (1755–1793) had her lady-in-waiting wear kid gloves while picking 5 perfect tarragon leaves every morning to marinate in 5 teaspoons (25 ml) of lemon juice in preparation for dinner. It was tarragon that is said to have saved the life of Great Britain's King George IV (1762–1830) when he was Prince of Wales. His chef, the renowned Marie Antoine Carême, put him on a diet with no other seasoning. His father, George III, failed to credit this remedy, but the prince rewarded 'Carême with a gold snuff box. The species name, *dracunculus,* means "little dragon" in Latin, which became *herbe au dragon* in French and *dragoncello* in Italian. Its modern name probably derives from a combination of its French and Arabic labels. The dragon per-

Artemisia dracunculus var. *sativa*
TARRAGON

haps describes its sharp taste, its reputed ability to cure poisonous bites, the Russian species' curled root, or even tarragon's reputation for killing intestinal parasites.

CULINARY: Tarragon is used in salads, pickles, fish, and especially with chicken. It makes delicious herb butters and mustards and is famous for how it flavors vinegar. According to author Alexander Dumas, "There is no good vinegar without tarragon." In fact, it is best used fresh, or preserved in vinegar, since the fragrance is easily lost once the herb is dried. Syrians have enjoyed eating young tarragon shoots for centuries.

MEDICINAL: Tarragon has few medicinal uses, but is chewed to numb a toothache or to improve digestion.

AROMATHERAPY: The essential oil, mainly produced in southern France, is known as "estragon oil" and is used in perfumery.

Artemisia vulgaris • Mugwort

FAMILY: Compositae.

DESCRIPTION: Single-stemmed, with floppy leaves. Height: To 6 feet (1.8 m). Width: 1 to 2 feet (30 to 60 cm). Flower: Tiny, red-brown, woolly, clustered on stem tips. Leaves: Elongated oval, but deeply toothed on end into points; green top with fuzzy silver-white underneath, to 4 inches (10 cm) long. Blooms: July to August.

HABITAT: Europe, Asia, naturalized in the United States.

CULTIVATION: Perennial. Zone: 2 to 3. Germination: 10 to 24 days. Space: 1 foot (30 cm). Soil Temperature: 65° to 70° F (18° to 21° C). Soil: Dry or moist, likes nitrogen. pH: 5 to 8.5. Sun: Full sun. Propagation: Sow from seed or divide large clumps. In moist garden soil, it will spread rapidly by runners.

GARDEN DESIGN: This is a good specimen for a silver or "moon" garden, to blend with other silver leaves or to contrast with deeper colors.

CONSTITUENTS: Essential oil, bitters, flavonoids, sesquiterpene lactone.

RELATED SPECIES: Related to wormwood *(A. absinthium)* and tarragon *(A. dracunculus)*. There are also American species and a variegated cultivar.

HISTORY: Once known in Europe as the Mother of Herbs, or *Mater Herbarum,* mugwort appears in ancient lore long before Dioscorides praised it in the 1st century. It was one of the 9 healing herbs of the Anglo-Saxons and is thought to be the girdle worn by St. John the Baptist in the Bible. For a while, when black tea prices rose in early-19th-century Cornwall, England, it became a popular tea. The origins of its name appear to be as confused as the intoxicated state mugwort produces. Some suggest it originated with *mygge,* meaning "midge"—any small insect, such as a gnat—or with the old English *magat,* or "maggot." However, it is the wool moth that mugwort deters, and a better possibility would be *mothe,* Anglo-Saxon for "moth." On the other hand, a few authors claim it comes from the Irish *mugan,* a mug that holds beer—mugwort beer, of course! As long as others are guessing, I wonder about a connection to the Gaelic *mugach,* meaning a "cloudy sky" or "gloomy condition" (which became our English "muggy"), perhaps descriptive of mugwort's gray color, its folkloric associations with water, or the "muggy" state resulting from drinking or even smelling the herb! *Wort* simply means "plant."

CULINARY: Although mugwort is very bitter, it finds its way into European stuffing and dumplings. In Germany, it has flavored sausage for centuries. The Japanese eat the boiled young shoots in spring and flavor rice cakes and a rice-type patty called *mochi* (available in natural-food stores in the United States) with mugwort. Sheep eat it, and mugwort may have been the "Artemesia of Ponatos" that the ancients fed them. Mugwort serves as a bitter and a clarifying agent in beer. It was still flavoring English countryside brews well into the 19th century.

MEDICINAL: Mugwort has long been used in the West to promote menstruation (yet is found in Chinese formulas to prevent miscarriage). A tea or compress was used to speed labor and help expel the afterbirth. My goats—who seem to have more healing instinct than anyone I know—would gulp down fresh mugwort during labor until their afterbirth was delivered, then never touch it again until their next pregnancy. Mugwort decreases external inflammation and, in both China and Europe, a poultice is tradi-

Artemisia vulgaris
Mugwort

tionally placed on rheumatic and arthritic pains. Gerard said, "Mugwort cureth the shakings of the joynts inclining to the Palsie" and also prescribed it for hysteria. In Russia, it is extracted in vodka for swellings, wounds, and various skin problems. It is also a fairly effective poison oak treatment. The Chinese use their native mugwort *(A. moxa* and *A. sinensis)* for nausea and roll the fuzzy leaves into *moxa cones* for an acupuncture treatment that penetrates with heat instead of needles. Mugwort also helps digestion, kills intestinal roundworms, and promotes liver detoxification. In the 17th century, Culpeper suggested mugwort in vinegar as an antidote to poisonous mushrooms and henbane. Once used as a tobacco substitute, it was smoked by asthmatics to clear their lungs.

CONSIDERATIONS: Avoid large amounts or continued consumption, which can adversely affect the nervous system. Don't use while pregnant.

OTHER: Mugwort sleep pillows have been used for centuries to induce dreams. (It is often combined with hops to magnify the effect.) It is a moth repellent. It can be poisonous to livestock, especially when they dine on it exclusively—usually occurring only when land has been overgrazed.

Asclepias tuberosa. **Butterfly weed earned its name because its abundant flowers attract butterflies. The orange-yellow flowers turn to a deep red as they mature.**

Asclepias tuberosa • Butterfly Weed

FAMILY: Asclepiadaceae.

DESCRIPTION: A showy herb that contains none of the milky juice that gives the name milkweed to many others in this genus. Height: 3 feet (90 cm). Width: 2 feet (60 cm). Flowers: Orange-yellow, clustered in bunches. Leaves: Stiff, lance-shaped, 2 to 5 inches (5 to 12.5 cm) long, alternating and standing from the hairy stems. Fruit: Long, narrow, furry pods, jutting out at right angles. Root: Spindly, fleshy, stout, white with an acrid smell. Blooms: June to August.

HABITAT: Found in dry, sandy locations in North America.

CULTIVATION: Perennial. Zone: 3. Germination: 3 to 4 weeks. Space: 12 to 18 inches (30 to 45 cm). Soil Temperature: 68° to 75° F. (20° to 24° C). Soil: Sandy, well drained. pH: 4 to 5. Sun: Full sun. Propagation: Plant by seed or divide the roots in the spring or autumn. Mature plants are difficult to transplant because their fleshy, long taproots break easily, but with extra care, they can be moved. It takes about 3 years for a colorful flower display.

GARDEN DESIGN: Butterfly weed shows off its attractive flowers in ornamental landscaping as well as in herb gardens. The flowers tower on the herb's top, making it a good background plant. Use it to draw the eye to the far reaches of the garden. It is suitable for a "wild" section, rambling off to the side of the garden or on a gravel-strewn or rocky slope. It also looks lovely in a distinguished location in a formal perennial flower bed.

CONSTITUENTS: Glycosides (asclepiadine), resins, essential oil, bitters (asclepione).

RELATED SPECIES: Seed companies offer strains with different colored blossoms. The Mexican *A. curassavica* was tested as a potential chemotherapeutic drug in the early 1970s and is naturalized in many areas of Australia.

HISTORY: An old medicinal herb first used by Native Americans, butterfly weed was included in Samuel Stern's *American Herbal* of 1772. It soon found its way into the European herbalism

Asclepias tuberosa
Butterfly Weed

and was cataloged in Germany by 1787. For a short while, it was official in the *U.S. Pharmacopoeia*.

CULINARY: Various Native American tribes did eat milkweed pods, but a number of authors state they were never collected from this species. According to historian Charles Millspaugh, the very young shoots were boiled and eaten by Canadian Indians, although there are mixed reports concerning this. The root was chewed raw for medicinal purposes.

MEDICINAL: Although it has fallen into disuse, butterfly weed, also called milkweed and pleurisy root, was a well-recognized remedy for all sorts of lung ailments, including bronchitis, consumption, typhoid fever, and, of course, pleurisy. It is a lung tonic that relieves congestion, inflammation, and difficult breathing. A warm tea of butterfly weed increases sweating and relieves digestive disturbances, diarrhea, and dysentery. The settlers learned of its use from the Native Americans, who chewed the raw root to alleviate lung problems. They also put the powdered roots on wounds to stop bleeding and pounded fresh roots into a poultice to place on bruises, rheumatism, inflammation, and lameness in the legs. It has also been used to treat certain uterine problems and estrogenlike components have been reported.

CONSIDERATIONS: Butterfly weed, as well as other milkweeds, contains potent cardiac glycosides. Very large dosages of the root can be toxic, causing diarrhea and vomiting. The fresh leaves cause nausea.

OTHER: Butterfly weed's flowers produce a yellow dye and were used by eastern Native Americans to color their baskets. The interesting seedpods are used in wreaths and other dried flower arrangements. Some American Indian tribes made fiber and bowstrings from the stalks. In the larval stage, monarch butterflies feed exclusively on milkweed and contain a considerable quantity of the glycoside (females 24% more than males). Research from Amherst College in Massachusetts shows that birds who dine on the monarch suffer poisoning and vomiting for up to 30 minutes afterwards.[1]

Atropa belladonna • Belladonna

FAMILY: Solanaceae.

DESCRIPTION: Small bush. Height: 2 to 3 feet (60 to 90 cm). Width: 2 feet (60 cm). Flowers: Purple-brown, bell-shaped, and drooping, about 1 inch (2.5 cm) long. Leaves: Smooth, green in assorted sizes to 6 inches (15 cm) long, with prominent veins. Fruit: Shiny, smooth, black, jewellike, ripen in September. Blooms: June to July.

HABITAT: Europe, Asia, and northern Africa, but naturalized in other places, mostly in wooded areas.

CULTIVATION: Perennial. Zone: 6. Germination: 12 to 24 days. Space: 18 to 20 inches (45 to 50 cm). Soil Temperature: 70° F (21° C). Soil: Deep, moist, suitable for vegetables. Good drainage essential. pH: 4.5 to 7.5. Sun: Full sun or partial shade. Propagation: By root division or seed.

Atropa belladonna
BELLADONNA

RELATED SPECIES: *A. belladonna* 'Lutea' has pale, green-yellow flowers.

GARDEN DESIGN: This bush makes an attractive backdrop, especially when in flower or berry, but place it out of the reach of pets and children.

CONSTITUENTS: Alkaloids (hyoscymaine, atropine).

HISTORY: Venetian beauties used an eyewash of belladonna leaf to dilate their pupils and make them more attractive, and the herb came to be known as *herba bella donna,* or "herb of the beautiful lady." A potent plant used for more than vanity, it poisoned Marcus Antonius's troops during the Parthian wars and was Juliet's sleeping potion in Shakespeare's *Romeo and Juliet.* It later earned the name deadly nightshade because it belongs to the nightshade family. *Solamum* comes from *solar* ("I ease") and describes a practice of sixteenth-century herbalists who laid moistened leaves on the head to induce sleep. In the late 19th century, a liniment of the root relieved the pain of sciatica, rheumatism, gout, and nerve problems.

MEDICINAL: A belladonna derivative, atropine is used to dilate eyes prior to eye operations and for some eye exams, as with the Venetian beauties. It has been official in the *U.S. Pharmacopoeia* since 1820.

CONSIDERATIONS: Belladonna increases heartbeat and is too poisonous for common use. On the average, only 4 berries can produce poisonous effects in adults. The berries can be dangerously attractive to children. Cats and dogs are sometimes poisoned by them, although other animals eat them without harm.

Baptisia tinctoria • False Indigo

FAMILY: Leguminosae.

DESCRIPTION: Branched bush. Height: 4 feet (1.2 m). Width: 2 feet (60 cm). Flowers: Yellow, 1 inch (2.5 cm), pealike in clusters. Leaves: Rounded, 3 leaflets. Fruit: Short, oblong pods containing blue-black seeds. Root: Black and woody, with yellow inside, many rootlets. Blooms: May to July.

HABITAT: Canada to South Carolina, on dry, hilly woods.

CULTIVATION: Perennial. Zone: 3. Germination: 2 to 3 weeks. Herb grower Mark Wheeler recommends first sanding with light sandpaper, then soaking overnight. Space: 8 to 12 inches (20 to 30 cm). Soil temperature: 70° to 75° F (21° to 24° C). Soil: Well drained, acid, dry. pH: 5 to 8.7. Sun: Full sun or light shade. Propagation: By seed or division. Remove the seeds from the pods and soak overnight before planting.

GARDEN DESIGN: False indigo is attractive when flowering, but turns somewhat unsightly later in summer, so plant colorful summer-flowering herbs in front of it.

CONSTITUENTS: Alkaloids (baptoxin), glycosides, coumarins, polysaccharides.

Baptisia tinctoria
FALSE INDIGO

RELATED SPECIES: The dye plant indigo *(Indigofera tinctoria)*, though not in the same genus, is in the same family.

HISTORY: The herb is named from the Greek *baptein*, "to dye" —the Western world's primary use of false indigo. It is also known as wild indigo.

MEDICINAL: Although false indigo is not as well known, in many ways it is comparable to *Echinacea*. The root is used to enhance the immune system and to combat infection. The polysaccharides it contains have been shown to stimulate antibody production.[1] A few Native American tribes used the roots and sometimes the leaves both internally and externally to treat cancer. Herbalists recommend false indigo for lingering fevers, especially when there is general weakness accompanied by swollen lymph nodes, tonsillitis, or pharyngitis. It was once used to treat typhoid and scarlet fevers. According to writer Harvey Wickes Felter, in the *Eclectica Materia Medica, Pharmacology and Therapeutics* (1922), "Baptisia is not, as a rule, a remedy in acute diseases showing great activity, but rather for . . . capillary enfeeblement and a tendency to ulceration." An astringent and antiseptic, it is an ingredient in ointments, poultices, and washes for skin ulcerations, infections, boils, and even staph infections. It is also added to douche formulas for vaginitis and taken as a tea, as well as a douche, for cervical ulcerations. False indigo has been recommended to reduce inflammatory diseases, including arthritis.

CONSIDERATIONS: Large doses can be emetic and purgative.

OTHER: The pods can be used in dried wreaths.

Borago officinalis • Borage

FAMILY: Boraginaceae.

DESCRIPTION: Prickly, bushy herb. Height: 2 feet (60 cm). Width: 2½ feet (75 cm). Flowers: Star-shaped, blue, about 1 inch (2.5 cm) wide, with hairy backs, growing in great profusion. Leaves: Prickly, wrinkled, elongated oval, coming to a point. Fruit: Relatively large black seeds. Blooms: May to September.

HABITAT: Originally from Aleppo, in Syria, but naturalized throughout Europe and in parts of North America and Australia.

CULTIVATION: Annual, sometimes biennial. Germination: 7 to 10 days. Needs darkness to germinate. Space: 12 to 18 inches (30 to 45 cm). Soil temperature: 60° to 70° F (15° to 21° C). Soil: Dry, poor. pH: 5 to 8. Sun: Full sun or light shade. Propagation: The seeds freely self-sow throughout the garden. But it's an easy-to-weed plant. The taproot makes it difficult to transplant fully grown plants. There are usually some autumn volunteers. It can survive a light frost.

GARDEN DESIGN: Borage's abundant flowers bloom throughout the summer and will attract many bees. In fact, keep an eye out for them while picking the flowers, which droop and easily conceal insects. Place it here and there in the garden, or allow it to spread out and cover a lot of ground between young perennials or in undeveloped areas. The succulent, hollow stems can get ungainly as the plant grows. Try not to push the stems into order, as they easily snap off.

CONSTITUENTS: Essential oil, mineral acids (potassium, calcium), alkaloids (pyrrolizidine, 2 to 10 ppm).

HISTORY: The name borage is often said to come from the Latin *cor* ("heart") and *ago* ("I stimulate"), but in a less picturesque reality, it is probably derived from the Latin *borra,* meaning "hair of the beast" and referring to its bristly leaves. Borage has an old reputation of cheering people, especially when added to wine. They even whisper in Lebanon that it's an aphrodisiac. The 1st-century Roman Pliny called it *Euphrosinum* because it "maketh a man merry and joyfull." He claimed that borage steeped in wine was the famous Nepenthe of Homer, which brought absolute forgiveness when drunk. The Latin verse from Roman times is still repeated,

> *Ego Borage*
> *Gaudia semper ago.*
> *(I, Borage, Bring always courage.)*

John Evelyn suggested in the 17th century that borage would help hypochondriacs. The candied flowers were given to persons recovering from long illnesses and those prone to swooning—most appropriate, considering its reputation for cheering up people. The herb is still often called "cool-tankard" in England, where an old verse relates,

> *To enliven the sad with a joy of a joke,*
> *Give the wine with some borage put in to soak.*

CULINARY: The whole plant has a delicate, cucumbery taste. The prickly leaves discourage even the most adventuresome cook, but the flowers are delicious decorating the top of a salad or floating on a cold soup or punch. They can also be crystallized into candy. Be sure to pop off the prickly backs before serving them to company. Borage flowers were once used to flavor claret and ciders. Nineteenth-century English author Charles Dickens was particularly fond of borage punch and gave the recipe to American friends while visiting them. The recipe is very similar to that for a "Cool Tankard" from Dr. William Kitchiner's *The Cook's Oracle* (1823).

MEDICINAL: In Latin America, a borage tea is drunk for lung problems.

CONSIDERATIONS: While some scientists question the advisability of sitting down to a plate of borage leaves because of their pyrrolizidine alkaloids, eating a few flowers can hardly be considered risky. So far, no evidence points directly to borage, but these alkaloids are related to those found in comfrey and coltsfoot. The alkaloid content is *much* higher in fresh leaves; to play it safe, avoid eating the leaves fresh until more of the facts are in. Some people have an allergic reaction, usually a rash, after handling the prickly leaves.

OTHER: The blue flowers are dried in silica to glue on dried wreaths.

CRYSTALLIZED BORAGE FLOWERS

1   *cup (240 ml) fresh borage flowers*
¹/₂ *teaspoon (2.5 ml) water, cold*
1   *egg, separated*
      Granulated sugar

Wash borage flowers and remove excess moisture by setting on absorbent paper towels. Combine water and egg white; beat well. Dip flowers in mixture, then in sugar. Place on waxed paper to dry. Store in a tightly covered jar.

Borago officinalis
BORAGE

CHARLES DICKENS PUNCH

Charles Dickens often made and enjoyed this potent cider punch with borage.

2   *cups (500 ml) water*
¹/₂ *cup (120 ml) sugar*
2   *tablespoons (30 ml) lemon peel*
¹/₄ *cup (60 ml) borage flowers*
2   *cups (500 ml) sherry*
1   *cup (240 ml) brandy*
4   *cups (1 l) apple cider*

Pour boiling water over the sugar, lemon peel, and borage, and let sit 10 minutes. Strain and add sherry, brandy, and cider.

© Derek Fell

Borago officinalis. Borage's bright blue flowers are a favorite of bees. A friendly herb, it will self-seed rapidly throughout your garden.

Calendula officinalis • Calendula

FAMILY: Compositae.

DESCRIPTION: Rounded bush. Height: 2 feet (60 cm). Width: 1¹/₂ feet (45 cm). Flowers: Large, yellow or orange with many petal rays. The double-petaled hybrid is most popular. Leaves: Long, oblong, pale green, soft, 2 to 6 inches (5 to 15 cm) long. Root: Long, spindly taproot. Bloom: June to winter.

HABITAT: Throughout southern Europe.

CULTIVATION: Annual, sometimes biennial. Germination: 10 to 14 days. Needs darkness to germinate. Space: 10 to 14 inches (25 to 60 cm). Soil Temperature: 55° to 70° F (13° to 21° C). Soil: Fairly fertile, well watered to prevent straggly growth. pH: 4.5 to 8. Sun: Full sun or partial shade. Propagation: The plants are so hardy, they can be put out before the last frost and will flower throughout the winter in warm climates or protected places, such as a glassed-in porch. Cool weather, plenty of water, and picking the flowers actually promote flowering. Sown in autumn, they will bloom in March, or even earlier in warm climates. Be careful not to injure the long taproot when transplanting.

GARDEN DESIGN: Calendula provides the garden with a constant supply of color. It can be placed not only in the herb garden to fill in open blocks, but finds a place in the flower or even vegetable garden. The cultivar 'Chrysantha' is by far more popular even in herb gardens than the original single-petaled calendula.

CONSTITUENTS: Essential oil, carotenoid, flavanoids, sterol, mucilage, saponins, bitters.

RELATED SPECIES: Calendula, also known as pot marigold, has been commonly called "marigold" since Elizabethan times, creating confusion with the unrelated *Tagetes* genus of marigold, which is planted as an ornamental and to deter garden pests.

HISTORY: Known as the "herb of the sun," Shakespeare speaks in *A Winter's Tale* of calendula "that goes to bed wi' th' sun, and with him rises weeping." Since ancient times, the East Indians, Arabs, Romans, and Greeks all noted how calendula's flowers open in the morning and close in the evening and how the flowering season extends for many months. The Latin word *calends,* or "calendar," refers to this trait. Calendula once held a prominent place in European kitchen gardens where it was grown for use in soups and broths.

For centuries, the English and Germans believed that eating the flowers maintained health throughout the winter. Stevens, author of *Countrie Farme* in 17th-century England, claims that "no broths are well made without dried marigold [calendula]." Sweet flower conserves were also served in the morning before breakfast. The practice of coloring butter made from autumn and winter milk— low in vitamin A and pale compared to spring butter—with skin-healing calendula was so common that butter became widely known as a burn ointment.

CULINARY: Calendula petals provided an inexpensive, though less vivid, saffron substitute to color soups, stews, and sauces. A few petals, pulled off the main flower head, give color and flavor to salads. The leaves, too, have been eaten raw in salads, but they are a bit stiff and acrid for my taste.

MEDICINAL: Calendula flowers were once as common on the medicine shelf as they were in the soup pot. Recommended in the past to heal liver ailments and duodenal ulcers, they were only occasionally suggested for these purposes today. Calendula is a popular salve and cream ingredient because it decreases the inflammation of sprains, stings, varicose veins, and other swellings and soothes burns, sunburn, rashes, and skin irritations. A strong tea can be washed over skin eruptions, including chicken pox and measles. Laboratory studies show it kills bacteria and fungus.[1] A remedy against candida, calendula is gentle enough to be applied (as a tea) to thrush (a type of candida) in children's mouths. Taken internally, it has been used traditionally to promote the draining of swollen lymph glands, such as in tonsillitis, and as part of the therapy for uterine or breast cancer, both as a poultice and as a tea. Modern herbalists report success in using a swab of calendula preparation or calendula boluses to treat abnormal cervical cells. Some antitumor activities have been observed in scientific studies.[2]

COSMETIC: A calendula hair rinse brings out yellow and gold highlights. Calendula, usually combined with herbs like chamomile, comfrey, and lavender, is the most popular herb for making baby oils, creams, and salves. It is also used in creams and lotions for sensitive skin.

OTHER: The flowers produce a bright yellow dye in a boiling bath. They are also grown commercially as cut flowers.

> *Open afresh you round of starry folds.*
> *Ye ardent marigolds!*
> *Dry up the moisture from your golden lids.*
> —"I STOOD TIP TOE UPON A LITTLE HILL," JOHN KEATS (1795–1821), ENGLISH

Calendula officinalis. Calendula, sometimes called pot marigold, is often confused with the common marigold. Its radiant yellow blooms are so bright, they were once said to be reflections of the sun.

Calendula officinalis
CALENDULA

Caltha palustris
Marsh Marigold

Caltha palustris • Marsh Marigold
(Previously *C. parnassifolia*)

FAMILY: Ranunculaceae.

DESCRIPTION: Low, saucerlike leaves. Height: 1 foot (30 cm). Width: 1 foot (30 cm). Flowers: Resemble giant buttercups, bright yellow, 2 inches (5 cm) across. Open and close with the sun. Leaves: Kidney-shaped, to 7 inches (17.5 cm) wide, on hollow, tall stems, shiny. Blooms: March to June.

HABITAT: Eurasia, Newfoundland to Alaska, and south to North Carolina.

CULTIVATION: Perennial. Zone: 5. Germination: 2 to 3 weeks. Soak seeds overnight before planting. Space: 1 foot (30 cm). Soil Temperature: 65° to 75° F (18° to 24° C). Soil: Moist; loves marshes and streams. Sun: Shade. Propagation: Root division in the autumn.

GARDEN DESIGN: Place this showy plant where you can take advantage of its eye-catching spring flowers. Good for areas that are too wet for many other herbs.

RELATED SPECIES: *C. palustris* 'Monstruosa' with double flowers.

HISTORY: On May Day (May 1), the ancients hung garlands of marsh marigold over doors. In the Middle Ages, the flowers were dedicated to the Virgin Mary for spring church festivals. Their caustic juice was used to get rid of warts. The buds have been pickled and the leaves cooked and eaten as a potherb, but since they can cause indigestion, we will leave this comment in a historical context.

MEDICINAL: Dr. Withering described a case in which a large bouquet of marsh marigolds brought into the sickroom of a spasmodic girl stopped her fits. The cure was presumed a result of whatever the flowers exude. Since then, infusions have also been used to prevent fits.

CONSIDERATIONS: Every part of the plant is a strong irritant, and it should not be used internally.

OTHER: The petal juice with an alum mordant produces a nonpermanent yellow stain.

The seal and the guerdon of wealth untold
We clasp in the wild marsh marigold.
—"NATURE'S COINAGE," ELAINE GOODALE (1863–1900), AMERICAN

Capsicum annum • Cayenne
(Previously *C. frutenscens*)

FAMILY: Solanaceae.

DESCRIPTION: Small, rather stiff plant. Height: 2½ feet (75 cm). Width: 15 inches (38 cm). Flowers: White drooping, ½ inch (12 mm) long. Leaves: Narrow, bright green, ¼ inch (6 mm) long, with a pointed tip, 1 to 6 inches (2.5 to 15 cm) long. Fruit: Fleshy pods, 1 inch (2.5 cm) or longer, bright red when ripe, pointed. Blooms: June to September.

HABITAT: Like all *Capsicum* peppers, cayenne is native to subtropical America.

CULTIVATION: Annual. Germination: 21 to 25 days. Seeds need light to germinate. Space: 9 to 12 inches (22.5 to 30 cm). Soil Temperature: 70° to 75° F (21° to 24° C). Soil: Good soil with even moisture. pH: 4.5 to 8.5. Sun: Full sun or partly shady. Propagation: Sow indoors 6 to 8 weeks before last frost, early enough to assure a long growing season. The pods can be hung to dry by stringing a heavy thread through the base of their stems.

GARDEN DESIGN: The colorful pepper pods call attention to the plants, which otherwise would be too straggly for the focus in an herb bed. Take advantage of bright red pods, not found in many herbs, for summer and autumn color.

CONSTITUENTS: Alkaloid (capsicin, 0.1% to 1.5%), carotenoids, essential oil, flavonoids, vitamins A and C, steroidal saponins in seeds.

HISTORY: South American Indians were enjoying hot pepper meals by 5000 B.C.. Cayenne, so popular in the hot cuisines of India, China, Indonesia, and South Africa, was unknown to those regions before European explorers stumbled on America while searching for a route to India. The pungent chilies were brought home instead of black pepper. German botanist Leonhard Fuchs dubbed them "Calcutta" pepper anyway, even though the Portuguese would

Capsicum annum
CAYENNE

not introduce cayenne to India until 1611, over 50 years later. As *Capsicum* spread throughout the world, it was hybridized and adapted by each culture—from the mild Hungarian paprika to mouth-blistering East Indian varieties. Over 90 varieties have been described, but most authorities narrow it down to a manageable 5. The degree of heat they produce is rated from 1 to 120 BTUs— amazing when you consider that the fairly hot jalapeño only registers 15. We call them cayenne after the former capital of French Guiana in South America. Their history and folklore are included in the beautifully illustrated *Peppers, The Domesticated Capsicums* by Jean Andrews (University of Texas Press, 1985).

CULINARY: Enjoyed in the traditional hot, spicy dishes of tropical and subtropical countries, cayenne is the main heating ingredient in Tabasco brand hot sauce and most salsas, curries, and mandrams, a West Indies condiment used to relieve indigestion. Recipes for "medicinal" drinks have been inspired by Caribbean cooking, such as Dr. William Kitchiner's Hot Sauce, which was mixed with quinine water. Cayenne also gives ginger ale and some beers an extra zing. You can join a "pod" chapter of the International Connoisseurs of Green and Red Chilies, Box 33467, University Park, Las Cruces, NM 88003.

MEDICINAL: Anyone who is fond of hot peppers knows that only a few bites can clear the sinuses. Mexican Indians and the Hunan and Szechwan Chinese, who steep their meals in hot peppers, have less chronic obstructive lung disease than the British with their blander diet. Cayenne also brings blood (and body heat) to the surface, stimulating sweating and cooling the body. It's little wonder, then, that it is so popular in hot climates. Dieters should note that eating hot spices temporarily boosts the body's metabolic rate by about 25% through a "diet-induced thermic effect." Researchers at Oxford Polytechnic in England found that 6 grams (.21 ounces) of cayenne burned an average of 45 (and up to 76) extra calories. (So did mustard, but ginger didn't). Cayenne acts as an energy stimulant, slightly encouraging the adrenals to produce cortisone.[1] Dr. Rozin from the University of Pennsylvania theorizes that the pain inflicted by cayenne also stimulates endorphins, which create a feeling of pleasure.

Capsicin has been found to reduce "substance P," a chemical that carries pain messages from nerve endings in the skin to the central nervous system. Clinical trials showed that 75% of the people who applied a capsicin cream on their shingles disease experienced substantial pain relief, with only an occasional burning sensation.[2] It is being investigated for use on other painful skin problems, such as diabetic nerve damage, psoriasis, and postsurgical pain, and has been developed into Zostrix, an over-the-counter cream. A small amount of cayenne stabilizes blood pressure and reduces excessive bleeding anywhere in the body. Contrary to popular belief, ulcer patients in a New Delhi, India, hospital experienced the same rate of healing after 4 weeks of eating 3 grams (¹/₂ teaspoon) a day as those who abstained. A scientific literature review is available.[3]

CONSIDERATIONS: Capsicin produces a strong alkaline skin reaction that can result in intense pain, dizziness, and a rapid pulse. Researchers at the University of Chicago Hospital, who dubbed the phenomenon "Hunan hand," say soaking peppers in vinegar for a few hours neutralizes the reaction. McCormick and Co. spice manufacturers found that fats and alcohol also reduce cayenne's painful sting. In light of this, try a sip of milk or beer the next time you have a painful reaction to cayenne.

OTHER: Cayenne is used in Cap-stun, a self-defense product manufactured by Lucky Police Products of Columbus, Ohio. It may be safer than mace since the symptoms of blindness, choking, and nausea disappear in 30 minutes without harmful effects.

MANDRAM CHUTNEY

Cayenne peppers
Cucumbers, thinly sliced
Onions, finely chopped
Chives, chopped
Lemon juice
Madeira wine

Mash or blend the cayenne peppers. Mix in other ingredients. Refrigerated, it keeps for weeks.

DR. KITCHINER'S HOT SAUCE

This recipe comes from Dr. William Kitchiner's nineteenth-century work, *The Cook's Oracle*. It is quite hot, but can be cooled down by replacing some or all of the cayenne powder with paprika.

- ¹/₄ **pound (112 g) fresh hot peppers**
- ¹/₂ **cup (120 ml) sherry**
- ¹/₂ **cup (120 ml) brandy**
- ¹/₂ **cup (120 ml) fresh lime juice, strained**
- ¹/₂ **teaspoon (2.5 ml) salt**
- ¹/₄ **teaspoon (1.25 ml) cayenne powder (or paprika)**

Rinse and drain peppers, being careful not to touch your hand to your eye. Cut off stems, but keep the core and seeds intact. Chop in a food processor or blender, and gradually add sherry and brandy until pureed. Add lime juice, salt, and cayenne powder.

Scrape into a jar and cover the top with 2 layers of cheesecloth, held in place with a rubber band. Keep in a warm place in the kitchen for at least 2 weeks. Then pour into a blender, and process it to make it as smooth as possible. Strain seeds out with a sieve. Store in the refrigerator or a cool cupboard indefinitely. Shake if it separates.

Makes about 1 cup (240 ml).

Carthamus tinctorius • Safflower

FAMILY: Compositae.

DESCRIPTION: Stiff, sparsely branched herb. Height: 3 feet (90 cm). Width: 1 foot (30 cm). Flowers: Orange-yellow, thick base, thistlelike. Leaves: Somewhat oval with spiny edges, prickly to the touch. Blooms: August to September.

HABITAT: Eurasia, cultivated in Europe, some in California, and extensively in India.

CULTIVATION: Annual. Germination: 10 to 14 days. Space: 1 foot (30 cm). Soil Temperature: 65° to 70° F (18° to 21° C). Soil: Average, well drained. Can tolerate very dry, but prefers slightly moist. Sun: Full sun. Propagation: By seed, 8 weeks before last frost to assure a long growing season for flower production. Easy to sprout.

GARDEN DESIGN: Safflower's prickly nature leads to it being set back from pathways. Use it in beds to add spots of bright color.

© Derek Fell

Carthamus tinctorius. The thistle-like flower of safflower is an attractive addition to the herb garden and can be dried for everlasting flower arrangements or herbal wreaths. Commercially, the seeds produce safflower oil.

CONSTITUENTS: Fixed oil, pigment (carthamone), lignans, polysaccharide.

RELATED SPECIES: Not related to saffron *(Crocus sativus)*, although the two herbs have similar, but not identical, properties.

HISTORY: For centuries, safflower—also known as "false saffron"—has offered the peoples of Europe and Asia a less expensive alternative to saffron.

CULINARY: Safflower is mostly grown to produce an inexpensive cooking and salad oil, which is very unsaturated. The tender, young shoots are also edible.

MEDICINAL: The flowers of safflower are laxative and diuretic. Although they are rarely used medicinally in Western countries, a tea was once given to children with fevers, measles, and other eruptive skin diseases. The tincture is widely used in China on sprains and wounds to decrease inflammation. The Chinese also use *hoang-chi,* their word for this plant, usually combined with other herbs, to treat problems relating to heart disease, circulation, menstruation, and blood congestion.

Safflower is also used to inhibit blood clotting. So far, no clinical studies have been done to support laboratory tests indicating that safflower's polysaccharides stimulate the formation of immune system antibodies. The East Indians, who know it as *koosumbha,* also use safflower medicinally and employ the oil as the base of some Ayurvedic medicinal body oils.

COSMETIC: Safflower was once mixed with finely powdered talc to color natural rouge.

OTHER: The flower heads yield an important dye that produces both yellow and red and imparts silk shades of rose and scarlet. The dried flower heads are a brilliant addition to wreaths.

Carum carvi • Caraway

FAMILY: Umbelliferae.

DESCRIPTION: Slender, feathery plant. Height: 1 to 2 feet (30 to 60 cm). Width: 1 foot (30 cm). Flowers: Lacy, creamy white, platelike heads up to 5 inches (13 cm), composed of tiny, individual blooms. Leaves: Short-stemmed, carrotlike, and mostly feathery, to 3 inches (7.5 cm) long. Fruit: Small, ¼ inch (6 mm) long, oval, slightly curved, with 5 distinct ridges. Root: Spindly, tapered taproot, similar to a parsnip. Blooms: July to September.

HABITAT: Found today throughout northern and central Europe and Asia, but according to the Roman historian Pliny, caraway originated from Caria in Asia Minor. Cultivated mostly in Holland, Germany, and Morocco, but the latter is considered inferior quality.

CULTIVATION: Biennial. Zone: 3 to 4. Germination: 10 to 14 days. Space: 8 to 10 inches (20 to 25 cm). Soil Temperature: 65° to 70° F (18° to 21° C). Soil: Prefers good drainage, but will grow in clay. pH: 4.8 to 7.8. Sun: Full sun. Propagation: Sow directly into garden if possible, in spring or fall. Fall plantings produce flower and seed the next year. Spring plantings occasionally don't bloom until the third summer. The plant will handle light frost, but a snowpack can kill it. The plant is strong enough to hold up fruiting heads without supports.

GARDEN DESIGN: Caraway does not attract much attention in the garden until the lacy flowers begin blooming. It can be set away from the path in a culinary garden since the seeds are not harvested until fall.

CONSTITUENTS: Seed: Essential oil (3% to 7%) includes carvone (40% to 60%), fixed oil (8% to 20%), polysaccharides, calcium oxalate, carlinene.

HISTORY: Caraway's history goes back at least 5,000 years, to the Mesolithic Era, as evidenced by fossilized seeds discovered in an old campsite. The ancient Arabs gave them the name *karawya.* The seed was so revered by the 6th century Persians that "They paid the taxes with bagsful of that most wanted coin—karawya." The story of Persia's King Khosru (died 579) relates that he offered his favorite wife 10% of the taxes to buy jewelry. When she checked a bag, she was enraged to find not gold, but caraway seeds. The king assured her that they were worth *more* than gold since they could cure illness. Indeed, the wealthy appreciated the seeds because they cured the indigestion suffered at banquets.

In 120 B.C., an anonymous Greek wrote of *karon* seeds: "The seeds were in great favor; Three years after, they held a savor." The roots, too, were baked with milk and yeast to make the *chara* bread favored by Julius Caesar and his troops, who considered the young roots sweeter than parsnips. They also ate the leaves as a spring potherb. Hassan Bedreddin of the *Arabian Nights* became world famous for his cheesecake. His secret? The oil of *karawya* was blended into the butter. Caraway was not well known in medieval Europe except in recipes for nut jams, sweet cakes, and a spiced wine known as "compost water," and sometimes seed-filled apples were roasted. It didn't gain popularity in the 16th century when Ann Boleyn's romance with King Henry VIII (which caused him to abandon both wife and church) began with the comforting "carwy" seeds that she slipped him at dinner to stop his hiccups and indigestion.

CULINARY: The seeds are found in crackers and breads, especially in Norway and Sweden, where black caraway bread is so common. *Karuij* seeds flavor some of the most famous Dutch cheeses. The Scots make a cheeselike gruel called *crowdie* that was immortalized by Scottish poet Robert Burns.

> *Oh that I had ne'er been married*
> *I wad never had nae care,*
> *Now I've gotten wife and weans,*
> *and they cry Crowdie ever nair.*
> —"Crowdie," **Robert Burns (1759–1796)**

They also still dip bread into caraway seeds and tea, a dish called "salt water jelly." Caraway seeds are an important addition to sauerkraut and other cabbage dishes, a custom possibly begun because caraway helps digestion. Long-term cooking makes it bitter, so whenever possible, add them no more than 30 minutes before a dish is done. The English custom of serving a dish of caraway seeds with roasted apple dates at least to Shakespearean days. It is also traditional to tuck a seed inside each sugarplum confection. "It was only to put a core of Truth within the ornaments that every Sugar Plum might have a Caraway Seed in it," wrote Henry David Thoreau (1817 to 1862) in *Walden*.

MEDICINAL: By the 20th century, caraway was mostly used to improve the taste of children's medicines, but a cordial and distilled water were once common indigestion remedies. One ounce (28 g) of seeds was infused for 6 hours in cold water, strained, and up to 3 teaspoons (15 ml) given every hour to infants with colic. Powdered seeds provided a poultice for bruises.

COSMETIC: A famous caraway cordial was called *Huile de Venus*, or "Oil of love" — probably because caraway was considered a love potion. Women of the 1300s smoothed out rough skin and wrinkles and toned their muscles . . . and discreetly sipped the cordial. Today, caraway is still used in complexion soaps, perfumes, and mouthwashes.

OTHER: Caraway slipped into their food is supposed to magically keep pigeons from straying. The "magic" may be their extreme fondness for the seeds. A 1907 recipe to cure mange on dogs calls for caraway (¼ teaspoon [1.25 ml]) in castor oil (4 teaspoons [20 ml]) and alcohol (¼ teaspoon [1.25 ml]).

Carum carvi
CARAWAY

CARAWAY RUSKS

Consider serving these delicious bread slices with an herbal tea or with soup and cheese.

3¹/₂ cups (840 ml) flour
4 teaspoons (20 ml) baking soda
³/₄ teaspoon (3.7 ml) salt
2 teaspoons (10 ml) caraway seeds, slightly bruised
1 teaspoon (5 ml) celery seed
¹/₂ teaspoon (2.5 ml) nutmeg, ground
2 eggs
2 tablespoons (30 ml) milk
¹/₃ cup (80 ml) honey
¹/₂ cup butter (120 ml), melted

Sift together flour, baking soda, and salt, and stir in seasonings. In a separate bowl, beat eggs and milk together, and then beat in honey. Stir in butter, then mix in dry ingredients. Knead by hand a few times. On a baking sheet, divide the dough into 2 parts and form flat-topped loaves, 12 inches (30 cm) long and about 2¹/₂ inches (5 cm) wide. Place well apart. Bake in a preheated oven at 325° F (162° C) until firm and golden, about 20 minutes. Reset the oven to 275° F (135° C), and remove loaves. Cool 20 minutes.

With a serrated knife, cut at a slight diagonal into ¹/₂-inch (1.25 cm) slices. Lay slices flat on the baking sheet. Rebake for 10 minutes, turn over, and bake another 10 minutes or until crisp and golden. Turn off oven and let cool inside with door open. When cool, store in an airtight container so they remain crisp. Will keep for weeks unrefrigerated.

Makes about 3 dozen.

NEW POTATOES

This recipe comes from Rome, circa 23 B.C.

10 small new potatoes, boiled or baked
1 teaspoon (5 ml) caraway seeds
¹/₄ stick butter
1 cup (240 ml) white wine
1 cup (240 ml) sour cream
1 tablespoon (15 ml) fresh parsley, minced

Sauté caraway in butter. Add wine. Bring to a boil, and then simmer, uncovered, for 5 minutes. Gradually add sour cream, 1 tablespoon (15 ml) at a time, stirring constantly. Add parsley. Pour over potatoes.

SCOTCH CROWDIE

This recipe comes from *The Scots Book*, written by MacDonald Douglas, circa 1520.

Pitcher (about 2 quarts or 2 l) of sour milk
Half a handful caraway seeds
Salt and pepper to taste

Heat the milk slowly, without boiling, until it separates. Strain off the liquid. Season the solid curds with caraway, salt, and pepper. Press in a muslin bag to drain out extra moisture. Chill 3 days.

Caulophyllum thalictroides • Blue Cohosh

FAMILY: Berberidaceae.

DESCRIPTION: Erect plant with tall flower stem. Height: To 3 feet (90 cm). Width: 1¹/₂ feet (45 cm). Flowers: 5 petaled, yellow-green, on the top of tall stalks. Leaves: Thin, bluish green, oval shape with lobes, 1 to 4 inches (2.5 to 10 cm) long. Fruit: Blue-black, ¹/₃ inch (8 mm) in diameter. Rhizome: Knotty, branched, brownish gray, white inside. Tastes bitter and acrid. Blooms: June to August.

HABITAT: Eastern United States and Canada, in moist deep woodlands.

CULTIVATION: Perennial. Zone: 3. Germination: 2 to 4 weeks. Space: 1¹/₂ to 2 feet (45 to 60 cm). Soil Temperature: 65° to 70° F (18° to 21° C). Soil: Fairly rich, moist. pH: 5 to 8. Sun: Filtered shade. Likes humidity. Propagation: Stratify 4 weeks first.

GARDEN DESIGN: Grow in a position to show off both the leaves and flower stalks.

CONSTITUENTS: Alkaloids (caulophylline), saponins (caulo-saponins), resin.

HISTORY: Cohosh, a name given to both the unrelated blue and black cohosh because of their similarity in looks and actions, is a Native American name from the Algonquian tribe. Rafinesque, in his 1898 *Medical Flora*, reported, "This is a medical plant of the Indians, and although not yet introduced into our official books, deserves to be better known." The root was widely used among Native American women 2 to 3 weeks in advance to promote easy labor. Before the wide use of forceps, it was also used by American doctors, especially when birth was delayed due to weakness or fatigue. Blue cohosh was a main ingredient in the popular "Mother's Cordial," officially known as Syrup of Mitchella (it also included partridgeberry, *Mitchella repens*). Blue cohosh remained an official *United States Pharmacopoeia* drug until 1936, although by 1915, black cohosh had largely replaced it.

MEDICINAL: The Eclectic doctors (a popular, turn-of-the-century group of healers) used blue cohosh to reduce labor pains, painful menstruation, stomach cramps, and joints stiff from arthritis or rheumatism. Herbalists also use it to help with irregular menstruation or a weak uterus.

CONSIDERATIONS: The powdered herb is a strong irritant to mucous membranes, so avoid inhaling it. Taken internally, blue cohosh can increase high blood pressure. The berries are poisonous.

Caulophyllum thalictroides. **The blue-green cast of blue cohosh's leaves create a soft visual effect in the herb garden. It is happily at home among the ferns and other shade-loving plants.**

Centella asiatica
GOTA KOLA

Centella asiatica • Gota Kola

FAMILY: Umbelliferae.

DESCRIPTION: Trailing plant. Height: To 6 inches (15 cm). Width: 6 inches (15 cm). Flowers: Small, buried under the leaves, reddish and rising from the center, 3 to 6 inches (7.5 to 15 cm). Leaves: 3 to 6 inches (7.5 to 15 cm) long, roundish with slight serration along the edge. Blooms: Summer.

HABITAT: Subtropics of India, Sri Lanka, South Africa, Malaysia, in wet, marshy areas.

CULTIVATION: Perennial, but grown in cool climates as an annual. Zone: 10. Germination: 7 to 10 days. Space: 6 to 10 inches (15 to 25 cm). Soil Temperature: 70° to 75° F (21° to 24° C). Soil: Moist, rich. pH: 6 to 6.5. Sun: Partial shade preferred. Needs humid air. Propagation: Suited for subtropical climates or a greenhouse.

CONSTITUENTS: Saponins (asiaticoside), triterpene acids (indocentoic acid), alkaloid (hydrocotylin), bitters (vellarin), tannin (9%), essential oil, vitamin C.

RELATED SPECIES: Gota kola is *not* related to kola nuts *(Cola spp.),* an herbal stimulant that contains caffeine.

HISTORY: The East Indians call this herb *Brahmi,* after the god Brahma, in honor of its qualities. Traditionally, gota kola was a treatment for insanity and leprosy, for which it is still used in Madagascar. It is reputed to improve the memory, and East Indians point out that elephants—supposedly famous for their memories—eat gota kola.

MEDICINAL: Gota kola leaves stimulate the appetite and correct digestive and bowel problems. They are also found in remedies for fever, rheumatism, and gastric complaints, such as dysentery. Gota kola is regarded as a tonic and used as blood purifier in venereal diseases and tuberculosis. Ayurvedic medicine recommends gota kola to treat asthma, anemia, and other blood disorders to reduce inflammation and fever. It considers it a "balancing" tonic that both increases energy and relaxes the body, being especially suited to overcoming insomnia and making one calm for yoga and meditative practices. Gota kola does contain 2 sedatives, saponin glycosides and an abundance of B vitamins, the "antistress" vitamins. Studies show it has tranquilizing, sedative, and antispasmodic actions. In one study, it also improved the general ability and behavior patterns of mentally handicapped children.[1]

Gota kola's effectiveness in killing the leprosy bacteria *(Mycobacterium lepre)* is thought due to its dissolving the waxy, protective substance around the bacteria. In both India and the Philippines, the juice of the roots is heated and applied to cuts. Studies have shown that when applied externally, it prevents scarring, especially from burns, and that it helps to heal post-operative incisions.[2] Patients treated with gota kola also noted improvement in varicose veins and other leg circulation problems.[3] In Brazil, it is used for uterine cancer, and it has been shown to inhibit the growth of human cells, at least in the test tube.[4]

CONSIDERATIONS: Large doses are narcotic, producing vertigo.

Chrysanthemum balsamita • Costmary
(Previously *C. majus* and *Tanacetum balsamita*)

FAMILY: Compositae.

DESCRIPTION: Upright leaves form the plant. Height: 3 feet (90 cm). Width: 1 foot (30 cm). Flowers: yellow, petaled, $1/2$ inch (1.25 cm) wide. Leaves: Long, 6 to 12 inches (15 to 30 cm) thin and very flat with a finely serrated edge, sometimes lobed at the base. Blooms: July to September.

HABITAT: Western Asian native, but naturalized throughout Europe and in parts of North America.

CULTIVATION: Perennial. Zone: 4. Space: 1 to $1^1/2$ feet (30 to 45 cm). Soil Temperature: 70° F (21° C). Soil: Dry, fairly rich since it is a heavy feeder. pH: 4 to 6. Sun: Partial shade; costmary usually only flowers in full sun. Propagation: Costmary often doesn't flower or make mature seed. Propagate by root division. Once established, it will spread rapidly enough by runners.

GARDEN DESIGN: Costmary is a good filler and background herb. The leaves make a solid contrasting backdrop for more variegated, lighter leaves such as those of a wormwood. Like most chrysanthemums, the center of the clump will die out in a few years and need replanting to keep it from looking straggly.

CONSTITUENTS: Essential oil.

RELATED SPECIES: It is often confused with *C. balsamita* var. *tanacetoides*, which has smaller, buttonlike flowers without petals.

HISTORY: In ancient days, costmary was called "balsam herb" in several different languages because of its pleasant, light scent. Its common name comes from *kostos,* after a perfumery herb from Asia with a similar fragrance. Costmary has found a place in English gardens since it was introduced in the 16th century. It has a reputation of keeping away bugs, especially the tiny ones that eat paper. A costmary leaf was often pressed into the Bible to repel destructive, paper-eating pests. Eventually it came to be known as Bible leaf.

CULINARY: Costmary leaves were a favorite flavoring for ale and sometimes beer, so it was commonly called alecost. The very young leaves used to be eaten in salad, but are quite bitter. They are best added whole in *very* small quantities to soup, then removed. Italians swish a leaf in the butter being melted for omelets to add just a hint of flavor.

MEDICINAL: Costmary is rarely used medicinally today, but it was included in the *British Pharmacopoeia* until 1788, for its use treating dysentery and other digestive problems. The 17th-century writers suggested the leaves to relieve headaches and gout pain, to increase menstruation, and as a diuretic. It was also used for conditions of "excessive coldness." Costmary is slightly astringent and antiseptic on wounds and burns and was also used with other herbs in ointments for dry, itchy skin and skin parasites.

AROMATHERAPY: A cosmetic water from the leaf was used to improve the complexion, as a hair rinse, and in bath water to make a fragrant "sweet washing water." The dried leaves lend their balsam fragrance to potpourri. Bundles of costmary leaves were tied with lavender stalks to sweeten linens in the 19th century.

Chrysanthemum balsamita
COSTMARY

Chrysanthemum cinerariifolium • Pyrethrum
(Previously *Pyrethrum cinerariifolium*)

FAMILY: Compositae.

DESCRIPTION: Short, bush herb. Height: To 15 inches (37 cm). Width: 15 inches (37 cm). Flowers: Daisylike, with a yellow disk in the center and white ray petals, heads to 1½ inches (3.7 cm). Leaves: Oblong, to 1 foot (30 cm) long, silky silver hair underneath. Blooms: May to June.

HABITAT: Commercially cultivated in Dalmatia, Yugoslavia, and in Japan, Kenya, South Africa, and parts of central Europe.

CULTIVATION: Perennial. Zone: 2. Germination: 20 to 24 days. Space: 15 inches (37 cm). Soil Temperature: 70° F (21° C). Soil: Moist, lime, with dry air. pH: 7.5 to 8.5. Sun: Full sun. Propagation: By seed. Pyrethrums tend to be short-lived perennials, often losing strength after only 3 years, then needing to be lifted and the younger, strongest sections replanted.

GARDEN DESIGN: The large, daisylike flowers are a bright addition to either herb or flower garden. They mix well with other large-flowering herbs, such as purple cone flower *(Echinacea).*

CONSTITUENTS: Pyrethrins (ketoesters cinerin I and II), chrysanthine, chrysanthene.

RELATED SPECIES: The painted daisy *(Chrysanthemum coccineum),* most commonly sold by nurseries as pyrethrum, is cultivated for use in insecticides. The original flowers were red, but hybrids now come in a rainbow of colors. It is also related to costmary *(C. balsamita)* and tansy *(Tanacetum vulgare)*—as well as 200 other chrysanthemums. These include chop suey greens *(C. coronarium)* and the Taoist elixir of immortality *(C. indicum).*

HISTORY: What the ancient Greeks called chrysanthemum was another flower, but the true chrysanthemum has been cultivated in China at least since the time of Confucius, about 500 B.C. Chinese scholar Chang Yee noted, "Crabs, chrysanthemums, wine and the moon are the four autumn joys of our scholars, artists, and poets." They arrived in Japan, probably in the 4th century, and went on to become the national flower. Chrysanthemum seems to have come to Europe in the 17th century. Persian insect powder from Persia's *P. roseum* and *P. carneum* (now both classified as *C. coccineum*) was used until Dalmatian insect powder was found to be more active. It has become the most important commercial chrysanthemum.

MEDICINAL: The flower heads contain a weak antibiotic, although are not used traditionally in medicine.

CONSIDERATIONS: Prolonged contact can result in contact dermatitis, asthma, and allergy reactions.

OTHER: Pyrethrum is the source of one of the best-known natural insecticides, pyrethrin. It rapidly paralyzes many different insects, but unlike most insecticides, is nontoxic to mammals. It is used in commercial products to control bedbugs, mosquitos, cockroaches, aphids, spider mites, ants, and the domestic common fly, although it kills many helpful insects as well. Lotions, diluted in 10 parts water, are applied to the skin as a repellent. Even the smoke from the burning flowers keeps bugs away. It retains its properties when powdered but will decompose rapidly, especially in sunlight. Pyrethrum is sold by itself or combined with other ingredients in commercial products. Maude Grieve, in *A Modern Herbal,* notes that only a teaspoon of the pure powder set under an upside-down glass will stupefy a captured fly in 1 minute.

Chrysanthemum cinerariifolium
PYRETHRUM

PYRETHRUM SPRAY

1   ounce (28 g) pyrethrum powder
²/₃   cup (160 ml) denatured alcohol
1   gallon (4 l) water

The active constituents in pyrethrum are not water soluble, so soak the powder for 4 days in the denatured alcohol, then strain, then dilute with the water. Spray at dusk to avoid injuring bees.

© Derek Fell

Chrysanthemum coccineum. Pyrethrum is one of a number of closely-related flowers that go by the name "painted daisy." Pictured is *Chrysanthemum coccineum,* which contains insecticidal properties.

Cichorium intybus • Chicory

FAMILY: Compositae.

DESCRIPTION: Stemy, upright plant. Height: 2 to 5 feet (10 cm to 1.5 m). Width: 2½ feet (75 cm). Flowers: Azure blue, 1½ inch (3.7 cm), close at midday. Leaves: Oblong, bristly, and mostly near the bottom. The young toothed leaves are sometimes mistaken for dandelion leaves but are much more bristly. Blooms: July to September.

HABITAT: A European native, it grows commonly in England, where it is known as succory. Chicory has naturalized itself in surrounding locations, in North America, and in temperate areas of Australia.

CULTIVATION: Perennial. Zone: 3. Germination: 7 to 14 days. Space: 10 to 12 inches (25 to 30 cm). Soil Temperature: 70° F (21° C). Soil: Calcium-rich, well drained. Tolerates poor conditions, but has less flavor. pH: 6 to 8. Sun: Full sun. Propagation: By seed. Roots can be harvested all winter digging them up in the fall, and trimming them to 10 inches (25 cm). They are replanted in sand or light soil in a protected area, often in a shed or cellar, away from light and freezing temperatures. The leaves are also blanched a creamy white by "forcing" them and growing them without sunlight so that they won't develop the bitterness of wild plants. The young heads are harvested when 6 inches (15 cm) tall.

CONSTITUENTS: Inulin (58%), sugar, mineral salts, vitamins (B, C, K, P), sesquiterpene lactones (lactucine and lactupicrine).

Cichorium intybus
CHICORY

65

HISTORY: Through the ages, chicory and its Asian relative, endive, have been cultivated as vegetables. The ancient Greeks served *kichoreia* leaves and the Romans cooked with *cichorium*. Fifteenth-century Europeans called chicory *sponsor solis* because its rayed flowers open and close by the sun. Carolus Linnaeus described chicory in his floral clock since he found it opened regularly at 7 A.M. and closed at noon. Elizabethan shops sold a "Syrup of Succory." Novelist Charles Dickens, in *Household Words*, describes chicory cultivation in 19th-century England. More than 20 cultivars have been developed in Italy.

CULINARY: Chicory, especially in its specially prepared state, is a very popular vegetable in Belgium, France, and Italy. Roots and "forced" leaves are cooked or eaten raw to provided fresh vegetables throughout the winter. The chopped root can also serve as a coffee substitute when roasted in an oven at 325° to 330° F (162° to 165° C) for about 30 minutes. Roasting provides a bittersweet taste that resembles but, coffee lovers will agree, does not duplicate that of coffee. Originally done for economic reasons, extending coffee with chicory has become a traditional Louisiana specialty. The unroasted root has also been ground into flour. The flowers can be candied for cake decorations.

MEDICINAL: As a tea or extract, chicory root is a bitter digestive tonic that also increases bile flow and decreases inflammation. It makes an ideal coffee substitute since 2 of its constituents sedate the central nervous system.[1] Egyptians treated rapid heartbeat with chicory root, and scientists have discovered a digitalislike principle in both the dried and roasted root that decreases the heart rate and amplitude.[2] It also has been found to significantly lower cholesterol and blood sugar levels. The sesquiterpene lactones found in roasted root kill bacteria.[3]

> In coffee, we used the scorched root,
> In salads, it's the blanched shoot.
> In love potions are seed,
> Of this blue-flowered weed;
> A Biblical bitter to boot.
> —"CHICORY," JAMES A. DUKE (b. 1929), AMERICAN

Cimicifuga racemosa • Black Cohosh

FAMILY: Ranunculaceae.

DESCRIPTION: Graceful, towering plant when in bloom. Height: 3 to 6 feet (.9 to 1.8 m). Width: 2 feet (60 cm). Flowers: Small, creamy white supported on very tall stalks, with a strong aroma. Leaves: Thin, rich green, multidivided with 1- to 4-inch (2.5- to 10-cm) leaflets with blue-green color. Rhizome: Thick, hard, knotty, with short branches and a bitter, acrid taste. Blooms: July to August.

HABITAT: Canada and eastern United States.

CULTIVATION: Perennial. Zone: 3. Germination: 2 to 4 weeks. Best if stratified. Space: 2 to 3 inches (5 to 7.5 cm). Soil Temperature: 55° to 65° F (12° to 18° C). Soil: Fairly rich, humus, moist. Likes humidity. pH: 5 to 8. Sun: Filtered shade. Propagation: By seed or root division.

GARDEN DESIGN: A graceful addition in the back of a shade garden where its white flowers seem like stars floating over the other herbs. Or place as a front edging plant since most of its height is a thin stalk.

Cimicifuga racemosa
BLACK COHOSH

CONSTITUENTS: Triterpene glycosides, resin (cimifugun), salicylates, isoferulic acid, essential oil, sterols, alkaloids.

RELATED SPECIES: The Chinese use a number of species called *sheng ma,* especially *C. foetida,* to treat headaches, measles, and prolapses of the uterus, stomach, intestines, and bladder and also to raise the *chi* or "vital energy."

HISTORY: Originally used by the Native Americans, black cohosh was introduced to the medical world in 1844 by Dr. John King for rheumatism and nervous disorders, and it became a favorite herb with the Eclectics medical practitioners. It was widely used to treat scarlet fever, whooping cough, and smallpox.

MEDICINAL: Black cohosh root improves blood circulation and lowers blood pressure and body temperature by dilating blood vessels. The constituents responsible for these actions are so resinous, they are much more soluble in an alcohol-based tincture than in tea.[1] A central nervous system depressant, black cohosh also directly inhibits vasomotor centers that are involved with inner ear balance and hearing. In fact, one of the few remaining uses for black cohosh recognized by doctors is for relief of ringing in the ears.[2] The Native Americans knew that it encouraged uterine contractions and used it to facilitate labor. It is also used to reduce the inflammation and muscular pain of rheumatism and to treat problems of the respiratory system.

CONSIDERATIONS: Black cohosh should be used carefully since large doses can produce vertigo, tremors, low pulse, vomiting, and nervous system irritation. Don't use during pregnancy.

Citrus limon • Lemon

FAMILY: Rutaceae.

DESCRIPTION: Small tree. Height: To 20 feet (6 m). Width: 5 to 12 feet (1.5 to 2.7 m). Flowers: White with a red tint, to 2 inches (5 cm) across. Leaves: Oblong, 4 inches (10 cm) long, yellow-green, stiff. Fruit: Bright yellow, oblong, ending in a nipple. Blooms: Almost throughout the year.

HABITAT: An Asian native, probably from India, it is now cultivated widely, especially in Italy, California, and Australia.

CULTIVATION: Perennial. Zone: 10. Soil: Fairly rich, heavy soil, but well drained. Sun: Full sun, although subject to sunburn. pH: 5 to 8. Propagation: Cultivated varieties don't grow true from seed, so propagate them from cuttings or by grafting. A tender subtropical, it likes moisture, but too much rain encourages disease. It is injured by sudden temperature changes, especially drops below 20° F (–6° C), although new cultivars are more adaptable. All this fickleness makes lemon trees well suited for a temperate seacoast with overcast skies.

GARDEN DESIGN: Lemon trees are a nice addition to the herb garden in a mild climate. Otherwise, they can be grown in pots and wintered in a greenhouse. Their somewhat dense growth allows them to be trimmed and shaped into hedges.

CONSTITUENTS: Juice: citric acid, pectin, hesperidin, vitamins (A, B, C); peel: essential oils (2.5%), d-limonene (70%), citral, citronellol, sesquiterpenes; calcium oxalate.

RELATED SPECIES: Related to lime *(C. aurantifolia),* sweet orange *(C. sinensis),* and bitter orange *(C. aurantium),* which yields the essential oil neroli, and to its subspecies bergamot *Bergamia,* which yields bergamot oil.

HISTORY: The lemon may have originated in the Indus Valley (where a lemon-shaped earring dating from 2500 B.C. was discovered). Ancient India knew it as *nimbuka,* which became the Hindi *nimbu* and *limbu.* Many authorities claim the lemon was unknown to ancient Greece and Rome, but although rare, Virgil knew it as "median apple" and it was depicted on a mural in Pompeii. It probably arrived there in 185 B.C. with Roman soldiers returning from Asia Minor. By the 3rd century, groves were established in Palestine, and in the 8th and 9th centuries, Arabs planted lemon in the Sahara and Moorish Spain. It appeared in China by the 10th century, when two bottles of exotic lemon juice were presented to the emperor. Northern Europeans probably discovered the lemon when 13th-century Crusaders returned home. Eventually, a *Merchands d'Aigrun* (Merchants of Acid) was established in France and held a monopoly on selling citrus fruits. A cookbook dating from 1474 suggested lemon juice to replace the excessive use of spices in vogue at the time, even though lemons themselves weren't cheap. Lemon was suggested to counteract poisons such as opium and to prevent scurvy. English ships were required to give each seaman an ounce (30 ml) of lemon or lime juice a day. In the United States, extensive cultivation began in Florida in the 17th century. Today, the drier southern California climate produces 80% of the United States crop.

CULINARY: Lemons are salted and spiced in Morocco, dried black in the Middle East, and preserved in spices when young and green in India. The English adopted "hotted-up" lemons pickled with horseradish and mustard from India. Its cooling flavor made lemon one of the first soda-water flavors in 1840. It is used in desserts and soufflés, and the peel is an ingredient in many recipes, not only for flavor, but also color. Lemon flowers are also floated on top of soups.

Citrus limon
LEMON

© Derek Fell

***Citrus limon.* The lemon has a well-traveled history of being sought by people in cold climates.**

MEDICINAL: Lemon is said to "cool" the body and has been substituted when quinine wasn't available to treat fevers. Even in the United States, lemon water is often given to feverish patients. Lemon's essential oil comes in handy as a powerful germ fighter, killing staph, strep, typhoid, and meningitis bacteria. It has been shown effective when used as a gargle, inhaled in steam vapor, or taken in a .2% dilution.[1] Lemon was once even used to disinfect doubtful drinking water. Even though it is acidic itself, the diluted juice neutralizes excessive stomach acidity and improves digestion. The juice has even been used to reduce the size of kidney stones and acidify the urine to prevent infections. As an antihistamine, it decreases inflammation.

AROMATHERAPY: Lemon's "clean" fragrance is the most popular scent for all types of cleaning products.

COSMETIC: Lemon scents soaps and other cosmetics and is an excellent complexion astringent. Applied to sunburn, it reduces redness and inflammation. Ladies in Louis XIV's court bit into lemons to keep their lips an appealing red.

OTHER: Lemon is an antioxidant and natural food preservative. Musicians say you can throw off trumpeters by sucking a lemon in front of them—their lips will pucker too much to play.

PICKLED LEMON

4   lemons
1   teaspoon (5 ml) cumin seed
1/3   teaspoon (1.6 ml) turmeric
1   tablespoon (15 ml) sea salt
1   cup (240 ml) vegetable oil
4   dry chili peppers, whole
1/2   teaspoon (2.5 ml) mustard powder

Cut lemons into 4 sections, but not all the way through, so pieces are not separated. Remove seeds. Mix cumin, turmeric, and salt into

enough oil to form a paste. Stuff this into the lemons and close the sections. Slightly press lemons, chilies, and remaining spice paste into a glass jar. Mix mustard powder into oil, and cover lemons with enough oil to submerge. Keep in a warm place 2 weeks, or until lemons are tender. Pickled lemons may be cut up (like pickles) and served as a condiment.

> *Knowest thou where the lemon trees flourish,*
> *where amid the shadowed leaves the golden oranges glisten,*
> *—a gentle zephyr breathes from the bluye heavens,*
> *the myrtle is motionless, and the laurel rises high?*
> *Dost thou know it well?*
> *Thither, thither, fain would I fly with thee, O my beloved!*
> —"MIGNON'S LIED," JOHANN WOLFGANG VON GOETHE (1749–1832), GERMAN

Cnicus benedictus • Blessed Thistle
(Previously *Carduus benedictus*)

FAMILY: Compositae.

DESCRIPTION: A prickly, rounded bush. Height: 2 feet (60 cm). Width: 1 1/2 feet (45 cm). Flowers: Yellow, 1 1/2 inches (3.7 cm), partially concealed by the leaves. Leaves: Prickly with pale veins, deeply indented with veins and surrounded by sharp, 1-inch (2.5-cm) spines. Fruit: Sharp spines surround the seed pods filled with small seeds. Blooms: July to September.

HABITAT: Originally from the Mediterranean and Near East, naturalized in waste places in the United States, Australia, and other regions.

CULTIVATION: Annual. Germination: 1 to 3 weeks. Space: 12 to 14 inches (30 to 35 cm). Soil Temperature: 65° to 70° F (18° to 21° C). Soil: Dry, fairly poor is suitable. Sun: Full sun. Propagation: Start by seed.

CONSTITUENTS: Essential oil, bitters (cnicin), alkaloid.

HISTORY: The Greeks called this herb *knekos*, or thistle, which became *cnicus* to the Romans. In medieval days, it was called *carduus benedictus*, or "blessed thistle," because its virtues made it considered a cure-all. Many different formulas through the centuries used blessed thistle, including plague treatments. Monks in medieval Europe were very fond of blessed thistle and added it as a tonic to their elixirs. It was even said to strengthen the emotions, as Shakespeare knew when he wrote in *Much Ado About Nothing,* "Get you some of this distilled Carduus Benedictus and lay it to your heart; it is the only thing for a qualm . . . I mean plain holy thistle."

CULINARY: Like most thistles, the spines can be trimmed and the leaves steamed, although this is labor-intensive dining! Some sources suggest eating it in salads, but the merits of this are dubious.

MEDICINAL: Blessed thistle leaves are considered one of the best herbs for increasing mother's milk. Small dosages improve appetite, stimulate the liver, and reduce fevers by encouraging sweating. In the past, it was considered interchangeable with milk thistle *(Silybum marianum),* which has been shown to have liver-regenerating properties. Blessed thistle is antibiotic, destroying staph and other infections, although it has not proved very effective against harmful intestinal bacteria.[1]

CONSIDERATIONS: Avoid large dosages, which are emetic and laxative.

Cnicus benedictus
BLESSED THISTLE

Collinsonia canadensis • Stone Root

FAMILY: Labiatae.

DESCRIPTION: Tall bush, with straight, rigid stems. Height: 1 to 4 feet (30 to 120 cm). Width: 2 to 3 feet (60 to 90 cm). Flowers: To ⅝ inch (6 mm) long, lemon-scented. Leaves: Oval, coarsely toothed, 4 to 10 inches (10 to 25 cm) long. Pungent lemon scent when crushed, especially in spring. Rhizome: Brown-grey, and "stone" hard. Blooms: July to September.

HABITAT: North America, from the rich, moist woods of Ontario and Vermont, to Florida and Arkansas.

CULTIVATION: Perennial. Zone: 2 to 3. Germination: 2 to 4 weeks. Improved by stratification. Soil Temperature: 65° to 70° F (18° to 20° C). Space: 3 feet (90 cm). Soil: Moist, rich, with humus. Sun: Full sun, but will grow in partial shade. Propagation: By seed or root division. To divide the root, cut segments off with a sharp shovel and replant. The root is best prepared fresh.

GARDEN DESIGN: Used in wild gardens.

CONSTITUENTS: Saponin, essential oil, possibly an alkaloid.

HISTORY: Stone root's very hard, knobby root (technically a rhizome) is most likely responsible for its name. It needs to be processed fresh, and even then has a reputation as probably the hardest-to-grind root. Its condensed shape is also stone-like. The first time I dug one up, for a second I thought I had popped out a rock by mistake. Its name may also refer to its popular use as a hemorrhoid remedy. The plant is also known as knob-root, horse-balm, horseweed, and clergyman's friend, the last because it helps a sore or hoarse throat. It was also used in veterinary practices as a diuretic. Native Americans used the fragrant leaves to scent their bodies and brewed the root and leaves into washes for cuts and wounds. They taught the European settlers about it and it eventually found its way into the pharmacies. The early 19th century Eclectic doctors greatly valued stone root. The genus was named after London botanist Peter Collinson, who took a great interest in Native American herbs.

MEDICINAL: Usually combined with other herbs, the root of stone root is used to strengthen weak veins, such as varicose veins. It also tones and improves the functioning of mucous membranes throughout the body, but particularly in the pelvic region. It is suggested for use when there is insufficient circulation in the pelvic region and a sense of "heaviness." Herbalists most often turn to it to reduce hemorrhoids, spasms, or fissures in the rectum. A syrup was once advised for inflammation or constriction of the throat, especially in cases of laryngitis and chronic coughs, and also for middle ear disorders. Indigestion, especially when accompanied by constipation, is often remedied by stone root. A sedative, it relieves muscle spasms, especially those in the digestive tract. The root has occasionally been used as a remedy for headaches caused by digestive sluggishness. An external poultice is placed on wounds, sores, bruises, inflammation.

Collinsonia canadensis
STONE ROOT

Coriandrum sativum • Coriander

FAMILY: Umbelliferae.

DESCRIPTION: Skinny, feathery herb rises up on a few, branched stems. Bees collect its pink pollen. Height: 2 to 3 feet (60 to 90 cm). Width: 1 foot (30 cm). Flowers: Small, flat umbels of white to pale mauve with a reddish accent. Tiny groups surrounded by enlarged, outer petals. Leaves: At first rounded with toothed edges and large lobes, mature leaves are finely divided, feathery. Fruit: Clusters of small, green globes that turn brown as they ripen. The smell of the fruits (technically not seeds) changes from pungent to spicy as they mature. Blooms: July to September.

HABITAT: It has now spread beyond its native Mediterranean and Caucasian regions. Grown commercially in India, Morocco, Poland, Romania, and Argentina. Some is grown in Kentucky for the liquor industry, but the United States imports more than 3 million pounds (1,350,000 kg) annually.

CULTIVATION: Annual. Germination: 7 to 14 days. Space: 12 to 18 inches (30 to 45 cm). Soil Temperature: 55° to 68° F (12.5° to 20° C). Soil: Average with good drainage, but lush if kept well watered, otherwise it produces less flowers. pH: 5 to 8.2. Sun: Full sun or partial shade in hot areas. Propagation: Coriander dislikes transplanting, so sow the seeds directly into the garden. Give it plenty of room to develop, since enclosed groupings can stunt it. Mature fruits appear in about 3 months. It requires staking if the heavy seeds begin to pull the plants over.

GARDEN DESIGN: Coriander plants provide a succession of shapes and smells as they grow. They are best grouped together. If you are fond of fresh cilantro, plant by the edge of a path or near stepping stones for easy access.

CONSTITUENTS: Fruits: essential oil includes borneol, coriandrol (55% to 74%) terpinene, geraniol, camphor, carvone, anethole); leaves: vitamins (A, C), minerals (calcium, phosphorus, potassium, iron), coumarins.

RELATED SPECIES: Hispanic markets sell pointed cilantro— *cilantro de punta (Eryngium foetida)*—which is unrelated, but has a similar taste and is used interchangeably.

HISTORY: Probably one of the first cultivated spices, coriander was in use by 1550 B.C. as a spice and medicine. Seeds were found in Bronze Age ruins on Aegean Islands of Thera and Therasia. The Egyptians, who mentioned coriander in the *Papyrus Ebers* (circa 1550 B.C.), added them to wine to increase intoxication, and seeds were found in King Tut's tomb from 1323 B.C. Grown in Babylon, Assyria, Cyprus, and Egypt, coriander is discussed in ancient Sanskrit texts and in Numbers 11:7 and Exodus 16:31, and King Merodach-baladan II (721–710 B.C.) included it in his treatise on gardening. Romans boiled coriander leaves with greens and barley porridge, and Virgil mentions a seasoning (which sounds very potent) of coriander seeds, rue, savory, mint, wild celery, onion, thyme, pennyroyal, and garlic. The Greek doctor Hippocrates (460–377 B.C.) devoted an entire treatise to *korion*—named after *koris,* or "bedbug," because the leaves' strong smell reminded the Greeks of the bug. Others have been more appreciative of the scent. Coriander was used in love potions in the Middle Ages and is an aphrodisiac in *The Arabian Nights*. The Spanish introduced it to Latin America, where the seeds, and especially the leaves, have become an integral part of their seasoning. It arrived in Massachusetts before 1670, but never gained the same fame in northern America, except to flavor liquor.

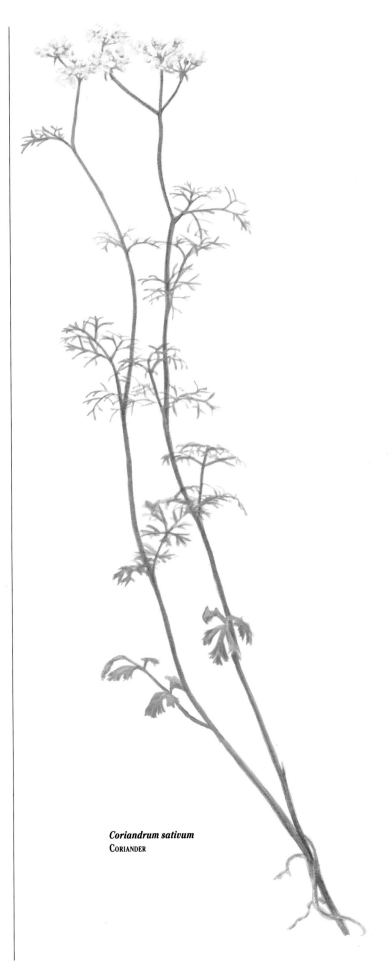

Coriandrum sativum
CORIANDER

CULINARY: Coriander is still one of the most widely used herbs in the world. The seeds are the basis of curries and salsas and are a secret ingredient in apple dishes. The fresh leaves, also known as cilantro, give their distinctive taste to Mexican, South American, Chinese, southeast Asian (especially Thai and Vietnamese), Philippine, North African, and East Indian cuisine. Ethiopians add the leaves to breads, sauces, and tea. The Chinese use them so much, raw in salads and to garnish food, that Westerners call it "Chinese Parsley." Even Caribbean markets sell bouquet garnis that include cilantro leaves and sweet peppers for their famous *sofrito* sauce, added to rice and bean dishes. Algerians still preserve their food in coriander mixed with pepper and salt, as Europeans once did. The seeds flavor the Basque drink *izzara,* melissa cordial, Chartreuse, Benedictine, Ratafia (with angelica, celery, and fennel), and some brands of gin and brandy. The root has been cooked and eaten like a vegetable. The seeds are used in baked goods and sweets and are the traditional center in "jawbreaker" candies.

MEDICINAL: Coriander seeds make many medicines taste better, especially bitter laxatives like senna syrup, and were official in the *U.S. Pharmacopoeia* from 1820 to 1980. They aid digestion, reduce gas, and improve the appetite. At one time, the seeds were made into candies for children's indigestion, and coriander water was used to relieve colic. The Chinese still employ coriander tea to counter dysentery and measles. East Indians make the seeds into an eyewash to prevent blindness in smallpox patients. The oil is an antiseptic and was suggested by Dioscorides to treat urinary tract restrictions and inflammation.

AROMATHERAPY: Coriander seeds, along with lemon balm and other herbs, were an ingredient in the famous Carmelite toilet water that was first made by Carmelite nuns of St. Just in 1379 and remained a principle complexion water, especially in France, until the 17th century. Other French toilet waters of the period incorporated coriander, including *Eau de Carnes,* a Paris favorite. Today, it provides raw materials for the manufacture of synthetic perfume scents. The fragrance is also used in soaps and natural deodorant. Its seeds make a flavorful dentifrice.

CONSIDERATIONS: Coriander can be narcotic in extremely high dosages. The juice of freshly picked plants produces an effect like that of alcohol—excitement, then depression.

OTHER: The seeds are a spicy ingredient in potpourri and are also used to flavor tobacco.

EAST INDIAN GARAM MASALA

1	*tablespoon (15 ml) cumin seeds, whole*
1	*tablespoon (15 ml) cloves, whole*
2	*tablespoons (30 ml) coriander seeds, whole*
2	*tablespoons (30 ml) peppercorns, whole*
2	*bay leaves, whole*
1	*teaspoon (5 ml) cinnamon, powdered*
2	*cardamom pods, whole*

Combine all ingredients and dry-roast by heating in a heavy frying pan over moderate heat for about 10 minutes, stirring constantly. When the spices smell strongly aromatic, remove from heat and grind. Store in an airtight container.

Crataegus laevigata • Hawthorn
(Previously *C. oxyacantha* and *C. oxyacanthoides*)

FAMILY: Rosaceae

DESCRIPTION: Dense tree with small, sharp thorns. Height: To 25 feet (7.5 m). Flowers: Small, white, with 5 rose-like petals, in clusters of 5 to 12. Leaves: Flat, small, lobed, maple-like; 2 inches (5 cm) long. Fruit: Bright red, round berries, 1/3 inch (8 mm) in diameter, with one large seed. Blooms: May.

HABITAT: Europe, with closely related species found in North Africa and Western Asia in hedges and open deciduous woods.

CULTIVATION: Perennial. Zone: 4. Germination: 2 to 3 years, may require scarification with acid. Stratify about 90 days. Space: 8 feet (2.4 m) from other trees, or grow shade-loving herbs underneath. Soil Temperature: Can vary. Soil: Average, alkaline garden preferred, but will tolerate most conditions. Sun: Full sun or partial shade in forested areas (although shady conditions produce fewer flowers and fruit). Propagation: Most species self-seed and come true from seed. Cuttings don't always take but can be grafted. Transplant seedlings in the autumn or very early spring. They can be dug in the wild, although their surprisingly long tap root makes transplanting tricky. (For technical details on germination, see *The Reference Manual of Woody Plant Propagation* by Dirr & Heuser, Varsity Press, 1987.)

GARDEN DESIGN: Hawthorn is considered one of the most beautiful spring-flowering shrubs and has inspired many poets. Even in late autumn, its bare, spiny branches are filled with attractive red berries. It makes a tall hedge that is useful as a protective barrier to isolate the herb garden.

RELATED SPECIES: About 1,000 species were once identified by botanists, who have since reduced the count to a more manageable selection. Traditional Chinese medicine used the berries to improve digestion and blood and, as a result of modern research, now uses it for treating heart conditions. Russian studies on a number of wild hawthorn species found they all contain at least some active flavonoids.

CONSTITUENTS: Flavonoids, saponins, procyanidines, phenolic acids. Flowers: Flavonoids, amines. Berries: vitamin C.

HISTORY: Hawthorn, or hedge-thorn, has been a well-loved tree throughout the ages. To the Greeks, it symbolized hope, and the flowering branches decorated weddings. In England, where it was called the mayflower after the month in which it blooms, it provided branches for the maypole. The *Mayflower* pilgrims sailing to America named their boat after this tree to symbolize their hope. *Al-Samarquandi* mentions a Mediterranean hawthorn *(C. azarolus)* in the 13th century as "useful for the stomach and yellow gall," but Western herbalists have had remarkably little to say about hawthorn's medicinal qualities. In 1917, Eclectic physician John Uri Lloyd chronicled its introduction into popular herbalism in the *Treatise on Crataegus:* "A well-known physician, the late Dr. Green, of Ennis, County Clare, Ireland, attained an extended reputation in the treatment of Heart Disease, but kept the remedy a secret. Upon his death in 1894, his daughter revealed the famous cure to be a tincture of the ripe berries of *Crataegus oxycanthus.*" Two years later a *New York Medical Journal* article brought hawthorn to the attention of physicians and the Lloyd brothers began producing an extract. They declared one American species superior, but never identified it.

Crataegus laevigata
HAWTHORN

The Hawthorne whitens; and the juicy Groves
Put forth their buds, unfolding by degrees,
Till the whole leafy Forest stands displayed,
In full luxuriance, to the sighing gales.
—"SPRING," JAMES THOMSON (1700–1748), SCOTTISH

CULINARY: The berries are eaten both raw and cooked in all parts of the world where they are found and are turned into tasty jam, jelly, wine, and liqueur.

MEDICINAL: Hawthorn normalizes the heart and circulation, lowering or raising blood pressure according to need. It is found in most herbal preparations for heart weakness, irregular heart beat, hardening of the arteries, artery spasms, and angina. In one of many clinical studies, after 52 patients with heart disorders caused by age or disease took hawthorn, their hearts required 77% less oxygen when under stress as compared to a 25% improvement offered by standard treatments.[1] In another study, hawthorn normalized heart action and efficiency and seemed to strengthen contractions in almost all the patients with primary heart disease and even some with more severe secondary heart disease. It also improved heart problems caused by hepatitis or other liver disease.[2] Hawthorn lowers blood pressure by dilating surface blood vessels, as opposed to directly acting on the heart as does the more dangerous digitalis (foxglove). Its action is less severe, but it takes longer to achieve.[3] Unlike digitalis, hawthorn does not have a cumulative effect on heart tissue. It makes the body more sensitive to digitalis, so the prescribed dose of digitalis may eventually be cut in half.[4] Originally only the berries were used, but higher concentrations of active flavonoids have been discovered in the flowers and leaves when hawthorn is in full bloom. One study found spring shoots to be the most active of all.[5] The flavonoids dilate coronary and external arteries while procyanidines, which are most prevalent in the leaves around August, apparently slow the heart beat and are antibiotic.[6] To cover all the bases, many herbalists now use the flowers, young stems, and berries together. The booklet *The Hawthorn Berry for the Heart,* by J.I. Rodale (Rodale Books, 1971) contains informal case histories. A scientific abstract on hawthorn is available from the Herb Research Foundation, Longmont, CO 80501.

OTHER USES: Hawthorn wood is strong and ideal for boxmaking. It is an even hotter fuel than oak.

© Kathi Keville

***Crataegus lavigaetus.* Hawthorn is dramatic in the autumn when it is covered with bright red berries. The berries make a delicious jam and are collected by herbalists for a heart tonic.**

Crocus sativus • Saffron

FAMILY: Iridaceae.

DESCRIPTION: Grass clumps with striking flowers. Height: 1 foot (30 cm). Width: 4 feet (1.2 m). Flowers: Fragrant, spreading 1½ to 2 inches (3.7 to 5 cm) long, usually lilac-purple, with bright orange-red, threadlike stigmas. Leaves: Thin, grasslike, numerous, appear in the fall. Blooms: September to November for about 15 days.

HABITAT: Native to central Europe and Asia Minor, but no longer found in the wild. Cultivated commercially in Spain, France, Italy, India, China, and the Middle East.

CULTIVATION: Perennial. Zone: 6 to 10. Germination: 8 to 10 weeks. Space: 8 to 10 inches (20 to 25 cm). Soil Temperature: 70° to 75° F (21° C to 24° C). Soil: Well drained, sandy, fertile, but not too rich. Low rainfall (about 15 inches [37 cm]) best. pH: 6 to 7.8. Sun: Sun or partial shade. Propagation: Plant corms 3 to 4 inches (7.5 cm to 10 cm) deep, in spring or early summer. They can survive cold weather, but mulch if there is danger of the ground heaving and disturbing the bulbs. One dozen corms should supply you with a year of culinary delights. Although plants live 15 years, dig the corms every 2 to 3 years after flowering and replant since they progressively work their way deeper in the soil, taking longer to flower and weakening the plant. Lift and divide them after the foliage dies back in the spring, then store in a cool, dry place for several weeks before replanting. They will flower again in the autumn.

GARDEN DESIGN: Plant saffron in a location that shows off the colorful autumn flowers. It makes an excellent border flower.

CONSTITUENTS: Essential oil (8% to 10%) includes terpenes, safranol (which produces the warm, spicy taste); glycosides are crocin (which provides the distinctive color), picrocrocin.

RELATED SPECIES: The numerous crocus species planted in flower gardens are all related.

HISTORY: Saffron has been harvested since at least 1600 B.C., when it was depicted in a wall painting in Crete. To the Greeks, *krocus* symbolized life, beauty, and youth, and so it was given to newlyweds. *Kroke* means "thread," probably describing the stigmas. Romans sprinkled saffron water on cushions at home and benches at the theater; strewed banquet floors with the leaves as they dined on luxurious yellow foods; and at least one emperor, Heliogabalus, bathed in saffron-scented water. Saffron crocuses are the Hebrew *karcom* mentioned in the Song of Solomon, 4:14; "Thy plants are an orchard of pomegranates, with pleasant fruits; . . . Spikenard and Saffron . . . ." Persia and Asia Minor exported saffron to India, where its color signified the highest caste and its water was sprinkled on guests to welcome them. When the Moors brought it to Spain in the 10th century, the Spanish called it *azafrano,* after the Arabic *azzafaran,* or "yellow-colored." In that same century, Arab Muhammed Ibn Zaka Riya al Rasi (Latinized to Rasis) wrote in his *Mensa Philophica* that saffron infused in wine was a stomach tonic that improved shortness of breath and "produces a most satisfactory elevation of spirits." China was familiar with saffron by the Yuen Dynasty (A.D. 1280–1368), and it appeared as *Sa-fa-lang* in the 16th-century *Pun Tsaou* pharmacopoeia. The French Office of Safran established severe penalties, even death, in the 14th century for those who adulterated saffron—usually with safflower or marigold petals. Although crocuses were growing in France, Italy, and Germany by the 12th century, tradition says that

Crocus sativus
SAFFRON

CULINARY: An early cookery book proclaimed, "Saffron should be put into all Lenten sauces, soups, and other such dishes; also without Saffron, we cannot have well-cooked peas." Eighteenth-century aristocrats nibbled on honeyed saffron balls and sprinkled saffron on salads. One of the most expensive spices in the world, the stigmas must be hand-harvested, as they have been for over 3,600 years, at an exorbitant retail cost per pound. Fortunately, only small quantities are needed to flavor the traditional French fish soup bouillabaisse, the Spanish *paella* (meat, fish, rice, and vegetables), the Milanese *risotto* (with cinnamon and lemon peel), or English Cornish cakes. The Schwenkfelder family were already saffron growers when they emigrated to the United States, bringing with them recipes that became well established in their Pennsylvania Dutch community, which still uses homegrown saffron in noodle and chicken dishes, soups, sauces, pastries, and "Schwenkfelder" cake. Saffron is potent: To use it, mix $^1/_4$ teaspoon (1.25 ml) of saffron in 2 tablespoons (30 ml) hot water for 5 cups (about 1 kg) of flour, or 6 servings of sauce.

MEDICINAL: Saffron used to be given to children to encourage sweating, especially during measles and scarlet fever. The Chinese still use it—to treat depression, shock, and menstrual problems, such as chronic, excessive bleeding, pain, irregularity, infertility, and menopause problems. They regard it as a catalyst to be combined with other herbs. Its actions are also related to the liver, spleen, and heart.

AROMATHERAPY: Saffron adds a warm, spicy scent to Oriental-style perfumes.

OTHER: Saffron produces a colorful, although unstable, golden yellow cloth dye used for East Indian ceremonial garb and bridal veils and also Irish bed linen. In medieval days, wealthy women dyed their hair with saffron and monks mixed it with *glair* (egg white glue), making a golden yellow, transparent coloring to illuminate manuscripts. They also mixed it with green colors to enhance them.

BOUILLABAISSE

This recipe is traditionally served with garlic bread. It also makes a good vegetable soup if you omit the fish.

$^1/_4$ cup (60 ml) onions, finely chopped
4   leeks, finely chopped, white parts only
4   medium tomatoes, diced
5   garlic cloves, minced
1   tablespoon (15 ml) fresh fennel, finely chopped
$^1/_2$ teaspoon (2.5 ml) saffron
2   bay leaves, pulverized
1   teaspoon (5 ml) orange rind, grated
2   tablespoons (30 ml) tomato paste
$^1/_8$ teaspoon (.6 ml) celery seed
3   tablespoons (45 ml) parsley, chopped
1   teaspoon (5 ml) black pepper, chopped
1   tablespoon (15 ml) salt
$^1/_4$ cup (60 ml) olive oil
4   pounds (1.8 kg) fresh fish, in 1-inch (2.5-cm) cubes
$2^1/_2$ cups (600 ml) water

Heat oil in large skillet, and cook all ingredients, except fish and water, until the vegetables are transparent. Add fish and water and boil for 20 minutes.

Sir Thomas Smith, Secretary of State to Edward II, risked his life to smuggle a corm through Arab customs in his cane around 1330. However it got to England, saffron was so well established by the 16th century that John Gerard wrote, "Saffron groweth plentifully . . . as corne in the fields" in Saffron Walden, in Essex. In 1670, J. F. Hertodt acclaimed its virtues in his German treatise *Crocologin.*

Risotto a la Milanese

2   cups (480 ml) rice, cooked
¹/₄   cup (60 ml) butter or oil
10   cups (2.5 l) soup stock
      Pinch of saffron
1   small onion, minced
      Grated Parmesan cheese

Sauté the rice in the butter or oil, then add 1 cup (240 ml) stock. Continue to stir for 10 minutes, adding 6 more cups (1.4 l) of stock. Dissolve the saffron in ¹/₄ cup (60 ml) of stock and slowly add while stirring, along with the rest of the stock during the next 5 minutes, by which time the rice should have absorbed the liquid. Serve warm, topped with grated Parmesan cheese.

Serves 8 to 10.

Saffron Nut Sauce

This recipe comes from *De Re Coquinaria,* by Apicius, who lived in the first century A.D.

¹/₂   teaspoon (2.5 ml) ground black pepper
1   teaspoon (5 ml) parsley, ground
1   teaspoon (5 ml) lovage seed (or celery), ground
¹/₂   teaspoon (2.5 ml) spearmint, ground
      Pinch of saffron
¹/₂   cup (120 ml) white wine
¹/₄   cup (60 ml) hazelnuts (or almonds), grated and roasted
1   tablespoon (15 ml) honey
1   tablespoon (15 ml) vinegar
1   cup (240 ml) soup stock
1   teaspoon (5 ml) olive oil
1   stalk celery, finely chopped
      Sprig of fresh mint

Combine the pepper and herbs with wine. Add nuts, honey, vinegar, and stock. Heat oil in pan, bring to a boil, and simmer 25 minutes on low, stirring constantly with celery and mint sprig.

> *Pale saffron plot*
> *Forget him not;*
> *His dwelling made trim*
>   *look shortly for him.*
> *When harvest is gone*
>   *then saffron comes on;*
> *A little of ground*
>   *brings saffron a pound.*
> **Five Hundred Points of Good Husbandry,**
> **Thomas Tusser (1527–1580), English**

> *SAFFRON, 'tis said, brings comfort to mankind,*
> *By giving rise to cheerfulness of mind.*
> *Restores weak limbs, the liver also mends,*
> *And normal vigor through its substance sends.*
> —"Of Saffron," *Regimen Sanitatis Salerni,* **10**th-century Italy

Cuminum cyminum
Cumin

Cuminum cyminum • Cumin
(Previously *C. odorum*)

FAMILY: Umbelliferae.

DESCRIPTION: Slender herb. Height: 8 inches (20 cm). Width: 6 inches (15 cm). Flowers: Tiny, white, sometimes slightly pink, in sparse umbel heads. Leaves: Thin, divided leaves. Fruit: ¹/₃ inch (.83 cm) long, narrow fruits. Blooms: June to July.

HABITAT: A native to Egypt and the Mediterranean, cumin is now cultivated in North Africa, the Middle East (primarily Iran), India, Malta, and China.

CULTIVATION: Annual. Germination: 10 to 14 days. Space: 6 to 10 inches (15 to 25 cm). Soil Temperature: 70° F (21° C). Soil: Well drained, average. pH: 4.5 to 8.2. Sun: Full sun. Propagation: Plant the herbs close together so that they can hold each other up and keep down competitive weeds.

CONSTITUENTS: Essential oil (2.5% to 4%) includes aldehydes, pinenes, cuminic alcohol; fatty oil, pentosan (25% to 35%).

HISTORY: Cumin is thought to be one of the oldest cultivated herbs. The Myceanes seasoned their food with it around 2000 B.C., and it is found in the earliest tombs of Egyptian pharaohs, including King Tut's tomb from 1323 B.C. Later, the ancient Romans imported *cuminum* from Egypt, sprinkling ground cumin on their food as liberally as Westerners use black pepper today. Cumin is recommended by Susruta the Older in the 4th-century B.C. herbal medicine text *Mushkakadigana* as a treatment for obesity and urinary and liver problems (along with cardamom, ginger, pepper, and mustard). Greek herbalist Dioscorides, in the 1st century A.D., suggested *kyminon* for pale girls (although it also had a reputation for keeping them pale!), and young scholars reportedly smoked cumin to make their complexions appear as though they were always studying. The prophet Isaiah mentioned the *fructus cumini* in the Bible (Isaiah 28:25, 27), and the tithes Jesus discusses in Matthew 23:23 were not money, but cumin.

CULINARY: Cumin became one of the favorite herbs of Europeans in the Middle Ages, but it eventually lost its popularity and much of its distinction. Today, the French *carvi* and German *kümmel* can refer to either caraway or cumin seeds. Both are ingredients in the liqueur *kümmel* and other cordials. Cumin remains a well-used seasoning for flavoring curries and beans in the Middle East, India, and Mexico.

MEDICINAL: Cumin seed is used for diarrhea and indigestion and was said by some medical herbalists to be superior to fennel or caraway, although the pleasing taste of these herbs has made them more popular. It is a specific for headaches caused by indigestion.

AROMATHERAPY: Small amounts of cumin oil are found in perfumery.

MIDDLE EASTERN HUMMUS

2   *cups (480 ml) garbanzo beans, cooked and strained*
2   *tablespoons (30 ml) sesame seeds*
2   *tablespoons (30 ml) sesame oil*
3   *tablespoons (45 ml) fresh lemon juice*
1   *large garlic clove, whole*
1/4   *teaspoon (1.25 ml) cumin, ground*
    Broth from cooking beans
    Salt and pepper to taste

Combine ingredients—except broth, salt, and pepper—in a blender. Pour in broth gradually to achieve the consistency of heavy batter. Season with salt and pepper.

TURNIPS IN CUMIN SAUCE

This recipe originated in Rome during the first century A.D.

1   *pound (500 g) turnips, peeled and cubed*
1/2   *teaspoon (2.5 ml) cumin*
    Pinch of rosemary (or rue)
1/4   *teaspoon (1.25 ml) ginger*
1   *teaspoon (5 ml) honey*
2   *teaspoons (10 ml) olive oil*
1/4   *cup (60 ml) white wine*
1   *cup (240 ml) turnip stock*
1   *tablespoon (15 ml) flour*
    Freshly ground pepper to taste

Steam turnips until half-cooked, drain, and save the stock. Mix remaining ingredients, except flour and pepper, and add to turnips. Finish cooking until tender. Thicken stock with flour and sprinkle with pepper before serving.

EAST INDIAN CURRY POWDER

Traditionally, curry is prepared by lightly cooking it in oil for several hours before adding it to foods. It also can be made into a paste or sauce with a water or coconut-juice base.

1   *ounce (28 g) each:*
    cumin
    coriander
    turmeric
1/2   *ounce (14 g) each:*
    ginger
    dried chili peppers
    black mustard seeds, whole
    fennel seed

Blend ingredients. Add to recipes as needed.

Cymbopogon citratus • Lemon Grass

FAMILY: Gramineae.

DESCRIPTION: Tall grass growing in dense clumps. Height: To 4 feet (120 cm). Width: To 2 feet (60 cm). Flowers: Seldom. Leaves: Grasslike, sharply tapered on the ends, 3 feet (90 cm) long, 1/2 inch (1.25 cm) wide, growing from a slightly bulbous base. Strongly lemon-scented when broken.

Cymbopogon citratus
LEMON GRASS

HABITAT: South India and Sri Lanka. Widely cultivated in the tropics (Central America, Mexico, Brazil) as well as in China, Florida, California, and Australia.

CULTIVATION: Perennial. Zone: 10. Space: 1 foot (30 cm). Soil Temperature: 70° to 75° F (21° to 23° C). Soil: Well drained, dry, even poor. Excessive watering lowers the oil content. pH: 4.3 to 8.4. Sun: Full sun. Propagation: From root divisions of clumps. Often the fresh lemon grass sold in some produce markets for Indonesian cooking has roots attached and can be grown. In cold climates, the roots can be dug up and brought in to overwinter.

GARDEN DESIGN: The most interesting feature of lemon grass isn't design quality, but the fragrance of the leaves when broken. Use as a backing for more delicate plants.

CONSTITUENTS: Essential oil (70% to 85%) includes citral (75% to 80%), geraniol, farnesol, nerol, citronellol, myrcene.

RELATED SPECIES: Citronella *(C. nardus; C. wintrianus)* from Sri Lanka, palma rosa *(C. martini),* and Cochin oil *(C. flexuosus),* from the port of Cochin, produce essential oils.

HISTORY: There are reports that lemon grass was being distilled for export as early as the 17th century in the Philippines. The first samples of the closely related citronella oil were displayed at the World's Fair at London's Crystal Palace in 1851.

CULINARY: An integral flavor in Sri Lanka and Thai cooking, lemon grass is also found in East Indian dishes and makes a very popular beverage in tropical countries. It commercially flavors dairy desserts, candy, and baked goods.

MEDICINAL: In East India and Sri Lanka, where it is called "fever tea," lemon grass leaves are combined with other herbs to treat fevers, irregular menstruation, diarrhea, and stomachaches. Lemon grass is one of the most popular herbs in Brazil and the Caribbean for nervous and digestive problems. The Chinese use lemon grass in a similar fashion, to treat headaches, stomachaches, colds, and rheumatic pains. The essential oil is used straight in India to treat ringworm or in a paste with buttermilk to rub on ringworm and bruises. Studies show it does destroy many types of bacteria and fungi and is a deodorant.[1] It may reduce blood pressure—a traditional Cuban use of the herb—and it contains five different constituents that inhibit blood coagulation. A scientific review of its uses is available.[2]

AROMATHERAPY: Lemon grass produces one of the 10-largest-selling essential oils in the world, with over 1500 tons (1524 tonnes) produced annually. It is used as the natural starting point to produce the fragrance component citral. In East India, the oil is mixed with coconut oil to rub on lumbago, rheumatism, and painful nerve conditions. In the Caribbean, lemon grass baths ease soreness.

COSMETIC: The lemonlike scent is a major fragrance in cosmetics and soaps.

OTHER: Lemon grass is a fly, flea, and mosquito repellent. It is used as the starting point in the manufacture of vitamin A. Lemon grass adds a citrus fragrance to potpourri.

Cypripedium calceolus var. *pubescens* • Lady's Slipper
(Previously *C. parviflorum* var. *pubescens*, *C. pubescens*)

FAMILY: Orchidaceae.

DESCRIPTION: A striking flower set amidst a few leaves. Height: 2 feet (60 cm). Width: 1 foot (30 cm). Flowers: Green-yellow, sometimes streaked with purple, fragrant. The lower lip forms an inflated, balloonlike sack. Leaves: Elongated ovals, broad, to 8 inches (20 cm) long, red-brown, odor slightly resembles valerian. Root: Fleshy, to 6½ inches (16 cm) long. Blooms: May to June.

HABITAT: North America, from Yukon territory south to Georgia and Louisiana, also Arizona and Oregon. Endangered and protected —do not dig in the wild and only purchase cultivated stock.

CULTIVATION: Perennial. Zone: 2. Germination: The tiny seeds in the fruits must be infected with a beneficial fungi found in soil that enlarges the root system and helps pull in nutrients. Space: 1 foot (30 cm). Soil: Moist, but not too wet, rich. pH: 4 to 4.5. Sun: Shade. Propagation: By division of plant root crowns, 2 inches (5 cm) below the surface. The fragile roots may extend 1 foot (30 cm) around the plant, so dig a large rootball when moving. They can be grown in pots, if adequate drainage and peat moss are provided. Indoor temperatures should average about 60° to 70° F (15° to 21° C).

GARDEN DESIGN: A beautiful addition to any garden, lady's slipper belongs in the herb garden more for its beauty and historical usage than practical use.

CONSTITUENTS: Essential oil, glycosides, resins.

RELATED SPECIES: There are many varieties. Small yellow lady's slipper (*C. calceolus* var. *parviflorum*) and pink lady's slipper *(C. acaule)* are used interchangeably. There are other species in North America, Japan, Asia, and Europe.

HISTORY: Used as a sedative, lady's slipper was also called "nerve root" or "American valerian," with which it is often compared. Rafinesque introduced it to European medicine in his 1828 *Medical Flora* stating, "all species are equally medicinal; they have long been known to the Indians and were used by the Empiric [physicians], . . . particularly Samuel Thompson. . . . The best substitute for American Valerian in almost all cases." The Native name was moccasin flower since the blossom resembles a slipper. The whites followed suit, naming it lady's slipper. It was a favorite of Native women to wear in their hair. In 1977, ninety countries, including the United States formed a treaty called the Convention of International Trade in Endangered Species of Wild Fauna and Flora, which restricted commercial trade of endangered species, including the lady's slipper orchid, and required export permits.

MEDICINAL: Lady's slipper used to be a specific remedy to overcome depression, mental anxiety, and troubled sleep. It was often recommended for women for both emotional and physical imbalances relating to menopause or menstruation, such as nervous tension, headaches, or cramps. Lady's slipper is said to increase nervous tone after a long disease and to relax nervous muscle twitches. It is almost always given as an alcoholic tincture, since some constituents are not water-soluble. Lady's slipper is often compared to valerian, although valerian doesn't create the uncomfortable side effects.

CONSIDERATIONS: Large doses may cause headaches and also disorientation. Contact dermatitis is also possible.

Cypripedium calceolus var. pubescens
LADY'S SLIPPER

Dianthus caryophyllus • Clove Pink

FAMILY: Caryophyllaceae.

DESCRIPTION: A branchy and bushy clump. Height: 12 inches (30 cm). Width: 8 inches (20 cm). Flowers: 1¹/₂-inch (3.7-cm) diameter, 2 to 5 flowers per stem with a very sweet fragrance that increases in the evening. Layers of purple-pink to pale rose petals with fringed edges. Leaves: Thick, straight, pointed and jutting upwards. Blooms: July to September.

HABITAT: Native to Europe and India, it is found growing on open, calcareous soils.

CULTIVATION: Perennial. Zone: 3. Germination: 5 to 10 days. Space: 10 to 12 inches (25 to 30 cm). Soil Temperature: 70° F (21° C). Soil: Rich, well drained. pH: 8 to 9. Sun: Full sun. The newer hybrids can better stand hot, dry summers. Propagation: Seed or cutting. Keep flowers cut to extend flowering season. It can also be spread by ground layering. It is easy to cultivate, even in a pot, but is subject to mildew so, in humid climates, provide plenty of room for air circulation around the plants.

Dianthus × allwoodii, a popular hybrid of clove pink.

GARDEN DESIGN: Clove pinks provide the herb garden with delightful spots of color. Plant them here and there to draw the eye through the garden or use them to edge and frame a specific point of interest. They lend themselves not just to lines, but to circles and squares. Medieval gardeners liked to place them next to and even on walls, taking advantage of the dirt-filled areas in between stones. A few varieties even earned the name wallflower.

CONSTITUENTS: Essential oil (eugenol).

HISTORY: The most popular of all cut flowers, the carnations have been hybridized from this less showy, but more aromatic, clove pink. Theophrastus called them *dios* ("divine") *anthos* ("flower"). Many sources claim the English name, gilly flower, came from the old name for July, the month they begin blooming, but the medieval *gyllofer* is really derived from the Greek *karyophyllon*, or "nut leaf." This ancient name for the cloves, a fragrance that clove pinks closely resemble, also gives them their species name *carophyllus* (and was once the species name for cloves themselves). John of Gaddesden recorded a heart remedy in 1314 that sounds good enough for a facial water: "Virify the heart with a powder made of roses, liquid aloes, saffron and gillyflower, all in rosewater. Soak the shirt of the sufferer in this." Clove pinks were also used to disguise the taste of strong medicines.

CULINARY: Petals from the fresh flowers are decorative additions to salads, soups, sauces, and open sandwiches. Gilly cordials, syrups, and conserves used to be popular, and the flowers still flavor some liqueurs and wines. An herbal vinegar from the flowers turns distilled vinegar a delicate pink and imparts its decidedly clovelike taste. Pickled gilly flowers and the vinegar were a favorite from the 14th through the 18th centuries. The flowers steeped in white wine were also used as culinary flavorings and were thought to be aphrodisiac.

AROMATHERAPY: A flower vinegar has been inhaled to ease headaches and used as a massage oil for sore muscles.

OTHER: The dried petals are added to potpourri and occasionally to cosmetics.

> *Take clove-gillyflowers, when just blown, clip the white*
> *bottoms from them, when taken out of the Husks, lay them to*
> *steep a little in fair water, boil up some White wine Vinegar....*
> *squeeze the water out of your Gillyflowers, and the Vinegar*
> *being cool, put them into it; then melt as much Sugar as*
> *convenient...; with a little Cinnamon, and Mace; stop them up*
> *close, and when you use them, mince them small, and putting*
> *a little fresh Vinegar to them, strew a little white Sugar finely*
> *beaten and they are excellent sauce.*
> "GILLY FLOWERS TO PICKLE," *THE FAMILY DICTIONARY*,
> WILLIAM SALMON (1705), ENGLISH

> *Your breath is sweeter than balm, sugar or licorice...*
> *And yourself as sweet as the gillyflower*
> *Or lavender seeds strewn in a coffer to smell.*
> —ANONYMOUS, LATE 14TH CENTURY

Dianthus caryophyllus
CLOVE PINK

Digitalis purpurea • Foxglove

FAMILY: Scrophulariaceae.

DESCRIPTION: Soft mound of leaves with spike flower stalk. Height: 4 to 8 feet (1.2 to 2.4 m). Width: 2½ feet (75 cm). Flowers: Bell-shaped, pale purple with crimson spots inside, hang along one side of flower spike. Leaves: Soft, 6 to 12 inches (12.5 to 30 cm), oval-shaped, blue-green. Blooms: June to August.

HABITAT: Western Europe and Moroccan native, it is naturalized in the Americas and widely cultivated.

CULTIVATION: Biennial. Zone: 4. Germination: 7 to 14 days. Space: 1 to 2 feet (30 to 60 cm). Soil Temperature: 65° to 70° F (18° to 21° C). Soil: Moist humus, very well drained. Must be acid. pH: 4.5 to 8.2. Sun: Partial shade or even total shade preferred, but will grow in full sun if well watered, especially in cooler climates. Propagation: By seed, which are very tiny so mix them with sand for a better distribution in flats.

GARDEN DESIGN: Foxglove may not provide many herbal home uses, but it finds a welcome place in the herb garden for its flowers alone. It is often grown with perennial flowers and in old-fashioned cottage gardens. Plant it where both the leaves and flowers can be noticed.

CONSTITUENTS: Glycosides (digitoxin, gitoxin, gitaloxin).

RELATED SPECIES: A number of cultivars have been hybridized with different coloring and marking on their flowers.

Digitalis purpurea
FOXGLOVE

Digitalis purpurea. **The tall stalks of flowers produced by foxglove make this beautiful, but potentially toxic, herb a favorite for both flower and herb gardens.**

HISTORY: The Anglo-Saxons called the herb *foxes glofa,* or "foxglove." It was also called "folk's glove," referring to a folk's (fairy's) glove, which somehow is easier to picture. Foxglove has been cultivated since at least 1000 A.D., but its now famous properties for heart ailments were not recognized, at least in texts. The 13th-century Welsh Physicians of Myddvai used foxglove poultice externally. They also used it to stain the lines engravèd into their stone floors to give them a mosaic appearance. In the 16th century, Gerard recommended using foxglove on those who have fallen from high places, and Dodoen boiled it in wine as an expectorant and a cough syrup for swollen glands. Then, in 1775, Dr. William Withering, an English physician, examined a woman suffering from dropsy. He found her condition was so serious, he expected her to die shortly. Imagine his surprise on hearing only a few weeks later that she had fully recovered. He discovered she drank an herbal tea containing foxglove that had been given to her by a "backwoods" Yorkshire female herbalist. It turned out that some lay herbalists had long known about the herb's properties. In 1785, Withering published *An Account of the Foxglove,* describing the herb's effects. In celebration of the two hundredth anniversary of Withering's document, *An Account of the Foxglove and its Medicinal Uses 1785–1985,* by J. K. Aronson (Oxford University Press, 1985) was published. The author makes notes on the original text and also includes the history and modern uses.

MEDICINAL: Foxglove yields *digitoxin,* which is still used today to increase the force of the heart's contractions. As a result, blood pressure in the veins is reduced and the pulse is slowed and stabilized.

CONSIDERATIONS: Extremely poisonous, digitalis is too dangerous to use without medical supervision. It can cause blurred vision, dizziness, vomiting, diarrhea, convulsions, and death. While low doses reduce the pulse, large doses produce a very rapid heartbeat. Continued use of digitalis may also cause depression. Researchers speculate that it affects depression-related brain chemicals.

OTHER: The flowers produce a yellow-green dye.

Echinacea purpurea • Purple Coneflower
(Previously *Brauneria purpurea* and *Rudbeckia purpurea*)

FAMILY: Compositae.

DESCRIPTION: Stately plant with a striking flower. Height: 3 feet (90 cm). Width: 2½ feet (75 cm), sometimes larger. Flowers: A few flowers on each stalk, bright pink-purple, petals 3 inches (7.5 cm) long, around a raised center disk of orange. Heads to 6 inches (15 cm) wide. Leaves: Sparse, narrow, pointed, and very hairy, 3 to 6 inches (7.5 to 15 cm) long. Fruit: Brown, papery seeds. Root: Long, spindly, grouped together in older plants. Fleshy, white inside covered by a dark skin. Blooms: July to August.

HABITAT: Central and southeastern United States, Ohio to Oklahoma, south to Georgia, in thin woodlands and open prairies.

CULTIVATION: Perennial. Zone: 3. Germination: 10 to 20 days —best if stratified 4 weeks in the refrigerator. Plant shallow; needs sunlight to germinate. Space: 1.5 to 2 feet (45 to 60 cm). Soil Temperature: 70° to 75° F (21° to 24° C). Soil: Well drained, fairly poor, can be fairly dry. pH: 6 to 8. Sun: Full sun, or light shade in very hot climates. Propagation: Plant from seed or divide the crowns on 2-year-or-older plants. It will bloom the first year from seed if started early. Root division is not suggested too often, but young plants can be removed from the main rootstock and replanted. It takes 3 to 4 years to develop roots large enough for a substantial harvest.

GARDEN DESIGN: Echinacea presents a tall and stately presence wherever it is placed. It is often grown as an ornamental in flower gardens. Place it in informal patches or as a tall back border among other tall perennials such as butterfly weed and false indigo. Even a small herb garden can include one or two echinacea plants.

CONSTITUENTS: Essential oil includes humulene, caryophylene, sesquiterpenes, polyacetylenes, isobutylalkamines, glycoside, polysaccharide, betain, inulin.

RELATED SPECIES: *E. angustifolia, E. pallida,* and other species have slightly different chemistry but all were used by Native Americans for similar medicinal purposes. Herbalists carry an ongoing debate over the most effective species. Cultivars popularly sold in nurseries include *E. purpurea* cv. 'Alba' with a greenish center and white petals. In the 1980s, it was discovered that much of the North American commercial echinacea was actually *Parthenium integrifolium,* another tall meadow plant with white flowers. Eventually the herb companies cleaned up their act.

HISTORY: Echinacea is usually referred to by its botanical name, but it is also called Purple or Missouri Coneflower. Botanists name it after the hedgehog *(Echinus)* to describe its prickly, con-elike center. The Plains Indians used various species for treatment of sore throats, toothaches, infections, wounds, snakebites, and skin problems, as well as mumps, measles, smallpox, and cancer. When these illnesses occurred, they would suck on the root. Samples of echinacea were uncovered in campsites from the 1600s, but its use probably goes back much further. In the late 19th century, H. C. F. Meyer began selling "Meyer's Blood Purifier," a patent medicine that contained *E. angustifolia.* In 1887, he enthusiastically offered to prove its abilities to the Eclectic doctors, John King and John Uri Lloyd, by having a rattlesnake bite him. The Eclectics knew about echinacea but at first dismissed Meyer as a quack. Once they did begin experimenting with it, Lloyd predicted, "the probabilities are that in time to come, it will be ardently sought and

© Kathi Keville

Echinacea's name comes from the Latin word for hedgehog; describing the prickly and vibrant center of its flower.

widely used . . ." Echinacea did find its way into the medical journals and the *Materia Medica,* but Lloyd's prediction really came true in the 1980s when echinacea became one of the top-selling herbs in the United States. Since 1930, over 300 scientific articles have been written about it. It has become so popular, many herbalists are concerned that overharvesting may lead to this once-prolific herb becoming endangered, and efforts are made to purchase only cultivated roots.

MEDICINAL: Echinacea root is a popular medicinal herb because it activates the body's immune system, increasing the chances of fighting off almost any disease; it is also very nontoxic. Clinical studies show that extracts improve white blood cell count and create other immune responses. Echinacin, found in echinacea, stops bacteria from forming the hyaluronidase enzyme, which helps makes cells more susceptible to infection.[1] Echinacea is a mild natural antibiotic—6 milligrams (.09 grains) of one glycoside equals 1 unit of penicillin—that is effective against strep and staph infections. A study done with over 200 children found that the group who took echinacea, along with two other herbs, had fewer colds and, when they did get sick, had fewer days of fever.[2] Similar results were observed in studies with upper respiratory tract infections and viral infections. It is obvious to researchers that echinacea contains a number of immune-stimulating constituents, although the mechanism is not fully understood. Some components are better extracted into water, others into alcohol, but personally, I have seen both the tea and extract of echinacea work wonders. Small amounts (a cup of tea, or 30 drops of extract) taken a few times daily work better than larger doses. Echinacea is also more stimulating to immunity when taken in an on-off regime, say 2 weeks on, 1 week off. To learn more, consult the following: *Echinacea, Nature's Immune Enhancer* by Steven Foster (Inner Traditional Press, 1990), which gives an overall treatment, including cultivation; *Echinacea: The Immune Herb!* by Christopher Hobbs (Botanica Press, 1990), for the medical perspective; and *The Echinacea Handbook* by Christopher Hobbs (Eclectic Medical Publications, 1989), which contains a complete scientific review of the literature.

© Kathi Keville

Eucalyptus globulus • Blue Gum Eucalyptus

FAMILY: Myrtaceae.

DESCRIPTION: Tall tree with a bluish, peeling bark. Height: 70 to 90 feet (21 to 27 m) in twenty years, and much larger in the wild. Flowers: Creamy yellow, to 1 1/4 inches (3 cm) across. Leaves: Leathery, slightly curving, elongated blue-green ovals that come to a point. Juvenile leaves are blue-gray. Strongly scented in caps. Fruit: Warty, ridged caps. Blooms: June to November.

HABITAT: Australia. Naturalized and cultivated in California. It has also been established in India, South America, Africa, and southern Europe and is grown commercially in Spain, Portugal, and India.

CULTIVATION: Zone: 9. Soil: Adapts to a variety of soil conditions, but prefers well drained and rich loam. Sun: Full sun. Propagation: By grafts or seed. Prefers temperatures over 60° F (15° C) and will freeze at temperatures below 27° F (–3° C). The tree exudes a substance that repels other plants (as well as insects).

GARDEN DESIGN: Eucalpytus may not be your average garden herb, but it can be grown in pots, which will restrict the growth so the trees don't become full-sized. In warm climates, eucalyptus trees can be grown directly in the garden and serve as an impressive backdrop. Otherwise, bring the potted plants into a greenhouse for the winter.

RELATED SPECIES: Eucalyptus represents over 600 species and varieties. A few hybrids have also been developed. One of my favorites is the lemon-scented gum *(E. citriodora)*. One of the tallest known broad leaf trees is *E. regnans,* an example of which stands at 327 feet (98 m) in the Tasmanian forest. The cultivar 'Compacta' originated in California, and has a dense, compact style.

MAJOR CONSTITUENTS: Essential oil (cineol, pinene) cuminaldehyde, aromadendrene, tannins. The 'gum' or material that oozes from knots in eucalyptus trees is called kino and contains tannins.

HISTORY: Eucalyptus is the most important genus of many Australian forests, composing 75 percent of all the trees. The blue gum is the most widely cultivated of all the species in the world. In the 1850s, botanist Baron Ferdinand von Muller, director of the botanical gardens in Melbourne, Australia, suggested that the leaves were antiseptic because their aroma closely resembled that of cajeput trees. The French government planted eucalpytus in Algeria in 1857 as a possible remedy for tropical diseases. In five years, the trees turned the marshy lands where they were planted dry, eliminating the mosquito's habitat and giving eucalpytus the name "fever tree." The trees were then planted in other areas infested with malaria, such as Italy, Corsica, and Spain. They did save the Ethiopian capital of Addis Ababa—although not from malaria. The region's timber had all been cut, creating a serious fuel shortage. The supply was reestablished in a few years, however, by these fast-growing trees. Eucalpytus arrived in California in the 1880s, along with the hope that they would absorb the "noxious gasses" then thought to be the source of malaria. The trees made themselves more than at home, invading farm and pasture land with their rapid growth and shallow root system.

MEDICINAL: Eucalpytus has long been used by the Australian aborigines to treat fevers and as an antiseptic dressing on wounds and burns. Kino from several eucalyptus species was used to treat dysentery in Australian convicts. The leaves cool the body and reduce fever. A tea with 1 to 2 teaspoons (5 to 10 ml) of dried leaves helps ease bronchitis. Inhaling the vapor, by placing a couple of drops of the essential oil in a pan of simmering water or in a vaporizer, will help clear sinus and bronchial congestion. Small amounts are found in many commercial cough syrups and especially in cough drops. Eucalyptol, derived from eucalpytus oil, is one of the main ingredients in Vicks Vapor Rub, which is used as a chest rub during a cold. The essential oil found in eucalpytus is strongly antibiotic, destroying not only a wide range of bacteria, but also viruses and fungi. It is a specific treatment for candida infections and for viral skin eruptions like herpes. Eucalpytus oil is also used as a counter-irritant in liniments that are rubbed on sore muscles or used to heat rheumatism. Kino drinks were once used as a tonic and a mouthwash for toothache. The manna from some eucalypts was used as a laxative.

AROMATHERAPY: The stimulating scent of eucalpytus is used to keep awake and alert. It is found in some aftershaves and in inexpensive colognes. Industrial preparations use it for a clean fragrance. The oil has a drying effect on the skin and is used in cosmetic preparations to treat oily skin and acne.

CONSIDERATIONS: Large dosages can lead to dizziness, stupor, vomiting, convulsions, and delirium, and eventually death. Some people are sensitive to the scent (essential oil).

OTHER: Eucalyptus supplies some of the world's best hardwood, used for building and furniture-making. The wood is used for making tool handles and other farm implements, in ship building, and for wood pulp. The leaves and seed caps are added to potpourris. The oil is a potent flea repellant and is found in natural flea collars and liquid flea repellents. I've also seen the seed caps strung on a string to make dog and cat flea collars. Veterinarians use the essential oil to treat flu in horses, distemper in dogs, and parasitic skin problems such as lice in many animals. The leaves preserved with glycerine are used in dried floral arrangements and wreaths. The blue gum is Tasmania's floral emblem.

Eupatorium purpureum • Joe-Pye Weed

FAMILY: Compositae.

DESCRIPTION: Tall, branched herb with hollow stems, stem nodes tinged with purple. Height: To 10 feet (3 m). Width: 3 to 4 feet (90 to 120 cm). Flowers: Pale, pink-purple, occasionally white, in clusters of 5 to 7. Leaves: In whorls of leaves, each to 1 foot (.9 m) long around the stem. Foliage releases a vanilla scent when bruised. Rhizome: To 1½ inches (3.7 cm) in diameter, very hard, with thin, gray-brown bark. Tastes bitter and astringent. Blooms: July to September.

HABITAT: Eastern North American woodlands, from southern New Hampshire to Georgia and Oklahoma.

CULTIVATION: Perennial. Zone: 3 to 4. Germination: 2 to 3 weeks, better if stratified. Plant fresh or refrigerate. Space: 2 to 3 feet (60 to 90 cm). Soil Temperature: 65° to 75° F (18° to 24° C). Soil: Well drained. Sun: Partial Shade. Propagation: By root division in the autumn. The crowns can be divided and set out. They will produce substantial roots in 2 to 3 years.

GARDEN DESIGN: Use joe-pye weed in the background of your garden, highlighting other herbs in front. However, the leaves are also sparse enough so that you'll be able to see beyond it, with its outline emphasized, if placed in the middle of a bed.

CONSTITUENTS: Essential oil (.07%) includes flavonoid (euparin), oleoresin (eupurpurin), produced by pouring tincture into cold water.

RELATED SPECIES: When boneset *(E. perfoliatum),* also called thoroughwort, was given to 53 flu patients, its effect on symptoms was equal to the aspirin compound, acetylsalicylic acid.[1] Smokeweed *(E. maculatum)* is also sometimes called joe-pye weed.

HISTORY: The name *Eupatorium* refers to Mithridates Eupator, King of Pontus, Greece, who is said to have used one of his local species of this genus in a 1st-century medicine. Native Americans taught the white settlers about the uses of both joe-pye weed and boneset to reduce the symptoms of flus and fevers (including the "break-bone" fever responsible for boneset's name). They also carried a piece for luck in gambling. Rafinesque commented in his 1828 *Medical Flora* that "Joepye, gravel root has the same properties as boneset and has been used in fevers and gravel." Boneset he describes as "one of the most powerful remedies of the native tribes for fevers." He also says that Joe-Pye was an Indian who was famous for curing typhoid, but the most accepted story says the herb was named after the 19th century white promoter of a boneset remedy for typhoid and other fevers. Another claim is that one Indian tribe called typhoid fever *jopi* and the herb *jopi weed.* The herb's impressive height and attractiveness gave it the more becoming name "queen of the meadow."

MEDICINAL: The leaves of joe-pye weed stimulate circulation and sweating and reduce inflammation. It has been used to tone the entire reproductive tract, helping with pelvic inflammatory disease, menstrual cramps, and also prostate and urinary infections. Herbalists also treat gout and rheumatism with it. One of its common names, gravel root, describes its use in treating kidney and urinary stones, especially those caused by excess uric acid. Nineteenth-century Eclectic doctors sold a concentrated root extract called "eupuruin." They felt joe-pye weed would not eliminate, but rather relieve, the painful irritation of urinary tract stones and infection, as well as prostate inflammation. Modern research indicates that the lactones and flavones in both joe-pye weed and

Eupatorium purpureum
JOE-PYE WEED

boneset may have anticancer effects.[2] At least in boneset, immune-stimulating polysaccharides encourage white blood cells to consume foreign agents in the blood. German researchers think this contributes to its effectiveness against infectious diseases.[3]

CONSIDERATIONS: It can cause vomiting if taken in very large doses.

OTHER: The fruit produces a pink or red dye.

Euphorbia lathyris • Gopher Purge
(Previously *Galarhoeus lathyris* and *Tithymalus lathyris*)

FAMILY: Euphorbiaceae.

DESCRIPTION: Upright, stiff plant that resembles green antennas! Contains a milky sap that exudes when broken, characteristic of *Euphorbia* genus plants. Height: To 3 feet (90 cm). Width: 6 to 8 inches (15 to 20 cm). Flowers: Yellow-green, on stems jutting from top of plant; to ³/₄ inch (2 cm) wide. Leaves: Narrow, pointed, blue-green, succulent, sticking straight out from the main stems in whorls, 2 to 6 inches (5 to 15 cm) long. Blooms: June to July.

HABITAT: Native to Europe, naturalized in the United States.

CULTIVATION: Annual, sometimes biennial. Germination: 1 to 2 weeks. Space: 1 foot (30 cm). Soil Temperature: 65° to 75° F (18° to 24° C). Soil: Average, but will grow in poor. pH: 7 to 8. Sun: Full sun or partial shade. Propagation: Grows easily from seed and readily self-seeds.

GARDEN DESIGN: Gopher plants have a habit of choosing their own garden locations and begin popping up everywhere, much like the animals for which they are named. Their linear angles contrast well with softer herb forms. They are suited for hot spots or sunny rock gardens where the warmth might wilt other herbs. Or plant them near ginseng beds and by vegetables to protect them from gophers. Don't plant gophers on the edge of fish ponds or streams since their roots exude a substance that is poisonous to fish.

CONSTITUENTS: Seed: protein (15%); fat (40% to 17.5%); sterols, 7-hentriacontane, daphnetin, glyceride.

HISTORY: The genus name comes from Euphorbos, physician to the king of Mauretania, who used spurges—the common name of many plants in this genus—in his healing concoctions. Other common names include caper and myrtle spurge. This is the most popular garden plant of the many species in this family believed to repel moles, gophers, and other underground pests. Opinions vary to its effectiveness. Kent Taylor of Taylor's Herb Gardens in Vista, California, tells an amusing story of seeing its narcotic effect produce a drunken stupor in gophers! Quite a few plants seem to be required in an average-size garden. The leaves can cause skin reactions and historically were used by beggars to produce lesions in order to create more sympathy.

MEDICINAL: Gopher purge has been applied externally in folk remedies to remove skin cancers and warts. The French have also used it as a purgative, but its action is too harsh for common use. The seed oil is used on burns. Herbal researcher Dr. James Duke states in the *Handbook of Medicinal Herbs,* "I believe that if all plants are studied in detail, they will be found to contain both carcinogens and antitumor or cytotoxic compounds. This one contains the antitumor compound beta-sitosterol and the cocarcinogen lingenol-3-hexadencanic acid ester . . . ." Duke also mentions that it is said to contain some L-Dopa, which is used to relieve symptoms of Parkinson's disease.

CONSIDERATIONS: The seeds used to be a coffee substitute, but are poisonous, and the plant should not be taken internally. Dermatitis is often caused by contact with the sap.

OTHER: Nobel laureate Melvin Calvin has suggested that gopher purge could be a profitable petroleum plant, since it produces a hydrocarbon much like gasoline. He feels it could possibly be used directly by a refinery, once separated from the water content, and estimates that ten to fifty barrels of oil could be produced per acre (.405 hectare) per year, which is 10 times the production of guayule, another plant that provides a fuel source.[1]

Euphorbia lathyris
GOPHER PURGE

Filipendula ulmaria • **Meadowsweet**
(Previously *Spiraea ulmaria*)

FAMILY: Rosaceae.

DESCRIPTION: Stout, upright herb. Height: To 6 feet (1.8 m). Width: To 2¹/₂ feet (75 cm). Flowers: Creamy-white, ¹/₈-inch- (3-mm-) long petals, in tight clusters. Leaves: 1 to 8 feet (30 cm to 2.4 m) long composed of 2 to 5 pairs of main leaflets, each 1 to 3 inches (2.5 to 7.5 cm) long, with dark green tops and whitish, downy undersides. Fragrant, almondlike scent. Blooms: June to September.

HABITAT: Europe, Asia, naturalized in eastern North America.

CULTIVATION: Perennial. Zone: 2 to 3. Germination: 1 month. Space: 2¹/₂ feet (75 cm). Soil Temperature: 65° to 75° F (18° to 24° C). Soil: Moist. Sun: Sun; partial shade in hot areas. Propagation: By seed, or divide older plants. More popular in Europe, the plants can be difficult to find in North America. Needs sufficient water to bloom.

GARDEN DESIGN: Grown as a border plant in flower gardens.

CONSTITUENTS: Salicylates (spiraein, salicin, gaultherine), tannin (to 10%), flavonoids, essential oils, vitamin C.

RELATED SPECIES: *F. ulmaria* 'Aureo-variegata,' has yellow variegated leaves, and 'Plena' is double-petaled.

HISTORY: Meadowsweet was one of the Druids' sacred herbs and one of the 50 herbs in a drink known as "save," which Geoffrey Chaucer (1342–1400) mentioned in his 14th-century "Knight's Tale" in *The Canterbury Tales*. At that time it was called "medwort" or "meadwort," being a principal ingredient in the honey-wine drink known as mead. It also came to be known as "queen of the meadow" in several European languages, a title it well deserves, considering the way it reigns over a damp meadow. The fragrant flowers were strewn on floors and, according to Gerard, made 16th-century "hearts merrie and joyful" while it "delighteth the senses" in the process. In 1838, an Italian professor isolated the first salicylic acid from meadowsweet flowers and from willow bark *(Salix alba)*. Fifty years later, the Bayer Drug Company synthesized a new drug (acetylsalicylic acid) based on the structure of salicylic acid and named it aspirin, a combination of acetyl and meadowsweet's old botanical name, *Spirea*.

CULINARY: The flowers were once added to herb beers and wines, and the leaves were placed into claret cups.

MEDICINAL: Meadowsweet is used to treat rheumatism, fevers, and pain in much the same way as aspirin is used, but it contains buffering agents that counter the drug's side effects, such as gastric bleeding. In fact, it prevents overacidity in the stomach and is considered one of the best herbal treatments for heartburn. It also improves digestion and helps to heal ulcers. An antiseptic diuretic that promotes uric acid excretion, it is used for urinary tract problems.[1] It was once the treatment of choice for children's diarrhea.

OTHER: A black dye is produced with a copper mordant.

Filipendula ulmaria. **Meadowsweet only recently began appearing in North American herb gardens and on herb shelves, but it has long been a popular herbal pain remedy in Europe.**

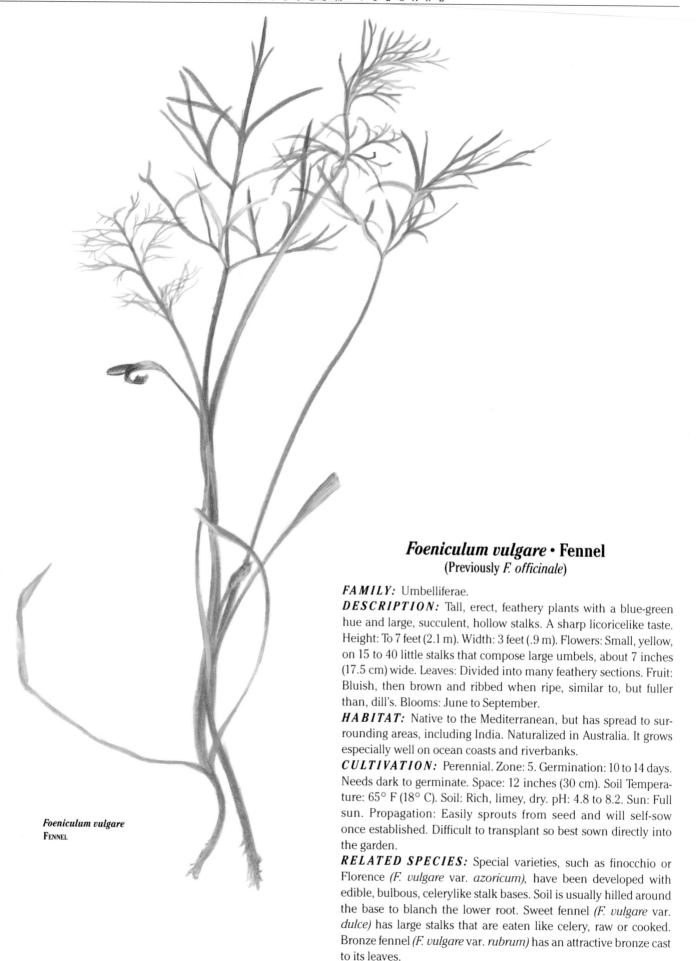

Foeniculum vulgare
FENNEL

Foeniculum vulgare • Fennel
(Previously *F. officinale*)

FAMILY: Umbelliferae.

DESCRIPTION: Tall, erect, feathery plants with a blue-green hue and large, succulent, hollow stalks. A sharp licoricelike taste. Height: To 7 feet (2.1 m). Width: 3 feet (.9 m). Flowers: Small, yellow, on 15 to 40 little stalks that compose large umbels, about 7 inches (17.5 cm) wide. Leaves: Divided into many feathery sections. Fruit: Bluish, then brown and ribbed when ripe, similar to, but fuller than, dill's. Blooms: June to September.

HABITAT: Native to the Mediterranean, but has spread to surrounding areas, including India. Naturalized in Australia. It grows especially well on ocean coasts and riverbanks.

CULTIVATION: Perennial. Zone: 5. Germination: 10 to 14 days. Needs dark to germinate. Space: 12 inches (30 cm). Soil Temperature: 65° F (18° C). Soil: Rich, limey, dry. pH: 4.8 to 8.2. Sun: Full sun. Propagation: Easily sprouts from seed and will self-sow once established. Difficult to transplant so best sown directly into the garden.

RELATED SPECIES: Special varieties, such as finocchio or Florence *(F. vulgare* var. *azoricum),* have been developed with edible, bulbous, celerylike stalk bases. Soil is usually hilled around the base to blanch the lower root. Sweet fennel *(F. vulgare* var. *dulce)* has large stalks that are eaten like celery, raw or cooked. Bronze fennel *(F. vulgare* var. *rubrum)* has an attractive bronze cast to its leaves.

GARDEN DESIGN: Fennel is suitable in the back of beds, where it provides interesting contrasts in color and texture to set off the other herbs. It is ideal for providing a screen to conceal a fence or road or to divide a large garden into sections.

CONSTITUENTS: Essential oil includes anethole; flavonoids (rutin), vitamins (A, C), minerals (calcium, phosphorus, and potassium).

HISTORY: The Latin word *foeniculum,* or "little hay," is said to describe fennel's feathery leaves, but I suspect it may refer to its use as animal fodder, since it was fed to goats to increase the quality and fat content of their milk. The Greek battle of Marathon in 490 B.C. was fought in a field of *marthron,* or fennel. (The "r" was misplaced somewhere along the centuries.) The runner Pheidippides, who ran to Sparta to warn of the Persian invasion, was presented with a fennel sprig upon his return, with which he is shown in all his statues.

> *Let this, foreshadowing the place, be the pledge!*
> *Gay, the liberal hand held out this herbage I bear*
> *I grasped it a-tremble with dew—whatever it bode.*
> — *"PHEIDIPPIDES,"* ROBERT BROWNING (1812–1889), ENGLISH

There are reports of fennel being eaten by people at least 2,000 years ago, athough the stem was then more popular than the seeds. Roman bakers placed the leaves under bread as it baked to provide flavor. The 1st-century Roman gourmet Apicius thought the seeds should be in every kitchen, and he used them in his famous sauces. Roman warriors dined on fennel for courage, and symbolically wore wreaths of the leaves, as Longfellow portrayed in the following poem:

> *Above the lowly plants it towers*
> *The fennel, with its yellow flowers,*
> *And in an earlier age than ours,*
> *Was gifted with the wondrous powers,*
> * Lost vision to restore.*
> *It gave new strength, and fearless mood;*
> *And gladiators, fierce and rude,*
> *Mingled it in their daily food;*
> *And he who battled and subdued,*
> * A wreath of fennel wore.*
> — *"THE GOBLET OF LIFE,"*
> HENRY WADSWORTH LONGFELLOW (1807–1842), AMERICAN

In the 2nd century, Galen (the famous Greek physician) declared fennel one of the 4 warming seeds (with celery, parsley, and asparagus). In the 8th century, fennel's popularity traveled north, and Charlemagne had it planted on his imperial farms in Germany. It was included in the medieval 4 "warming seeds" (with anise, caraway, and coriander) and was one of the 9 holy herbs the Anglo-Saxons used to combat the 9 causes of disease. A poultice of powdered fennel seeds was used on snakebites—a remedy still used by the Chinese today. The wealthy and poor alike ate fennel, not only for strength, but to appease their appetite on religious fast days. Sixteenth-century Italians complemented each other with *dare finocchio,* which means "to give fennel," or "to flatter."

CULINARY: Mediterranean seaside restaurants wrap fish in dried fennel leaves before grilling and place fennel twigs in the fire. The leaves are added to salads, sauces, and soups and, in Italy and France, finely chopped to garnish sauces and puddings. Fennel is also fed to rabbits to flavor their meat. Italians peel the stalks to make *cartucci,* a salad served with a vinegar-and-pepper dressing. In Provence, the flower buds are added to pickled olives, cucumbers, and capers or to season boiled chestnuts, and the stems are preserved in brine. It is found in Ethiopia's fiery berberé sauce, its universal seasoning, and in Oriental curry. It is also an ingredient in Chinese 5-spice (with anise seed, Szechwan pepper, cloves, and cinnamon).

MEDICINAL: Fennel seeds relax the smooth muscles, aid digestion and are said to be particularly helpful in digesting fat. In 1578, Li Shen-Chen, in the *Pen T'sao,* described them as good for children's indigestion, as well as backache and toothache. A popular European carminative water is still made from fennel, chamomile, caraway, coriander, and bitter orange peel. Dioscorides correctly noted fennel's diuretic effects and recommended it for urinary tract inflammation and restriction to help eliminate urinary stones. Fennel has even been used as a popular weight-loss herb as far back as ancient Greece. This use may tie in with its ability to increase milk production in nursing women and its hormonal substances, which have shown estrogen-like actions.[1]

Fennel is reported to be a mild stimulant, and John Evelyn in his *Acetaria* (1680) said that the peeled stalks produced a pleasant effect and make one sleepy. I did know one elderly woman who loved to eat the inside of the stalk, claiming it created a restful state. As the main ingredient in an excellent eyewash, fennel seed is said to improve eyesight. 17th-century herbalist Culpeper used the seeds to help the liver neutralize poisons. It is also reputed to reduce the effects of alcohol on the body.

CONSIDERATIONS: Extremely high dosages can overexcite the nervous system. The essential oil must be used very carefully since it is easy to overdose on this concentrated oil, which can cause convulsions.

COSMETIC: Fennel is used in facial steams to cleanse pores and has found its way for centuries into antiwrinkle cream, perhaps due to its hormonal actions. It also scents perfume and soap.

OTHER: The powdered herb is said to deter fleas, but you may not want to try this on your watchdog—fennel has a long-standing reputation for making animals timid! The swallowtail butterfly caterpillar likes to feed on the leaves.

FENNEL SAUCE

This recipe comes from Apicius and was created in the first century A.D.

- *¹/₈ teaspoon (.6 ml) fennel seeds*
- *¹/₄ teaspoon (1.25 ml) pepper, ground*
- *2 teaspoons (10 ml) parsley*
- *¹/₂ teaspoon (2.5 ml) mint*
- *1 teaspoon (5 ml) honey*
- *1 teaspoon (5 ml) vinegar*
- *1 cup (240 ml) water or soup stock*

Combine ingredients and bring to boil. Gently simmer 20 minutes. Serve warm or cold.

> *Downe by a litel path*
> *I fond of mintes and fennell greene.*
> —DE LORRIS (1237), FRENCH, TRANS. BY GEOFFREY CHAUCER

Galium odoratum • Woodruff
(Previously *Asperula odoratum*)

FAMILY: Rubiaceae.

DESCRIPTION: Ground cover on a creeping rhizome. Height: 6 inches (15 cm). Width: 6 inches (15 cm). Flowers: White, funnel-shaped, small, to 1/4 inch (6 mm) wide, in loose bunches. Leaves: elongated, 1 1/2 inches (3.7 cm) long, with bristle tips, in whorls of 6 to 8 around the stem. Not fragrant until dried or starts to die back. Blooms: May to June.

HABITAT: Europe, North Africa, Asia, in mixed woodlands. Introduced elsewhere.

CULTIVATION: Perennial. Zone: 3. Germination: Slow, can take 6 months. Stratify first. Seeds must be fresh. Space: 6 to 8 inches (15 to 20 cm). Soil Temperature: 55° F (12° C). Soil: Fairly rich humus, well-drained. Prefers some moisture, especially in hot climates. pH: 6 to 8.3. Sun: Partial shade. Full sun yellows leaves and decreases flowering. Propagation: By seed or root division. Most growth of the shallow root system occurs in the autumn, so only divide roots when there are several months before a frost to re-establish itself. It can be grown indoors. Dry the leaves carefully to maintain the best scent and color.

GARDEN DESIGN: Woodruff is a great ground cover for shady areas or for underplanting with tall perennial hedges. Show it off by planting it around and under a bench, birdbath, or statuary, or in a planter. Woodruff is easily grown in a pot.

CONSTITUENTS: Coumarin, which is developed upon drying; iroids (asperuloside, about .05%, monotropein); flavonoids; anthroquinones; organic acids (citric, rubichloric).

RELATED SPECIES: Relatives include yellow bedstraw (*G. verum*).

HISTORY: The Anglo-Saxons named it *wudurofe*, from *wudu*, or "woods." *Rove* is probably associated with the French *rovelle*, a "wheel," describing the leaves' spokelike formation, although in Old French, it was known as *muge-de-boys*, or "musk of the woods." *Asperula* is the Latin word for "rough," which also describes the texture of the leaves. Woodruff was strewn on the floors of medieval churches. Garlands of the leaves decorated statues, especially those of the Blessed Virgin, on St. Barnabas's Day (June 11) and St. Peter's Day (June 20), as well as sweethearts during spring and summer festivals. In Germany, where it grows wild in the Black Forest, it is called *waldmeister*, or "master of the woods."

CULINARY: Woodruff's main culinary role has been to flavor wines and liquors. The traditional German May wine, or *mai-trank*, always enjoyed at May Day (May 1) celebrations, is made from it. A favorite fruit bowl called *mai-bowle*, or "may bow," used the wine as a base. Woodruff cakes, soups, salads, and sauces have also been made.

MEDICINAL: One reason that woodruff leaves were added to wines was because they aid the digestion and are helpful in treating liver obstructions and hepatitis. At one time, woodruff leaves made a popular diuretic and remedy to reduce bladder stones. Woodruff reduces inflammation and the asperuloside it contains has been suggested as a starting point for manufacturing prostaglandin drugs. The herb also provides coumarin, used to produce anticoagulant drugs. Considered a light sedative, it comes in handy for treating nervous tension, especially in the elderly and children.

AROMATHERAPY: Woodruff's scent, described as a new-mown-hay fragrance, is produced by coumarin, and makes it useful in potpourris and perfume. It was once laid among linens and placed in bed pillows to scent them, and was added to snuffs. The back of many 18th-century pocketwatches held a whorl of woodruff leaves that would scent the air when the back door was opened.

CONSIDERATIONS: Very large amounts can cause dizziness and nausea. Studies with test animals show large amounts of coumarin stunt their growth and cause liver damage, although this is no cause for alarm since such dosages would never occur in normal use of the herb. The FDA has approved its use in alcoholic beverages.

MAI-TRANK (TANKARD)

1	*quart (1 l) white wine (or cider)*
1	*cup (240 ml) woodruff*
2	*ounces (56 g) sugar*
1/4	*pint (140 ml) water*
1	*orange, peeled and sliced*

Pour wine over woodruff and let sit at least 7 days. Strain, add other ingredients, and serve cold.

MAI-BOWLE (FRUIT BOWL)

This recipe is a variation of the previous and used any type of fresh fruits, although strawberries are the traditional choice. Instead of seltzer, you might use champagne, Benedictine, or cognac.

1	*quart (1 l) Mai-Trank*
4	*ounces (112 g) of mixed fresh fruit, chopped*
2	*cups (480 ml) seltzer (carbonated) water*

Add fruit to the Mai-Trank and let steep. Add seltzer just before serving.

WOODRUFF SAUCE

Incorporating the Mai-Bowle recipe, this sauce is a lovely accompaniment for pudding or cake and can also be served as a custard.

5	*egg yolks*
1/2	*cup (120 ml) sugar*
2	*cups (480 ml) Mai-Bowle*

Blend ingredients in double boiler, stirring constantly until it coats the spoon.

MAY WINE

1	*quart (1 l) woodruff blossoms and leaves*
2	*lemons, sliced*
2	*gallons (9 l) water*
6	*pounds (2.7 kg) sugar*
1/2	*ounce (14 g) yeast*

Add half the woodruff and lemons to water and boil 20 minutes. Strain into a jar or barrel and dissolve sugar in it. Add remainder of woodruff. Dissolve yeast in small amount of water and add. Cover and let sit 2 weeks, then strain into bottles. Let stand 1 year before drinking.

Galium odoratum
WOODRUFF

Lenten is come with love to toune
With all blosmen and with briddes roune,
     That all this blisse bryngeth.
Dayes-eyes in this dales,
Notes suete of nythegales;
     Uch fowl song singeth.
The threstelcoc him threteth oo;
Away is here wynter woo
     when woderove springeth.
—LATE 13TH CENTURY SONG, BRITISH

Gaultheria procumbens • Wintergreen
(Previously *G. repens*)

FAMILY: Ericaceae.

DESCRIPTION: Small, stiff, creeping herb. Height: 6 inches (15 cm). Width: 6 inches (15 cm). Flowers: Small, solitary, nodding, white, 1/4 inch (6 mm) long. Leaves: Elongated ovals, to 2 inches (5 cm) long, with dark green, shiny tops. Fruit: Scarlet, round berries, about 1/3 inch (8 mm) in diameter. Blooms: June to August.

HABITAT: Canada, through the Midwest, to Georgia.

CULTIVATION: Perennial. Zone: 3 to 4. Germination: 3 to 4 weeks, but can last up to a year (protect from seed-eating rodents). Stratify at 40° F (4° C) for 1 to 2 months. Space: 6 to 8 inches (15 to 20 cm). Soil: Sandy and moist, but will tolerate dry. Sun: Partial or full shade. Propagation: By seed, cuttings, root division, or layering stolons, which grow just below surface.

GARDEN DESIGN: An attractive groundcover for partially shady places where the passing light on the shiny leaves will catch the sun. The "winter" green leaves and berries provide garden interest in the fall when other herbs are dying back.

CONSTITUENTS: Essential oil (0.5% to 1%) methyl salicylate (98%) is produced through the action of enzymes of the glycoside gaultherin when the leaf is broken or fermented, then distilled.

RELATED SPECIES: North American and Asian *Pyrola* species are often called wintergreen but aren't in the same family.

HISTORY: When Quebec physician Dr. Gaultier (circa 1750) named *Gaultheria* after himself, thinking he was introducing it to the medical community, he probably wasn't aware that Mother Marie de L'Incarnation had already described this "miracle herb" shown her by the Native Americans in the 16th century. Rafinesque, in his 1828 *Flora,* lists wintergreen as "a popular remedy in many parts of the country. . . . The tea is used as a palliative in asthma, to restore strength, promote menstruation, also in cases of debility. . . . It is a very agreeable and refreshing beverage, much preferable to imported China Teas. The Indians make great use of this plant as a stimulant, cordial. . . ." They also smoked the leaves with their tobacco. It was used so much in liniments and to disguise strong flavors of patent remedies around the turn of the 20th century, that even today, most people regard its scent as "medicinal."

CULINARY: Wintergreen was such a popular tea herb, it was called tea berry and mountain tea. The berries are eaten raw and also made into pies, certainly by patient cooks with lots of time to pick the small berries. The leaves are an important flavoring in root beer, traditionally made in the spring or fall from freshly harvested roots.

MEDICINAL: The methyl salicylate found in wintergreen leaves is closely related to salicylic acid. Accordingly, the leaf tea is given for the same conditions treated by aspirin, such as colds, flu, fever, muscle pain, arthritis, and rheumatism. It has also been used to treat asthma and skin problems. In contrast to aspirin, small amounts relieve stomach indigestion instead of causing it. Wintergreen made a short appearance in the *U.S. Pharmacopoeia,* but it has mostly been used to disguise strong-tasting herbs. Native Americans chewed wintergreen leaves to improve their breathing while carrying loads or running and on long treks. In some regions, Early American settlers had their children chew the roots for 6 weeks every spring to reduce tooth decay. They also steeped the berries in brandy for a winter tonic. It is a skin softener that will smooth rough, callused skin. In liniments, it eases muscular, arthritic, and rheumatic pains and is readily absorbed into skin.

AROMATHERAPY: Wintergreen oil was once true wintergreen, but it is difficult to produce and now comes from birch bark *(Betula lenta)* or synthetic methyl salicylate. "Iceland Wintergreen" was well loved by 19th-century women as a handkerchief perfume. The wintergreen-based "Russian Leather" fragrance (actually derived from birch) became so popular that, for many years, the Russian government closely guarded the secret recipe. Wintergreen oil was originally used by bookbinders to keep leather soft.

CONSIDERATIONS: The straight essential oil can irritate the skin. Overdoses taken internally can cause stomach inflammation and have resulted in death. Excessive doses of salicylates can cause ringing in the ears and nausea.

OTHER: Wintergreen is a popular flavoring for toothpaste and other dental preparations. Herbal trivia: Wintergreen absorbs ultraviolet waves, especially in the presence of sugar. Chew a wintergreen candy in the dark and it will release a bright blue-green light.

ROOT BEER

1 1/2	gallons (7 l) molasses
5	gallons (23 l) water
4	ounces (112 g) wintergreen leaf
8	ounces (240 ml) sassafras root bark
1/2	cup (112 g) dry yeast

Heat molasses and water to 160° F (71° C) and let stand 2 hours. Add herbs and yeast and let ferment 12 hours at room temperature, and bottle (or refrigerate).

ICELAND WINTERGREEN

1/2	teaspoon (3 ml) each of essential oil of:
	rose
	lavender
	neroli (or petitgrain)
	vanilla
	cassia (related to cinnamon)
1	minum (drop) wintergreen oil

Blend ingredients.

Gaultheria procumbens
WINTERGREEN

Gentiana lutea • Gentian

FAMILY: Gentianaceae.

DESCRIPTION: Height: 3 feet (90 cm), sometimes taller. Width: 1 foot (30 cm). Flowers: 1-inch (2.5-cm) pale yellow blooms in clusters of 3 to 10. It takes about 3 years to flower. Leaves: Shiny, to 10 inches (25 cm) long, tightly clasped on upright stems. Root: Thick taproot. Blooms: May to June.

HABITAT: Europe and Asia Minor, in cool, moist, shaded locations, such as alpine mountain forests. Commercially cultivated in eastern Europe and North America.

CULTIVATION: Perennial. Zone: 3. Germination: 14 to 28 days. Stratify for 3 weeks. Space: 10 to 14 inches (25 to 35 cm). Soil Temperature: 70° to 75° F (21° to 24° C). Soil: Rich humus, moist, with good drainage and heavy watering. pH: 5.5 to 6.5. Sun: Light shade. Prefers cool climate. May be difficult to establish, but plants can live over 50 years. Propagation: For best results, sow fresh seeds in the autumn to naturally stratify. Established plants can be divided.

GARDEN DESIGN: Gentian is perfect for the shade garden, or plant it by a tree or large bush. It is usually placed toward the back of a bed due to its height, but in a position where its long blooming season can be enjoyed.

CONSTITUENTS: Gentiopicrine, one of the most bitter substances known, converts when the herb is dried to glycosides such as gentiin, alkaloids, essential oil.

RELATED SPECIES: The Chinese use a number of other species with similar constituents, all called *longdan,* for treating urinary and skin problems. Other Western species are similarly employed.

HISTORY: King Gentius of Illyria (180 to 67 B.C.) is said to have introduced gentian to medicine and given the herb his name after it cured his army of a mysterious fever. It is a bitter flavoring used for alcoholic drinks, especially in Germany and Switzerland, where gentian flavored beer before the introduction of hops. Gentian wine was served as an aperitif at 18th-century dinner parties to encourage the guests' digestion.

CULINARY: Gentian is found in any liquor store as the chief flavor in vermouth, and in Stockton bitters and Angostura bitters, both originally hailed as digestive tonics. Angostura bitters does not contain the bark of that name, but was produced in Angostura, Argentina (now Ciudad Bolivar), by Dr. J. G. B. Siegert, Chief Surgeon at the U.S. Military Hospital, in 1824. The label describes it as a "pleasant and dependable stomachic" and suggests adding it to soups, stews, vegetables, ice cream, and about every other imaginable food!

MEDICINAL: One of the most bitter of the bitter digestive tonics, gentian is appropriately called "bitter root." It remains bitter even at a 1 part per 20,000 dilution! Taken 30 minutes before eating, it increases the appetite, stimulating digestive juices, pancreas activity, the blood supply to the digestive tract, and intestinal peristalsis. It also decreases intestinal inflammation and kills worms. Digestive juices begin flowing about 5 minutes after the herb reaches the stomach, and the level achieved in 30 minutes is maintained for 2 to 3 hours. It is especially helpful in fat and protein digestion and slightly raises stomach acidity. A German study found it extremely effective in curing indigestion and heartburn when volunteers were given gentian with small amounts of cayenne, ginger, and wormwood.[1] Gentian is also used to treat liver and spleen problems, and to promote menstruation. At times, its

Gentiana lutea
GENTIAN

fever-lowering action has been considered superior to Peruvian bark. There is some evidence that it makes the body more sensitive to adrenalin and may indirectly stimulate more than appetite. It was once used externally to clean wounds.

CONSIDERATIONS: Large doses can produce nausea and even vomiting. Note that the skin infection treatment *gentian violet* is not prepared from gentian, as many people believe, but from a chemical called hexamethylparaosaniline, derived from coal tar.

OTHER: Veterinarians use gentian to improve animals' appetites.

With uses too many to mention,
Malaria's one target of gentian.
Connoisseurs are surer
To sip Angostura,
Which helps many things more than tension!
—"GENTIAN," JAMES A. DUKE (b. 1929), AMERICAN

Ginkgo biloba • Ginkgo
(Previously *Salisburia adiantifolia*)

FAMILY: Ginkoaceae.

DESCRIPTION: Large tree. Height: To 120 feet (36 m). Flowers: Small. Leaves: Fan-shaped with lobes, up to 2 to 3 inches (5 to 7.5 cm) long, with radiating veins. Fruit: Small, round, yellow with a strong smell of rancid butter. Blooms: Summer.

HABITAT: Native probably to China, possibly to Japan, but there are no wild trees living.

CULTIVATION: Perennial. Zone: 5. Space: 20 feet (6 m) from other trees, or grow herbs underneath. Germination: 3 weeks or longer. Stratify 1 month first. Soil Temperature: 65° to 75° F (18° to 23° C). Soil: Average, fairly well drained. Sun: Full sun. Propagation: Plant seedlings. Very resistant to infection and pollution, gingko trees have been known to be over 1,000 years of age. The medicinal flavonoid content is strongest in the autumn, when the leaves begin to turn color.

GARDEN DESIGN: If you have the room, ginkgo is one of the most ornamental trees for the herb garden, as well as a useful shade specimen. Some gardeners keep ginkgo small by growing it in a small pot or purchasing a bonsai tree. Often the male tree is planted to avoid the smelly fruits produced by mature female trees.

CONSTITUENTS: Lignans (ginkolides, bilobalide), flavonoids, essential oil, uroshiols.

HISTORY: The ginkgo is the world's oldest living tree species, dating to the Permian period, 200 million years ago. No one knows when ginkgos last grew wild, but for centuries, Chinese monks have grown ginkgo as a sacred tree and are credited with keeping the tree in existence. It was first brought to Europe around 1730, and its interesting leaves made ginkgo a cultivated favorite. The name comes from the Chinese *yin-hing,* meaning "silver apricot," and refers to the resemblance of the orange fruits to miniature apricots. The leaves look like maidenhair fern leaves, giving it another name, the maidenhair tree. Originally spelled "gingko," from the Japanese *ginko,* it is now known in print as ginkgo.

CULINARY: The strong smell and taste of the fruit does not deter the Chinese, who consider it a great delicacy. I've found ginkgo porridge in Chinese restaurants strong, but tasty—at least when sweetened. The nuts or inner kernels, which are sold in Oriental markets, are roasted and eaten.

MEDICINAL: Ginkgo is rapidly gaining recognition as a brain tonic that enhances memory. It increases blood flow, metabolism efficiency, regulates neurotransmitters (chemicals that relay electrical signals between neurons), and boosts oxygen levels in the brain, which uses 20% of the body's oxygen. Scores recorded for healthy, young women performing challenging memorization tests improved dramatically after they took a large dose (600 milligrams or .6 grains) of extract. From this double-blind study, researchers concluded that ginkgo has "a specific effect on the memory process."[1] Ginkgo's potential in treating mental disorders, including Alzheimer's disease, is currently being studied. When 112 geriatric patients with atherosclerosis were given 120 milligrams (.12 grains) of ginkgo every day, they had less dizziness, fewer headaches, and less ringing in the ear, short-term memory loss, awareness loss, depression, and other symptoms resulting from poor blood circulation in the head. The ginkgo produced no side effects and was not

Ginkgo biloba. **Ginkgo is also called the maidenhair tree because its interesting leaves are similar in shape to those of the tiny maidenhair fern. The golden autumn leaves are the ones prized by herbalists for their medicinal properties.**

habit forming.[2] The extract also relieves hearing loss.[3] It is speculated that ginkgo may help other circulation-related disorders, such as diabetes, Raynaud's syndrome, hemorrhoids, and varicose veins. When it was given to patients with leg circulation problems in a double-blind study, it increased blood flow in their legs and improved their ability to walk distances. Many were able to walk pain-free. The only previous treatment available for them had been physical therapy. The ginkolides in ginkgo have been shown to subdue allergic inflammation, anaphylactic shock, and asthma.[4] One study showed its effectiveness in treating asthmatic children.[5] Ginkgo is most effective when taken 3 times daily to keep a constant blood level. The science of ginkgo is presented in *Ginkgolides, Vol. I,* edited by I. P. Braquet (J. R. Prous Science Publishers, 1988). An easier-to-read booklet is *Ginkgo: The Elixir of Youth* by Christopher Hobbs (Botanica Press, 1991).

CONSIDERATIONS: The fruit pulp, which contains catechols similar to those found in poison ivy and oak, can cause dermatitis. No toxicity has been found in the leaves; however, there are reports of irritability, headaches, heart palpitations, and diarrhea with large doses of standardized extracts (in which isolated active compounds are added to whole plant extracts). Germany's BGA (similar to the United States FDA) has asked manufacturers to conduct more clinical studies. The symptoms are possibly a result of contaminants added to the isolated compounds during processing.

OTHER: The leaf and fruit are used for control of aphids and grubs in China.

Ginkgo biloba
Gɪɴᴋɢᴏ

Gɪɴᴋɢᴏ Pᴏʀʀɪᴅɢᴇ

Here is a delightful dish from the kitchen of herbalist Christopher Hobbs.

1	cup (240 ml) rice
2	cups (480 ml) water
10 to 15	ginkgo nuts
	Honey to taste

Cook rice, water, and nuts over a slow heat for about 1 hour, until the rice is done. Blend into a creamy consistency and serve warm. Add honey to sweeten.

Glycyrrhiza glabra
Licorice

Glycyrrhiza glabra • Licorice

FAMILY: Leguminosae.

DESCRIPTION: Bushy herb. Height: To 3 feet (90 cm), occasionally taller. Width: 2 to 3 feet (60 to 90 cm). Flowers: Small, blue-violet, resemble miniature pea flowers. Leaves: Oblong in 4 to 8 pairs. Fruit: Small, reddish pods, clustered into a prickly seed ball almost 1 inch (2.5 cm) long. Root: Thick, fleshy, long, 3- to 6-foot (.9- to 1.8-m) taproot. Blooms: June to August.

HABITAT: Mediterranean and southwest Asia, northern India, in deep sandy soils, often in river valleys. Extensively cultivated in Russia, Iran, Spain, and India.

CULTIVATION: Perennial. Zone: 8. Germination: 10 days. Soak 24 hours before planting. Space: 1¹/₂ feet (45 cm). Soil Temperature: 65° to 75° F (18° to 23° C). Soil: Sandy soil, near streams, moist, well drained. pH: 5.5 to 8.2. Sun: Full sun. Propagation: By seed, or divide roots in the fall. Also propagated from stolons (aboveground, spreading stems). It will handle only a light frost. Harvest the roots (before it goes to seed) of 3- to 4-year-old plants. Older ones are woody. Dryness and heat increases their sweetness, and cold weather makes them woody. A legume, it fixes nitrogen in the soil.

GARDEN DESIGN: Licorice can be easily lost among other tall herbs. The small flowers don't distinguish it, so accent the interesting pealike foliage.

CONSTITUENTS: Glycyrrhizin (5% to 10%), flavonoids, polysaccharides, chalcones, coumarins, saponoids, sterols, starch (30%), sugar (to 14%), amino acids, amines (asparagine, betaine, choline), gums, essential oil.

RELATED SPECIES: Spanish or Italian licorice *(G. glabra* var. *typica),* Persian or Turkish licorice *(*var. *violacea),* Russian licorice *(*var. *glandulifera),* and Chinese licorice *(*var. *uralensis)* seem to have similar properties. So does the hardier wild American licorice *(G. lepidota,* which is sometimes sold by herb nurseries as *G. glabra).* Nurseries also often sell an unrelated (except by family) Eurasian herb called goat's rue *(Galega officinalis)* as licorice! Goat's rue has 1¹/₂-inch- (3.7-cm-) long pods. The roots of Indian licorice or jequirity *(Abrus precatorius),* a native twining shrub of tropical Asia and Australia, have been used as a licorice substitute and medicinally, but the seeds are poisonous.

HISTORY: The first mention of licorice was recorded on ancient Assyrian tablets and Egyptian papyri. The Greeks learned about the sweet root from the Scythians, so Theophrastus named it scythian in the 3rd century B.C., declaring it good for lung disease. Later, it descriptively became glycyrrhiza *(glykys,* meaning "sweet," and *rhiza,* "root"*).* Widely cultivated in 15th-century Italy, it was sold in apothecaries, and it remains a common pharmaceutical sweetener and pill binder today. About this time, the plants also found their way into northern Europe. The Latin *liquiritia* turned into *lycorys* in Old French. The Dominican Black Friars introduced it into England, where *lycorys* extract was later sold as lozenges called "pomfrey cakes."

CULINARY: Licorice flavors candies, liqueurs, ice cream, chewing gum, and baked goods for good reason—its constituent glycyrrhizin is 50 times sweeter than sugar. It also enhances the flavor of cocoa, which can be reduced 25% in manufactured products. It increases the amount of foam in Guinness beer. East Indians chew it with betel after a meal. The flavor of most American "licorice" candy really comes from anise *(Pimpinella anisum)*. English versions, however, contain strong licorice extracts.

MEDICINAL: The complicated chemistry in licorice gives it a wide spectrum of properties. Literally hundreds of studies have been done on its ability to correct problems with the liver, adrenals, hormonal imbalances, and peptic ulcers. In China, where it is one of the most often prescribed herbs, second only to ginseng, it is suggested for the spleen and kidney and to protect the liver from disease. The Japanese use a licorice preparation to treat hepatitis. Studies show it helps the liver neutralize toxins produced by diphtheria, tetanus, cocaine, and strychnine and also increases glycogen storage. Another property of licorice is to stimulate the adrenals. Several studies have compared its action to that of hydrocortisone, but without the side effects.[1] Like cortisone, it decreases inflammation and relieves arthritic and allergy symptoms, but it also regulates adrenal-related low blood sugar, and is effective for Addison's disease (in which all 3 adrenal hormones are not being produced). Unlike drug therapy, which makes adrenals "lazy," licorice helps them recover normal function. One woman with adrenal failure who was treated solely with herbs experienced rapid improvement that was attributed to licorice.[2] Studies with extracts on licorice's estrogenlike substances show contradictory results, suggesting it has regulating actions. Women treated for infrequent menstruation due to hormonal imbalances found that licorice normalized their cycles.[3] The use of licorice for stomach and intestinal ulcers goes back at least to Dioscorides in 1st-century Greece, but modern clinical use began in the 1930s. Licorice covers the stomach wall with a protective gel, lowers acid levels, and reduces intestinal spasms. In the 1960s, doctors began using the constituent, glyceyrrheinic acid (carbenoxoloen sodium) instead of licorice root because, although it produced side effects, it worked faster. They switched to DGL, an extract with 97% glycyrrheinic acid removed, when researchers discovered it was almost as effective.[4]

Licorice—which also reduces throat irritations, lung congestion, and bacteria—is used for coughs and bronchial problems. Antitumor effects were observed in cultured human cells and an increase of immune-stimulating interferon occurs in people.[5] Studies in 1986 in India found that a 5% solution of licorice dropped into the eyes was as effective as the drug chlorophenical in treating conjunctivitis, which improved within 7 days.

CONSIDERATIONS: Although licorice candy sounds perfectly safe, large doses can cause sodium retention and potassium loss, leading to water retention, high blood pressure, headaches, and shortness of breath. (Its action is similar to the ACTH hormone.) In a controlled study, 3½ ounces (100 grams) of licorice twists daily (which equal .002 to 0.14 ounces) [1 to 1.4 grams] of pure glycyrrhizin) for 1 to 4 weeks resulted in serious symptoms, which disappeared when discontinued.[6] The concentrated extracts in laxative preparations can aggravate potassium loss when used daily. Avoid if pregnant or if you have high blood pressure or a kidney disease.

OTHER: Ninety percent of imported licorice in America goes into tobacco, with some containing 10%. The pulp is mixed into mushroom compost, insulating mill board, and cattle and horse feed.

Hamamelis virginiana • Witch Hazel
(Previously *H. macrophylla*)

FAMILY: Hamamelidaceae.

DESCRIPTION: Small tree. Height: To 15 feet (4.5 m). Width: 15 feet (4.5 m). Flowers: Golden yellow, petals to ³/₄ inch (2 cm) long, graceful, spiderlike form, in tight clusters. Roll up when caught in a cold spell to wait for warmer weather. Leaves: Oval, to 6 inches (15 cm) long, coarsely indented. Fruit: Seed capsules contain 2 shiny black seeds that pop out when mature. The seeds ripen the following autumn. Bark: Light brown to gray, with light circular spots. Blooms: September to April.

HABITAT: Eastern North America, from New England south to Georgia and west to Minnesota.

CULTIVATION: Perennial. Zone: 3. Germination: 1 to 2 years. Stratify for 3 months at 40° F (4° C). Space: To 15 feet (4.5 m). Soil: Well drained, cool, slightly sandy with organic matter; moist preferred, but not fussy. pH: 5.5–6.5. Sun: Partial shade, or full sun suitable in cold climates. Propagation: By seed, layering, or suckers. Plant trees in November or March. Witch hazel seems to have a high tolerance for polluted city air.

GARDEN DESIGN: This small tree can be planted within a large herb garden, or off to the side in smaller plots. It is an excellent choice to provide a shady section in the garden. The bright yellow and red leaves are striking in the autumn. If possible, plant it where you can see it from the house and enjoy it late in the season. The flowering branches can be brought into the house.

CONSTITUENTS: Leaves: up to 10% tannin, saponins, flavonoids; bark: up to 6% tannin, essential oil (eugenol, carvacol).

RELATED SPECIES: Other species and cultivars are often grafted on to *H. virginiana* stock. The Chinese witch hazel *(H. mollis)* is considered the most beautiful of the 8 species.

HISTORY: First brought to Europe by Collinson in 1736, it was christened witch hazel, probably after England's wych elm *(Ulmus glabra)*, which was named *wicen,* "to bend", by the Anglo-Saxons. Coincidentally, witch hazel branches are used as divining rods to "witch" water. The botanical name came from *hama,* meaning "same time," and *mellon,* or fruit, signifying any fruit-bearing tree. (Although rarely eaten, the oily, inner seed is edible.) Cadwallader Colden's 18th-century report describes an Indian treatment of "almost blindness occasioned by a blow cur'd by receiving the warm steam of a Decoction of the Bark of the shrub through a funnel upon the place . . ." Some American tribes drank the tea to promote a sweat in their sweat lodges.

MEDICINAL: Witch hazel water (from young flower-bearing twigs), lotion, ointment, and suppositories are sold in drugstores around the world. Witch hazel acts mostly on the veins and circulation. It has been shown to decrease the inflammation and pain of bruises, sore muscles, bleeding, hemorrhoids, varicose veins, phlebitis, and nosebleeds, as well as insect bites, poison ivy, and poison oak.[1] Native Americans washed wounds with it and placed a witch hazel poultice over painful inflammations, as well as rubbed it on the legs of their athletes to protect their muscles from strain. It is also antibacterial, and a weak tea makes a good wash for inflamed eyes. Although the tannins were originally thought responsible for witch hazel's astringency, the tannin-free water is still very astrin-

Hamamelis virginiana
WITCH HAZEL

gent and effective. One of witch hazel's effects on circulation is to lower blood pressure and increase respiration.[2] It has also been taken to relieve congestion and infection in the female organs, both as a tea and as a douche.

COSMETIC: Witch hazel is found in aftershaves and mouthwashes.

CONSIDERATIONS: Extracts made from the bark or leaves are too astringent to be used on the skin undiluted. The commercial water is poisonous to drink because it is made with rubbing alcohol, but it can safely be used externally.

Hepatica americana. **While liverwort makes a very attractive groundcover because of its pretty lavender-blue, rose, or white flowers, it also has been used throughout history to treat kidney problems and bronchitis, and has been proven to have antibiotic qualities.**

Hepatica americana • Ker-Gawl Liverwort
(Previously *H. tribola*)

FAMILY: Ranunculacae.

DESCRIPTION: Small rambling herb. Height: To 6 inches (15 cm). Flowers: Lavender-blue to rose and white colored, $^1/_2$ to 1 inch (1–2.5 cm) across, with 8 overlapping petals and delicate stamens in the center. Leaves: Flat, leathery, with three definite lobes, supported by thin hairy stalks. Blooms: An early spring flower.

HABITAT: Eastern Canada south to northern Florida and Missouri, in moist, shaded wooded areas.

CULTIVATION: Perennial. Zone: 3–7. Germination: About 2 weeks. Stratify first 2–4 weeks, or overwinter in outside, but shaded, seed beds. Space: 8 inches (20 cm). Soil Temperature: 60° to 70° F (15° to 21° C). Soil: Moist, semi-rich, with humus, calcium-rich. pH: 6 to 7.5. Sun: Semi-shade or shade, especially in hot climates. Propagation: From seed or by root division. Divide the rootstock in autumn, being careful not to break off the leaves, which stay on throughout the winter and provide nourishment. Plant so the leaf buds are just at the soil surface, then mulch lightly for the winter. Must have a cold winter for survival.

GARDEN DESIGN: Liverwort forms an attractive groundcover in shady garden areas. It is sometimes used in landscaping.

MAJOR CONSTITUENTS: Protoanemonin (which changes to anemonin upon drying), flavonoids, anthrocyanins, and glycoside (hepatrilobin).

RELATED SPECIES: The similar European species is *H. nobilis*. The sharp-lobed liverwort (*H. acutiloba*), with pointed leaves was also used by Native Americans medicinally for the same purposes.

HISTORY: The name liverwort originated from the liver-shape of the related European herb. This is a classic example of the Doctrine of Signatures, which held that an herb cured the ailments of the part of the body it physically resembled. The Greeks originally called the plant *heper*, meaning liver, and prescribed it for liver disorders, which at that time included not only jaundice and certain indigestion problems, but cowardliness, or feeling "liverly." The 17th century herbalist, Culpeper, suggested that liverwort be boiled in beer for similar problems. It was also considered "cooling" to the body and was given to people who were feverish. The Native Americans used their species as a tea for these purposes, and also to soothe coughs and sore throats and as a wash for sore breasts. In 1828, the botanist Rafinesque commented that having fallen into disuse in Europe, it "has lately been brought to use in America." By 1859, it had gained repute as an ingredient in "Dr. Roder's Liverwort and Tar Sirup." It was also part of the self-prescribed "kidney cure." The increasing popularity of liver tonics in the late 19th century resulted in the use of 450,000 pounds (202,500 kg) of dried leaves of American species for use in the United States and exports to other countries in 1883 alone. All along, doctors were debating its effectiveness, and it again eventually fell into disuse.

MEDICINAL: While liverwort is rarely found in herbal remedies today, it is a mild astringent and a diuretic. Reports indicate that it stimulates gall bladder production and, as a result, is a mild laxative. Its astringency has also served to stop bleeding in the digestive tract and the resultant spitting of blood. Historically, liverwort has also been used for kidney problems and bronchitis. Liverwort's active constituent, protoanemonin, has been shown to have antibiotic action. The Russians use it in their folk medicine, and also to treat cattle with "mouth sickness." Various Native American tribes also use it to prevent convulsions in children and as a wash for easing for facial contortions and dizziness.

CAUTIONS: Although they will stop any bleeding, the leaves and flowers are irritating to skin and should not be placed on wounds. Large doses can produce symptoms of poisoning.

> All the woodland path is broken
> By warm tints along the way
> And the low and sunny slope
> When there comes the silent token
> Of an April day
> Blue hepatica!

"HEPATICA"—DORA READ GOODALE (1866–1915), AMERICAN

Humulus lupulus • Hops
(Previously *H. americanus*)

FAMILY: Cannabaceae

DESCRIPTION: Tall, spindly, clinging vine. Height: 15 to 30 feet (4.5 to 9 m). Flowers: Green-yellow catkins. The female flowers are enclosed in strobiles. The male flowers hang in 6- to 10-inch (15- to 25-cm) clusters. Female flowers on separate plants form long narrow bract pairs. Leaves: Bright green, opposite, usually 3 to 5 heart-shaped lobes with coarsely serrated edges resembling grape leaves, with long twirling petioles. Fruit: Conical strobile, 11 inches (27 cm) long. Blooms: July to August.

HABITAT: In Europe, hops are found wild in thickets with damp, deep, humus-rich soils. Cultivated in Europe and Chile.

RELATED VARIETIES: *H. japonica* 'Variegatus' has huge, 10-inch (25-cm) leaves that are lime green accented with white.

CULTIVATION: Perennial. Germination: 25 to 30 days. Space: 3 feet (90 cm). Soil Temperature:70° to 75° F (21° to 23° C). Soil: Deeply dug, rich, light, well drained; tolerates dry but prefers frequent watering. pH: 7 to 8. Sun: Full sun or partial shade, likes heat. Propagation: Propagate by young shoots or from cuttings or underground stems in late summer. Cut back stems after they die down from frost.

GARDEN DESIGN: Use hops as an upright vine to provide garden height or as a rambling groundcover that will quickly fill in an area. Grown on a lattice or other support, it will cover a shed or an unsightly fence.

MAJOR CONSTITUENTS: Lupulin; essential oil (0.3–1%) includes humulene; bitter resin (3–12%); also flavonoids (astralagin, quercitrin, rutin); estrogenic substances, asparagin; GLA.

HISTORY: The Roman historian Pliny dubbed hops *lupus*, or wolf, after noticing the way it twines tightly around other plants. The word hops comes from *hoppan*, "to climb." Hops were grown by the Romans but were not widely cultivated until the 9th and 10th centuries, mostly in France and Germany. In less than one hundred years, a new drink called *bier* made from Bavarian hops became famous. It was developed after hops was added to bread to encourage fermentation and preservation. Since bread was sometimes used in brewing, it was discovered that hops increases beer's alcohol content. The English, however, continued to make the traditional ales, flavored with bitters like alehoof and alecost (costmary and ground ivy), and preferred to sleep on hops pillows instead. In the 15th century, Henry VIII warned that *humele* was a wicked weed that "would spoil the taste of the drink and endanger the people" and forbade its use. In the 17th century, English herbalist John Evelyn was still claiming that ingesting hops could result in disease, melancholy and a shorter life. In Russia, the word *hmel* describes both the herb and a slightly drunk person.

CULINARY: The young shoots of hops can be boiled, steamed, or eaten raw and served like asparagus. The Romans ate them this way and also blanched the young tops.

MEDICINAL: The strobiles of hops are mildly sedative and diuretic. They are a bitter digestive that is especially suited for treating nervous indigestion, ulcers, insomnia, irritable bowel syndrome, and Crohn's disease. They relax nerves and smooth muscles, especially in the digestive tract, within 20 to 40 minutes after ingestion. A 1980 study suggested that they contain a muscle-relaxing constituent in addition to lupulin, which had been assumed to be the only active chemical.[1] Hops' antibacterial agents, responsible for preserving bread and beer, also fight digestive tract infections. Hormonal effects from estrogen-like compounds were first noted when female hops pickers experienced changes in their menstrual cycles (some even stopped menstruating) after absorbing quantities of the essential oil through their hands.[2] Aphrodisiacal effects were observed in men. Regular doses of the herb can help regulate the menstrual cycle. GLA (gammalinoleic acid), which also occurs in evening primrose oil, has been found in hops, suggesting its usefulness for PMS and menstrual problems, especially muscle cramps, headaches, and sore breasts. Hops also helps insomniacs. A hops poultice can relieve the pain and inflammation of earache or toothache. Experiments in Germany have shown that hops tinctures are more stable than dried hops, which quickly degrades with exposure to light and humidity.

AROMATHERAPY: A hops "sleep pillow" encourages a sound sleep. Europeans used to fill a whole bed pillow with the strobiles, but a small hops pillow tucked under the usual bed pillow is all that is needed. Apparently the fragrance is responsible for the soporific action. Other fragrant, relaxing herbs, like lavender, may be included in the pillow. Hops oil is used in some perfumes.

COSMETIC: Used in skin softening creams and lotions, its effectiveness is possibly due to hormonal actions.

CONSIDERATIONS: Up to 30% of hops pickers experience some degree of dermatitis, with pollen from the strobiles causing skin eruptions in about 1 out of every 300.

OTHER: Hops can be used for basketry and wickerwork. The fiber is also good for producing paper.

HOPS SLEEP PILLOW

4 *parts hops strobiles (for sleep)*
1 *part lavender flowers*
1 *part thyme (to prevent nightmares)*

Combine herbs and use as stuffing for a small pillow.

Humulus lupulus
HOPS

Hydrangea arborescens
HYDRANGEA

Hydrangea arborescens • Hydrangea

FAMILY: Saxifragaceae

HABITAT: Eastern United States from New York to Florida.

DESCRIPTION: Large bush. Height 4 to 8 feet (1.2 to 2.4 m). Flowers: White, sometimes tinged pink or purple, thin petaled, in tight, round clusters held on many small branches. Leaves: Broad ovals, to 6 inches (15 cm). Blooms: July to September.

CULTIVATION: Perennial. Zone: 5. Space: 5 to 6 feet (1.5 to 1.8 m). Soil: Rich, porous, well-drained, but somewhat moist. pH: 6.5. A soil this acid or lower on the scale will tinge the flowers blue-purple. A more alkaline soil will turn them pink. Sun: Full or partial shade. Propagation: By cuttings of the tender wood, usually in the late winter since it produces mostly sterile seeds. Prune back rather severely in the autumn or very early spring before the leaf buds form.

GARDEN DESIGN: Although most often found in the ornamental garden, hydrangea is equally suitable for the herb garden, where it provides a colorful backdrop for an herb garden large enough to contain bushes. It makes an excellent background hedge or can divide a large garden into sections.

CONSTITUENTS: Glycoside (hydrangin), saponoin, resin, rutin, essential and fixed oils.

RELATED SPECIES: There are a number of subspecies, all very similar in appearance. The variety 'Grandiflora,' and occasionally other varieties, are also called hills of snow. Peegee *(H. panicu-lata)* found in China and Japan, is an oriental folk remedy for coughs and is used to treat malaria.

HISTORY: The Native Americans called hydrangea seven barks, since the stems are covered with thin layers of different colored bark. They used it as a diuretic and later taught the settlers about its properties. The Cherokee also chewed the bark to relieve upset stomach and lower high blood pressure. They placed the antiseptic bark on burns, wounds, sprains, and swellings.

MEDICINAL: Hydrangea's primary medicinal use is to help in passing kidney and bladder stones. It is also used to decrease pain and inflammation in the urinary tract and when stones are passed. The dried root is considered strongest, but the leaves are sometimes also used. According to the Eclectic doctors of the early 20th century, it does not actually dissolve the stones but helps them to pass and prevents their reoccurrence. Unlike many herbs of its nature, they felt it was safe to use during an acute infection. Modern herbalists use it in combination with other herbs to treat inflamed and enlarged prostates. The roots have a laxative effect.

CONSIDERATIONS: Overdoses are said to cause dizziness and indigestion. There is one report in *Poisonous Plants of the U.S. and Canada* by J. M. Kingsbury, of food poisoning when children added hydrangea buds to the family's picnic salad. The wood has been reported to cause skin reactions in woodworkers.

OTHER: The pith inside the stems can be removed to make pipe stems. Carefully air-dried, the flowers are a beautiful addition to dried wreaths.

© Derek Fell

Hydrangea arborescens. You may not imagine hydrangea as a suitable addition to the herb garden, but it is a medicinal plant and is also dried for herbal wreaths. The paper-thin flowers turn reddish in alkaline soil and bluish in acid soil.

Hydrastis canadensis
GOLDENSEAL

Hydrastis canadensis • Goldenseal

FAMILY: Ranunculaceae.

DESCRIPTION: Low, solitary plant on single stem. Height: 1 foot (30 cm). Width: 1 foot (30 cm). Flowers: single, greenish white flower, without petals, 3/4 inch (2 cm) wide. Leaves: 1 to 2, maple-shaped, with 5 to 9 lobes, 8 inches (20 cm) wide. Fruit: Small, indented, bright red berry contains 10 to 20 hard, black, shiny seeds. Root: Somewhat cylindrical, very knotted, bright yellow inside, acrid smell and taste. Grows horizontally. Blooms: June to July.

HABITAT: Canada and Eastern United States, from Vermont to Georgia and into Minnesota and Arkansas, in shady, rich woodlands.

CULTIVATION: Perennial. Zone: 4 to 5. Germination: Stratify 3 months. Needs to be fresh. Space: 1 to 2 feet (30 to 60 cm). Soil Temperature: 55° F (13° C). Soil: Rich humus, moist. pH: 6 to 7. Sun: Filtered, 75% shade. Likes air humidity. Propagation: Can be planted from seed, but it is easier to plant small rootlets purchased from a nursery in the autumn. Similar growing conditions to ginseng, but easier. Once established, propagate it by root division.

GARDEN DESIGN: Goldenseal is a compact plant that can be grown in pots. If you do plant it in the garden, be sure to place it somewhere where you can keep an eye on it. Patches are easiest grown under a lath or cloth shading.

© Steven Foster

Hydrastis canadensis. **The berberine in the roots of goldenseal makes them a bright yellow, and gives the plant part of its name. The once large, natural stands of this high-priced herb are being depleted, so herbalists strive to buy only cultivated stock.**

CONSTITUENTS: Alkaloids (hydrastine [1% to 3%], berberine [2%], canadine), fixed oil, essential oil.

HISTORY: The Native Americans taught the settlers about this valuable herb. Jesuit LeMoyne provided the first English account of goldenseal in 1650, reporting "it closed up all kinds of wounds in a short time." Rafinesque, who first coined the major alkaloid "hydrastine," noted in his *Medical Flora* that Native Americans also used it to treat urinary infections. It was introduced to England in 1760, and eventually found its way into both the *British Pharmacopoeia* and the *U.S. Pharmacopoeia* (1860). The Eclectics spoke very highly of it, and John U. Lloyd published an extensive review in his 1930 work, *Drugs and Medicines of North America* (Bulletin of the Lloyd Library, No. 29, Series No. 9). Most goldenseal is still wildcrafted, and prices are escalating as supplies diminish. Herbalists fear that if precautions are not taken, wild goldenseal will soon be an endangered species.

MEDICINAL: Early American medicine primarily used goldenseal root for treating uterine lining inflammation, but it is now considered valuable for treating any infection, inflammation, and congestion of mucous-lining areas, such as the lungs, throat, digestive tract, and sinuses. The primary constituents are hydrastine and berberine. Similar in action, they lower blood pressure and destroy many types of bacterial and viral infections.[1] Goldenseal salve helps to heal herpes, ringworm, impetigo, hemorrhoids, canker sores, and inflamed gums. The powdered root is sniffed for sinus congestion or gargled for sore throat, and a strong (and well-strained) eyewash is used for conjunctivitis. The tea also makes an effective douche for thrush *(Candida albicans)* and trichomonas. A bitter digestive, goldenseal stimulates appetite and bile production, and it also helps in the treatment of severe diarrhea caused by various diseases, including cholera.[2] Berberine effectively treats intestinal parasites, including giardia, a threat to campers and those living in rural areas. It proved as effective as, and sometimes even better than, the established drugs.[3] It is also used to help restore patients after long bouts with fevers and flus. Goldenseal is a beneficial but overused herb. Herbalists find it most effective used to treat an active infection, then discontinued, since it does not show the long-range adaptogenic actions of ginseng. History and cultivation information are found in *Goldenseal/Etc.* by Veninga and Zaricor (Ruka Publications, 1976).

CONSIDERATIONS: Very large doses can cause oversecretion of mucous membranes. Not for use during pregnancy because large amounts are a uterine stimulant. It is most effective when taken for short periods of time. The fresh plant causes dermatitis in sensitive individuals.

OTHER: Goldenseal roots produce a bright yellow dye and stain. The erroneous idea that goldenseal can mask urine tests for drugs became so widespread that clinical studies were done on people (1975) and on racing horses (1985). They determined it was only a rumor. The idea was, however, similar to the plot of the Eclectic herbal pharmacist, John U. Lloyd, in his novel *Stringtown on the Pike* (Dodd Mead, 1890). In the story, Red Head is convicted for murder after Professor Drew determines with an assay test that "strychinine" was in the dead man's stomach. But when the heroine later studies chemistry, she discovers that a combination of hydrastine and morphine results in the same assay—although not accurate, it makes for a good botanical murder mystery.

Hypericum perforatum • St.-John's-Wort

FAMILY: Hypericaceae.

DESCRIPTION: Many-branched herb, rising from underground runners. Height: 2 to 3 feet (60 to 90 cm). Width: 1 foot (30 cm). Flowers: Star-shaped, yellow, in clusters, with tiny black dots near edge on back, 3/4 inch (2 cm) across. Leaves: Oblong, to 1 inch (2.5 cm) long. There appear to be holes through the leaves when held up to light (thus the species name, *perforatum*). Blooms: June to August.

Hypericum perforatum
St.-John's-Wort

HABITAT: Europe, naturalized in North America and Australia.

CULTIVATION: Perennial. Zone: 3. Germination: 20 to 30 days. Stratify. Space: 1 foot (30 cm). Soil Temperature: 70° F (21° C). Soil: Well drained, fairly dry, drought tolerant, although oil content increases with some moisture. pH: 6 to 7. Sun: Full sun, or semishade tolerated, but fewer flowers. Propagation: By seed or root division. The constituents vary with locality.

GARDEN DESIGN: It can become weedy and needs to be controlled but is an interesting-looking herb in its own right.

CONSTITUENTS: Essential oil includes hypericin, pseudo-hypericin; flavonoids, procyanidins, tannin (8% to 9%). According to the *Merck Index,* hypericin dissolves in alkaline water, although one study found extracts were more effective than tea.

RELATED SPECIES: Many species are grown as ornamentals, such as the popular Aaron's beard *(H. calycinum),* which forms a lush, 15-inch- (37-cm-) high groundcover. It contains no hypericins but is high in procyanidins. *H. hirsutum* and *H. puctatum* are high in all active constituents. Tutsan *(H. androsaemum),* whose name comes from *toute-sante,* meaning "heal-all" in French, has been used for nervous and mental disorders and skin problems.

HISTORY: In Greek, *hypericon* means "over an apparition," since it was thought to protect one from evil. Later, the same attributes were transferred to Christianity, in which the herb became *Herba Sancti Ionnis,* the herb of St. John. The flowers are traditionally collected on St. John's Day, June 25, and soaked in olive oil for a few days to produce a vivid, blood-red anointing oil known as "blood of Christ." The word *wort* simply means herb and may denote herbs used in beer making. At one time, St.-John's-wort did flavor brandy, and bakers added a pinch to flour to improve bread's texture.

MEDICINAL: Studies show that hypericin (and a close variant, pseudohypericin) found in St.-John's-wort is a potent antiviral and antibacterial. They also suggest that other constituents (there are at least 50) have similar actions. St.-John's-wort counters herpes simplex and flu viruses[1] and possibly even the AIDS virus, according to research presented to the 1988 Proceeding of the National Academy of Sciences. The hypericins also inhibit monoamineoxidase (MAO), an action similar to drugs prescribed for depression.[2] It helps disturbed sleep patterns, and in one clinical study, women experienced significant relief from anxiety symptoms after 4 to 6 weeks of taking a St.-John's-wort extract.[3] The most well-known action of St.-John's-wort is in repairing nerve damage and reducing pain and inflammation. It is taken to relieve the pain of menstrual cramps, sciatica, and arthritis. The oil is applied to inflammations, sprains, bruises, and varicose veins. St.-John's-wort also treats circulation problems, bronchitis, gout, and incontinence, especially bedwetting at night.

CONSIDERATIONS: St. John's-wort was placed on the "unsafe herb list" by the FDA in 1977 because animals that ingest it (especially the young plants) develop a poisoning, phototoxic reaction when exposed to the sun. In Russia, it is even known as *zveroboi,* or "beast killer." However, no cases of human poisoning exist.

OTHER: An alcoholic extract produces violet-red dyes on silks and wools but doesn't color cotton. Both pills and the herbal extract are used in homeopathy.

Hyssopus officinalis
HYSSOP

Hyssopus officinalis • **Hyssop**
(Previously *H. aristata* and *H. vulgaris*)

FAMILY: Labiatae

DESCRIPTION: Small, greyish bush. Height: 2 feet (60 cm). Width: 18 inches (45 cm). Flowers: Blue, 1/2-inch (1.2-cm), whorls on one side on stem. Leaves: Soft and usually hairy, almost grey. Blooms: June to October.

HABITAT: Found in the Mediterranean region, in dry soils in sunny locations. Commercially cultivated in Europe, Russia, and India.

CULTIVATION: Perennial. Zone: 3 to 4. Germination: 7 to 10 days. Space: 12 to 18 inches (30 to 45 cm). Soil Temperature: 60° to 70° F (15° to 21° C). Soil: Well drained, dry. pH: 7.5 to 8.5. Sun: Full sun or light shade. Propagation: By seed, root division, or cuttings.

RELATED CULTIVARS: Dense-growing cultivars are showy with red (*H. officinalis* 'Rosea') or white (*H. officinalis* 'Alba') flowers.

GARDEN DESIGN: An excellent hedge herb with tight growth, which allows it to be shaped without looking straggly. It was once commonly trimmed into patterned knot gardens requiring constant pruning. Also used in rock gardens.

CONSTITUENTS: Essential oil (up to 2%) includes pinenes, camphene, and terpinene; flavonoids (hyssopin); tannin (5–8%); organic acid; bitter lactones (marrubiin, ursolic acid).

HISTORY: The hyssop referred to in the Bible is thought to be a King James version mistranslation of marjoram, since hyssop doesn't grow wild in Palestine. So much of it did grow in 1st-century Greece, however, that Dioscorides said that he didn't need to describe it, although he, too, may have been referring to marjoram. A common strewing herb, it was placed on packed dirt floors as a room freshener.

CULINARY: Hyssop was a culinary herb that flavored soups and meat dishes, but the flavor is too strong for most modern tastes. The tips boiled in soup were eaten by asthmatics. It is one of the herbs in Chartreuse liqueur and a French honey is famous for its hyssop flavor. Dried hyssop flowers are placed in soups, and the leaves are used in fruit dishes.

MEDICINAL: The flowering tops and the leaves are tonic and stomachic. Hyssop contains marrubiin, also found in horehound. Like horehound, hyssop is an expectorant, used to treat lung conditions, specifically bronchitis. In fact, these two herbs were often together in old formulas, although modern herbalists generally prefer horehound. Hyssop also contains ursolic acid, which reduces inflammation, so the tea makes a good sore throat gargle. Studies also show it to be an antiviral that is especially effective against the herpes simplex virus (at least in the test tube).[1] Hyssop is included in some flu and cold remedies to reduce congestion and fevers.

AROMATHERAPY: The fairly expensive essential oil is found in expensive perfume and eau de cologne. Aromatherapists used the fragrance to stimulate mental clarity and alertness. Hyssop baths were an English country cure for rheumatism.

CONSIDERATIONS: Use only in small doses. Pregnant women and people with high blood pressure should avoid it. Epileptics should not use the essential oil at all.

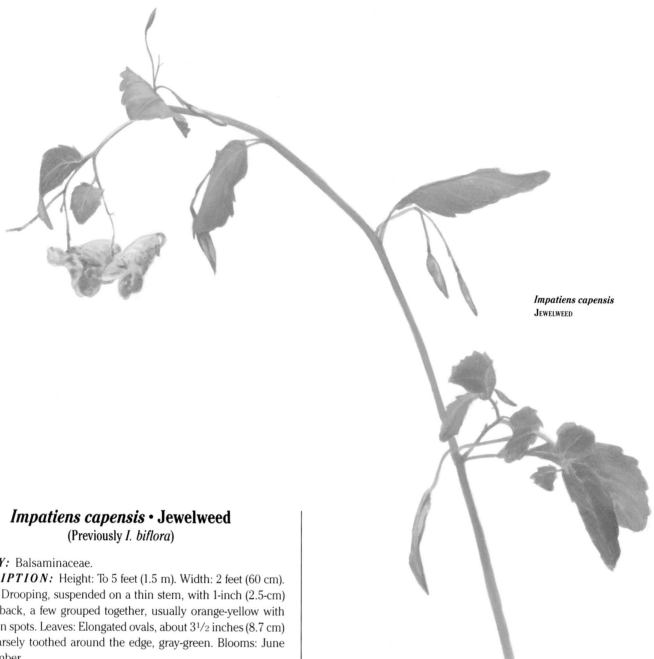

Impatiens capensis
JEWELWEED

Impatiens capensis • Jewelweed
(Previously *I. biflora*)

FAMILY: Balsaminaceae.

DESCRIPTION: Height: To 5 feet (1.5 m). Width: 2 feet (60 cm). Flowers: Drooping, suspended on a thin stem, with 1-inch (2.5-cm) spur on back, a few grouped together, usually orange-yellow with red-brown spots. Leaves: Elongated ovals, about 3½ inches (8.7 cm) long, coarsely toothed around the edge, gray-green. Blooms: June to September.

HABITAT: Canada south to Alabama and Oklahoma.

CULTIVATION: Annual. Germination: 10 to 18 days. Needs light, but not direct sunlight, to germinate. Space: 3 feet (90 cm). Soil Temperature: 65° to 70° F (18° to 21° C). Sun: Semishade. Propagation: By seed.

GARDEN DESIGN: The small flowers are its most interesting feature. The plant is suitable in the herb or wildflower garden.

CONSTITUENTS: Not investigated.

RELATED SPECIES: Part of a very large genus of perhaps 500 species. About 20 are cultivated in flower gardens. Pale touch-me-not *(I. pallida),* with yellow flowers and few spots, grows in the same regions. *I. balsamina,* from India, China, and Malaysia, is a popular garden annual and is used to dye silk. Other species are used by Ethiopian women to stain their feet and hands and by Japanese women to paint their nails.

HISTORY: The names impatiens and touch-me-not describe how the seed capsules burst open even when lightly touched. Native Americans, noting the flower's form, called it crowing cock.

MEDICINAL: The juice from the broken stem is a well-known folk remedy for poison ivy rash. It also works on the western United States poison oak, although there are fewer reports of its effectiveness since this eastern plant doesn't grow in the same region. In 1957, one physician was impressed when 108 of the 115 poison ivy rashes he treated with jewelweed cleared up in 2 to 3 days. If you tend to run into poison ivy or oak, you can keep jewelweed on hand by freezing it into small ice cubes. Even if you never need it for poison ivy, the herb also relieves the pain of insect bites, nettle stings, burns, sprains, ringworm, and various skin diseases. The juice is also made into an ointment for hemorrhoids, warts, and corns. It used to be taken for jaundice and asthma, although it is rarely used internally today.

CONSIDERATIONS: Large doses taken internally induce vomiting.

OTHER: The whole plant produces a yellow dye.

Inula helenium • Elecampane

FAMILY: Compositae.

DESCRIPTION: Tall, striking herb. Height: To 6 feet (1.8 m). Flowers: Daisylike, yellow with thin petals, to 4 inches (10 cm). Leaves: Stiff, large, to 16 inches (40 cm), hairy, with velvety undersides, on thick, hairy stems. The smaller, top, heart-shaped leaves clasp the stem. Roots: Light gray, hard, grow from a crown. Aromatic, the taste is both bitter and sweet. Blooms: May to August.

HABITAT: Probably native to central Asia and possibly central Europe, naturalized in the United States and southern Europe, where it is found along roadsides, in woodlands, and in damp places.

CULTIVATION: Perennial. Zone: 3. Germination: 6 to 8 weeks. Space: 2 to 3 feet (60 to 90 cm). Soil Temperature: 65° to 75° F (18° to 24° C). Soil: Heavy loam, well dug, well drained, moist. pH: 4.5 to 7.4. Sun: Full sun or partial shade. Propagation: Start seed in spring about 7 weeks before the last frost. Also by dividing the buds, or eyes, on the roots of at least 2-year-old plants in the fall, or cut the root into 4- to 6-inch (10- to 15-cm) pieces, and plant in the spring. The best rooting temperature is 50° to 60° F (10° to 15° C).

CONSTITUENTS: Inulin (44%), essential oils (1% to 4%) are camphor (azulene upon distillation), sesquiterpene lactones (alantolactone).

HISTORY: Elecampane was a common medicinal herb of the early Greeks, Saxons, Welsh, and Celts. The Romans used it as both food and flavoring, adding it to sauces for its bitter, camphorlike flavor and to counter the effects of overeating. As the wealthy Roman gourmet Apicius suggested, probably only the leaves of *E. helenium* were eaten, while the culinary roots came from *E. ensifolia*. *Inula* probably derives from the Greek goddess Helen, and the Latin *campania*, which means "campus" or "field," where it grows wild. Thought to improve general well-being, the ancients believed *Inula campana reddit praecordia sana* ("Elecampane will the spirits sustain"). Elecampane candy is said to have been a favorite of Julia, daughter of Augustus Caesar (63 B.C.–A.D. 14). The Romans mixed the dried root with raisins, dates, and honey or vinegar for dessert. Pliny called it "extremely wholesome." Even in the late Renaissance, hard elecampane confections were molded into shapes and English children were given bottles of a sweet drink composed of elecampane, licorice, sugar, and water to enjoy on Easter Monday.

In Europe elecampane is typically found near the ruins of monasteries, where it was once cultivated. At one time used for skin diseases by both doctors and veterinarians, it was given the names scabwort and *hors helene* ("horse healer") because it so effectively healed sheep scab and cutaneous horse diseases. It was also used in surgical dressings by the Spanish.

CULINARY: Until about 1920, elecampane root was a common flavoring in English sweets, such as sugar cakes colored red with cochineal, and the root itself was candied. Asthmatics would chew a piece in the morning and evening. Those who traveled by a polluted river sucked the root to protect them from the poisonous air. It is still used in some European wines and liqueurs, particularly vermouth, Absinthe, and the French Vin d'Aulnée.

MEDICINAL: A bitter-aromatic tonic, elecampane root increases appetite and promotes digestion. Europeans with indigestion still sometimes sip on a cordial made by infusing the roots, sugar, and currants in white port. In Russia, the whole root is preserved in vodka to store it for winter use. A common ingredient in cough medicines and lung remedies, elecampane is a decongestant that helps to reduce coughing. Usually mixed with other medicines, it has been used for bronchitis, coughs, catarrh, shortness of breath, diphtheria, and it was once a specific for tuberculosis, its effectiveness shown in 1885 experiments by Korab. One lactone elecampane contains expels intestinal worms and two others are powerful germ and fungus fighters.[1] It is also used to promote menstruation and to treat anemia. Pliny of Rome said that elecampane, "being chewed fasting, doth fasten the teeth," and subsequent herbalists agreed. While the Europeans have always favored using the root, the Chinese prefer the flowers, which they use to treat certain types of cancers.

OTHER: A blue dye is made by mixing elecampane with ashes and whortleberries.

Inula helenium
ELECAMPANE

Iris x *germanica* var. *florentina* • Orris Root
(Previously *I. florentina, I. violacea*)

FAMILY: Iridaceae.

DESCRIPTION: Tall leaves growing in clumps. Height: 2½ feet (75 cm). Width: 1 foot (30 cm). Flowers: Typical iris flowers, with large, very thin petals that fall back, white with traces of blue or purple inside. Leaves: Stiff, sword-shaped, pointed, and standing upright. Blooms: April to June.

HABITAT: Perhaps from the Mediterranean or Syria, naturalized in various parts of the world, including central Europe, Iran, and North India. Cultivated commercially in Italy and Morocco.

CULTIVATION: Perennial. Zone: 4 to 5. Space: 1 foot (30 cm). Soil: Well drained, dry, limey and acrid, deep, rich. pH: 7.5 to 8.5. Sun: Full sun, or partial shade in hot climates. Propagation: By seed, which is sown in summer, but more often by rhizome division, best done immediately after flowering. It is best to divide them every 3 to 4 years since they are heavy feeders and produce fewer blooms in the center patch. Don't bury the rhizomes deeply, or they will produce more foliage than flowers. Rhizomes are ready to harvest in 3 years and should be aged at least 2 years to develop their violetlike aroma. Individual flowers live 3 to 5 days.

GARDEN DESIGN: Orris, like most irises, looks best when growing in informal groupings or clumps.

CONSTITUENTS: Essential oil includes (0.1%) myristic acid (85%), methyl myristate; ketone (irone), which develops a violet-like scent upon drying.

RELATED SPECIES: Related to the common garden blue flag *(I. versicolor)*, which was used for indigestion and liver problems when dried (the fresh root is toxic). The Florentine orris, with the finest fragrance, is often confused with *I.* x *albicans,* a natural sterile hybrid with white flowers and a yellow "beard," and sometimes confused with *I.* x *germanica* and *I. pallida* with lavender-blue flowers and yellow-tipped white "beard." All are used in perfumery.

HISTORY: Macedonia, Elis, and Corinth were famous for their iris unguents. Orris was used for perfume in ancient Greece, Rome, and Egypt. We know the iris was being used medicinally in Egypt in 1540 B.C., when pharoah Thatmosis I had it depicted on the walls of the temple of Theban Ammon at Karnak. A stylized iris also appears on the brows of the sphinx statues. Iris, which means "rainbow" in Greek, describes the varied colors of the flowers, although their *iris* may have referred to all plants with swordlike leaves. Both Dioscorides and Pliny agree that the best roots came from Illyricum, or Dalmatia, Yugoslavia (probably *I. germanica*). Arabs planted them in Moorish Spain, and the 13th-century writer Petrus de Crescentiis of Bologna described the use of the white iris medicinally. Orris was one of the favorite flowers in medieval English and French gardens. It had been the coat of arms of the Frankish king, Clovis I (481 to 511). One version of his story is that orris saved his army when he saw it growing in a river as a sign they could safely cross. In 12th-century France, it became the *fleur-de-lys,* or "flower of Louis VII." The flower was also adopted by England's Edward III when he claimed the French throne in 1339 and then by Charles V of France, and it remained in the Royal Arms until 1800 (when it was replaced by the Irish harp). Still called fleur-de-lys, it remains the heraldic arms of Florence, which hosts the International Iris Trials. By the nineteenth century, orris cultivation had become a major Italian industry. Orris

Iris x *germanica* var. *florentina*
ORRIS ROOT

flavors brandy and drinks. An orris, honey, and ginger drink was once sold on Russian street corners.

MEDICINAL: The dried root is used for lungs, for coughs, and for hoarseness. It was formerly used to treat dropsy and chronic diarrhea and has also been used as a snuff for congestive headaches.

AROMATHERAPY: The fragrance of aged orris roots closely resembles that of violets. Historically, most violet products have really been scented with the less-expensive orris root. Orris, with anise, perfumed the Elizabethan "swete clothe." The isolation of the constituent irone in 1893 led to the manufacture of a synthetic ionone with a scent even closer to that of violets.

COSMETIC: Orris used to provide an "instant" shampoo that removed grease and scented the hair. In the 18th century, it was one ingredient in hair-whitening powder. It is chewed as a breath freshener and included in some dentifrice powders.

CONSIDERATIONS: Although it has been used for centuries, reports of occasional allergic reactions to smelling or touching dried orris root has resulted in a decline in its use. The fresh root is a powerful cathartic when ingested and can cause nausea.

OTHER: Orris is a popular fixative for potpourris and is found in most 19th- and 20th-century formulas. It is carved into fragrant rosary beads and provides teething sticks for babies. The rhizome produces a gray-black dye when used with an iron mordant.

O flower-de-luce, bloom on, and let the river
  Linger to kiss thy feet!
O flower of song, bloom on, and make forever
  The world more fair and sweet.
—"Flower-De-Luce,"
Henry Wadsworth Longfellow (1807–1882), American

Isatis tinctoria • Woad

FAMILY: Cruciferae.

DESCRIPTION: Small bush. Height: 3 feet (90 cm). Width: 2½ feet (75 cm). Flowers: Small, yellow. Leaves: Elongated oblongs, to 4 inches (10 cm) long. Fruit: Deep purple pods, suspended from stems. Blooms: June to September.

HABITAT: Europe, cultivated in western Europe until the 1930s.

CULTIVATION: Biennial. Zone: 4. Germination: 2 to 3 weeks. Space: 2 feet (60 cm). Soil Temperature: 60° to 70° F (18° to 21° C). Soil: Well drained, rich. Sun: Full sun. Propagation: From seed. Reseeds easily in the garden. It exhausts the ground, so the garden location should be alternated every other year. In climates with a long growing season, you can harvest 3 to 4 crops a summer, but the first two are the best quality.

GARDEN DESIGN: Woad is interesting visually, especially with its deep purple seedpods.

CONSTITUENTS: Indigo, which ferments into isatin; sitosterol, glycoside.

RELATED SPECIES: Dyer's rocket or weld, also called wild woad *(Reseda luteola)*, is unrelated.

HISTORY: Woad was cultivated in Europe for over 2,000 years, mostly by seminomadic peoples, because it exhausts the soil and crops are poor if replanted in the same place. The Greeks used woad to stop bleeding. When the Britons went into battle against the Romans, their naked bodies were painted blue with "waad"—certainly enough to scare any enemy. As an extra benefit, woad would help staunch any wounds they received. Julius Caesar (100–44 B.C.), in his *Gallic War,* recorded that, "All Britons do dye themselves with woad which sets a blue color upon them." English poet Sir Samuel Garth (1661–1715) wrote, "When dress was monstrous, And fig-leaves the mode, And quality put on, No paint but Woade." The relatively sunfast color was used to dye Oriental carpets, as well as fabrics. In the 17th century, comments were made concerning "the deep woad of intense displeasure"—which has turned into the contemporary saying that someone has "the blues." Woad provided the chief blue dye before indigo *(Indigofera tinctoria)* was introduced in the early 19th century.

MEDICINAL: The Chinese and East Indians use woad as both a dye and a medicine. They considered it a broad-spectrum antibiotic and used it to treat many different infections and also for inflammation. Both leaves and roots are used when there are swollen glands, such as in cases of mumps, tonsillitis, or laryngitis. High fevers, diphtheria, and hepatitis are other problems that respond to woad, but it should be used only by professionals—see Considerations.

CONSIDERATIONS: Poisonous, not for internal use.

OTHER: The blue dye is obtained by fermenting, drying, and refermenting the crushed leaves, then adding limewater.

Isatis tinctoria
Woad

Jasminum officinale • Jasmine

FAMILY: Oleaceae.

DESCRIPTION: Climbing, vinelike bush. Height: Up to 40 feet (12 m). Width: To 10 feet (3 m). Flowers: White, tight, with a long tubed back, $2/3$ inch (6 mm) long. The very fragrant scent increases at night and for days after being picked. Leaves: Thick, shiny, coming to a point, with leaflets in 3 pairs, to $2^1/_2$ inches (6.5 cm) long. Blooms: June to October.

HABITAT: Originally, probably Iran, now widely distributed in north India and China and acclimatized in southern and central Europe. It is cultivated in France and Italy, and about 80% of the world's production occurs in Egypt.

CULTIVATION: Perennial. Zone: 6. Germination: 20 to 25 days. Space: 4 to 6 feet (1.2 to 1.8 m). Soil Temperature: 70° to 75° F (21° to 24° C). Soil: Rich, light, sandy, well drained; keep moist, although too much water reduces the scent. pH: 6.5 to 7.5. Sun: Full sun. Propagation: By cuttings or layering. Prune in the fall, right after flowering. Next year's flowers will appear on the new shoots. It is deciduous in cooler climates.

GARDEN DESIGN: Jasmine adds its beauty, charm, and exquisite scent to any garden. Grow outdoors on a trellis in warm regions or in a greenhouse.

CONSTITUENTS: Essential oil, containing over 100 aromatic chemicals.

RELATED SPECIES: There are about 200 species of tropical and subtropical jasmines, as well as many cultivars. About 20 are generally cultivated for their beauty and fragrance. Spanish jasmine *(J. grandiflorum)* is also used in essential oil production and to treat liver disease. It is often grafted to the less delicate *J. officinale* rootstock. An 18th-century double form existed, but seems to have been lost.

HISTORY: "Poet's jessamine" inspired the Persians to designate *Yasmin* (meaning "white flower") as king of the flowers, to rule next to the rose as queen. They prepared an oil by soaking the flowers in sesame oil, which scented the bodies and hair of Persian and Indian women for centuries. Various cultures have considered the fragrance an aphrodisiac. By the 3rd century, China had also grown familiar with the scent of *yeh-hsi-ming.* Jasmine was not accurately described in Italy until Rino mentioned it in his *Liber de Simplici-lius* in 1415. Even then, it was not formally introduced in Europe until explorer Vasco da Gama brought the plant from India in 1518. Not long afterward, the Duke Cosimo de Medici of Italy acquired one and was so jealous of his jasmine plants, he forbade even a twig to leave his garden. However, a young gardener presented a cutting of *J. sambac* to his fiancée, and they later became wealthy selling the illicit plant in the Florentine market. Since then, Tuscan brides have worn sprigs of jasmine for their weddings. Jasmine came to France during a new interest in perfumery that arose in Renaissance times, and some of the finest jasmine oil still comes from the French districts of Carnes and Grasse. The British took up the fashionable perfume as early as the 16th century, wearing jasmine-scented gloves.

CULINARY: Jasmine flowers add a light perfumey flavor to Chinese black tea and are found in other beverages.

MEDICINAL: Although it is rarely used in Western medicine, a jasmine flower syrup for coughs and lungs was once made. The East Indians do use it, chewing the leaves to heal mouth ulcers and softening corns with the juice. They also make a leaf tea to rinse sore eyes and wounds. Traditional Chinese medicine states that jasmine clears the blood of impurities. Headaches and insomnia have been relieved with a tea made from the root.

Jasminum officinale
JASMINE

AROMATHERAPY: The oil is produced by a costly process called *enfleurage* in which fresh flowers are placed on refined, warm fat for several days. Thirty-six separate batches of flowers are placed on the same fat, which is then separated off, resulting in "Ointment Number 36." With the retail price of jasmine absolute over $1,500 US a pound (1989), it is used in only the most expensive perfumes. Much East Indian oil is economically diluted with the less expensive sandalwood oil. Seventeenth-century herbalist Nicholas Culpeper recommended a jasmine massage "for hard and contracted limbs."

COSMETIC: Jasmine is good for skin types that are hot, dry, and overly sensitive.

OTHER: The male Oriental fruit fly produces a pheromone scent for the female moth that is almost identical to a blend of jasmine and cinnamon.

> *Jas in the Arab language is despair,*
> *And min the darkest meaning of a lie.*
> *Thus cried the Jessamine among the flowers,*
>   *How justly doth a lie*
>   *Draw on its head despair!*
> *Among the fragrant spirits of the bowers*
> *The boldest and the strongest still was I.*
>   *Although so fair,*
>   *Therefore from heaven*
> *A stronger perfume unto me was given*
> *Than any blossom of the summer hours.*
>
> *Among the flowers no perfume is like mine;*
>   *That which is best in me comes from within.*
> *So those in this world who would rise and shine*
>   *Should seek internal excellence to win.*
> *And though 'tis true that falsehood and despair*
>   *Meet in my name, yet bear it still in mind*
> *That where they meet they perish. All is fair*
>   *When they are gone and nought remains behind.*
> —"JESSAMINE." **CHARLES GODFREY LELAND (1824–1903), AMERICAN**

Laurus nobilis • Bay

FAMILY: Lauraceae.

DESCRIPTION: Stout tree. Height: To 25 feet (7.5 m) in cool climates like Britain's but up to 60 feet (18 m) in warmer areas. Width: To 30 to 40 feet (9 to 12 m). Flowers: Small, yellow, in umbel clusters of 3 to 4. Leaves: 3 inches (7.5 cm) long, deep green, stiff, leathery, oblong, and pointed on the end. Shiny on top, gray-green underside. Breaking the leaf produces a pungent aroma. Fruit: Dark purple to black berries, about 1/2 inch (1.25 cm) in diameter. Blooms: June to July.

HABITAT: Native to the Mediterranean, but cultivated in Europe since the 16th century; also grown in Morocco.

CULTIVATION: Perennial. Zone: 8. Germination: 3 to 6 months. Soil Temperature: 70° F (21° C). Soil: Well drained, sandy, with some moisture. pH: 4.5 to 8.2. Sun: Sun or partial shade. Propagation: Usually by cuttings from new growth. Be patient; it grows slowly at first. It can handle temperatures down to about 28° F (–2° C), but an extended freeze will kill it.

Laurus nobilis
BAY

GARDEN DESIGN: Bay prefers a sheltered location. The trees were traditionally grown in pots in European gardens so they could be brought indoors during the winter. This practice also kept them "garden size." Place the potted trees in strategic locations to add height, such as by a walkway or the corner of a bed. Be sure the pot has good drainage.

CONSTITUENTS: Essential oils are geraniol, cineol, eugenol, terpenes; tannic acid, bitters; berries: glyceryl laurate, essential oil similar to leaves.

RELATED SPECIES: The larger leaf of the American bay *(Umbellularia californica)* makes a good substitute, even though it has a different family and chemistry. Its flavor is stronger and more camphoraceous, so use a little less. Don't confuse bay with the poisonous cherry laurel *(Prunus laurocerasus),* which many people plant in their gardens—it is the source of the narcotic laurel water.

HISTORY: Bay, the *Laurus* ("to praise") *nobilis* ("the famous") of ancient Greece, crowned Olympic winners (776 B.C.), scholars, and poets—as well as Julius Caesar. It appears on a 342 B.C. Greek coin and, later, the head of James I on a 1619 gold coin. The tradition continues. Bay wreaths are still placed on Boston Marathon winners and occasionally on symphony conductors. Baccalaureate and "bachelor's" degrees come from the French *baccae lauri,* or "noble berry tree." It still remains an honor to "win laurels." The emperor Tiberius (42 B.C. to A.D. 37) found another use for it. He had a phobia that led him to always wear a bay wreath during thunderstorms, because lightning was said to never strike bay trees. The fragrance of bay became very popular in the late 19th century, especially for men's colognes and aftershaves.

CULINARY: Bay leaves are especially popular with French cooks, who liberally use bouquet garni, a bouquet of fresh herbs tied together, in soups, stews, and bean dishes. Unlike most culinary herbs, whose flavors rapidly depart, bay releases its flavor for hours. It is found in most pickling spices.

MEDICINAL: Formerly a French antiseptic, bay is rarely used medicinally except by the Lebanese, who steep the berries and leaves in brandy in the sun for a few days and drink it to calm queasy stomachs. Liniments containing bay oil warm sore muscles when rubbed on them.

AROMATHERAPY: An experimental convalescent home in Russia encourages patients to smell bay leaves to sharpen the memory. The ancient Romans and Greeks also used it for improving memory, and when bothered by headaches, they placed a rolled bay leaf in the nose or stuck a leaf on the forehead. Either remedy not only provided fragrance, it was an obvious warning to everyone that the wearer was probably not in the best mood! Greek priestesses at ancient Delphi sat over fumes of what were probably burning bay leaves to inspire prophetic visions. Nero (A.D. 37 to 68) fled to Laurentium during a plague outbreak to breath air purified by bay trees.

COSMETIC: A 1526 recipe in the *Grete Herbal*, by Peter Treveris, called for a paste of bay and honey to be applied to blemishes. The 17th-century herbalist Culpeper added that it "helpeth other skin problems and bruises." The scent in modern "bay" rum aftershave and most "bay" soap now comes from the West Indian bay rum tree *(Pimenta racemosa)*, a relative of allspice *(P. dioica)*.

OTHER: The wood is used for making bowls and cabinets.

BAY RUM COLOGNE

Here is a fragrant cologne developed circa 1914.

2   ounces (28 g) bay leaves
1/4   ounce (7 g) cardamom, ground
1/2   teaspoon (2.5 ml) cinnamon, ground
1/2   teaspoon (2.5 ml) cloves, ground
1   pint (500 ml) Jamaican rum

Crush the bay leaves (a blender or coffee grinder will do nicely), and add them to the rum and spices. Shake, then let stand for 7 days. Strain out the leaves, and bottle the cologne. At room temperature, it will keep indefinitely.

BAY RUM AFTERSHAVE

1   pint (500 ml) bay rum
2   ounces (56 g) glycerine
2   ounces (56 g) rose water
2   ounces (56 g) violet flower tincture (optional)

Mix ingredients and shake well.

BOUQUET GARNI

Use fresh herbs, if possible, for this recipe, but dried can also be used. Use a bouquet garni to flavor foods while they are cooking.

3   sprigs fresh chervil
3   sprigs fresh parsley
1/2   bay leaf
2   sprigs fresh thyme

Tie together into a bundle with a thin white string. If only dried herbs are available, tie them inside a 4-inch (10-cm) square of cheesecloth so that pieces don't break off.

Lavandula angustifolia • Lavender
(Previously *L. vera, L. officinalis*)

FAMILY: Labiatae.

DESCRIPTION: Woody stemmed shrub with a rounded form. Height: 2 to 3 feet (60 to 90 cm) Width: 2 to 3 feet (60 to 90 cm). Flowers: Vivid gray-purple, clustered on tall spikes to 3 1/2 inches (9 cm) long. Very fragrant. Leaves: Gray-green, linear, to 2 1/2 inches (6 cm) long by 1/4 inch (6 mm) wide. Blooms: June to August.

HABITAT: The Mediterranean, cultivated in France and elsewhere.

CULTIVATION: Perennial. Zone: 5. Germination: 2 to 4 weeks. Space: 2 to 4 feet (60 to 120 cm). Soil Temperature: 70° F (21° C). Soil: Sandy, very well drained. pH: 6.4 to 8. Sun: Full sun. Propagation: Lavender is difficult to grow from seed, but can be propagated by cuttings and root divisions. Cutting off the first-year blooms strengthens the plant. Young plants in cold climates are subject to winterkill unless mulched and planted in a well-drained soil. Only *L. angustifolia* survives a hard freeze well. Flowers are harvested as tight buds so they will hold their scent for many years.

GARDEN DESIGN: Lavender makes a fragrant pathway hedge where passersby brush it and release its scent. It provides extra height in raised beds. The flowers contrast especially well with pink-flowering herbs such as yarrow or roses.

CONSTITUENTS: Essential oil (to 1.5%) includes linalol, eucalyptol, limonene, cineole; coumarins, flavonoids.

RELATED SPECIES: There are many subspecies and cultivars, including *L. angustifolia* 'Alba,' with white flowers; *L. angustifolia* 'Hidcote,' with deep purple flowers; and the slightly hardier dwarf lavender *(L. angustifolia* 'Munstead'). French lavender *(L. dentata)* has dark green foliage and is best suited to excessive moisture. Spanish lavender *(L. stoechas)* has gray-green leaves. Spike lavender *(L. spica* and *L. latifolia)* was the source of an inferior, less expensive essential oil that was once promoted to grow hair.

HISTORY: Lavender has scented washing water and baths since the Romans named it after *lavare*, "to wash." English lavender is actually a Mediterranean herb that is cultivated primarily in France.

MEDICINAL: A compound tincture of lavender (also known as "Palsy Drops") was officially recognized by the *British Pharmacopoeia* for over 200 years, until the 1940s. Used to relieve muscle spasms, nervousness, and headaches, it originally contained over 30 ingredients. Tests show that lavender's essential oil is a potent ally in destroying a wide range of bacterial infections, including staph, strep, pneumonia, and most flu viruses.[1] It is also strongly anti-fungal. A lavender-flower douche is an effective treatment for vaginal infections, especially candida-type yeast infections. Lavender ointments are rubbed into burns, bruises, varicose veins, and other skin injuries. The straight oil dabbed on stops the itching of insect bites.

AROMATHERAPY: The fragrance of lavender scents many sweet perfumes. It is used as a mental relaxant that raises the spirits. The 16th-century herbalist William Turner suggested wearing a quilted cap containing lavender for head colds and to "comfort the braine." Victorian women prone to fainting sniffed lavender-scented hankies to revive themselves and placed lavender swooning pillows on the settee (with the hope they would land upon it). Rubbing a drop of lavender oil into the temples is often all that is

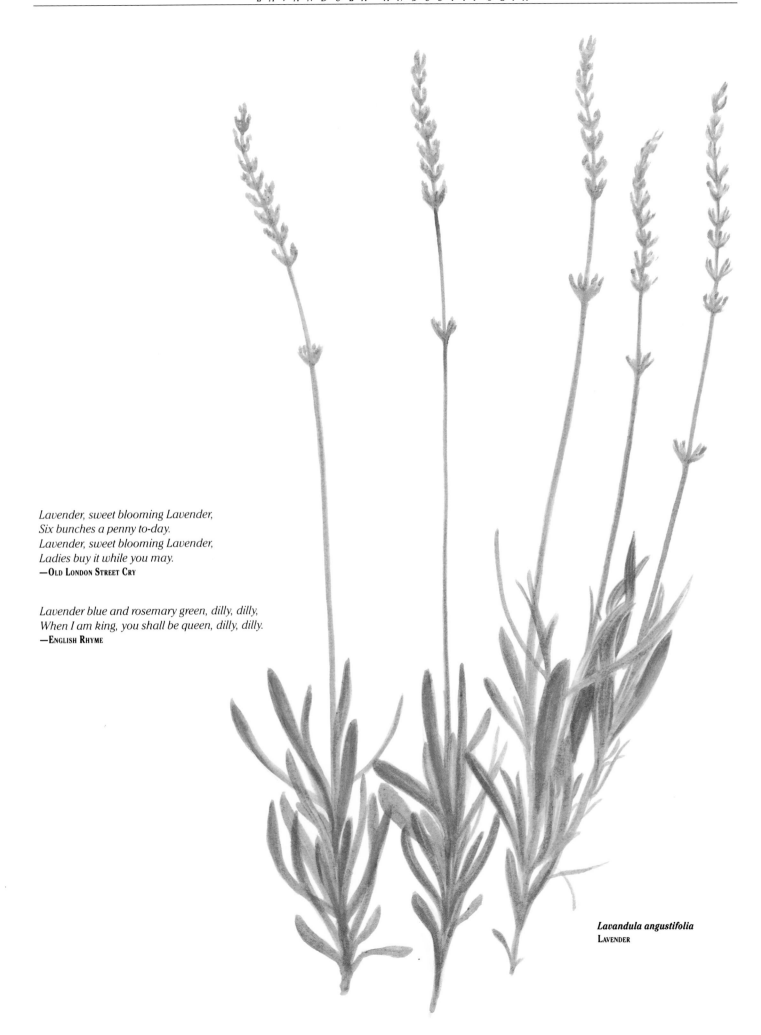

Lavender, sweet blooming Lavender,
Six bunches a penny to-day.
Lavender, sweet blooming Lavender,
Ladies buy it while you may.
—OLD LONDON STREET CRY

Lavender blue and rosemary green, dilly, dilly,
When I am king, you shall be queen, dilly, dilly.
—ENGLISH RHYME

Lavandula angustifolia
LAVENDER

needed to relieve a headache. In massage and bath oils and as a liniment, lavender relaxes sore muscles. During childbirth, a poultice of the heated flowers wrapped in cheesecloth was traditionally placed on the small of the back to relieve muscle and emotional tensions. The scent alone is said to make lions and tigers docile.

COSMETIC: Lavender is one of the most popular cosmetic ingredients in skin creams, lotions, and hair conditioners.

OTHER: Lavender is one of the most popular fragrances for scented sachets and potpourris. For centuries, lavender sachets have been placed among clothes to keep them fragrant. The stalks are woven into Victorian-style lavender "wands" and "fans." It is a fairly successful insect repellent that deters wool moths and mosquitoes, as well as parasites on animals.

Lavandula angustifolia. **Lavender is especially appealing when grown as a border hedge, which will be covered with purple spikes of fragrant flowers in mid-summer.**

PALSY DROPS

This version of Palsy Drops comes from the *London Pharmacopeia,* published in 1746.

1   *ounce (28 g) each:*
      lavender
      rosemary
      cinnamon
1/2   *ounce (14 g) each:*
      nutmeg
      red sandalwood
16   *ounces (480 ml) brandy*

Combine ingredients and let sit for 7 days, then strain.

VICTORIAN SACHET

Here is a fragrant blend from *The Era Formulary,* published in 1914.

1   *pound (500 g) lavendar flowers*
1   *ounce (30 ml) dried thyme leaves*
1/2   *ounce (15 ml) dried mint leaves*
1/8   *ounce (.6 ml) lavender oil*
1/2   *ounce (15 ml) cloves*

Powder ingredients and mix.

Leonurus cardiaca • Motherwort

FAMILY: Labiatae.

DESCRIPTION: Upright prickly bush. Height: To 5 feet (1.5 m). Width: 2 feet (60 cm). Flowers: Pale pink to purple, very hairy, in whorls of 6 to 12, alternating up the stems with leaves. Leaves: Dark green above, pale below, oak-shaped—deeply lobed into three, especially at the bottom, prickly. Blooms: August.

HABITAT: Europe, naturalized on waste grounds and along roadsides.

CULTIVATION: Perennial. Zone: 3. Germination: 2 to 3 weeks. Space: 2 to 3 feet (60 to 90 cm). Soil Temperature: 65° to 75° F (18° to 24° C). Soil: Light, well drained, fairly poor. pH: 7.7. Sun: Full sun. Propagation: More than easily self-sows once established.

GARDEN DESIGN: Although motherwort creates a striking hedge, I set it back from the path where it won't prickle visitors. It is an interesting plant to view from afar, with its slightly drooping leaves. Actually, what motherwort plants resemble from afar is marijuana—a fact I learned one day after being stopped by police while transporting a number of them in my pickup truck!

CONSTITUENTS: Essential oil, alkaloids (stachydrine, leonurinine), glycosides (leonurine, leonuridin), flavonoids, tannins, vitamin A.

RELATED SPECIES: Chinese research shows that a tea of *L. heterophyllus* is as effective as the drug ergotamine to encourage uterine contraction after childbirth.[1] In a clinical study in China, 105 patients showed "significant improvement" in red blood cell structure, blood flow, and a reduction in blood clotting. There was also over 80% recovery for numb limbs and insomnia and over 60% less dizziness and headaches.[2] The Japanese consider their species *(L. sibiricus)* an "herb of life" and have a Motherwort Festival on the ninth day of the ninth month, which is known as Kikousouki, or "Month of Motherwort Flowers." During the festival, the flowers are eaten with rice and stirred in saki cups while blessings for a long life are exchanged.

HISTORY: The early Greeks gave motherwort to pregnant women suffering from anxiety. This use continued and gave the herb the name mother wort, or "mother's herb." Its other prominent action is on the heart, giving it the species name *cardiaca,* or the Greek *kardiaca,* or heart. Nicholas Culpeper suggested it "to drive away melancholy vapours from the heart" in the 17th century. There is an old tale about a town whose water source is a stream flowing through banks of motherwort. Many of the townspeople lived to be 130 years old and recall one who reportedly lived to 300 years.

MEDICINAL: Motherwort is primarily an herb of the heart. Several species have sedative effects, decreasing muscle spasms and temporarily lowering blood pressure. Chinese studies found that extracts decrease clotting and the level of fat in the blood[3] and can slow heart palpatations and rapid heartbeat.[4] German Dr. Rudolf Weiss, M.D., states in *Herbal Medicine,* "My own investigations have shown that there is indeed a medicinal action mainly for functional heart complaints." Another of motherwort's uses is to regulate menstruation, improve fertility, and reduce anxiety associated with childbirth, postpartum depression, and menopause. It also reduces fevers, and is especially suggested for illnesses associated with nervousness or delirium. Motherwort was formerly used to treat rheumatism and lung problems, like bronchitis and asthma.

CONSIDERATIONS: Motherwort leaves occasionally produce skin dermatitis when touched.

Leonurus cardiaca
MOTHERWORT

Levisticum officinale
LOVAGE

Levisticum officinale • Lovage

FAMILY: Umbelliferae.

DESCRIPTION: Tall, stout herbs with large leaves and hollow stems. Height: 4 to 6 feet (1.2 to 1.8 m), sometimes even taller. Width: 3 feet (90 cm). Flowers: Small, green-yellow, in umbels, 2 to 3 inches (5 to 7.5 cm) across, stiffly held above the plants. Leaves: Celerylike, broad, flat, and with deep indentations, coarsely toothed around the edge at the base—2 feet (60 cm) long. Fruit: Narrow, elliptical seeds, $1/3$ inch (8 mm) long, with winglike appendages. Rhizome: Fleshy, thick, 3 to 5 inches (7.5 to 12.5 cm) long, aromatic, with side rootlets to 8 inches (20 cm) long. Blooms: June to July.

HABITAT: Southern Europe, but no longer wild. Naturalized in the United States, from New Jersey to New Mexico.

CULTIVATION: Perennial. Zone: 5. Germination: 10 to 14 days. Space: 2 feet (60 cm). Soil Temperature: 60° to 70° F (15° to 21° C). Soil: Rich, deep, moist, and very well drained. pH: 5.5 to 6.5. Sun: Full sun, or partial shade, especially in the south. Propagation: By seed or by root division in spring or fall, or by offshoots in the fall. It reaches full size in 3 to 5 years, then should be divided to encourage better growth. Aphids are attracted to it, so be armed with a garlic spray to deter them! Cold winters promote dormancy and the best growth. Cut the flower stalks to prevent seeding if you prefer keeping the leaves in a usable state. To dry, cut off the stems, and lay the leaves on a screen.

GARDEN DESIGN: Placed toward the back of a bed, lovage makes a statement with its height alone.

CONSTITUENTS: Essential oil (.6% to 1%) includes phthalides, pinene, phellandrene, terpinene, carvacol; isovaleric acid, angelic acid, coumarins.

HISTORY: The Romans' name for lovage, *levisticum*, is said to come from the Italian province of Liguria, where it grew abundantly. The ancient Greeks chewed *ligustikon* seeds to help them digest their meals. In Europe, Medieval tavernkeepers and Benedictine monks grew it in their gardens to make beer and cordials to settle the stomach, often combining it with yarrow *(Achillea ligustica)* and tansy *(Tanacetum vulgare)*. Lovage beer remained popular in England until the early 19th century. 12th-century Hildegard of Bingen used lovage not as a medicinal herb but as an important cooking spice. Considered a love charm, lovage was also known as "love parsley" or love "ache."

CULINARY: Lovage seeds once seasoned breads, and the powdered root was sprinkled on meals like pepper, but these are rarely used in cooking today. The leaves are occasionally added to soups, stews, and fish sauces, then removed before serving. The leaves, which have a strong, celerylike flavor, can be eaten as a vegetable and the leaf stalks blanched. Stems were once candied like angelica but they don't produce the same spicy bite. They are delicious added dry to herbal "salt" blends. Lovage is found in some alcoholic beverages.

MEDICINAL: Hot lovage root tea induces sweating. It is the main ingredient in many European diuretic preparations and is added to urinary tract formulas. Since it can irritate kidneys, it isn't suggested when an infection is present. It is also used to promote menstruation and to ease migraine headaches. Lovage has been employed as a mouthwash for soothing tonsillitis and mouth ulcers. At one time it also treated jaundice, pleurisy, and malaria.

CONSIDERATIONS: Pregnant women and those suffering from kidney disease or with weak kidneys should not use lovage. Dermatitis due to a photosensitive reaction to light has been observed in animals but never in people.

© Derek Fell

Levisticum officinalis. **Lovage leaves give a warming, celerylike flavor to soups and stews.**

Lobelia inflata • Lobelia

FAMILY: Lobeliaceae.

DESCRIPTION: Erect, hairy herb with angled stems that branch near the top. Height: 3 feet (90 cm). Width: 1 foot (30 cm). Flowers: Blue-violet to white, very small, 1/4 inch (.63 cm) long. Leaves: Elongated ovals, serrated around the edges, 2 1/2 inches (6.25 cm) long. Fruit: Seed capsules resemble an inflated bladder (thus its name) filled with tiny, rough, black, oily seeds. Blooms: June to September.

HABITAT: Northeastern America, Labrador to Georgia.

CULTIVATION: Annual. Germination: 2 to 3 weeks. Needs light, preferably sunlight, to germinate. Sow on the surface. Space: 8 to 12 inches (20 to 30 cm). Soil Temperature: 70° to 75° F (21° to 24° C). Soil: Rich, cool, moist. pH: 5 to 7. Sun: Full sun in colder climates, otherwise, partial shade. Propagation: Tap down seed into premoistened soil. Mulch well to protect it in cold climates.

GARDEN DESIGN: Even if lobelia seems too potent to use for anything but its beauty, still it does make a beautiful edging plant along semishaded pathways.

CONSTITUENTS: Piperidine alkaloids (.3% to .4%), glycoside (lobelacrin), essential oil (labelianin), chelidonic acid. The seeds contain lobelinein.

RELATED SPECIES: *L. radicans* and *L. chinensis* are used for similar purposes by the Chinese and to treat snakebite. The vivid red blooms of the cardinal flower *(L. cardinalis)* and the blue cardinal flower *(L. siphilitica)* make these popular garden perennials. The nonpoisonous *L. succulenta* is eaten as a vegetable by the Japanese.

HISTORY: The first lobelias were brought to Europe and named in honor of the 16th-century Flemish botanist Matthias de L'Obel, physician and botanist to James I. Samuel Thomson, founder of the physiomedical Thomsonian Medicine, promoted lobelia after "discovering" it in 1793, although 8 years earlier, a Dr. Manasseh Cutler had published a report on lobelia in *Account of Indigenous Vegetables,* delivered to the American Academy of Arts and Sciences. Thomson called lobelia the "number one herb" in a system that promoted purging to rid the body of toxins. Strongly emetic, it induced such vomiting and sweating that it was known as gag root and purge weed. Thomson was arrested for murder in 1809 after a patient died, apparently of a lobelia overdose, but after a stormy trial, he was acquitted due to lack of evidence—of intent or even that lobelia was indeed a poison. Small amounts were added to herbal formulas to activate the other ingredients. Lobelia was promoted in the 20th century by Jethro Kloss, author of *Back to Eden* (1939), and later by Dr. John Christopher, who wrote *School of Natural Healing* (1926), both of whom carried on the legacy of Thomsonian medicine.

MEDICINAL: Lobelia leaves reduce spasms by relaxing tissues rather than by producing a narcotic effect on the brain, as does opium, for example. They first stimulate the nervous system, but then depress it. The constituent lobeline stimulates the respiratory system, dilating bronchials and relieving lung congestion. Native Americans smoked it like tobacco for respiratory problems, and it gained the name Indian tobacco. It does contain properties that are similar to, but less potent than, those of nicotine and has been used to reduce tobacco-withdrawal symptoms. Both drinking the tea and

Lobelia inflata
LOBELIA

smoking lobelia, usually with other herbs to modify its intense reaction, have been employed to treat asthma, bronchitis, and whooping cough. Plasters and liniments for sprains, muscle spasms, and insect bites and poultices for breast cancer sometimes contain lobelia.

CONSIDERATIONS: The herb is toxic, so should only be used in minute doses by qualified professionals. Overdoses can be fatal. Large doses cause vomiting, convulsions, respiratory failure, and depression of motor functions in the brain and nervous system. It is on the FDA's restricted list, but the administration allows it in pills to stop smoking.

Lonicera caprifolium
HONEYSUCKLE

Lonicera caprifolium • Honeysuckle
(Previously *L. verna*)

FAMILY: Caprifoliaceae

DESCRIPTION: Climbing shrub that often wraps around other plants. Height: To 20 feet (6 m). Flowers: Fragrant, pale yellow tinted pink, 2 inches (5 cm), tubular. Leaves: Thin, opposite, oval, 2 to 4 inches (5 to 10 cm), upper ones in pairs of 2 or 3, united at base, around stem. Fruit: Orange-scarlet, round berries in clusters. Blooms: May to July.

HABITAT: Southern central Europe and western Asia.

CULTIVATION: Perennial. Zone: 5 to 6. Germination: 4 to 8 weeks. Space: 3 feet (90 cm). Soil: Moist, porous, and loamy. Soil Temperature: 65° to 75° F (18° to 23° C). Sun: Partial shade or sun if planted in a cool area of the garden. Propagation: Take woody cuttings in autumn and root in sand or peat. Layer in the summer. Prune in autumn if they die back. Avoid growing the vines in hot garden spots.

GARDEN DESIGN: A beautiful visual and fragrant accent to the herb garden, honeysuckle is graceful when grown on fences, trellises, or hedges. If you happen to have a garden gazebo, follow the 19th century fashion of adorning it with honeysuckle vines.

RELATED SPECIES: At least a dozen of the 150 species of *Lonicera* are used medicinally. Woodbine *(L. periclymenum)* is a taller honeysuckle with properties similar to those of Italian honeysuckle. *L. japonica*, a Japanese species that actually originated in China, is used like echinacea in Traditional Chinese medicine as a broad spectrum antibiotic for treating flus, fevers, and colds. Recent studies show some promise for treating breast cancer.

CONSTITUENTS: Glycoside, salicylic acid, invertin.

HISTORY: Known as Italian honeysuckle, this is the most common honeysuckle grown as an ornamental. The name honeysuckle, or *honysocle* from medieval days, comes from the delight that children (and supposedly, faeries) took in sucking the nectar from the flowers. The Romans called it *caprifolium*, probably because goats *(capri)* like to eat the leaves *(folium)*. During the 19th century, honeysuckle was encouraged to grow tightly coiled around tree limbs that would later be turned into contoured walking sticks.

MEDICINAL: Honeysuckle is diuretic, laxative, and increases sweating. At one time, it was a popular medicinal, but today it is rarely used. Dioscorides suggested using the seeds and a flower syrup for liver and spleen problems, and recommended honeysuckle to relieve labored breathing. Italian honeysuckle has also been used for colds and flus and may have some antibiotic properties similar to those of Japanese honeysuckle, but it has not been investigated.

CONSIDERATIONS: The berries are poisonous.

COSMETIC: A honeysuckle wash was traditionally used to clear the complexion of freckles and sunburn.

And bid her steal into the pleached bower,
Where honeysuckles, ripen'd by the sun,
Forbid the sun to enter, like favorites,
Made proud by princes, that advance their pride
Against that power that bred them.
—*MUCH ADO ABOUT NOTHING*, ACT III, SCENE I, **WILLIAM SHAKESPEARE (1564–1616), ENGLISH**

I plucked a honeysuckle where
    The hedge on high is quick with thorn,
    And climbing for the prize, was torn,
And fouled my feet in quag-water;
    And by the thorns and by the wind
    The blossoms that I took was thinn'd,
And yet I found it sweet and fair.
—"THE HONEYSUCKLE," **DANTE GABRIEL ROSSETTI (1828–1882), ENGLISH**

Fair Lonicera prints the dewy lawn,
And decks with brighter blush the vermeil dawn;
Winds round the shadowy rocks, and pansied vales,
And scents with sweeter brath the summer gales.
With artless grace and native ease she charms,
And bears the horn of plenty in her arms.
Five rival swains their tender cares unfold,
And watch with eye askance the treasured gold.
—"THE BOTANIC GARDEN," **ERASMUS DARWIN (1731–1802), ENGLISH**

© Steven Foster

Lonicera dioica. **The heady scent of the fragrant honeysuckle flower will waft through the herb garden on warm summer days.**

Marrubium vulgare • Horehound

FAMILY: Labiatae

DESCRIPTION: Small, rounded shrub. Height: 1½ feet (45 cm). Flowers: Small, whitish, in dense whorls that circle around the stems, getting smaller near the top. Leaves: Pale green, wrinkled, and very woolly, giving the appearance of being white, somewhat oval-shaped, to 2 inches (5 cm). Blooms: June to September.

HABITAT: Wild in southern Europe, northern Africa, western Asia, and the Azores; introduced in other areas, including the United States and Australia, in dry, grassy fields.

CULTIVATION: Perennial. Zone: 3 to 4. Germination: 10 to 12 days. Space: 8 to 12 inches (20 to 30 cm). Soil Temperature: 55° F (13° C). Soil: Light, sandy, dry. pH: 4.5 to 8. Sun: Full sun. Propagation: By seed or root division. Its deep roots require careful transplanting. Blooms in the second year.

GARDEN DESIGN: Horehound can be clipped and maintained into a fairly good border. It is a good herb to place in hot spots where other herbs would droop during the day.

CONSTITUENTS: Essential oil includes pinene, limonene, and campene; diterpene alcohols (marrubiol); sterols; saponin; bitter lactone; vitamin C.

HISTORY: Horehound has been used at least since the early Egyptians brewed it into a cough remedy and respectfully referred to it as the "Seed of Horus." It was also considered an antidote for poison, being particularly effective against the bites of mad dogs and serpents. Horehound was probably one of the bitter Passover herbs—the word *marrubium* is thought to be derived from the Hebrew *marrob*, for "bitter juice." *Har hune* (which later became horehound) is old English for "downy plant."

CULINARY: Horehound has been used as a bitter condiment and as a candy, but is too bitter for most tastes.

MEDICINAL: Horehound's bitterness stimulates the appetite and also promotes bile, making large doses laxative. The whole herb and its derivatives are used in thousands of lung medications around the world, especially for treating bronchitis and coughs. The essential oils and marrubiin dilate the arteries and help to ease lung congestion.[1] Marrubiin also normalizes the heart beat and is a weak sedative. At one time, horehound was suggested for relieving menstrual pain and slowing a rapid heart beat. Since it also induces sweating, it has been used to reduce fevers, even those associated with malaria. Old recipes call for the leaves to be boiled in lard and applied to wounds.

Marrubium vulgare
HOREHOUND

Matricaria recutita • Chamomile
(Previously *M. chamomilla*)

FAMILY: Compositae.

DESCRIPTION: Spindly, feathery, many-branched plants. Height: 2.5 feet (75 cm). Width: 1 foot (30 cm). Flowers: Small, daisy-like with white petals surrounding a raised, yellow center. Leaves: Very fine and feathery. Fruit: Tiny, straw-colored seeds. Blooms: June to July.

HABITAT: Grows wild in the open meadows of Europe and west Asia, with related species growing in North America and North Africa. Cultivated commercially in Egypt, Russia, Bulgaria, Hungary, Argentina, and Germany.

CULTIVATION: Annual. Germination: 10 to 12 days. Space: 6 to 12 inches (15 to 30 cm). Soil Temperature: 55° to 60° F (13° to 15° C). Soil: Dry, light, sandy, and well drained. A rich soil produces lush growth, although fewer flowers. pH: 5 to 8. Sun: Full sun. Herbalist Steven Foster found that time-consuming hand-harvesting is simplified by using a blueberry rake, which will gently pop off the flower heads. Propagation: Chamomile can be transplanted when young, but prefers to be seeded directly into the garden. Sow it early in the spring since the young plants become leggy if it gets too hot. Water the seedlings gently so they won't bend over into the mud.

GARDEN DESIGN: Chamomile is best grouped together, so that the plants can help support each other and the small flowers can make more of a visual impact.

CONSTITUENTS: Essential oil (to 1.75%) includes farnesene, bisabolol, chamazulene—upon distillation, flavonoids (rutin, quercimertrin), coumarins, plants acids (valerianic), glycosides, polysaccharides, salicylate, tryptophan, amino acids.

RELATED SPECIES: Fragrant English lawns have been covered with the low-growing Roman chamomile *(Chamaemelum nobile,* previously *Anthemis nobilis)* since Elizabethan times. It shares many medicinal properties with German chamomile, but its bitter taste makes it less popular, although a somewhat better digestive aid. Distilled, the resulting yellow oil contains almost no chamazulene.

HISTORY: The Greeks, inspired by chamomile's distinct apple-like fragrance, named it *kamai* ("ground") *melon* ("apple"), and the Spanish call it *manzanilla,* or "little apple." The ancient Egyptians dedicated it to their sun god and used it in their aromatherapy practice. They also rubbed it on sore muscles. Chamomile's legacy lives on, as children throughout the world hear how Peter Rabbit's mother gave him chamomile tea to calm him down after a tense night of eating Mr. McGregor's garden.

MEDICINAL: Chamomile flowers help to soothe indigestion, nervousness, depression, and headaches. It has also been recommended for hundreds of years to ease nerves and muscle pain, sciatica, and menstrual cramps. One clinical study noted that 10 out of 12 patients who drank chamomile tea instead of their regular pain medication went into a deep sleep within 10 minutes, even while undergoing a painful procedure.[1] It is ideal for emotion-related digestive problems such as peptic ulcers, colitis, spastic colon, colic, and plain old nervous indigestion. In testing its product Kamillosan®, the Chemiewerke Hamburg Pharmacy of West Germany found that chamomile reduces gastric acid and actually helps prevent ulcers. It also promoted tissue regeneration after patients

Matricaria recutita
CHAMOMILE

© Derek Fell

Matricaria recutita. **German chamomile flowers provide a tasty tea enjoyed by people all over the world as a beverage and medicine.**

had operations on their intestinal, urinary, and genital systems.[2] Chamomile decreases histamine, implicated in ulcers and the skin swelling, puffy eyes, and headaches brought on by allergies.[3] It is given to children for digestive and hyperactive problems, to discourage nightmares, and to prevent the convulsions that sometimes accompany children's high fevers. It binds and inactivates bacteria, fungus, and toxins, including staph and candida, even in low quantities.[4] Historically, chamomile poultices have been placed on cancers, and its sesquiterpene lactones do show immune system–stimulating and antitumor activity.[5]

AROMATHERAPY: The fragrance is used in massage and bath oils for those who are emotionally oversensitive or depressed. Monks in the Middle Ages placed patients on raised garden beds covered with Roman chamomile, so the scent would lift them from depression and illness. Herbalist Nicholas Culpeper noted that "bathing with . . . chamomile taketh away weariness, easeth pains to what part of the body soever they be applied. It comforteth the sinews that are over-strained, mollieth all swellin . . . by a wonderful, speedy property."

COSMETIC: Chamazulene, a strong anti-inflammatory, is produced when the essential oil is steam-distilled. It is used in expensive cosmetics to reduce facial puffiness. Chamomile creams are used on dry, sensitive skin, enlarged capillaries, acne, and for skin allergies. Herbalist Jeanne Rose notes that, as a rinse, it brings out highlights in her dark hair. Two chamomile tea bags, steeped in hot water a couple of minutes, can be placed on the eyes to relieve strain.

CONSIDERATIONS: A study found the likelihood of acute allergy to chamomile quite low. Two out of 25 people already allergic to other plants in the Asteraceae family were found to be allergic to chamomile as well.[6]

OTHER: The old herbals call chamomile "the plant's physician" and say in "9 out of 10 cases," it will revive an ailing plant when planted nearby.

> *To comfort the braine smel to camomill, eate sage…wash measurably, sleep resonably, delight to heare melody and singing.*
> —*RAM'S LITTLE DODOEN,* **17TH-CENTURY HERBAL**

Melissa officinalis • Lemon Balm

FAMILY: Labiatae.

DESCRIPTION: Bushy, rounded herb. Height: 3 feet (90 cm). Width: 2 feet (60 cm). Flowers: Small, white, tube-shaped, 1/3 inch (8 mm) long. Leaves: Oval, coming to a point, serrated around the edges, and strongly lemon-scented, 1 to 3 inches (2.5 to 7.5 cm) long. Blooms: May to August.

HABITAT: Southern Europe, naturalized throughout Europe and the United States.

CULTIVATION: Perennial. Zone: 4. Germination: 7 to 14 days. Space: 2 feet (60 cm). Soil Temperature: 70° F (21° C). Soil: Fertile, moist, and very well drained—wet ground can kill it. pH: 4.5 to 7.5. Sun: Full sun or partial shade for lusher plants. Propagation: The thick root clumps can be divided with some effort, but it is easier to take cuttings or plant seeds. Lemon balm is a prolific self-sower. It is susceptible to frost so plant in a protected location and mulch before a hard frost in cool climates.

GARDEN DESIGN: Lemon balm is a cooperative herb. It doesn't spread by runners or fall on its neighbors, and it can be trimmed. Plant it where garden visitors will be sure to smell its leaves but won't be bothered by the flurry of bees it draws. The flowers are inconspicuous, but the yellow-green foliage is set off next to deep greens.

CONSTITUENTS: Essential oil (to 0.2%) includes citral, citronellol, eugenol, geraniol, polyphenols; flavonoids, triterpenoids.

RELATED SPECIES: Golden lemon balm (*Melissa officinalis* 'Golden,' 'Aurea,' or 'All Gold') has golden leaves and there is a variegated cultivar (*M. officinalis* 'Variegata').

HISTORY: Lemon balm has been cultivated in the Mediterranean region for about 2,000 years. The Muslim herbalist Avicenna recommended lemon balm "to make the heart merry." A definite bee attracting plant, it was *melisophyllon* (*melissa,* "bee," and *phyllon,* "leaf") to the Greeks and *apiastrum* (from *apias,* or "bee") to the Romans. Paracelsus claimed this herb could completely revitalize the body, and 14th-century French King Charles V drank its tea every day to keep his health, as did Llewelyn, Prince of Glamorgan, who lived to a ripe old 108. The famous Carmelite Water, first made by 17th-century Carmelite nuns to treat nervous headache and neuralgia, combined lemon balm with lemon-peel, nutmeg, coriander, and angelica root. It was sold for centuries as *Eau de Mélisse de Carmes.* Germany's *Pharmacopoeia* still recognizes a "Compound Spirit of Melissa," but it no longer contains any lemon balm. It has been replaced with citronella oil (*Cymbopogon nardus*), which is said to have a similar action and is much cheaper (although it has a harsher, lemonlike fragrance). The true Carmelite water is still sold in Germany as *Klosterfqu Melissengeist.*

CULINARY: Wine cups, teas, beer, medieval cordials, and Chartreuse and Benedictine liqueurs have all been flavored with lemon balm. It finds its way into soups, salad dressings, and sauces, especially lending a lemony taste to fish sauces. Lemon balm tea was so well enjoyed in France that the tea became known as *thé de France.* Much of the fragrance and flavor are lost in drying, so use fresh leaves whenever possible.

MEDICINAL: Lemon balm's main action is as a tranquilizer. It calms a nervous stomach, colic, or heart spasms. The leaves are reputed to also lower blood pressure. It is very gentle, although effective, so is often suggested for children and babies. It may be gentle, but lemon balm is also potent. The hot tea brings on a sweat that is good for relieving colds, flus, and fevers, and an antiviral agent has been found that combats mumps, cold sores (*Herpes simplex*), and other viruses.[1] The tea has also been shown to inhibit the division of tumor cells.[2] The sedative actions of the "Spirit of Melissa" have been successfully used to help treat a number of psychiatric problems, including dystonia, in which restlessness, excitability, and headaches were reduced.[3] Studies indicate that the herb slightly inhibits the thyroid-stimulating hormone and restricts Grave's disease, a hyperthyroid condition.[4] Lemon balm's antihistamine action is useful to treat eczema and headaches and accounts for the centuries-old tradition of placing the fresh leaf on insect bites and wounds.

AROMATHERAPY: Balm, or balsam, means "sweet-smelling oil." Aromatherapists say just sniffing the sweet fragrance of a lemon balm tea or bath reduces depression, nervousness, and insomnia. The essential oil is very expensive, so commercial oils usually distill lemon oil over lemon balm or use a citronella oil base. A preparation called *Oleum Melissae Indicum* is actually citronella oil.

OTHER: Lemon balm is used in potpourris. In the 16th century, it was rubbed on beehives to encourage the bees to create honey.

Melissa officinalis
LEMON BALM

Mentha x *piperita*
PEPPERMINT

Mentha spicata
SPEARMINT

Mentha x piperita • Peppermint
Hybrid cross between *M. aquatica* and *M. spicata* (spearmint)

FAMILY: Labiatae.

DESCRIPTION: Spreading, very fragrant herb. Height: 3 feet (90 cm). Width: 1 foot (30 cm). Flowers: Lilac pink, sterile, forming whorls on the top of the stems. Leaves: Often purple-tinged, oval, smooth, slightly serrated along the edge, pungent, to 2½ inches (6.25 cm) long, on square, red-purple stems. Blooms: June to November.

HABITAT: Naturalized throughout Europe and in parts of North America and Australia. The United States supplies about three-quarters of the world's peppermint, most of which is grown in Michigan and Oregon. Cultivated in Australia for its essential oil.

CULTIVATION: Perennial. Zone: 3. Germination: 10 to 20 days. Stratify 40 days. Space: 8 to 12 inches (20 to 30 cm). Soil Temperature: Most growth occurs when temperatures are under 85° F (29° C). Runners grow best at 70° F (21° C). Soil: Moist, can handle excessive wetness. pH: 7 to 8. Sun: Full sun or partial shade, even full shade, although this reduces its oil content. Propagation: By dividing roots or stolons (aboveground stems). Tests at the Thailand Institute for Science and Technology Research in Bangkok found that Japanese mint *(M. arvensis* var. *piperescens)* is most potent when flowering.

GARDEN DESIGN: If you have space, peppermint makes a wonderful, tall groundcover. Peppermint spreads so easily, you many need to curb it by planting it in a contained pot.

CONSTITUENTS: Essential oil (to 2%) is menthol (responsible for cool sensation); flavonoids; phytol; tocopherols; carotenoids, azulene; rosmarinic acid; vitamins A and C; minerals (calcium and potassium).

RELATED SPECIES: Starting with about 25 true species—mostly from Eurasia—mints have hybridized extensively! Eau de cologne mint, or orange mint *(M. x piperita* var. *citrata),* with a citrus odor, is commonly called bergamot, but is not the same as orange bergamot or bee balm *(Monarda didyma).* One of my favorites is the miniature groundcover Corsican mint *(M. requienii)* with its very small, ¼ inch (6 mm), round leaves and delightful minty scent. It needs 50% shade and must be mulched during the winter in zone 4 or colder.

HISTORY: A relative newcomer to herbalism, peppermint doesn't even enter into herbal history until 1696, when English botanist John Ray (1628–1705) published a brief description of a pepper-tasting mint he found in a field. He called it *Mentha palustris* in his 1704 *Historia Plantarum.* By 1721, it was listed in the *London Pharmacopeia* as a digestive aid and flavoring agent.

CULINARY: Although many of us don't think of mint as a culinary herb, according to food historian Waverly Root, it is the most widely used of all aromatic herbs. Peppermint's popular flavor appears in desserts, beverages, ice cream, liqueurs, sauces, confections, candies, and, of course, the various types of afterdinner mints that bear its name. Most peppermint essential oil goes to flavoring chewing gum, candy, and "mints."

MEDICINAL: The sparkling flavor of peppermint, from its essential oil, not only brews a tasty tea, it helps with indigestion. Every time you drink a cup of mint tea or pop an afterdinner mint in your mouth, you relax the muscles of the digestive tract.[1] If peppermint is taken before eating, hunger pangs subside briefly, but then return with even more force, increasing the appetite. Studies show it relieves colon spasms.[2] It has also been found to be a specific remedy for irritable bowel syndrome.[3] The constituent azulene decreases inflammation and helps to heal ulcers.[4] Peppermint also eases nervous headaches,[5] including migraines. Menthol, peppermint's main constituent, helps kill any bacteria, parasites, or viruses lurking in the stomach, and balances intestinal flora.[6] It also destroys fungus infections, including ringworm and herpes simplex.

AROMATHERAPY: Aromatherapists use peppermint's scent to increase concentration, to simulate mind and body, and to stay awake. The British Medical Journal *Lancet* first drew attention to menthol in 1879 for relieving headaches and neuralgia. After that, menthol cones that evaporated into the air and scented candles to relieve sinus and lung congestion became popular. The steam from a strong tea or a drop of essential oil in a steaming pan of water can likewise be inhaled. Externally, the essential oil is used in balms and liniments as a combination cooling and heating agent that stimulates both hot and cold nerve endings and increases blood flow to the area.

OTHER: Dental products are often flavored with peppermint. Some brands of tobacco also incorporate it.

> *Mint falsifies its much-exalted fame,*
> *Unless it quick relieves, and can reclaim*
> *Our bowels from a strange and faulty state,*
> *Disposing them at times to verminate.*
> —"OF MINT," *REGIMEN SANITATIS SALERNI,* 10TH-CENTURY ITALY

Mentha suaveolens varigata. **The varieties of mint can seem almost endless. This pineapple mint offers an interesting variation on mint's popular taste.**

Mentha pulegium • Pennyroyal

FAMILY: Labiatae.

DESCRIPTION: Tall groundcover. Height: 1 foot (30 cm). Width: 1 foot (30 cm). Flowers: Pale purple, grouped in whorls on upper top of short flowering stalks. Leaves: Dark green, slightly hairy, oval, to 1 inch (2.5 cm). Blooms: July to August.

HABITAT: Native to Europe and western Asia and possibly northern Africa. Naturalized in southern Australia.

CULTIVATION: Perennial. Zone: 5 to 6. Germination: 10 to 14 days. Space: 8 to 12 inches (20 to 30 cm). Soil Temperature: 50° to 70° F (13° to 21° C). Soil: Well drained, slightly rich, sandy, prefers moisture. pH: 5.5 to 8. Sun: Full sun or partial shade. Propagation: By seed, cuttings, or root division. Pennyroyal spreads rapidly, and once established, clumps can be divided.

GARDEN DESIGN: Pennyroyal makes a fragrant groundcover. It grows well along and into pathways, where it will release a delightful fragrance. In a small garden, plant it inside a hollow brick or a pot to restrict the runners.

CONSTITUENTS: Essential oil (.5% to 1%) includes pulegone (80% to 90%).

RELATED SPECIES: Prostrate pennyroyal *(M. pulegium* var. *decumbens)* is a low-growing, aromatic groundcover used for English lawns, especially under trees where grass has a difficult time growing. It can be mowed and, although it won't tolerate constant traffic, it can be walked on. American pennyroyal *(Hedeoma pulegiodes)* has a similar aroma, chemistry (but with 2% essential oil), and use.

HISTORY: Pennyroyal is thought to be the *kykeōn* herb used during the Greek Eleusinian mysteries. In the Middle Ages, it was dubbed *puliol royale,* or "royal thyme," since it was thought to be related to thyme. Later, it was designated a mint, with the French calling it *la menthe pouliot.* Gerard said that pennyroyal was so antiseptic, it would purify bad water. It was so highly regarded by Europeans, it was one of the first herbs brought to America by the pilgrims.

CULINARY: Pennyroyal is rarely used today as a culinary herb, but one of its popular names is "pudding grass." This actually refers to a famous stuffing, not pudding, that was made with pennyroyal, pepper, and honey.

MEDICINAL: Probably pennyroyal's most famous role is as an insect repellent. The crushed leaves or essential oil are rubbed on insect bites to reduce their itch and to ward off future attacks. The vinegar can be put on bruises, burns, and skin marks, as suggested by the 17th-century herbalist Culpeper. Pennyroyal has also been taken to relieve headaches, indigestion, congestion from colds, and menstrual pain. Hot pennyroyal tea is one of the best herbs to produce sweating and reduce a fever.

AROMATHERAPY: One remedy for a nervous headache or hysteria was to dab pennyroyal waters on the forehead. Gerard, in the 16th century, recommended that a "garland of penny-royale made and worn about the head is of great force against the swimming in the head and the pains . . . ." Centuries before him, Romans wore *pulegium* wreaths, hoping to dispel drunkenness. The name actually comes from *pulex,* or "flea," since the smell of both the fresh plant and the smoke from burning leaves were used as a flea repellent. As far as insect "aromatherapy" is concerned, the pennyroyal is a fairly good insect repellent, providing you use it liberally.

Mentha pulegium
PENNYROYAL

CONSIDERATIONS: Occasionally, pennyroyal causes contact skin rashes. Large amounts of the herb can be irritating to the genitourinary tract. Even small quantities should not be used by those with kidney disease or by pregnant women. Pennyroyal got a bad reputation in 1978 when a woman died from an overdose (2 tablespoons, or 30 ml) of the essential oil while trying to encourage an abortion.[1] The FDA declared that not only the essential oil, but the herb itself must be declared "for external use only." The oil is a highly concentrated form of the herb, and according to Dr. Norman Farnsworth of the University of Illinois in Chicago, the effect of 2 tablespoons (1 ounce, or 30 ml) of pennyroyal oil equals roughly 75 gallons (285 l) of strong tea! He also notes that 1 ounce of almost any essential oil taken internally could be fatal.

OTHER: Pennyroyal is a dye plant, and small amounts are occasionally used in potpourri.

Mentha spicata • Spearmint
(Previously *M. viridis, M. longifolia, M. niliaca*)

FAMILY: Labiatae.

DESCRIPTION: Height: 2½ feet (75 cm). Width: 1 foot (30 cm). Flowers: Tiny, white, clustered in spikes. Leaves: Bright green, textured, intense aroma when crushed, oval, coming to a point, slightly hairy and toothed, to 2 inches (5 cm) long. Blooms: June to September.

HABITAT: Possibly native to southern Europe, but widely naturalized in Europe and Australia.

CULTIVATION: Perennial. Zone: 4. Germination: 2 weeks. Space: 1 foot (30 cm). Soil Temperature: 70° F (21° C). Soil: Moist. pH: 7 to 8. Sun: Full sun or partial shade. Propagation: By seed, but does not necessarily come true from seed. Also by root division, cuttings, or replanting the stolons (aboveground stems that sprout). Plants need some dormant period for best growth so take houseplants outside in the winter for at least 2 months before bringing back in to resprout.

GARDEN DESIGN: Well suited for damp areas of the garden. Be sure to place it in a container or a contained bed so it doesn't take over.

CONSTITUENTS: Essential oil includes carvone (50% to 70%), flavonoids (diosmin, diosmetin).

RELATED SPECIES: Curly spearmints *(M. spicata* var. 'Crispi' and 'Crispata') have extra crinkly leaves. A wild mint *(M. arvensis)* is found in New England.

HISTORY: The most likely parent of peppermint, spearmint is thought to be the oldest of all mints. It is probably the mint mentioned in the Bible (Matthew 23:23, Luke 11:42). Romans distinguished between the cultivated *mentha* and the wild *mentastratum,* liberally adding both to their cooking. Arabs were also fond of mint, calling it *tudanaj.* Throughout the ancient world, it was much used to keep milk from curdling. In the 16th century, it became *spere mynte,* to describe the spear-shaped flowers that distinguish it from many other mints.

CULINARY: Spearmint leaves are found in sauces, jellies, and hot and iced teas. They garnish cold drinks and flavor candy.

MEDICINAL: Spearmint leaves improve digestion and reduce muscle spasms, especially in the digestive tract. Spearmint is still listed in the *Hungarian Pharmacopoeia* as a medicine.

AROMATHERAPY: Similar to peppermint, but with a lighter action, the fragrance is energizing.

HOT MINT SAUCE

This recipe comes from *De Re Conquinaria* by Apicius and dates from the 1st century A.D.

- ½ **teaspoon (2.5 ml) celery seed (or lovage)**
- ⅛ **teaspoon (.6 ml) cumin**
- 3 **sprigs fresh mint or 1 tablespoon (15 ml) dried mint**
- ¼ **teaspoon (1.25 ml) oregano**
  Pinch thyme
  Pinch fennel seed
  Dash ground pepper
- ¼ **cup (60 ml) red wine**
- ⅛ **cup (30 ml) plums, finely chopped**
- 2 **tablespoons (30 ml) honey**
- ½ **cup (120 ml) vinegar**
  Olive oil

Grind herbs and spices together. Moisten with a little red wine. Blend with plums, honey, vinegar, and a few drops of olive oil. Bring to a boil, then simmer for 25 minutes.

Spearmint gets its name from the spear-like form of its flower.

Mitchella repens
Partridge Berry

Mitchella repens • Partridge Berry

FAMILY: Rubiaccae.

DESCRIPTION: Small, trailing vine. Height: 4 inches (10 cm). Width: 4 inches (10 cm). Flowers: Pale pink, an elongated tube, to ¹/₂ inch (1.25 cm) long, with hairs inside. Leaves: Small, roundish ovals, to ³/₄ inch (1.88 cm) long, dark green, shiny on top, often with fine, white lines. Remains green throughout the winter. Fruit: Double, red berry, to ³/₈ inch (.93 cm) diameter, edible. There is a form with white berries. Blooms: June to July.

HABITAT: Canada, through the midwestern United States, to Florida and into east Texas.

CULTIVATION: Perennial. Zone: 4. Germination: 2 to 3 weeks. Space: 6 to 10 inches (15 to 25 cm). Soil Temperature: 60° to 65° F (15° to 18° C). Soil: Humus, rich, cool, moist preferred, but dry tolerated. Likes pine needle mulch. pH: 4 to 6. Sun: Shade. Propagation: It is easiest to propagate by separating the trailing, fragile roots at the nodes. A terrarium favorite, it grows at 60° F (15° C) or less in the spring.

GARDEN DESIGN: A good herb to place in raised beds or pots so its delicate beauty can be appreciated. Often cultivated as a ground cover under the shade of trees.

CONSTITUENTS: Glycosides, alkaloids, tannins, mucilage.

HISTORY: Partridge berry is also called two-eyed berry and twin berry. It was one of the herbs, or "kinnikinnik," smoked by the Native Americans.

CULINARY: The Indians ate the berries and dined on a medicinal jelly when experiencing fever.

MEDICINAL: Partridge berry has been used to promote easy labor and prevent miscarriage. It is often combined with red raspberry leaf in women's tonic formulas. A well-known early 20th-century preparation, called Mother's Cordial, combined it with cramp bark *(Viburnum opulus),* blue cohosh *(Caulophyllum thalictroides),* unicorn root *(Chamaelirium luteum),* sassafras *(Sassafras albidum)* oil, brandy, and sugar. Partridge berry appeared in the U.S. National Formulary from 1926 to 1947 for treating uterine problems. It improves digestion and calms the nervous system. At times, it has been substituted for pipsissewa *(Chimaphila* spp.*)* as a treatment for urinary tract infections.

Monarda didyma
BERGAMOT

Monarda didyma • Bergamot
(Previously *M. coccinea*)

FAMILY: Labiatae.

DESCRIPTION: A bushy herb with many stiff, grooved stems. Height: 4 feet (1.2 m). Width: 2 feet (60 cm). Flowers: Scarlet, about 1¹/₂ inches (3.75 cm) long, in whorled heads like tasseled pompoms. Leaves: Rough, thin, oval with a sharp tip, and toothed edges tinged with red. About 3 inches (7.5 cm) long, growing opposite each other, aromatic. Blooms: July to September.

HABITAT: Bergamot grows wild in the eastern United States.

CULTIVATION: Perennial. Zone: 4. Germination: 15 to 20 days. Space: 12 to 15 inches (30 to 37.5 cm). Soil Temperature: 60° to 75° F (15° to 24° C). Soil: Well drained, light, moist. Will wilt with too much dry heat. pH: 5 to 7. Sun: Full sun or light shade. Propagation: Bergamot will easily spread itself around your garden by runners and seed once established, so weed it out to keep it controlled. Pinch back the tops if you want to encourage a bushier shrub. May flower the first year. Remove old flowers to extend the blooming. After a few years, the center dies out and will need replanting.

GARDEN DESIGN: This is the most popular of 17 species that are well adapted to being naturalized by streams and ponds or anywhere in a wild garden. For more formal groupings, combine different colored blooms together for a mass of summer color. It is a primary herb in a hummingbird garden.

CONSTITUENTS: Essential oil includes thymol, tannic acid.

RELATED SPECIES: Other species grow throughout the United States in an assortment of flower colors, such as the lavender-flowering *M. fistulosa.* I especially enjoy lemon bee balm *(M. citriodora)* from the Appalachian mountains. In the southwest, the smell and taste of "wild oregano" *(M. fistulosa* var. *'Menthifolia')* so closely resembles true oregano, it is sold for seasoning.

HISTORY: The genus *Monarda* was named in honor of the Spanish physician Nicholas Monardes, who wrote about it in his *American Flora,* published in 1571. Europe first became acquainted with wild bergamot in 1630 through the writings of John Tradescent the Younger (the "Elder" was Charles I's head gardener). It is the namesake of another bergamot, a member of the citrus family from Bergamo, Italy, that is used in perfumery. The unrelated plants share a citrus fragrance reminiscent of orange. Bergamot has also been called Oswego tea ever since John Bartram, a Quaker botanist from Philadelphia, encountered it at Fort Oswego, New York. The leaves became a popular Colonial tea, especially when the Boston Tea Party in 1773 forced the colonists to substitute native herbs for black tea—which probably resulted in the healthiest period in the colonies' history! It is also referred to as horsemint.

CULINARY: Try blending the leaves with mints and a touch of orange peel to bring out the citruslike flavor in tea. Native Americans used it as a food flavoring. The florets can also be added to an edible salad or become cake decorations.

MEDICINAL: Native Americans used the leaves of various *Monardas* as a poultice and compress on skin eruptions, as a tea for colds and flus, and inhaled as a steam, to relieve sinus and lung congestion. Scientific evidence shows that bergamot may inhibit the herpes simplex and the related chicken pox viruses. It is also combined with other herbs to treat urinary tract infections and indigestion.

Nepeta cataria • Catnip

FAMILY: Labiatae.

DESCRIPTION: Tall, erect bush with stiff, square stems. Height: 3 to 4 feet (.9 to 1.2 m). Width: 2 feet (60 cm). Flowers: Small, 1/2 inch (1.25 cm) long, whitish to blue with small reddish dots, in dense, prickly whorls that almost form a spike. Leaves: Downy gray, soft, heart-shaped, and toothed around the edges with white undersides, 1 to 2 inches (2.5 to 5 cm) long. Blooms: July to September.

HABITAT: Native of Europe, but naturalized throughout the temperate zone in rocky, open areas.

CULTIVATION: Perennial. Zone: 3 to 4. Germination: 7 to 10 days. Space: 14 to 18 inches (35 to 45 cm). Soil Temperature: 60° to 70° F (15° to 21° C). Soil: Well drained, but will grow in clay if well fed. More lush with consistent watering, but tolerates drought. pH: 5 to 7.5. Sun: Full sun best, but adjusts to shade, although will be less fragrant. Propagation: Seed, cuttings of soft stems, or root division. Once established, it freely self-seeds in amazing profusion. If your cats have adventure in their eyes, you may need to protect young seedlings under chicken wire cages until they are large enough so that the cats can't roll on them.

GARDEN DESIGN: Catnip makes a tall border than can be shaped somewhat by pruning back new growth. It blends nicely with blue flowering plants that pick up the blue-gray leaves. It looks good growing with more showy plants of similar stature that have deeper-colored leaves, such as anise hyssop and bergamot.

CONSTITUENTS: Essential oil (to 0.3%) includes nepetalactone (to 42%), nepetol, carvacrol, thymol, citronellol, geraniol, pulegone; iridoids.

RELATED SPECIES: *N. cataria* var. 'citriodora' has distinctly lemon-scented foliage and is slightly less hardy. Ground ivy *(N. glechoma,* now called *Glechoma hederacea)* is often used as a landscaping groundcover. Persian or Kashmir catnip sterile hybrid *(N. x Faassenii)* with low-growing gray foliage and purple blossoms is well suited to a rock garden or dangling from a hanging pot, safe from the reach of cats. Named after the Dutch nurseryman, Faassen, who hybridized it, it is mistakenly called *N. mussinii,* which is really its less glamorous parent.

HISTORY: The name *Nepeta* originates from the city of Nepi (called Nepete by the Etruscans) where one species grows in great profusion. For a time, the French considered catnip a culinary seasoning, but its pungency has mostly been restricted to medicine and for the pleasure of cats. The leaves reflect such a pale, soft color, the English developed their familiar expression, "as white as a nep."

MEDICINAL: Catnip leaves reduce a fever by increasing body heat and stimulating perspiration. A catnip tea is useful for many children's ailments, including measles, chicken pox, colic, fevers, indigestion, hives, nervousness, headaches, insomnia, and hyperactivity. For adults, it is mildly relaxant and digestive. The nepetalactone it contains is similar in structure to the valepotriates found in the well-known sedative, valerian.[1] Small dosages stop diarrhea. It is also an ingredient in enema formulas.

AROMATHERAPY: Catnip's name is a tribute to its well-known reputation for attracting cats, who will play for hours with cloth balls filled with dried catnip and will roll on garden plants. There is an old saying, "If you set it, the cats will eat it/If you sow it, the cats won't know it," referring to the aroma emitted by the cuttings. While it attracts cats, rats are repelled by the smell. As for insect aromatherapy, studies at Cornell University in New York State found that catnip vapors (due to the nepetalactone) also repel insects.

Nepeta cataria. **Catnip is a well-known herb to most people —and most cats. In the summer, the tops of the bushes are covered with spires of flowers that can be dried for herbal wreaths.**

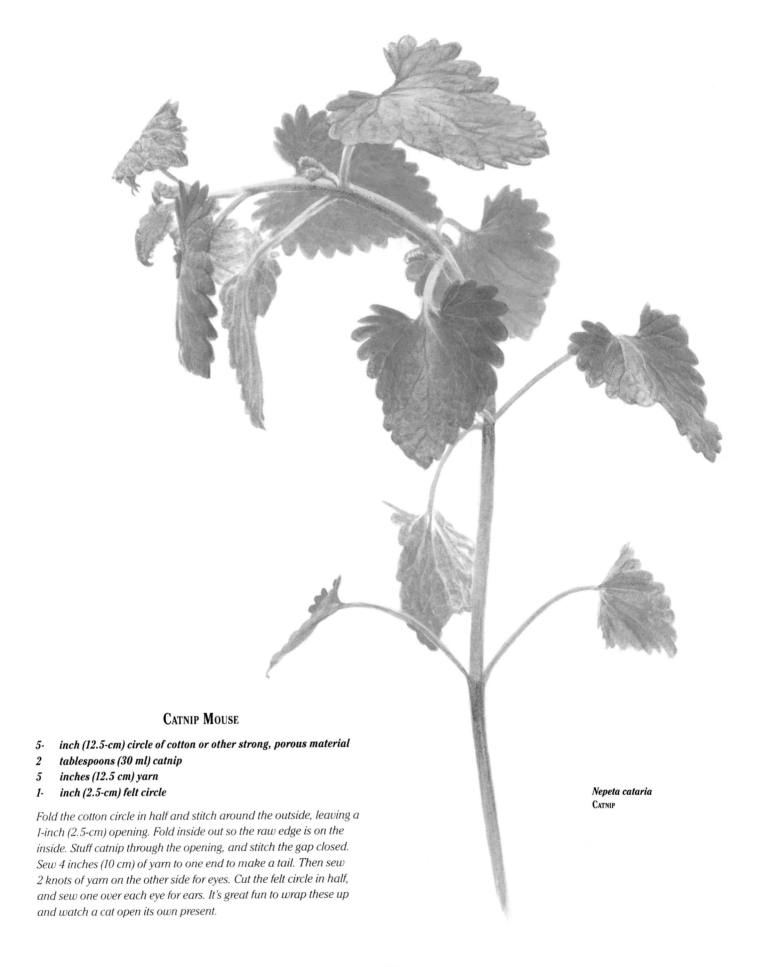

Nepeta cataria
CATNIP

CATNIP MOUSE

5- **inch (12.5-cm) circle of cotton or other strong, porous material**
2 **tablespoons (30 ml) catnip**
5 **inches (12.5 cm) yarn**
1- **inch (2.5-cm) felt circle**

Fold the cotton circle in half and stitch around the outside, leaving a 1-inch (2.5-cm) opening. Fold inside out so the raw edge is on the inside. Stuff catnip through the opening, and stitch the gap closed. Sew 4 inches (10 cm) of yarn to one end to make a tail. Then sew 2 knots of yarn on the other side for eyes. Cut the felt circle in half, and sew one over each eye for ears. It's great fun to wrap these up and watch a cat open its own present.

Ocimum basilicum • Sweet Basil
(Previously O. bullatum)

FAMILY: Labiatae.

DESCRIPTION: Small, rounded, bushy herb. Height: 2 feet (60 cm). Width: 1 foot (30 cm). Flowers: Small, white that whorl around the top of the stalk. Leaves: Flexible, fleshy, smooth, oval. Bright, yellow-green, about 2 inches (5 cm) long. Blooms: July to August.

HABITAT: Native to India, but cultivated in the Mediterranean for thousands of years. Produced commercially in France, Hungary, Bulgaria, Yugoslavia, Italy, and Morocco. A superior-quality plant comes from California.

CULTIVATION: Annual. Germination: 6 to 10 days. Space: 10 to 15 inches (25 to 37.5 cm). Soil Temperature: 70° F (21° C). Soil: Dry, medium rich, well drained. pH: 5 to 8. Sun: Full sun or partial shade, but plants will get "leggy" and spindly. Propagation: Plant seeds indoors 5 weeks before last frost. Don't set them out too soon since basil is subject to frost. Be careful with overhead watering followed by direct sun, which can produce water spots. Cutting back the blossoms and uppermost leaves will keep basil bushy and provide a succession of crops throughout the summer.

GARDEN DESIGN: Basil's bright leaves contrast nicely with any low-growing herbs. It grows quickly to fill empty spots or provide a low border along the edge of a path. If you don't have a garden, grow potted basil on the porch or windowsill like the Italians and Greeks. (A practice reputed in Italy and Morocco to repel flies and mosquitoes, but to also attract lovers!) It thrives indoors, provided it has adequate light.

CONSTITUENTS: Essential oil (1%) includes estagole (to 70%), eugenol, camphor, methyl cinnamate, others depending on species.

RELATED SPECIES: There are approximately 150 species of basil. Bush basil (O. 'minimum'), a compact, short version, is perfect for small spaces. Other favorites are lemon-scented basil (O. basilicum cv. 'Citriodorum') brought to the United States from Thailand by the Department of Agriculture in 1940, and holy basil, or tulsi (O. sanctum), used in Hindu religious ceremonies. Purple basil (O. basilicum cv. 'Purpurascens'), developed at the University of Connecticut in the 1930s, is the least hardy but makes a beautiful purple-colored basil vinegar. Eleven basils are described in The Cultivated Basils by Helen H. Darah (1980).

HISTORY: The ancient Egyptians burned a mixture of basil and myrrh to appease their gods, and embalmed their dead with it. The Greek physician and botanist Chrysippos declared it his favorite seasoning in 400 B.C. In Greece, it became a sign of mourning, but signified love for the Romans, and today an Italian suitor can still proclaim his serious intentions by wearing a basil sprig in his hair. The French were introduced to it by Catherine de Medici in 1533 when she married their King Henry II and brought with her Italian chefs and a taste for food well seasoned with basil. They dubbed it Herbe Royale. Dried basil provided a 16th-century snuff for relieving headaches and head colds.

CULINARY: Basileus means "royal," and indeed, many a cook regards basil as the royalty among culinary herbs. One of the herbs in the bouquet garni, the leaves accent any tomato dish, make delicious herbal vinegar, and are essential in making pesto and Soupe au Pistou, one of the most famous dishes from Provence, France. Italians serve fresh basil at the table set in a small vase of water to keep the cut leaves from darkening.

MEDICINAL: The leaves of basil are used to relieve indigestion and nausea, and are effective even when these are side effects from chemotherapy. They are considered a gentle sedative for mild disorders. Studies on patients at the King George Medical College, in India, have found that the closely related holy basil (O. sanctum) prevents peptic ulcers and other stress-related diseases like hypertension, colitis, and asthma.[1] In Japan, India, and western Africa, various species are used to treat colds and flus to reduce fever, congestion, and joint pain. Recognizing its bacteria- and fungus-fighting properties, East India's Ayurvedic medicine places basil poultices on itching skin, ringworm, and acne, as well as poisonous insect bites. Backing up the traditional use, one study in India showed that basil effectively cleared up acne.[2]

AROMATHERAPY: Ocymum is probably derived from the Greek "to smell," since simply sniffing the herb was said to rid one of a headache and more. According to herbalist Gerard, "The smell of basil is good for the heart...it taketh away sorrowfulness, which cometh of melancholy and maketh a man merry and glad." At one time, basil was made into a sweetly scented washing water for the face and hands. The fragrance is still used in soaps and other cosmetics, offering a less expensive perfume substitute for mignonette. Aromatherapists massage oils scented with basil into overworked muscles and use the fragrance to decrease mental fatigue and to clear the head. Basil also helps to restore the sense of smell lost from sinus congestion.

BASIL PESTO

Refrigerated, this pesto will last for months. Individual portions can also be frozen in ice-cube trays for long-term storage. Add a tablespoon or more to pasta, potatoes, or soup or spread on bread instead of butter or mayonnaise in sandwiches.

1 1/2 cups (360 ml) fresh basil leaves
2 cloves garlic
1/4 cup (60 ml) pine nuts or walnuts
3/4 cup (180 ml) Parmesan cheese, grated
3/4 cup olive oil

Chop the basil in blender. Add the nuts and garlic and blend into a puree, then add the cheese. Slowly add most of the olive oil until the consistency of creamed butter. Pack into a container, removing air pockets, and pour the remaining 2 tablespoons (30 ml) of oil on top to keep from darkening.

DRIED BASIL TOMATOES

1 pound (500 g) tomatoes
1 teaspoon (5 ml) salt
1 tablespoon (15 ml) basil

Choose firm tomatoes (a pear-shaped variety such as Roma, for example) with less juice but a sweeter taste. Cut tomatoes into slices about 1/2 inch thick. Sprinkle with salt and basil. Place in an oven preheated to 160° F (71° C) about 9 hours or in a 125° F (51.6° C) dehydrator for 18 to 24 hours. Or do it Italian style and lay it out on drying racks in direct sun.

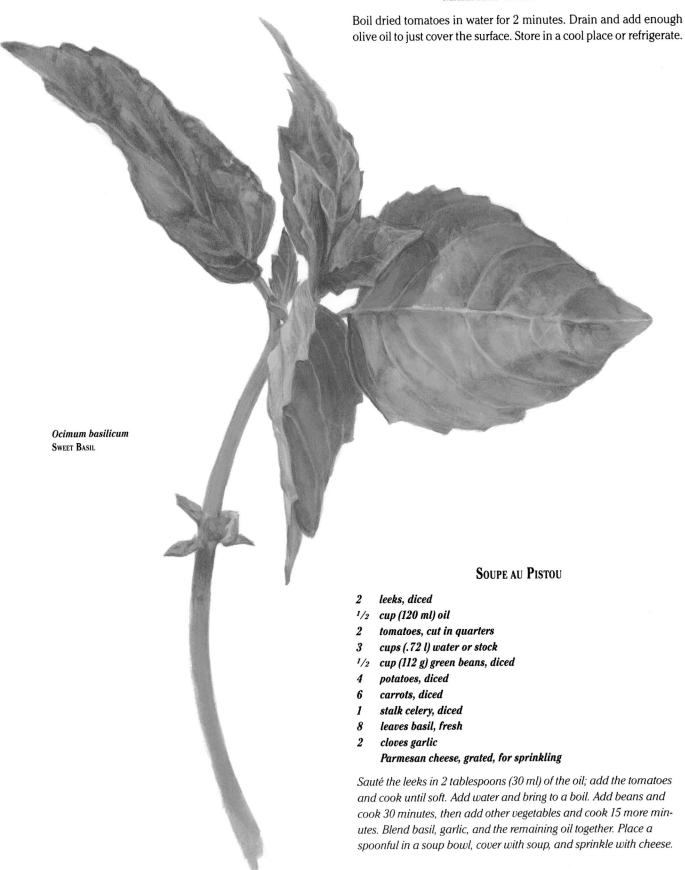

Ocimum basilicum
SWEET BASIL

MARINATED DRIED TOMATOES

Boil dried tomatoes in water for 2 minutes. Drain and add enough olive oil to just cover the surface. Store in a cool place or refrigerate.

SOUPE AU PISTOU

2	leeks, diced
$^1/_2$	cup (120 ml) oil
2	tomatoes, cut in quarters
3	cups (.72 l) water or stock
$^1/_2$	cup (112 g) green beans, diced
4	potatoes, diced
6	carrots, diced
1	stalk celery, diced
8	leaves basil, fresh
2	cloves garlic
	Parmesan cheese, grated, for sprinkling

Sauté the leeks in 2 tablespoons (30 ml) of the oil; add the tomatoes and cook until soft. Add water and bring to a boil. Add beans and cook 30 minutes, then add other vegetables and cook 15 more minutes. Blend basil, garlic, and the remaining oil together. Place a spoonful in a soup bowl, cover with soup, and sprinkle with cheese.

Oenothera biennis
EVENING PRIMROSE

Oenothera biennis • Evening Primrose
(Previously *O. muricata*)

FAMILY: Onagraceae.

DESCRIPTION: Mostly identified by its tall and dramatic flowering stalk. Height: To 6 feet (1.8 m). Width: 1½ feet (45 cm). Flowers: Fragrant, 4 yellow petals, 1 inch (2.5 cm) long, that stand out at a right angle from the plant. Flowers are grouped in bunches. Leaves: 3 to 6 inches (7.5 to 15 cm) long, soft, coming to points. Fruit: Elongated capsules filled with small black seeds containing the oil. Blooms: June to September. As its name implies, the flowers open in the evening.

HABITAT: Native to eastern North America, naturalized in Europe and Australia, mostly in wastelands, on dry, sandy, stony slopes.

CULTIVATION: Biennial, or annual in some climates. Zone: 4. Germination: 15 to 20 days. Space: 8 to 12 inches (20 to 30 cm). Soil Temperature: 70° to 85° F (21° to 29° C). Soil: Well-drained garden soil, can be dry. pH: 6 to 8. Sun: Full sun or light shade. Propagation: Plant directly into garden when possible. Reseeds easily.

GARDEN DESIGN: Evening primrose is often placed along flower borders. Since the flowers open in the evening, be sure to place it where it will be appreciated by evening strollers. It is a suitable addition to a theme moon garden containing night-flowering plants or to the flower garden.

CONSTITUENTS: Unsaturated fatty acids, including GLA.

HISTORY: Evening primrose arrived in Europe in 1619 and was planted in the Padua Botanic Gardens of Italy. The botanical name comes from *oinos*, since other members of this genus were used by the Greeks to flavor wine. It was not often used in folk medicine, and it only achieved medical acclaim in the 1980s, probably because the concentrated oil was not available until then.

CULINARY: The entire evening primrose plant is edible. The roots were eaten in Europe, and in the 19th century, either pickled or boiled as vegetables. The young shoots can be added to salads.

MEDICINAL: GLA, a constituent acid, is responsible for many of the herb's properties. It is an anticoagulant that is thought to reduce high blood pressure, prevent heart attacks, and guard against coronary artery disease. When a 1981 clinical study at the St. Thomas Hospital in London gave evening primrose oil to 65 women with premenstrual syndrome, 61% of the participants found their symptoms completely disappeared and another 23% felt partial relief. Those who suffered from sore breasts noted the most improvement.[1] There was noticeable improvement in the skin conditions of 99 people with eczema when they were treated with evening primrose oil in a double-blind study.[2] In another study, the oil was found to improve dry and brittle nails and, combined with zinc treatments, it helped acne and dry eyes, as well as nails.[3] In 1987, the Glasgow Royal Infirmary of Scotland saw improvement in 60% of its rheumatoid arthritis patients who took a combination of evening primrose and fish oil instead of their regular drugs. A study by the Highland Psychiatric Research Group at the Craig Dunain Hospital, Inverness, Scotland, found that evening primrose encouraged regeneration of liver cells damaged by alcohol consumption. Researcher Brian Leonard, from the University College in Galway, Ireland, thinks it may also prevent alcoholic poisoning, hangovers, postdrinking depression, and alcohol withdrawal. It is thought to stop alcohol from damaging brain cells by bolstering them with unsaturated fats. Professor Field, former director of multiple sclerosis research for the U.K. Medical Research Council, thinks it might also help multiple sclerosis patients. A New York City hospital found that more than 10% of overweight people tested with evening primrose oil lost weight. In still another study, two-thirds of hyperactive children studied responded favorably to the oil. More studies are reported in the booklets *Evening Primrose Oil* by J. Graham (Thorsons, 1984) and *Evening Primrose Oil Bibliography* by Christina Toplack (Efamol Research Institute, 1986).

CONSIDERATIONS: Headaches, skin rashes, and nausea have occasionally been reported. Not suggested for epileptics.

Origanum majorana • Marjoram
(Previously *Majorana hortensis*)

FAMILY: Labiatae.

DESCRIPTION: Small, bushy herb. Height: 2 feet (60 cm). Width: 1 foot (30 cm). Flowers: Small, white, sometimes pinkish, in tight, compact, $1/2$ inch (1.25 cm) spikes. Leaves: Oval, dusty green, to 1 inch (2.5 cm) long, very aromatic when crushed. Blooms: June to August.

HABITAT: Asia, naturalized in southern Europe. Cultivated commercially in Asia, central Europe, the Mediterranean, and some areas in the United States.

CULTIVATION: Perennial. Zone: 8 to 10. Germination: 1 to 2 weeks. Space: 1 foot (30 cm). Soil Temperature: 70° F (21° C). Soil: well drained, dry. pH: 7 to 8. Sun: Full sun. Propagation: By seed, which is tricky, or by cuttings or root division. Marjoram germinates easily, but the young plants are fragile, subject to damping-off disease and being knocked over by forceful watering. Often cultivated as an annual, although I've had mature true marjoram plants survive under snow when the ground didn't freeze and they were well mulched. When cut way back, it can winter indoors or grow in a pot all year.

GARDEN DESIGN: A good placement for marjoram is near the edge of a bed or terrace where its soft form will be noticed and the leaves can be easily pinched to release its scent, since it doesn't automatically perfume the air like many culinary herbs. It makes an attractive hanging basket on a porch or in a sunny location in the house.

CONSTITUENTS: Essential oil (to 2%) includes terpenes; cis- and trans-sabinese hydrate creates unique fragrance and taste, flavonoids.

RELATED SPECIES: The hardier pot marjoram *(O. onites)*, from southeast Europe and Turkey, is grown as a marjoram substitute, although its flavor is coarser and it is less aromatic. Marjoram was previously placed in its own genus before it joined the ranks of oregano. In fact, there exists much confusion in the genus, and pot marjoram or oregano itself is often sold as marjoram. Hardy sweet marjoram *(O. majorana* x *marjoricum)* is a recent sturdy hybrid.

HISTORY: In the ancient civilization of Crete (to 1600 B.C.), marjoram was a badge of honor worn by the most distinguished leaders, according to Greek physician-historian Galen (200 to 130 B.C.). The ancient Greeks used marjoram as a seasoning and a tea, placed pain-relieving fomentations on their bodies, and coated their hair and eyebrows with a pomade. The Romans, as well as the Greeks, crowned

Origanum majorana
MARJORAM

bridal couples with head wreaths of *amaracum* (marjoram) to symbolize love, honor, and happiness. (Perhaps Hippocrates's 4th-century B.C. recommendation of marjoram as an aphrodisiac was a factor.) The "hyssop" of the Bible is thought by some scholars to really have been marjoram, perhaps *M. syriaca*, which is found growing on Gebel Musa (Mt. Moses), thought to be the original Mt. Sinai. Medieval Europeans used marjoram both as antidote to narcotic poisons and convulsions and a seasoning for sweet porridge, puddings, and cakes. In the 16th century, it perfumed "swete bags and powders" for sachets, linens, and the bare floors in houses.

CULINARY: According to gourmet historian Waverly Root, modern Greeks, Italians, and North Africans prefer oregano, while the French and English seem partial to marjoram, although he admits there are exceptions. Marjoram often accompanies oregano, but has a sweeter taste and stands well on its own or mixed with other herbs in tomato, cheese, and bean dishes. It is an ingredient in bouquet garni. In Shakespeare's time, it was eaten in salads.

> *Indeed, sir, she was the*
> *sweet marjoram of the sallet,*
> *or, rather, the herb of grace.*
> —*ALL'S WELL THAT ENDS WELL,* **WILLIAM SHAKESPEARE (1564–1616), ENGLISH**

MEDICINAL: Marjoram tea is an age-old remedy to aid digestion, increase sweating (to reduce fevers or colds), and encourage menstruation. In laboratory tests, it inhibits viruses such as herpes 1[1] and is an antioxidant that helps preserve foods containing it.[2] As a steam inhalant, marjoram clears the sinuses and helps relieve laryngitis. European singers preserve their voices with marjoram tea sweetened with honey.

AROMATHERAPY: The essential oil of marjoram, blended into a massage oil, helps muscle cramps, especially menstrual cramps, and rheumatic pains. One of my favorite combinations is marjoram, clary sage, and lavender. A drop of marjoram oil can be rubbed directly on sore gums instead of clove oil. According to herbalist Dodoen (1517–1585), smelling marjoram "mundifieth [cleanses] the brayne," and modern aromatherapists say that the fragrance alone causes drowsiness, sleep, and in overdoses, can even be stupefying. A marjoram-scented bath is not only relaxing, it is good during a cold or flu. The aroma is used specifically to treat loneliness and grief.

COSMETIC: Marjoram provides a scent in body-care products and cosmetic waters.

OTHER: Marjoram dyes wool purple and linen red-brown, but unfortunately, the color is not long-lasting.

CRAMP OIL

2   *drops each:*
    essential oil of marjoram
    essential oil of lavender
1   *drop essential oil of clary sage*
1   *ounce (30 ml) almond oil*

Combine ingredients, and rub onto the afflicted areas.

Origanum vulgare
OREGANO

Origanum vulgare • Oregano

FAMILY: Labiatae.

DESCRIPTION: Bushy mounds. Height: 2¹/₂ feet (75 cm). Width: 2 to 3 feet (60 to 90 cm). Flowers: White-pink, held in small spikes, about 1 inch (2.5 cm) long. Leaves: Oval, to 1¹/₂ inches (3.75 cm), hairy, opposite each other. Blooms: July to September.

HABITAT: Native from Europe to central Asia and in the Middle East; introduced into the Far East. Cultivated commercially in southern Italy, the United States, Turkey, Greece, Italy, and Portugal.

CULTIVATION: Perennial. Zone: 5. Germination: 5 to 10 days. Space: 1¹/₂ feet (45 cm). Soil Temperature: 60° to 65° F (15° to 18° C). Soil: Well drained, slightly sandy, fairly dry. pH: 4.5 to 8. Sun: Full sun. Propagation: By seed, cutting, or root division. Heat and a dry soil increase the oil content.

GARDEN DESIGN: A tall, fragrant groundcover.

CONSTITUENTS: Essential oil (to 0.5%) includes thymol (to 15%), origanene, carvacrol; bitters.

RELATED SPECIES: There are about 20 species of oregano, with a great deal of confusion over which is which. Pot marjoram *(O. Onites)* with white, sometimes purple, flowers and *O. heracleoticum* with white, sometimes pink, flowers are also sold as common oregano. According to Gertrude Foster, who worked with the Bailey *herbarium* at Cornell University in New York State, *O. heracleoticum* is the winter marjoram of the English herbals that was cultivated in the 18th century for marketing earlier in the year than sweet marjoram. There is also golden oregano (*O. vulgaris* var. 'Aureum'). Dittany of Crete *(O. dictamnus)* is a very ornamental, and very tender herb used in wreath making, with pink-purple flowers that hang in loose panicles. To add to the oregano confusion, *Coleus amboinicus,* popular in Puerto Rico; *Monarda fistulosa* cv. *Menthifolia,* from New Mexico; *Thymus nummularius,* from Spain; and the Mexican *Lippia graveolens* all have an oreganolike flavor and have been sold as oregano.

HISTORY: The Roman cook Apicius frequently recommended *organy* to season sauces. While Europeans must have been vaguely familiar with it since 1597, when John Gerard called it "bastard marjerome of Candy [Ceylon]," according to Frederick Rosengarten in *The Book of Spices,* it was introduced to the United States only after World War II, when soldiers returned from Italy with a taste for pizza laden with oregano. In the 25 years that followed, the demand for oregano increased 6,000 times! Oregano has been substituted for marjoram, which gets a better price, or marjoram supplied when the more popular oregano was in short supply.

CULINARY: Oregano often accompanies marjoram and basil in cheese, tomato, bean, and egg dishes, and pizza. It became the *Thé Rouge Tisane* of France and was briefly used as a beer flavoring.

MEDICINAL: An expectorant and antiseptic, oregano improves digestion and reduces muscle spasms and inflammation. It also encourages menstruation and helps respiratory problems. A weak sedative, it is sometimes used to treat nervous headache, irritability, or menstrual cramps. It also has some ability to kill intestinal worms. The diluted oil can be rubbed on insect bites, toothache, and skin fungi such as athlete's foot.

AROMATHERAPY: Oregano is sometimes used in baths and as an inhalant steam for respiratory congestion.

OTHER: The leaves produce a dye. The dried flowers are used for wreath making.

Panax quinquefolius
GINSENG

O Great Spirit! do not go away.
I have come with a clean heart.
My soul is unstained.
It is purged of sin and wicked design.
Remain here, O Greatest of Spirits.
—CHINESE PRAYER TO JEN-SHEN

Panax quinquefolius • Ginseng

FAMILY: Araliaceae.

DESCRIPTION: One main stem supports a few side stems bearing leaf clusters. Height: 1 to 2 feet (30 to 60 cm). Width: 1 foot (30 cm). Flowers: Several, green-white. Leaves: Thin, green, leaflets divided usually in clusters of 4 to 5. Root: Fleshy, white taproot, up to 1 inch (2.5 cm) in diameter, with appendages that often have an uncanny, manlike appearance. A heel on the root indicates where stems from previous years grew. Fruit: Bright red, hanging berries, ¹/₂ to 1 inch (1.25 to 2.5 cm) in diameter, containing 2 seeds. Blooms: May to June.

HABITAT: Wild in the eastern United States; Quebec to southern Georgia, east to Oklahoma and Minnesota, in the shade of northern slope, hardwood forests, although rapidly disappearing and almost endangered. The United States government listed ginseng as a threatened (not endangered) species in the mid-1970s, and as a result, many states have initiated harvest restrictions.

CULTIVATION: Perennial. Zone: 3 to 4. Germination: 12 to 18 months. Must be scored with a razor, then stratified 8 months in moist sand. You may be able to buy prestratified seed, which will need only 7 to 10 months germination. Space: 2 feet (60 cm). Soil: Rich humus, well drained, moist. pH: 5 to 6. Sun: Filtered, 70% shade. Sunlight encourages root growth, although too much will kill it. Humid air. Propagation: Ginseng can be grown from seed, but it needs to be fresh and carefully stratified. Some growers slice the outer seed coat with a razor blade. It is easiest to purchase 1-year-old rootlets. Tricky to grow, it is subject to disease, and insects, gophers and moles favor it. Damage to its main stalk often kills the plant, although, in certain conditions, the root can lie dormant for up to 2 years. It takes 5 to 6 years to become mature enough to harvest, but older roots are preferable. Roots are fully grown at 18 to 20 years, after which they are most subject to diseases. If they stay healthy, they can live over 100 years. The age is determined by counting the nodes on top of the root, left from previous stalks. Older larger roots are preferred.

GARDEN DESIGN: Ginseng is a small but attractive plant that deserves to be a central feature of the shade garden. In late summer, its bright red berries are especially showy. Try growing ginseng in elevated boxes where you can give it special attention and protection.

CONSTITUENTS: Saponins (ginsenosides), sterols, vitamins (B₁, B₂, B₁₂, choline [part of the B complex group]), minerals (zinc, copper, magnesium, calcium, iron, manganese).

RELATED SPECIES: The Chinese consider their own ginseng *(P. pseudoginseng,* more commonly referred to as *P. ginseng* or *P. schinseng)* to be more warming and stimulating, but prefer American ginseng for treating certain body types and conditions. There are other species, including Japanese ginseng *(P. japonicus).* The well-studied Siberian ginseng *(Eleutherococcus sentiocosus)* shares the family and similar attributes with *Panax* genus.

HISTORY: Ginseng has an ancient and rich history. Emperors monopolized the rights to harvest it and wars have been fought over it. A 2,500-year-old Chinese myth from the Province of Sheni tells of villagers hearing a loud voice calling them from underneath a plant shaped like a man, which they named *Jen-shen* or *Ren-shen,* meaning "man root." Said to be a manifestation of Tu Ching, the Spirit of the Ground, the Chinese went on spiritual quests to find ginseng, reciting an ancient chant before digging it. Likewise, the Native North Americans considered the root sacred. The Iroquois named it *Garent-Oquen,* or "man's thighs and legs separated." It was a talisman for warriors and given to them to treat "old year's fire." The Cherokee, who call it *yunwiya usdi,* or "little men," consider it one of their most sacred herbs and add it to many herbal formulas to make them more potent. Today, it is rumored that some Indian medicine men have retained a secret art of processing a translucent root that is said to accentuate the properties. The Korean process to produce a pressed, red root is highly valued. Although there are claims that Chinese ginseng is superior, that country has imported large amounts of American ginseng since 1718, when the Jesuits of Canada first initiated trade with China.

"'Seng" hunting in the United States was a lucrative business that was often (and still is) run by fur traders who frequented the same areas. In 1876 alone, 550,624 pounds (250,000 kg) were exported. The first successful United States ginseng crop reported in an 1895 New York paper sparked interest in cultivating ginseng, and the Department of Agriculture printed a bulletin on growing ginseng. In 1902, a special crops publication began networking growers. Historic and cultivation information on ginseng (as well as goldenseal and other herbs) is provided in *Ginseng and Other Medicinal Plants* by A. R. Harding (1908, reprinted).

CULINARY: Small amounts of ginseng are chopped and added to soups and stews in the Orient, where the difference between foods and medicines often loses its distinction. The Polynesians used *P. fruticosum* as a food as well as a medicine.

MEDICINAL: As implied by its botanical name—*Pan* is Latin for "all" and *akos* means "remedy"—ginseng was considered for generations to be a panacea by the Chinese and Koreans, although there are some disorders, such as acute inflammatory diseases, for which it is not recommended. It usually is not taken alone, but combined in formulae with other herbs. One of ginseng's key investigators, Russian I. I. Brekhman, coined the term "adaptogen" to describe ginseng's ability to regulate many different functions. It can have different responses, depending on what an individual needs. This makes its properties difficult to pin down, and although hundreds of studies have been performed, many provide conflicting information. They do show that ginseng increases mental and physical efficiency and resistance to stress and disease. Psychological improvements were also observed according to Rorschach Tests given to volunteers before and after a regime of taking ginseng. When nurses in a London hospital in 1957 were given ginseng, their endurance and concentration significantly improved.[1] Studies done at the Chinese Academy of Medical Science in Beijing, China showed that the ginsenosides increase protein synthesis and activity of neurotransmitters in the brain.[2] They are also probably responsible for ginseng's dual role of sedating or stimulating the central nervous system, depending on the condition it is being taken to treat. Studies also show that ginseng improves carbohydrate tolerance in diabetics.[3] When volunteers were given 3 grams (about ⅛ ounce) of ginseng along with alcohol, their blood alcohol level was 32% to 51% lower than that of the control group.[4] The Ginseng Research Institute (500 3rd St., Suite 208–2, Washoe, WI 54401), sells a bibliography of 2,500 citations on ginseng.

CONSIDERATIONS: Large doses caused depression, nervousness, and high blood pressure in a 1979 clinical study, but the methods used are questionable.[5]

Passiflora incarnata • Passion Flower

FAMILY: Passifloraceae.

DESCRIPTION: A vine on a woody, hairy stem that hangs on twirling tendrils. Length: To 30 feet (9 m) long. Flowers: White or pale lavender, with pink or purple calyx, 2 to 3 inches (5 to 7.5 cm) across. The outer rings (corona) have pink or purple filaments; 5 stamens with hammer-shaped anthers surround the 3-part style; reddish stigmas emanate from flower's center. Leaves: Deeply lobed, toothed, 4 to 6 inches (10 to 15 cm) long. Fruit: Edible, yellow, oval, about 2 inches (5 cm) in diameter. Blooms: July to September. Takes 2 to 3 years to flower.

HABITAT: Australia, and in the United States, from Missouri and Texas east to Florida and Virginia.

CULTIVATION: Perennial. Zone: 7. Germination: Poor, to 2 years. Harvest seeds when berry puckers and use fresh, or keep refrigerated. Space: 2 feet (60 cm). Soil Temperature: 65° to 70° F (18° to 21° C). Soil: Sandy loam; if too rich, produces fewer flowers. pH: 7.5 to 8.5. Sun: Full sun. Propagation: From seed, or 6-inch

Passiflora incarnata
Passion Flower

(15-cm) cuttings, or divide runners in the autumn. Prune back by about one-third in the autumn, especially lateral growth. Passion flower is hardy, surviving temperatures down to about 15° F (–9.4° C), but will die back to the roots during a frost. Mulch the roots well if temperatures can drop below that. Otherwise, it is fast-growing and can be raised as an annual or wintered in a greenhouse. It also makes a suitable houseplant and actually flourishes in the restriction of a pot.

GARDEN DESIGN: Take advantage of passion flower's climbing abilities and outstanding flowers to decorate a trellis or arbor in any area with a long, warm growing season. Be sure to place it where the flowers can be admired.

CONSTITUENTS: Alkaloids (harman), flavonoids, sugars, sterols, gums.

RELATED SPECIES: Several different species produce edible passion fruits that are sold commercially. *P. caerulea* is grown as an ornamental in tropical climates and will bloom as a houseplant. The hybrid *P.* x *alatocaerulea* is used in perfumery. Australian native passion flowers include *P. aurantia*, with bright red or salmon flowers and *P. cinnabaria*, with large vivid red flowers.

HISTORY: In 1610, the Italian theologian Giacoma Bosio was completely amazed when he was presented with a stylized drawing of a passion flower from the New World. In his treatise on the Cross of Calvary, he noted that it "contains . . . not only the Saviour's Cross, but also the symbols of His Passion." The Spanish colonists had already dubbed it the "Flower of the Five Wounds." European cultivation began in 1699. It eventually reached the height of its popularity in the 19th century, both as a garden ornamental and medicine. The herb was introduced into United States medicine in 1867 as a sedative and was listed in the *National Formulary* from 1916 until 1936. A sedative passion flower chewing gum was even marketed in Romania in 1978. In 1990, a marked increase in passion flower sales was assumed to be a result of consumer concern over using the amino acid L-tryptophan as a sedative and sleep inducer after possible side effects were reported, although these were later attributed to a contaminant in some products.

CULINARY: Passion fruit, also known as maypops, is made into commercial drinks. South Americans use passion flower in cocktails, fruit punch, and dessert dishes, to top ice cream, and to make a very popular soup. Australians also use passion fruit *(Pediculus)* and cultivate it commercially. The flavor is described as a combination of pineapple, apricot, guava, and banana—with a hint of lime.

MEDICINAL: The leaves of passion flower are an ingredient in many European pharmaceutical products to treat nervous disorders, such as heart palpitations, anxiety, convulsions, epilepsy, and sometimes high blood pressure. They have been shown to make a nonaddictive sedative that relaxes the nervous system.[1] Passion flower seems especially helpful when physical or mental strain results in insomnia or stress. While it is not a strong pain reliever and it may take a while for its effects to be noticed, it seems to have a lasting and refreshing effect on the nervous system. It is used to prevent spasms from whooping cough, asthma, and other diseases. The unusual fruit has been historically considered a tonic.

CONSIDERATIONS: Large doses can cause nausea and vomiting. There are incorrect reports that it contains toxic cyanogenic glycosides like its relative, *P. caerulea*.

Pelargonium graveolens
Rose Geranium

Pelargonium graveolens • Rose Geranium
(Previously *P. terebinthiaceum*)

FAMILY: Geraniaceae.

DESCRIPTION: Small, fragrant, full shrub. Height: 1 foot (30 cm). Width: 2 to 3 feet (60 to 90 cm). Flowers: 1 inch (2.5 cm) mauve-pink, unscented. Leaves: Rounded, heart-shaped, fuzzy. Blooms: Summer.

HABITAT: South Africa, in dry areas, and commercially cultivated in Africa and the Mediterranean.

CULTIVATION: Perennial. Zone: 9–10. Space: 14 to 18 inches (35 to 45 cm). Soil Temperature: 70° to 85° F (24° to 29° C). Soil: Well drained. Should dry out between waterings. Very drought resistant. pH: 6 to 7. Sun: Full sun or light shade. Propagation: By cuttings. Cut so 3 stem nodes remain on stem. (Only *P. zonae* is propagated from seed.) The plant will winter at 50° to 55° F (10° to 13° C) indoors or in a well-ventilated greenhouse. Temperatures should not go past 90° F (32° C). Remove flower buds if it starts to get straggly.

GARDEN DESIGN: Scented geraniums are best planted where they can be touched and smelled. They make an excellent summer bedding plant if they can be kept fairly dry; otherwise, keep them in pots throughout the year. They will cascade over the edges of pots, either hanging on a porch or set in the garden.

CONSTITUENTS: Essential oils include geranyl tiglate, citronellol, isomenthone.

RELATED SPECIES: The rose-scented group is the most popular of the more than 230 scented geraniums, and rose geranium is a parent to many hybrids. Other popular species are the peppermint or woolly geranium (*P. tomentosum*), with large, heart-shaped, velvety leaves and a mint fragrance; coconut geranium (*P. grossularioides*), a trailing plant with small, rosy red flowers that is often hung in baskets; the ruffled-leaf apple geranium (*P. odoratissimum*), with white flowers veined in red. Some confusion exists in distinguishing between the scented and the true geraniums *(Geranium spp.)*—the latter being a hardier plant with a less agreeable scent—because of their resemblance to one another. Scented geraniums were even originally designated *Geranium.*

© Derek Fell

HISTORY: Both the Greek names *geranos*, "crane," and *Pelargonium*, "stork," describe the herb's bill-like, long seed. Scented geraniums were first sent to England in 1609 by the governor of Cape Colony, South Africa, but were officially introduced in 1632 by botanist and plant hunter John Tradescant. The Duchess of Beaufort imported rose "pink" geranium for perfume in 1700. Otherwise, scented geraniums went mostly unrecognized until the nurseryman Robert Sweet published his multivolume, richly illustrated treatise *Geraniaceae* from 1823 to 1830. In the 19th century, South Africa fell into British rule just when the English were gaining interest in greenhouse plants. Cultivation for perfume also began in the warm coastal areas of France and Spain and later in Algeria and the Belgian Congo. Scented geraniums reached the height of their popularity in Victorian England and were widely grown until 1914, when fuel for greenhouses was banned during the war. *Geraniums: Pelargoniums* by Helen Van Pelt Wilson (M. Barrows and Co., 1950) is a good reference on varieties. The most complete modern text is *Pelargoniums, Including the Popular Geranium* by Derek Clifford (Blandford, 1958).

CULINARY: Fresh leaves can be added to jellies, fruit dishes, and cold plates for a mild flavor. To lightly flavor a pound cake or angel food cake, lay the leaves flat on a buttered and floured pan just before pouring batter. Discard the leaves after the cake is baked.

MEDICINAL: The leaves were used in Africa to stop diarrhea, and an Italian study showed that scented geraniums stop bleeding.[1] The essential oil is made into preparations to treat lice, ringworm, and shingles, usually accompanied by other herbs. The pharmaceutical industry utilizes an antiseptic component of the essential oil called geraniol.

AROMATHERAPY: Called both rose geranium and geranium by aromatherapists, it is an important fragrance for men's products since it blends well with citrus and woodsy scents. Used in facial steams and creams, it is suitable for both dry and oily complexions and has long been reputed to have an "antiaging" effect. The fragrance is also used in bath salts, bath oils, and massage oils as an antidepressant and to counter insomnia. An inexpensive substitute for the true rose, rose geranium forms a starting point in the manufacture of synthetic rose oil.

OTHER: The oil repels mosquitoes.

ROSE GERANIUM JELLY

Other geranium scents and, in fact other herbs, can be substituted for the rose geranium leaves.

5 cups (1.2 l) apple juice, tart if available
3³/₄ cups (.9 l) sugar
12 rose geranium leaves

Bring the juice rapidly to a boil, gradually adding the sugar and stirring constantly. Boil until 2 drops hang on the side of cold spoon, or until a sugar thermometer registers 222° F (105.5° C). Place 1 small geranium leaf in the bottom of each sterilized jelly glass. Skim the juice if needed, and pour quickly into glasses. Float a second geranium leaf on top and cover immediately with melted paraffin.

Makes six 8-ounce (240-ml) jars.

Petroselinum crispum • Parsley
(Previously *P. hortense, P. sativum, Carum petroselinum*)

FAMILY: Umbelliferae.

DESCRIPTION: Soft, rounded, leafy mound. Height: 2 to 3 feet (60 to 90 cm). Width: 10 inches (25 cm). Flowers: Green-yellow, in umbels. Leaves: Divided, feathery, with strong aroma. Fruit: Oval, compressed. Root: Long taproot, spindly, thick, resembling small parsnips. Blooms: Second summer.

HABITAT: Probably northern and central Europe and western Asia. Naturalized elsewhere, including some subtropical regions, such as West Indies.

CULTIVATION: Biennial. Zone: 3. Germination: 2 to 3 weeks, sometimes 2 months—hastened by presoaking. Space: 6 to 10 inches (15 to 25 cm). Soil Temperature: 70° F (21° C). Soil: Fairly rich, moist, but well drained, especially in winter. pH: 6 to 8. Sun: Full sun or partial shade. Propagation: By seed, which can be planted 2 weeks before the last frost. It is difficult to transplant unless small. Seedlings can tolerate a light frost and can be cut through the winter in warm climates. I make a "cloche" by placing an inverted clay pot over my plants to extend their season into the winter. Parsley is often grown as an annual since it turns bitter, seeds, then dies the second year. The flowering stalks can be removed to extend its growth. To keep potted parsley in the winter kitchen, plant seeds directly into pot in midsummer and place near a sunny window or a grow light to provide sufficient light. The leaves tend to yellow when hung to air-dry, but drying can be hastened by placing on a nonmetallic surface (so it does not burn) in a 440° F (226° C) oven for a few hours. Alternatively, replace the oven light with a 100-watt (341-BTU) bulb and use that as the heat source. Stir every once in a while to redistribute.

GARDEN DESIGN: One of the most important culinary herbs to place within easy reach of the kitchen door for a constant, fresh supply.

CONSTITUENTS: Essential oil includes apiol, apiolin, myristicin, pinene; flavonoids (apigenin); glycoside; vitamins A, C; minerals (iron, manganese, calcium, phosphorus); protein (to 22%).

RELATED SPECIES: There are varieties of *P. crispum* with extra curly leaves, including 'Moss Curled'. Neapolitan (*P. crispum* var. *neapolitanum* [previously *P. latifolium*]) has flat, uncurled leaves, and thick stems that can be eaten like celery. This may be the ancients' Macedonian, or black, parsley. Turnip root parsley (*P. crispum* var. *tuberosum*) is tall, with fernlike leaves and a thick root that is cooked like parsnips. Known as Hamburg parsley, the Germans themselves call it Dutch parsley, in reference to its probable country of origin. It can be stored in moist sand in the cellar during the winter. Parsley piert (*Alchemilla arvensis*), a diuretic, is unrelated.

HISTORY: Pliny stated that every sauce should contain *apium* (parsley). The Romans spread parsley and soft cheese on bread, a predecessor of the modern European's parsley and cream cheese sandwich. The Greeks bordered their gardens with *petroselinon* (*petros* means "rock," among which the parsley grew) and used it to decorate graves and feed to chariot horses. The name may also refer to parsley's ability to relieve kidney and bladder stones. While Olympic winners were crowned with bay, the victors of the Nemena and Isthmian Games (500 B.C.–A.D. 67) wore crowns of wild parsley. Greek poet Anacreon (580–490 B.C.) sang, "Our wreaths of parsley spread their fadeless foliage round our head." The Greek physician Galen copied an old prescription from Hippocrates' temple of Asclepius on the Greek island of Cos, which contained parsley, thyme, fennel, anise, and other herbs that were powdered and mixed with wine. This is thought to be the basis of the many popular cure-alls of the Middle Ages. Parsley was also found in Mithradates' (132 B.C.–A.D. 63) famous poison antidote.

Emperor Charlemagne had it planted in his 9th-century gardens. Catherine de Medici is said to have brought parsley to France from Italy, and she probably did, although it had been there since the 12th century, according to the *Journal de Paris*. Gerard boiled the roots and seeds in his 16th-century ale to "cast forth strong venome or poyson" and noted that the seeds helped those who are "light-headed to resist drink better."

CULINARY: "To take parsley away from the cook," wrote Louis Augustin Bose d'Antic in the 18th century, "would make it almost impossible for him to exercise his art." Bouquet garni ingredients vary but always include parsley. Sometimes it is the only seasoning in *omelettes fines herbes*. Sauces, garnishes, tomato dishes, potatoes, and peas require parsley as well. The stems are used instead of leaves in white sauces and stocks because they don't impart a green color. Europeans prefer the plain, flat-leaved parsley with a strong taste, while Americans almost always choose curly parsley, except, that is, for southern Louisiana's Creole cuisine, which demands a stronger taste. In any dish, fresh parsley is always preferred, but dried flakes can be used in a pinch. It takes about 12 pounds (5.4 kg) of parsley leaves to produce 1 pound (454 g) of dehydrated flakes. Over a million tons are produced annually, mostly in California.

MEDICINAL: Parsley leaves, seed, and root (which is strongest) treat urinary tract infections and help eliminate kidney stones. The constituent apiol is used in some pharmaceutical medicines for kidney ailments and to induce menstruation. It also stimulates appetite and increases blood flow to digestive organs, as well as reduces fevers.[1] Another constituent, the flavonoid apigenin, reduces inflammation by inhibiting histamine and is also a free-radical scavenger.[2] The root and seed still appear in the pharmacopoeias of a number of countries.

AROMATHERAPY: The thick, green-yellow essential oil obtained from seeds is sometimes called "parsley camphor." It is used in creams for bruises, hemorrhoids, and varicose veins. It also scents Oriental-style perfumes and colognes.

OTHER: Parsley stems produce a green dye. According to Maude Grieve, in a *Modern Herbal*, rabbits love parsley, but it can be fatal to small birds.

Of many pilgrim hastow Cristos curs,
For many of the persly yet they fare the wors,
That they han eaten with the stubbelgoos;
For in thy shoppe is many a fly loose.
—GEOFFREY CHAUCER, 1340–1400, ENGLISH

Petroselinum crispum
PARSLEY

Phytolacca americana
POKEWEED

Phytolacca americana • Pokeweed
(Previously *P. decandra*)

FAMILY: Phytolaccaceae.

DESCRIPTION: Tall, narrow, treelike bush composed of a few thick, hollow stems. Height: 12 feet (3.6 m). Width: 3 feet (.9 m). Flowers: White or purplish, grouped on the tips of stems. Leaves: Long ovals, to 6 inches (15 cm) long, with an unpleasant scent. Fruit: Globular, black-purple, with red juice. Root: Large, thick main root with offshoots. Blooms: July to August.

HABITAT: Maine to Florida, introduced in the Mediterranean.

CULTIVATION: Perennial. Zone: 3. Germination: 2 to 3 weeks. First, stratify for 6 weeks. Space: 2 to 3 feet (60 to 90 cm). Soil Temperature: 60° to 70° F (15° to 21° C). Soil: Rich, well drained. Sun: Full sun. Propagation: Seed or by root division.

GARDEN DESIGN: A striking plant that is excellent set to the back of a bed. You may want to purposely plant it out of the reach of visitors, especially children, because the berries are poisonous.

CONSTITUENTS: Root: Triterpenoid saponins, alkaloid (phytolaccine), resins, phyolaccic acid; leaf: PAP, fatty oil.

HISTORY: During James Knox Polk's presidential campaign in 1845, when supporters wore poke twigs, it was erroneously reported that the herb was named after him. Poke is really an abbreviation of the Native American *puccoon*—meaning any plant that produced a red dye or stain, from *pak*, or "blood." According to John Burroughs, in a *Bunch of Herbs* (1881), "Thoreau coveted its strong purple stalk for a cane and the robins eat its dark crimson-juiced berries"—(as do pigeons; one of its other names is "pigeon berry"). Both the Pennsylvania Dutch and the Portuguese added berry juice to give wine the appearance of good port, but the practice was discontinued because it spoiled the taste.

CULINARY: A poke "salet" of leaves and shoots is a popular spring dish in parts of eastern United States, especially in the South. It is usually cooked twice, with a change of water to leach out potentially toxic properties. The canned greens are even sold commercially. In *Cross Creek* (1942), Marjorie Kinnan Rawlings describes the preparation: "I hunt through the grove after a spring rain, basket in hand, for the most tender shoots, cutting those from six to ten inches [10 to 25 cm] in length. I trim off the leaves and thin skin and cook the shoots exactly as I do asparagus, serving them on buttered toast with a rich cream sauce poured over, and strips of breakfast bacon round them. The flavor is delicate and delicious, with a faint taste of iron."

MEDICINAL: Pokeroot is said to stimulate the lymphatic system; it has been used mostly to treat tonsillitis, swollen glands, upper respiratory and lung congestion, and mumps, as well as to encourage the elimination of toxins from the tissues. Proteins found in poke are antiviral and have inhibited flu and polio viruses in scientific studies.[1] Native Americans and the early white settlers placed a root poultice on skin and breast cancers and mastitis. Pokeweed mitogen (PWM) has been designated as an effective immune system stimulant. The leaf contains an antiviral protein called PAP, which is similar to interferon, and is being studied for antiviral and antitumor compound. In the Appalachian region of the United States, the dried fruit is still placed on sores, ringworm, and scabies to reduce inflammation and to encourage healing.

CONSIDERATIONS: All parts of the plant can cause digestive irritation, vomiting, and decreased respiration and blood pressure, with overdoses sometimes being fatal. In 1981, 16 out of 51 campers became ill 30 minutes to 5 hours after dining on poke leaves, even though they had been boiled twice. The berries are relatively non-poisonous, except to children. One 5-year-old girl died after drinking a diluted poke juice drink.[2] The root dust is irritating to the eyes and causes sneezing. Even people handling the root are encouraged to wear gloves since absorbing large quantities of the juice could possibly produce cell abnormalities.

OTHER: Poke is a dye and stain that has been used as artist's paint. Researchers are investigating an Ethiopian species called *enod* that is effective in destroying African snails, which carry a parasitic disease called bilharzia.

Pimpinella anisum • Anise

FAMILY: Umbelliferae.

DESCRIPTION: A slender, feathery herb. Height: 18 to 24 inches (45 to 60 cm). Width: 8 inches (20 cm). Flowers: Small, whitish clusters on umbels. Leaves: The first, lower ones are rounded or lobed, toothed around the edge, 5 inches (12.5 cm) long. Secondary, feathery leaflets appear on mature plants. Fruit: Small, oval, brown-gray, 2-inch- (5-cm-) long seeds with ribs with a licoricelike taste. Blooms: July to August.

HABITAT: Asia Minor, Egypt; anise has established itself from Egypt through the eastern Mediterranean. Now cultivated commercially in India, Turkey, Mexico, Chile, the Soviet Union, Spain, Italy, and Germany.

CULTIVATION: Annual. Germination: 20 to 28 days. Space: 8 to 10 inches (20 to 25 cm). Soil Temperature: 70° F (21° C). Soil: Average garden soil, fairly rich but well drained. Do not let completely dry out. pH: 6–7.5. Sun: Full sun, but not excessive heat. Propagation: Plants will self seed. It is best to sow anise directly in the garden early. It produces seeds in 140 days. Seeds keep their viability a couple of years at most.

GARDEN DESIGN: Plant anise in an area where you can enjoy its light, feathery leaves, since its flowers are small and rather insignificant. It can be set away from the path in a culinary garden since it is only harvested once in the autumn for its seeds.

CONSTITUENTS: Essential oil includes transanethole, 70% to 90%, fixed oils, coumarins, flavonoid glycosides, fatty acids, sugars, sterols.

RELATED SPECIES: Star anise (*Illicium verum*), a bush from southeast Asia, is not related, but it has an almost identical chemistry and is often substituted for anise. Neither herbs are related to licorice (*Glycyrrhiza glabra*) or the similar-tasting fennel.

HISTORY: Anise was cultivated and well appreciated by the ancient Egyptians, Tuscans, Greeks, and Romans, and by the Arabs, who named it *anysun*. In 550 B.C., the Greek mathematician Pythagoras declared *anisonas* bread a great delicacy. Anisum gave flavor to Roman spice cake, *mustaceae*, made with new, unfermented wine and served at the end of banquets and sometimes weddings to counter indigestion. It is probably the forerunner of Europe's traditional spice wedding cake. Cultivation eventually spread to central Europe in the Middle Ages, when its feathery leaves gave anise the medieval name *dipinella,* "twice-pinnate," later to become *Pimpinella.* In 1480, King Edward IV had his personal linen scented with "lytil bagges of fustian stuffed with ireos and anneys [anise]." Turner, in his 1551 *Herbal,* recommended anise to "maketh the breth sweter," and the seeds are still occasion-

Pimpinella anisum
ANISE

Pimpinella anisum. Anise seed's flavor is delightful in sweets, candies, pastries, and cordials around the world. It does need a long, warm growing season to produce seed, so start it early.

ally served as afterdinner fresheners. The once-famous anise-flavored candies with a hard sugar coating called *dragati* are now the *dragée* candies enjoyed by the modern French. The term has also come to mean any sugar-coated medicine in the pharmacy.

CULINARY: Added to many sweet biscuits and cakes, anise seeds often become a substitute licorice flavoring that conveniently reduces the amount of sugar needed in recipes. They are one of the most popular liqueur flavorings—an interesting association, considering they are said to subdue the effects of a hangover. Anise is found in the French *anisette,* the Greeks' famous *ouzo,* as well as their stronger *anesone,* the Turkish *raki,* Latin America's *aguardiente* (distilled from sugarcane), the Latvian *kummel,* and the Spanish *ojen.* Its sweet, spicy taste can be added to almost any dish calling for dill or cumin, such as curry, or even to pickles or beans. Occasionally, the fresh leaves are used to sweeten salads.

MEDICINAL: The taste of anise seed, or aniseed, has made it a favorite medicine for relieving indigestion, gas, colic, and flatulence. It gives cough syrups and teas a pleasant taste while relaxing spasms in the chest and eliminating lung congestion.[1] It is thought to reduce coughing by sending messages to the brain. The mild hormonal actions (mostly estrogenlike) of anise may explain its ability to increase mother's milk and its reputation for easing childbirth and being an aphrodisiac.

AROMATHERAPY: Eau de cologne sometimes includes anise for its fresh, spicy fragrance, and derivatives of anise are used in perfumery. Aromatherapists use the fragrance of anise for relaxation and to reduce insomnia.

OTHER: The essential oil is an insecticide that is occasionally used to kill pests. On the other hand, cattle, mice, rats, dogs, and even fish are so fond of it that it flavors many animal foods and baits. Given to cows, it increases their milk production.

ANISE DROP COOKIES

These cookies are traditional Christmas fare that turn out best when prepared in cool weather and humidity under 50%.

2	medium eggs
1/2	cup (120 ml) sugar, sifted
1/4	teaspoon (1.25 ml) vanilla
1	cup (240 ml) pastry flour, sifted
1/2	teaspoon (2.5 ml) baking powder
1	tablespoon (15 ml) anise seed, crushed

Beat the eggs until light, and add the sugar gradually. Continue beating at least 3 to 5 minutes at a medium blender setting (longer if mixing by hand). Add vanilla. Add the flour and baking powder sifted together, then add the seeds. Beat the batter another 5 minutes.

Drop 1/2 teaspoonfuls (2.5 ml) of batter, well spaced, on a cookie sheet. These should flatten to 1-inch (2.5-cm) rounds. Dry at room temperature for 18 hours.

Bake in an oven preheated to 325° F (163° C) until the cookies begin to brown, about 12 minutes.

Makes about 45 puffed meringuelike cookies.

> *The sav'ry aniseed the stomach cheers,*
> *And human sight improves as well as clears.*
> *The sweeter kind all others overpeers.*
> —"OF ANISE," **REGIMEN SANITATIS SALERNI, 10TH CENTURY ITALY**

Plantago lanceolata • **Plantain**

FAMILY: Plantaginaceae.

DESCRIPTION: Flat, spreading leaves growing from a rosette center. Height: 2 feet (60 cm). Width: 1 foot (30 cm). Flowers: Tiny, white, clustered into a head 2 to 3 inches (5 to 7.5 cm) long, atop thin stalks. Leaves: Long, lancelike oblongs with predominant ribs running parallel along the leaf, to 9 inches (22.5 cm) long by 1¹/₂ inches (3.75 cm) wide. Fruit: Small, round seed covered with brown chaff. Root: Spindly, fleshy taproot. Blooms: May to August.

HABITAT: Native to Europe and naturalized throughout the world. Commercially cultivated in Eastern Europe.

CULTIVATION: Perennial. Zone: 2. Germination: 7 to 10 days. Space: 1 foot (30 cm). Soil Temperature: 60° to 70° F (15° to 21° C). Soil: Prefers slightly rich, moist ground, but definitely not fussy. Sun: Full sun or partial shade. Propagation: By seed, easily.

GARDEN DESIGN: Plantain is an attractive herb, although largely unappreciated in garden design since most people regard it as a weed. Chances are you won't need to cultivate plantain since it will arrive on its own. If you plant it in a fancy pot with rich soil, most people won't even recognize the lush plant at first glance!

CONSTITUENTS: Mucilage, flavonoid glycosides, tannins, iroids, silica.

RELATED SPECIES: Broadleaf plantain (*P. major*) is very similar, but has very wide leaves. More decorative cultivars, including a bronze-purple–leafed 'Atropurpurea,' are available. Psyllium (*P. ovata*) seeds are sold in drugstores as a bulk laxative and in products such as Metamucil.™ *P. psyllium* is also used in Europe. Australian native plantains include sago weed *(P. varia, P. cunninghamii)* and shade plantain *(P. debilis).*

HISTORY: Plantain is the Old French version of the Latin *plantago,* meaning "plant." In medieval days, it was often called *quinquenervia,* or "ribs," and today plantain is still called ribwort to describe its definite leaf veins. For centuries, children have "shot" plantain by popping off the heads, and English children still refer to it as "kemps," from the Anglo-Saxon word for soldier, *cempa.* Farmers planted it for their sheep to graze on. The gelatinous matter obtained from soaking the seedhead was once used to stiffen muslin.

CULINARY: The young leaves can be steamed or boiled and eaten as a potherb. The seeds, which contain protein, have a nut-like flavor and were ground and made into breads, usually mixed with flour. Early Australian settlers used plantain seeds to substitute for sago in puddings. Aborigines made a kind of porridge from shade plantain.

MEDICINAL: A plantain poultice or salve is used on wounds to stop bleeding and encourage healing with its proteolytic enzymes, which are active in the fresh leaf or the fresh or dried root. It also reduces inflammation and helps reverse allergic symptoms. Dr. Surge Duckett stated, "This treatment is a blessing for those who must have a constant supply of calamine lotion or cortisone" after applying the fresh leaf to poison ivy on 10 patients and seeing their inflammation and itching immediately reduce and not return.[1] Plantain leaves are also made into an eyewash. Traditional Chinese medicine uses plantain to treat urinary problems, dysentery, hepatitis, and lung problems, especially asthma and bronchitis. The seeds are used for bowel ailments. Plantain is also found in African and southeast Asian folk medicine. Research in India has shown its beneficial effects in treating coughs and colds. One study found it provided relief of the pain, coughing, wheezing, and irritation of chronic bronchitis.[2] The evidence that psyllium seeds lower cholesterol may apply to plantain seeds as well.

> Romeo: Your plantain leaf is excellent for that.
> Juliet: For what I pray thee?
> Romeo: For your broken skin.
> —*ROMEO AND JULIET.* **WILLIAM SHAKESPEARE (1564–1616), ENGLISH**

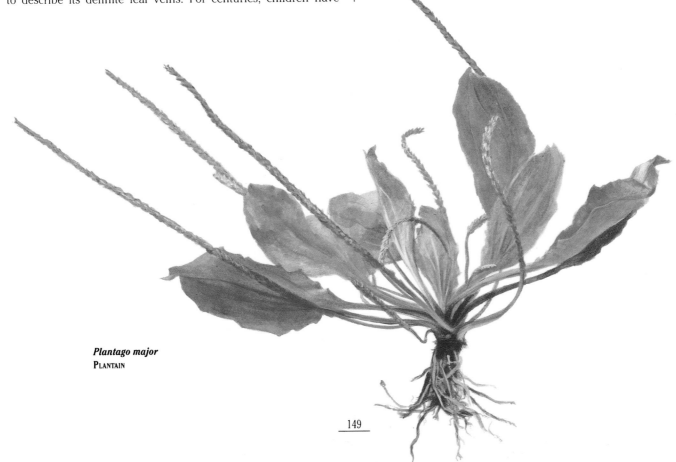

Plantago major
PLANTAIN

Podophyllum peltatum. **Underneath the mayapple's bold leaves blooms a delicate flower. Recently this herb has caught the attention of researchers searching for new medicines.**

Podophyllum peltatum • Mayapple

FAMILY: Berberidaceae.

DESCRIPTION: Large leaves supported on stems. Height: 1 1/2 feet (45 cm). Width: 1 1/2 feet (45 cm). Flowers: White or pale pink, 2 inches (5 cm) across, nodding and supported individually on stem. Leaves: To 1 foot (30 cm) across, 3 to 5 lobes, often with purple-brown spots. Younger plants bear 1 leaf, older plants 2. Fruit: Yellow, sometimes red, 2 inches (5 cm) across, sweet, and slightly acid. Rhizome: Knotty, red-brown, with whitish interior, long, cylindrical, 1/2-inch (1.25 cm) wide, acrid odor. Blooms: May to June.

HABITAT: North America, Quebec to Florida and Texas.

CULTIVATION: Perennial. Zone: 2–3. Germination: 4 to 6 weeks. Stratify 4 weeks. Space: 1 foot (30 cm). Soil Temperature: 60° to 70° F (15° to 20° C). Soil: Nitrogen-rich, must be moist. pH: 4 to 7. Sun: Partial shade. Propagation: By seed or root division. Spreads by clumps—can eventually overtake delicate neighboring plants.

GARDEN DESIGN: An attractive selection for the shade garden, mayapple is found in both wildflower and herb gardens.

CONSTITUENTS: Lignan (podophyllotoxin, about 4%), flavonoids (quercertin).

RELATED SPECIES: Although also known as American mandrake, it is not related to the more toxic mandrake (*Mandragora officinarum*). The Himalayan mayapple (*P. hexandrum*) from East India yields even more podophyllotoxin—10% to 12%.

HISTORY: Native Americans used mayapple to eliminate warts. The Cherokees treated deafness with it. Dr. Schöpf, a physician to German soldiers during the American Revolutionary War, introduced mayapple to modern medicine in 1787. The Philadelphia botanist William Barton called it to wider attention in the early 1800s. Mayapple entered the *U.S. Pharmacopoeia* in 1820, where it remains a source of podophyllum resin to remove venereal warts—usually mixed with compound tincture of benzoin.

CULINARY: Despite its laxative effects, the fruit is sometimes eaten and made into jelly and sweet drinks. They used to be sold in American markets. Plant researcher Dr. James Duke reports that he whips up a delicious mayapple fruit sauce and ice cream.

MEDICINAL: The wart-removing drugs are produced from podophyllotoxin—found in mayapple rhizomes. Its application must be restricted to abnormal tissue only. One product called Wartec® (derived from *P. hexandrum*) has been shown to be 94% effective. When another product, Pidofilox®, was applied in a clinical study, over 74% of the warts were gone in four weeks. The compound is thought to interfere with the wart's development and blood supply.[1] The podophyllotoxin in mayapple has been found to stimulate the immune system while suppressing lymph cells. It is more toxic to leukemia cells than to normal cells.[2] The tumor inhibitor was actually discovered in 1958, but the compound created digestive-tract irritations too severe to make it practical. Now a semisynthetic derivative, etoposide, is being used for chemotherapy in Europe and was introduced in 1985 under the trade name Vepeside®. Etoposide has also been approved by the FDA to treat testicular and small-cell lung cancer.[3] Studies also indicate its use in ovarian cancer.

CONSIDERATIONS: Poisonous, with the spring roots most toxic. A strong purgative, it is a digestive-tract irritant, causes vomiting, diarrhea, headaches, bloating, stupor, and lowered blood pressure. Fatalities have been reported. Even handling the powdered root can cause skin lesions and inflamed eyes. For professional use only!

Portulaca oleracea • Purslane

FAMILY: Portulacaceae.

DESCRIPTION: Thick, matlike groundcover, very succulent, with red stems. Height: 8 inches (20 cm). Width: 10 inches (25 cm). Flowers: Bright yellow, 3/8 inch (9 mm) across. Leaves: Thick, succulent, oval, to 1 1/4 inches (3.1 cm) long. Blooms: June to September.

HABITAT: Possibly native to India, but well established from Greece to China. Introduced elsewhere.

CULTIVATION: Annual, sometimes biennial. Germination: 7 to 15 days. Space: 6 to 8 inches (15 to 20 cm). Soil Temperature: 65° to 75° F (18° to 24° C). Soil: Well drained, well watered. pH: 5.5 to 8. Sun: Full sun. Propagation: From seed, ready to harvest in 6 to 8 weeks. Cultivation makes the leaves taste less sharp.

GARDEN DESIGN: Purslane makes a good ground cover, if you don't mind that most people consider it a weed. Indeed, Australians know it as pigweed! Watch out that it doesn't turn into one in your garden. Medieval gardens took advantage of its nature and grew it as a ground cover between upright herbs.

CONSTITUENTS: Alkaloids (.03%), glycoside, sterols, essential oil, resins, organic acids, vitamin C (700 milligrams per 100 grams of fresh plant), oxalic acid, potassium salts (1% in fresh plant, 70% in dried plant).

RELATED SPECIES: Giant purslane (*P. oleracea* var. *giganthes*) has double-petaled flowers 1 inch (2.5 cm) across and is grown

Portulaca oleracea
PURSLANE

MEDICINAL: The sticky, broken leaves of fresh purslane soothe burns, stings, and swellings. The juice was once used for treating earaches and to "fasten" teeth and soothe sore gums. In Europe, it is a treatment for painful urination and sometimes for stomachache and is turned into a cough syrup for sore throats. Purslane is the richest known plant source of Omega-3 acids, found mostly in fish oils. These fatty acids reduce blood cholesterol and pressure, clotting, and inflammation and may increase immunity. They were discovered in purslane in 1986 by Dr. Artemis P. Simopoulos who, one day in her kitchen, noted the similarity of the slimy leaves to fish oil. A former chairwoman of the United States National Institute of Health, who learned to cook purslane in her native Greece, brought some to the laboratory for investigation.

Potentilla anserina var. *sericea* • Cinquefoil

FAMILY: Rosaceae.
DESCRIPTION: Silvery mound. Height: 8 to 16 inches (20 to 40 cm). Width: 8 inches (20 cm). Flowers: Resemble buttercups

Potentilla anserina. **This attractive species, with its bright yellow flowers and deep green leaves with silvery undersides, is one of more than 300 related species. It is the species of cinquefoil most commonly used for medicinal purposes.**

as an ornamental. Garden purslane (*P. oleracea* var. *sativa*) was grown in Europe in the 16th through 18th centuries for food. The South African Zulu use *P. quadrifida* as an emetic. Several species grow throughout mainland Australia, including the inland species *P. intraterranea,* used for Aboriginal food.

HISTORY: The botanical name *oleracea* is Latin for "potherb." *Portulaca* may mean "milk carrier," from *potare,* Latin "to carry" and *lac,* "milk," describing the juice that exudes from the broken stems. Some scholars think it is derived from *portula,* a "little gate," due to the gatelike cover on the seed capsules. The Romans enjoyed puns and called purslane *porcella,* or "little pig," as a pun on its name. This became the Italian *porcellana,* the old French *porcelaine,* and eventually "purslane" in English. (White, eyed cowrie shells, also nicknamed *porca* for their resemblance to piglets, followed the same language progression. Their white patina reminded sailors of the newly imported "porcelain" fine china.) Brought north into Europe, purslane provided not only dinner, but was one of the four "cold" seeds of medieval medicine that cooled "hot" complaints, such as "heat in the liver." High in vitamin C, it used to be a scurvy remedy. By the 1700s, it had made itself so much at home in the United States, some regarded it as a native American plant. In Australia, Aborigines used the white hairs of native *P. filifolia* as a ceremonial decoration.

CULINARY: Sometimes compared to asparagus in taste, purslane is used in salads and soups, steamed as a garnish, or is pickled for winter salads. It has long been eaten in the Middle East and India and is found in the Middle Eastern salad *fattoush.* In China, the herb is boiled, then mixed with eggs. Australian Aborigines ground the seeds, making a paste eaten fresh or baked. Settlers boiled and ate the leaves. The French soup *bonne femme* combines purslane with French sorrel. It has become an abundant "weed" in my garden, where I find it a refreshing snack.

© Jessie M. Harris

with 5 petals, golden yellow, 1-inch (2.5-cm) diameter, borne individually on slender stems. Leaves: 4 to 8 inches (10 to 20 cm), silver white, hairy underneath, toothed around the edges, with 12 to 15 pairs running along each stem. Root: Short, thick rootstock. Blooms: July to September.

HABITAT: Asia and Europe, especially common along England's roadsides, on nitrogen-rich loamy soils. Naturalized in many areas, including Armenia, China, Australia, New Zealand, and Chile.

CULTIVATION: Perennial. Zone: 5. Germination: 15 to 20 days. Space: 12 to 18 inches (30 to 45 cm). Soil Temperature: 65° to 70° F (18° to 21° C). Soil: Moist, clay, fairly poor suitable. pH: 5.5 to 7.5. Sun: Full sun. Propagation: By seed.

GARDEN DESIGN: The silvery leaves of this cinquefoil make it the most popular cinquefoil in herb and rock gardens. It stands out strikingly against the herb garden's predominant greens.

CONSTITUENTS: Flavonoids (quercitin), alcohol starch.

RELATED SPECIES: There are over 300 species, including Tormentilla (P. *erecta*, previously P. *tormentilla*), a European astringent used as a tooth powder and to treat colic and fevers (it contains quinoric acid, also found in cinchona bark). It has been found to have some immune-stimulating properties. P. *anserina* (the non-variety) is less attractive with silver-gray on the underside only.

HISTORY: Called potent or powerful, from the Latin *potens*, cinquefoil is thought to be the "Myriophyllon" described by Dioscorides, who boiled it in salt water to treat hemorrhages. Old English herbals refer to it as *argentina*, from the Latin *argent*, or silver, and one of its modern names remains silverweed. The name *cinquefoil* is common to many herbs in this genus and describes their common trait of having 5 (*cinque*, or the Latin *quinte) foil*, or leaves. However, such is not the case with this particular species.

CULINARY: A wild edible, the root can be boiled, roasted, or eaten raw.

MEDICINAL: Cinquefoil is an astringent. A poultice of cinquefoil leaves can be placed on hemorrhoids, or the tea can be gargled to tighten spongy gums and loose teeth. A tea sweetened with honey is suggested for soothing a sore throat. In the past, it was found in formulas for uterine and stomach spasms and painful menstruation, and it was added to douche formulas. It is also diuretic, a folk remedy for gravel, and was once even used to treat tetanus. Rudolf Weiss relates in *Herbal Medicine* his experience of using it for dysentery while a prisoner of war, but adds that it was only moderately effective.

COSMETIC: Traditionally, those concerned about freckles, dark spots, pimples, or sunburn used a strong tea of cinquefoil to improve the complexion. Fomentations were used on fresh scars to prevent skin pitting from smallpox and acne.

OTHER: Cinquefoil is used in homeopathy. Animals, including cattle, horses, geese, and pigs, enjoy dining on it.

Poterium sanguisorba • Salad Burnet

FAMILY: Rosaceae.
DESCRIPTION: Forms a mounded clump. Height: 1¹/₂ feet (45 cm). Width: 1 foot (30 cm). Flowers: Tufted, round balls rising on thin stems, green with crimson tufts, about ¹/₂ inch (1.25 cm) wide.

Leaves: Run along stems in 7 to 15 leaflets, divided into many lobes. Blooms: June to August.

HABITAT: Native to Europe and Asia, salad burnet has naturalized itself elsewhere, including the United States, along roadsides, on the edges of woods, and in grassy, dry meadows.

CULTIVATION: Perennial. Zone: 4. Germination: 8 to 10 days. Space 8 to 12 inches (20 to 30 cm). Soil Temperature: 70° F (21° C). Soil: Sandy, well drained. It thrives even in poor soil, but is more bitter. pH: 7 to 8.5. Sun: Full sun. Propagation: By seed, or divide in the spring or fall. It can be transplanted when young, until the taproot develops. Once established, burnet will continue to appear every year.

GARDEN DESIGN: Salad burnet is suitable for filling in herb garden gaps around large perennials that are not full grown or as a ground cover. Elaborate Tudor herb and knot gardens used it for a low-growing border. It winters well and can be picked fresh most of the winter in areas where there is no snow.

CONSTITUENTS: Vitamin C, essential oil, tannins, flavones.

RELATED SPECIES: The old herbals often prefer the tall—3 to 5 feet (.9 to 1.5 m)—great burnet *(S. officinalis)*. Used in Chinese compounds, clinical studies show it to be effective against bacillary dysentery and skin diseases such as eczema and athlete's foot, cervical erosion, uterine bleeding, and gastrointestinal hemorrhage.[1]

HISTORY: The Greeks named burnet *Poterium* after *poterion*, their drinking cup that signifies its popularity in flavoring beverages. It was considered to be an especially cooling drink. Dodoen's 16th-century *Herbal* states that a couple of stalks of the leaves in wine "doth comfort and rejoice the hart and keep it from trembling!"

CULINARY: Salad burnet's flavor resembles that of cucumbers. Use it fresh since it loses much flavor when dried. As its name implies, it is used in salads, but the leaves are tougher than most salad greens, and I prefer blending them into salad dressing or using them as a garnish. The fresh leaves with cottage or cream cheese make a tasty dip. The leaflets removed from the stiff main stem can be added to sandwiches or can float in a punch bowl. Blended with water and frozen in icecube trays, burnet can flavor drinks throughout the year.

MEDICINAL: Gout and rheumatism sufferers in the 17th century drank burnet-flavored wine to ease their discomfort. *Sanguisorba* means to "absorb blood," and the dried, powdered leaves are indeed an astringent that stops bleeding. Chewing a leaf alleviates indigestion and drinking the tea stops diarrhea. Studies indicate that its properties are due to more than just the presence of astringent tannins. Chinese medicine uses the root on burns and wounds to reduce inflammation and infection. It has also been used to help heal ulcerative colitis. Used in dentifrice, it is said to prevent and treat periodontal disease.

BURNET DIP

1   cup (240 ml) cottage cheese
3   tablespoons (45 ml) milk
2   tablespoons (30 ml) chopped burnet, fresh
3   burnet leaves, whole

Whip cottage cheese, milk, and seasonings together in a blender until smooth. Serve garnished with a few whole leaves.

Potentilla anserina
CINQUEFOIL

Prunella vulgaris
SELF-HEAL

Prunella vulgaris • Self-Heal
(Previously *P. incisa*)

FAMILY: Labiatae.

DESCRIPTION: A slow creeper with a typical mintlike form. Height: To 1 foot (30 cm). Width: 6 inches (15 cm). Flowers: Violet-purple, occasionally pink. Leaves: Somewhat oval leaves, pointed at tip. Blooms: May to June.

HABITAT: Eurasia, but widely naturalized, including throughout much of North America and temperate eastern Australia.

CULTIVATION: Perennial. Zone: 3 to 4. Germination: 1 to 3 weeks. Space: 8 to 12 inches (20 to 30 cm). Soil Temperature: 60° to 70° F (15° to 21° C). Soil: Well drained. pH: 6 to 7. Sun: Full sun, or will grow straggly in partial shade. Propagation: By seed, cuttings, or divide root clumps. It reseeds abundantly, especially in garden soil, and also travels by runners, so be sure to keep it under control.

GARDEN DESIGN: Self-heal may be a weed in many gardener's eyes, but it looks right at home in an herb garden.

CONSTITUENTS: Triterpenes (ursolic, betulinic, oleanolic acids).

RELATED SPECIES: *P. grandiflora* grows to 2 feet (60 cm) and has a number of cultivars used in landscaping design.

HISTORY: Although its actions are considered weak by many modern herbalists, it once was held in such great esteem, it was christened both self-heal and allheal. It was said if self-heal grew in your yard, you didn't need a medicine chest. Self-heal's ability to stop bleeding gave it an assortment of other names, including Carpenter's herb, sicklewort, and woundwort. Cole tells us in his *Adam in Eden* (1657) that it is called "Brunella, from *brunellen,* which is a name given unto it by the Germans, because it cureth that inflammation of the mouth which they call *die Braüne* [quinsy], yet the general name of it in Latin nowadays is *Prunella,* as being a word of a more gentile pronunciation." In Germany, the herb is still called *Gemeine Brunelle.*

MEDICINAL: Astringency and germ-fighting capabilities have led to self-heal leaves' use as a mouthwash or gargle for sore throat and gum and other mouth inflammations. As a skin salve, they are applied on rashes, cuts, burns, and bruises. Self-heal was once used against gout and diphtheria and to stop diarrhea. The Chinese still find it useful in reducing fevers and as a diuretic.

Pulmonaria officinalis • Lungwort
(Previously *P. maculata*)

FAMILY: Boraginaceae.

DESCRIPTION: Groundcover of tall leaves. Height: 1 foot (30 cm). Width: 1 to 1¹/₂ feet (30 to 45 cm). Flowers: Rose-violet to blue as they mature, sometimes reddish, tube-shaped, open at end. Leaves: Rough, hairy, oval, coming to a point, white spots, 1 foot (30 cm) long. Blooms: March to April.

HABITAT: Europe in mixed woodlands, introduced elsewhere.

CULTIVATION: Perennial. Zone: 2 to 3. Germination: 2 to 6 weeks. Space: 8 to 12 inches (20 to 30 cm). Soil Temperature: 65° to 75° F (18° to 24° C). Soil: Well drained, calcium-rich. Prefers mois-

Pulmonaria officinalis
LUNGWORT

ture. pH: 6 to 7. Sun: Partial shade or full sun, if well watered. Propagation: Easily cultivated by seed or root division. Self-seeds so readily, you may want to clip off the old flowers before they go to seed.

GARDEN DESIGN: Lungwort is an old-fashioned, favorite landscaping plant, making an eye-catching groundcover for a shady part of the garden. Take advantage of its early blooming. It is sometimes used as a border, but spreads by runners and must be maintained.

CONSTITUENTS: Mucilage, saponin, allantoin, flavonoids (quercertin, kaempferol), tannin, silica, mineral salts (potassium, iron). Does *not* contain pyrrolizidine alkaloids found in other members of Boraginaceae family, such as comfrey and borage.

RELATED SPECIES: *P. officinalis* var. *immaculata* has entirely green leaves, and *P. picta* has gray-green leaves with white spots. Lungwort is sometimes confused with another lung herb called lung moss or lungwort *(Lobaria pulmonaria),* found growing on European oak trees.

HISTORY: Lungwort, or "lung-plant," was commonly used to treat lung problems in medieval days. According to the *Doctrine of Signatures* promoted by the Muslim Avicenna (980–1037), the spotted leaves resemble the lungs and are a key to its use.

MEDICINAL: As you might have guessed, lungwort has been used primarily for lung problems, especially in cases of bronchitis and laryngitis, and to reduce bronchial congestion. The silica it contains restores the elasticity of lungs, and made it an appropriate remedy when tuberculosis was common. Although it is not a common medicinal in the United States, it is a major ingredient in the English "Potters Balm of Gilead Cough Mixture." An astringent, lungwort treats diarrhea and hemorrhoids. Its properties are similar to those in comfrey. Both contain allantoin, which promotes wound-healing action. A well-known Russian folk medicine, lungwort was the subject of experiments conducted by the Moscow Medical Institute from 1963 to 1965 to substantiate the herb's beneficial actions on the lungs.

Rosa damascena • Damask Rose

FAMILY: Rosaceae.

DESCRIPTION: Prickly bush. Height: To 8 feet (2.4 m) Width: 4 feet (1.2 m). Flowers: Pink to red, double petals, soft, rounded, and slightly folded back on themselves. Very fragrant. Leaves: In groups of 5 leaflets, with rough edges, to 2¹/₂ inches (6.25 cm) long. Blooms: May to June.

HABITAT: Asia Minor. Cultivated mostly in Bulgaria, Iran, and India.

CULTIVATION: Perennial. Zone: 5. Germination: 2 to 3 months. Space: 3 to 4 feet (.9 to 1.2 m). Soil Temperature: 70° to 75° F (21° to 23° C). Soil: Fairly rich, well drained. pH: 5.5 to 6.5. Sun: Full sun. Propagation: Usually by cuttings. Dry, hot weather produces more fragrant flowers.

GARDEN DESIGN: Roses grace the herb garden like no other plant, with both beauty and fragrance.

CONSTITUENTS: Flower: essential oil includes geraniol, nerol, citronellol, eugenol; Rosehips: vitamins C (to 1.7%), B, E, K, nicotinamide, organic acids, pectin.

RELATED SPECIES: There are more than 10,000 cultivated roses. The damask rose is sometimes confused with *R. gallica* cv. 'Versicolor'—the apothecary rose. *Rosa damascena* is thought to be a natural seedling produced from *R. gallica* crossed with *R. phoenicia.* Sweetbriar *(R. eglanteria)* has delicate single pale pink petals and a strong fragrance. The clove-scented *R. rugosa* is very hardy and makes a good hedge plant; its hips contain high quantities of vitamin C.

HISTORY: Roses were cultivated at first in Persia—now Iran—then throughout the ancient world. *Rosa* comes from the Greek word for red, *rodon.* The Greek poetess Sappho first christened it "Queen of Flowers" around 600 B.C. The Romans' red Provins rose *(R. gallica)* lavishly covered banquet floors, statues, wedding couples, and the streets in front of victors. A rose suspended over the table signified that all talk beneath it would be confidential, or *sub rosa.* (The plaster rose once placed in the center of ceilings had the same intent.) There is a story that a Persian princess, Nour-Djihan, discovered rose oil while being rowed during her wedding procession in a canal filled with fresh roses. The hot day caused the oil to float on the water's surface. When the princess swept her hand into the water, it was covered with exquisite perfume. She begged her father to have his alchemist extract that essence, and thus began the manufacture of attar of roses in Persia in 1612. The plant probably came to Damascus from Persia.

Between 1254 and 1270 Robert de Brie brought it back from the Crusades to his castle in Champagne, France. In 1520, Dr. Linacre, court physician to King Henry VIII, brought the damask rose to England, where it was known as the "York and Lancaster," a symbol of the union of the warring houses of the Red and White Roses. By the 18th century, France began making rose oil, but its main product was the delicately scented rose water produced as a by-product of distilling rose oil. The damask rose reached its zenith in popularity in the 19th century, when over 300 varieties were introduced.

CULINARY: The rosehips, and even the petals themselves, make delicious jams, jellies, candies, and syrups. Rose petal sandwiches started with placing a hunk of butter with rose petals in a closed jar overnight. The delicately flavored butter was spread on thin slices of bread that were made into sandwiches with a few fresh petals showing around the edges. Medieval cooks served "holy water" of rose water, honey, marjoram, and ginger. Roses were also included in the liqueur Parfait d'Amour. *Lassi,* an East Indian yogurt drink, is flavored with rose water.

MEDICINAL: The *British Pharmacopoeia* only indicates *R. gallica,* but most old roses are medicinal. Honey of Red Rose was once an "official" pharmaceutical preparation in the United States for sore mouths and throats. Rose vinegar was used for headaches, especially those brought on by heat. The leaves are a mild, but seldom used, laxative. Rose oil is also very antiseptic.

AROMATHERAPY: Damask roses are the major source of attar of roses, mostly distilled from flowers grown in Bulgaria. The oil is distinguished by its incredible fragrance and the fact that it congeals at about 17° F (–8.3 C). The Turkish rose oil is slightly less expensive.

COSMETIC: Rose is said to be good for most skin types and is used in a wide range of cosmetics.

OTHER: Rose petals and rosehips add color and fragrance to potpourris.

> —In your world, said the little prince, men cultivate five thousand roses in one garden . . . and still they do not find what they seek.
> —That is true, I said.
> —And yet what they are seeking may be found in a single rose or a drop of water.
> —So it can, I answered.
> And, the little prince went on, but the eyes are blind: one must seek with the heart.
> —THE LITTLE PRINCE, ANTOINE DE SAINT-EXUPERY **(1900–1945),** FRENCH

ROSEBEADS

These instructions come from *Godey's Lady's Book.*

¹/₂ **pound (226 g) fresh rose petals**
¹/₄ **pound (113 g) fine salt**
¹/₂ **ounce (15 ml) each**
      cloves
      allspice

Pound the ingredients together in a mortar or grind in a meat or grain grinder. (If your rose petals are not moist enough to form balls, boil them in a small amount of water first.) Shape into balls, sliding a thick needle or toothpick through the center for a hole. They will shrink and dry in a few days and continue to harden with age. When very hard, they can be polished with vegetable oil.

> The Spring comes garland bearing.
> And wreath and blossom wearing;
> And we will aye be singing
> The Roses she is bringing.
> Come! Comrades! songs are ringing
> To Summer Rose! Sweet Summer Rose.
>
> This flower takes off diseases,
> In sickness gently pleases;
> Its old age cannot sever
> The scent it loses never;
> And dead we keep for ever
> The perfumed air of Roses fair.
> —ODE 51, ANACREON **(580–490** B.C.), GREEK

© Derek Fell

A rose is a rose is a rose is a rose.
—"GEOGRAPHY AND PLANTS" IN *SACRED EMILY,* 1922,
GERTRUDE STEIN (1874–1946), AMERICAN

*But the roses—they were the loveliest of all....In the early
morning, washed in the dew, they felt so soft, so pure, I could
not help wondering if they did not resemble the asphodels of
God's garden.*
—*THE STORY OF MY LIFE,* **HELEN KELLER (1880–1968), AMERICAN**

Rosemarinus officinalis • **Rosemary**

FAMILY: Labiatae.

DESCRIPTION: Tall, stout shrub. Height: 4 to 6 feet (1.2 to 1.8 m). Width: 4 feet (1.2 m). Flowers: Pale blue, sometimes pink or white. Leaves: Long, narrow, leathery, folded into themselves, deep green on top and white and slightly fuzzy underneath. Blooms: May to July.

HABITAT: The Mediterranean, Portugal, and Spain.

CULTIVATION: Perennial. Zone: 6–8. Germination: 15 to 20 days. Space: 2 to 3 feet (60 to 90 cm). Soil Temperature: 55° to 77° F (13° to 25° C). Soil: Well drained, fairly dry. pH: 5 to 8. Sun: Full sun. Propagation: By seed, cuttings, or layering. Avoid peat pots, which are too acid. Mulch in the winter if the ground freezes and temperatures dip below 20° F (–6.6° C). With adequate light and drainage, rosemary can be grown as a houseplant.

GARDEN DESIGN: Rosemary is one of the highlights of herb garden design. Its tall, graceful bush is interesting throughout the year and one of the earliest bloomers. It can be pruned into topiary shapes or trimmed into a hedge. Or you can copy the Tudor style and train it to grow in patterns against a wall. This serves a double purpose in protecting this sensitive plant from frost and wind. The rose gardens of Algiers and Morocco were once edged by low borders of clipped rosemary.

CONSTITUENTS: Essential oils include cineole, borneol, camphor, linalool, verbenol; flavonoids (diosmin), rosemarinic acids.

RELATED SPECIES: There are many cultivars, including the white flowering *R. officinalis* 'Alba', the groundcover 'Prostratus', and the bright blue-violet–flowered 'Tuscan Blue'. 'Aja' is a cultivar that tolerates temperatures as low as –10° F (–23° C).

HISTORY: The name comes from the Latin *ros maris,* or "dew of the sea," where it loves to grow. It was later called Rose of Mary, or rosemary, in honor of the Virgin Mary. The ancients said that it strengthens memory. Shakespeare remembered it when Ophelia says in Hamlet, "There's rosemary, that's for remembrance, pray you love, remember." Thought to encourage couples to remember their wedding vows, it was entwined into the bride's head wreath and, tied with ribbons, was presented to wedding guests. It was added to wine and used to toast the bride's special wishes. Anne of Cleves wore "a circlet of gold, precious stones set full with Twigs of Rosemary" when she married King Henry VIII. The custom of placing it in tombs to remember the dead dates back to ancient Egypt. It was laid on Shakespeare's Juliet, and in Australia today, a sprig is worn on Anzac Day in memory of the dead. Rosemary was burned for church incense and (until recently) purified the air in French hospitals. Its Old French name was *incensier.* Sixteenth-century Europeans carried it in pouches and in the heads of walking sticks to ward off the plague, and judges placed it on their benches to protect them from typhoid. The English statesman, Sir Thomas More (1478–1535), wrote in the 16th century:

> *As for Rosemarine,*
> *I lett it run all over my garden walls,*
> *Not onlie because my bees love it,*
> *But because 'tis the herb*
> *Sacred to remembrance*
> *And, therefore, to friendship.*

Rosemarinus officinalis
ROSEMARY

CULINARY: Rosemary is often eaten in Italy, where cooks are masters at using such strong flavors subtly. The classical Roman Easter dish, *abbacchio,* lamb, is flavored with rosemary. Rosemary is used mostly with peas, greens, meats, and eggs and is excellent with tofu. The French town of Narbonne is famous for its rosemary honey. Rutgers University in New Jersey has found that a dilution of .02% is a more powerful food preservative and antioxidant and is less toxic than the chemicals BHA and BHT. Research continues to develop a commercial preservative.

MEDICINAL: Rosemary leaves also deserve a place in the medicine cabinet. Studies show they increase circulation, reduce headaches, and fight bacterial and fungal infections.[1] The flavonoid diosmin strengthens fragile blood vessels, possibly even more effectively than rutin. German pharmacies sell rosemary ointment to rub on nerve and rheumatic pains and for heart problems. A traditional European treatment for those suffering from poor circulation due to illness or lack of exercise is to drink rosemary extracted into white wine. Rosemary improves food absorption by stimulating digestion and the liver, intestinal tract, and gallbladder. It is also used to inhibit kidney- and bladder-stone formation. It makes an antiseptic gargle for sore throats, gum problems, and canker sores. Researchers speculate that rosemarinic acid might even be a good treatment for septic shock.[2] In addition, it inhibited, although didn't destroy, 87% of the cancer cells tested in a laboratory study.[3] Asthma sufferers used to smoke it with coltsfoot and eat bread that had been baked over rosemary wood.

AROMATHERAPY: The original "Queen of Hungary's Water" was a secret formula said to be prepared by a hermit for the elderly Elizabeth, Queen of Hungary, in 1235. It not only cured her paralyzed limbs, it gave her such a beautiful complexion, a young man fell in love with her. According to Grieve, in *A Modern Herbal* (1931), the formula is preserved in Vienna in the queen's own handwriting. Women not only used the waters on their skin and hair but sweetened it with sugar for a "lady's" liqueur. Rosemary is added to baths and liniments to stimulate and warm the skin and relax muscles. Studies from the University of Tübingen, Germany, show that the essential oil is absorbed through the skin and into the blood system in a bath in about the same time as it would be through drinking a cup of rosemary tea. Rosemary's fragrance is said to prevent nightmares, and the smoke was inhaled for weakness of the brain. It is an ingredient in eau de cologne.

COSMETIC: Rosemary is found in hair shampoos and conditioners to decrease dandruff and stimulate as a tonic. In earlier times, the branches were used like hairbrushes. It has flavored tooth powders and toothpastes since medieval days.

Rosemarinus officinalis. **A close-up look at the tiny blooms of rosemary reveal its amazing flowers. Sprigs of the herb have traditionally been worn by brides.**

OTHER: Rosemary is also used in potpourri and as an insect repellent, especially for moths.

> And (she) took especial pride to sleek
> Her lightsome locks of hair;
> With rosemary when she wreathed them.
> —*THE STORY OF CYLLARUS AND HYLONOME,* OVID (43 B.C.–A.D. 17), ROMAN

HUNGARY WATER

The following is said to be close to the genuine formula. If you want to try making this recipe at home, replace the spirits and water with 100 proof alcohol, add the ginger with the other herbs, and strain instead of distilling.

1	pound (500 g) rosemary tops in bloom
1	ounce (28 g) sage, fresh
3	cups (850 ml) rectified spirits (160 proof alcohol)
1	cup (240 ml) water
1	ounce (28 g) Jamaican ginger

Combine ingredients, except ginger. Let sit 10 days. Distill with 1 1/2 pounds (.67 kg) common salt and pour off 6 pints (3.5 l). Add Jamaican ginger, let sit a few days, then filter.

HUNGARY WATERS

British perfumers used this 1866 recipe.

1/4	ounce (7.5 ml) rosemary oil
1/16	ounce (1.8 ml) English lavender oil
1	cup (240 ml) orange flower water
1 1/2	pints (720 ml) rectified spirits (160 proof alcohol)

Combine ingredients in covered container. Shake daily for one week.

ROSEMARY HONEY

This recipe hails from Narbonne, France.

1/2	cup (120 ml) honey
1/8	cup (30 ml) rosemary flowers

Heat the honey and mix in rosemary flowers.

ROSEMARY IN SNOW

Follow this recipe to make a "a Dyschefull of Snow." It is an adaptation from *A Proper Newe Booke of Cokerye,* which appeared in 1575.

1	quart (1 l) thick cream
5	egg whites
1/2	cup (120 ml) powdered sugar
1/2	cup (120 ml) rose water
	Thick branch of rosemary
	Apple

Whip egg whites and beat in sugar and rose water. When thick, place in a colander to strain. Cut an apple so that it is flat on the bottom. Use the apple as a support for the rosemary branch, and set it upright in a platter. Place the whipped "snow" on the branches and around the bottom. Serve at once with sweet wafers.

***Rubus* species**
BLACKBERRY

Rubus species • Blackberry

FAMILY: Rosaceae.
DESCRIPTION: Rambling, thorny shrub with woody stems. Height: To 4 feet (1.2 m) and higher if it climbs on old brambles. Width: 3 to 4 feet (90 to 120 cm). Flowers: 4 white petals. Leaves: 3 leaflets, edged in tiny prickles and feltlike underneath. Fruit: Shiny, black berries composed of many little spheres with large pips and a juicy, sweet taste. Blooms: July to August.
HABITAT: Western United States. Prefers moist ground or streambanks. Blackberry species have naturalized in Australia and become troublesome weeds.
CULTIVATION: Perennial. Zone: 6. Space: 4 to 6 feet (1.2 to 1.8 m). Soil: Rich, mulchy, and moist, especially when fruiting. It prospers when grown by streams. pH: 4 to 6. Sun: Full sun best. Propagation: Will grow from seed, but usually produced from root division or from suckers in the spring, or plant bare root in the autumn. Prune back excess growth during the winter since it flowers and fruits off second-year canes.
GARDEN DESIGN: Blackberries in the herb garden? Well, considering their passion for taking over an area, you might want to restrict them to a hedge or wall on the side of the garden, or use one of the improved cultivars. They are attractive and also provide a delightful reward for the gardener on a hot summer day.
CONSTITUENTS: Vitamin C, organic acids, pectins, tannins, sugars, flavonoids (kaempferol and quercertin).
RELATED SPECIES: There are about 250 species of blackberries, raspberries, boysenberries, loganberries, and related berries, growing mostly in the Northern Hemisphere. The leaves of raspberry *(R. idaeus),* recognized by its white, dusty stems and red berries, are used to strengthen the uterine muscle. It is suggested for most uterine disorders, including painful menstruation, and is a well-known pregnancy tea. Although the active constituents have been difficult to isolate, studies have found raspberry to have both uterine-stimulating and -relaxing actions.
HISTORY: For thousands of years, people—and other animals—have enjoyed eating berries. The blackberry was formerly called "bramble," or *brymbyl,* meaning prickly—certainly a descriptive name for it. In Germany it is still known as *brombere.* Many species are also called dewberry.
CULINARY: The berries easily find their way into pies, jams, jellies, and all manner of sweets. Blackberry wine and brandy have been enjoyed for centuries. In Australia, Aborigines and settlers ate the native raspberries from various species, including *R. gunnianus, R. parvifolius,* and *R. rosifolius.*
MEDICINAL: Early American pioneers encountering brambles enjoyed them both as food and as medicine, spreading the astringent jam on toast to remedy diarrhea. Australian settlers used *R. parvifolius* and *R. hillii* similarly. American salesmen used to carry blackberry wine for the same reason. Eating too many of the bulky pips or the unripe berries, however, will result in a laxative effect. The root bark is the strongest medicine; the gentler leaves are suggested for children. I like to incorporate all four seasons by combining blackberry syrup (made with blackberry honey) and an extract of the roots and leaves. Tannins are thought to be mostly responsible for the astringent action.

OTHER: The root makes an orange dye, the shoots a gray-black dye (due to iron), the vines a red-tan color, and the berries themselves blue-grays.

SPICED BLACKBERRY SYRUP

Here is a warming dessert liqueur to sip during cold winter nights by the fire or to serve on hot summer days over vanilla ice cream. It can be used straight as a syrup or added to carbonated water to make a blackberry soda. It will last for months, long after summer blackberry-picking days are just memories. The syrup can also be canned.

8	*cups (2 l) blackberries*
1	*cup (240 ml) water*
1/2	*cup (120 ml) honey*
1/2	*teaspoon (2.5 ml) cinnamon sticks, chopped*
1/8	*teaspoon (.6 ml) nutmeg*
2	*tablespoons (30 ml) lemon juice, strained*

Coarsely purée the berries in a blender, or mash by hand. Blend in water. Bring to a boil over medium heat, and simmer gently for 5 minutes. Pour through a sieve or jelly bag, and let the juice drain through. Measure 4 cups (1 l) into a pan and add warmed honey. Add spices and lemon juice. Store in very clean bottles in the refrigerator.

BLACKBERRY CORDIAL

This amazingly simple recipe is meant to be sipped with a friend or shared as a gift. Bottled, it will store indefinitely. By the way, don't throw out the strained berries—they are delicious eaten by themselves or combined with the cordial.

4	*cups (1 l) ripe blackberries*
1	*pint (500 ml) brandy*

Mash the berries in a blender or food processor or by hand using a potato masher. Cover the brandy and let stand for 2 to 4 weeks. Strain out the berries, and it is ready to serve, or you can bottle it.

Rubia tinctorium • Madder

FAMILY: Rubiaceae.
DESCRIPTION: Sprawling, many-branched bush with stiff, prickly stems. Height: 4 feet (1.2 m). Width: 2 to 3 feet (60 to 90 cm). Flowers: Green-yellow, clustered in small groups. Leaves: In whorls of 4 to 6, elongated, to 4 inches (10 cm), prickly on midrib and edges. Fruit: Globular, purple-black berry. Root: Slight acrid odor, 1/4 inch (6 mm) thick. Blooms: June, the second or third year.
HABITAT: Southern Europe and Asia Minor.
CULTIVATION: Perennial. Zone: 6. Germination: 2 to 3 weeks. Space: 2 to 3 feet. Soil Temperature: 70° to 75° F (21° to 24° C). Soil: Well drained, deep, loamy. pH: 7.5 to 8.5. Sun: Full sun or partial shade. Propagation: By seed or root division. Blooms second or third year.
GARDEN DESIGN: Madder is best to look at, because it is very prickly to the touch. Place it toward the back of a garden bed where

it can be contrasted with the softer leaf forms of other tall herbs, or grow it as a bristly ground cover or on a tripod.

CONSTITUENTS: Iridoid (asperuloside), anthaquinones [alizarin (red), purpurin (purple), rubiacin (orange), xanine (yellow)].

RELATED SPECIES: Wild European madder *(R. peregrina)* and Indian madder *(R. cordifolia)*, called *munjeet,* are also dye plants.

HISTORY: Both the Greek name, *erythodanon,* and the Roman *rubia* describe the red dye produced by madder root. The Latin botanical name, *tinctura,* also means "color." We get our name for madder from the Anglo-Saxons, who called it *maddre.* Later it became "Adrianople red" and "Turkey red," since it was first exported from these areas to the cloth centers of Holland, Germany, France, and sometimes England. Eventually, it was cultivated in Holland and France, where it dyed the red trousers of the French troops, who also used the bristly leaves to polish metal. The dye also colored the distinctive red fezzes of the Turks. In the 19th century, "maddering" was typically done by a messy process of placing cotton or wool cloth in fermenting baths of madder roots after first treating it with a series of alkali, oily emulsions, sheep dung, oak galls, then the mordant alum. Depending on the mordant used, shades of red, orange, purple, and black developed. The dye was called alizarin, from the active constituent, but since 1868, when a coal-tar derivative was produced, it has been replaced by synthetic alizarin.

MEDICINAL: Madder is still grown as a medicinal in central Europe and west Asia. The root eliminates and prevents the formation of kidney and bladder stones, increases bile production and menstruation, and is a laxative. The red coloring agent is so potent that it turns the urine red and eventually even stains the bones, although no health problems are associated with these phenomena. A madder poultice encourages wound healing. It is used in Ayurvedic medicine in east India and considered an important "blood-purifying" herb that "cleans" the body by improving liver functions.

OTHER: Madder is still used as a dye plant by people specializing in natural dyes, with the young, main roots considered the best.

Rubia tinctorium
MADDER

Rumex scutatus • French Sorrel

FAMILY: Polygonaceae.

DESCRIPTION: Large leaves that branch into several stalks. Height: To 3 feet (90 cm). Flowers: Small, clustered along the tall flower stalks, red-green, turning red-brown as they form into seeds. Leaves: Long, fleshy, ripply, with slightly rounded tips. Blooms: June to September.

HABITAT: Many areas of Europe.

CULTIVATION: Perennial. Zone: 4. Germination: 1 to 2 weeks. Space: 1 foot (30 cm). Soil Temperature: 65° to 70° F (18° to 21° C). Soil: Average, fairly dry garden soil. Sun: Full sun or partial shade will result in a lighter flavor. Shadier areas produce better foliage in hot climates. Propagation: By seed or root division, and it also expands by runners. Cut the flower stalks back if you wish to produce more abundant and less tart leaves. Hot weather encourages blooming, but the entire plant can be cut back to establish new growth.

GARDEN DESIGN: Adds a lush green to the herb garden.

RELATED SPECIES: The garden cultivars include "Large Belleville." A number of other species are eaten, including common yellow dock (*R. crispus*) and the common weed, sheep's sorrel (*R. acetosella*), which is smaller, but similar in appearance. Virgin sorrel (*R. montanus*) doesn't produce seed so remains less acid. It is not related to *Oxalis* species, which are also commonly called sorrel.

MAJOR CONSTITUENTS: Oxalic acid; oxalic salts, mostly potassium binoxalate (to 1%); tartaric acid; tannins.

HISTORY: The Egyptians were enjoying sorrel dishes around 3,000 B.C. Later, both the Romans and Greeks ate sorrel either before or after a large feast. It was first listed in England in 1217 by the Abbess of Cirencester, who included it among her 21 culinary herbs. The name comes from *sur,* meaning sour, from the Old French *surele.* There is much confusion over exactly which sorrel species is discussed in historical literature—and there are about 100 of them. Many of these species were (and still are) eaten. The smaller, more common sorrel (*R. acetosella*), was a common sight in European vegetable gardens of the Middle Ages. It seems to have reached its height of popularity in England during the 16th century reign of King Henry VIII. Sorrel juice was added to ales to give them more body. Sauces, jellies, and jams of sorrel accompanied mutton and poultry dishes. A dish of sorrel leaves mashed with vinegar and sugar called Greensauce was so well-liked, the herb itself went by the same name. Another name was "cuckoo's meate" because it was believed that this bird cleared its throat with sorrel. It was also known as *Herba Acetosa* by apothocaries, in whose formulae it was a common ingredient from the 15th to the 19th century. The lusher French sorrel seems to have been introduced around 1600. It quickly became more popular as a salad and pot herb. John Evelyn, in 1720, said sorrel added "so grateful a quickness to salad that it should never be left out." He also noted that it made "men themselves pleasant and agreeable." While sorrel eventually fell out of English culinary favor, it is still popular in France, where the Parisian Georges Gibault noted in his 1912 *Histoire des Légume* that there are few countries where sorrel is as much liked as in France. Records show that in 1895, 44 million pounds (20 million kilograms) of sorrel were delivered to the French markets. While it was a garden plant in the early 19th century, it is rarely seen for sale in the United States today.

CULINARY: The sharp, lemony taste of sorrel leaves comes from their combination of oxalic acid and vitamin C. They are often cooked like, or with spinach leaves, which also contain oxalic acid. Most traditional recipes mix sorrel with milk. The Irish have a sorrel and milk dish that is mixed with fish. Laplanders mix it with reindeer milk! The Germans enjoy it and Scandinavians add it to meal and eat it. The English still make a sauce of sorrel, blending it with butter and soup stock and thickening the dish with a little flour. Various species of sorrel are also eaten in China and Japan, in East India it is featured in soups and omelets. But by far the most famous dish is French sorrel soup, which is often served cold as part of a summertime meal. Sorrel also makes an appearance as the flavoring in *Fricassée* soup and *Soupe aux herbes,* as well as *potage germiny,* or cream of sorrel soup. The French used to boil the root with barley water to make it turn red and be more appealing to invalids eating the broth. By the way, sorrel is only cooked in stainless steel or enamel pans because the acid it contains turns metal black.

MEDICINAL: Sorrel leaves act as a diuretic. Research has shown them to be a mild antiseptic and a light laxative. They were once used to prevent scurvy due to vitamin C content. Sorrel was also once a popular "spring cure," usually in form of sorrel soup. Raw, the leaves are a cooling agent for fevers and relieve thirst. I always find them very refreshing to nibble on while gardening on hot days.

CONSIDERATIONS: Oxalic acid in large amounts is a kidney irritant and is poisonous. Even the small amounts found in sorrel are thought to be harmful if taken in large quantities. Anyone with a kidney disorder, gout, rheumatism, or who is pregnant should avoid it, just to be on the safe side. The acid is water soluble, so boiling and discarding the water greatly reduces it.

OTHER: The dried seed stalks are used in floral arrangements, although wild dock seed stalks are fuller and sturdier than those of French sorrel. The sorrels are used as a pre-dye, or mordant, since the oxalic acid they contain produces a more permanent black dye on fabric. Sorrel also served as an inkstain remover.

Potage Germiny, or Cream of French Sorrel Soup

2	cups (450 g) sorrel leaves, finely chopped
1	tablespoon (30 ml) butter or oil
2	shallots
3	cups (720 ml) soup stock
2	sprigs fresh (2 tablespoons or 60 ml dried) chervil, chopped fine
1/4	teaspoon (2 ml) black pepper, ground
3	tablespoons (90 ml) flour
3	egg yolks
1/2	cup (120 ml) cream
	fresh chervil for garnish

Lightly cook the sorrel and shallots in butter or oil for a few minutes, until sorrel becomes limp. Add soup stock and simmer 2 minutes. Let cool. Puree in blender with other ingredients. Return to stove, heating slowly until it thickens. Serve hot or cold. The traditional garnish is fresh chervil leaves.

Rumex scutatus
FRENCH SORREL

***Rumex scutatus.* French sorrel is the most lush and tasty of the sorrels, offering a tart, lemon-like flavor when used either raw or cooked.**

Ruta graveolens • Rue

FAMILY: Rutaceae.

DESCRIPTION: Small, rounded bush. Height: 3 feet (90 cm). Width: 2 feet (60 cm). Flowers: Yellow, with scooplike flowers. Leaves: Spadelike, to 1/4 inch (6 mm) long, blue-gray, with a powerful smell. Fruit: Globular seedpods, with deep indentations. Resembles a miniature green orange, to which rue is related. Blooms: June to September.

HABITAT: Southern Europe.

CULTIVATION: Perennial. Zone: 4. Germination: 10 to 14 days. Space: 1 foot (30 cm). Soil Temperature: 60° to 70° F (15° to 21° C). Soil: Well drained. (Wet soil during a cold winter can kill it.) pH: 6 to 8. Sun: Full sun or partial shade, although it will be more straggly. Propagation: From seed or cuttings. They grow larger and fuller in gardens in warm climates.

GARDEN DESIGN: The blue-green foliage is reason alone to include rue in your herb-garden plans. It contrasts well with the typical greens of many other herbs and also sets off the gray *Artemisias*. It is best grown in a partially sheltered location.

CONSTITUENTS: Essential oil (to 0.6%) includes methylnonylketone (to 90%), limone, cineole; alkaloids (fagarine, arborinine); coumarins (bergapten, xanthotoxin, psoralen); flavonoids (quercitin, rutin, named after rue).

RELATED SPECIES: Interestingly enough, rue belongs to the citrus family, and its seeds resemble miniature citrus fruits. *R. graveolens* cv. 'Variegata' has leaves variegated with white. *R. graveolens* var. *divaricata* has yellow-green leaves. The narrow-leafed *R. chalepensis* from Greece has a stronger scent and pointed seed capsules and is more likely to cause dermatitis. Rue is not related to Syrian rue *(Peganum harmala)*, or "harmel," which produces a red dye, harmala red.

HISTORY: Our name for rue comes from the Greek *rhutē*. Roman painters ate *R. graveolens* in an effort to preserve their eyesight. The Latin name means "strong smell"—an accurate description! It was the herb used by John Milton's angel, along with eyebright *(Euphasia)*, to purge Adam's sight in *Paradise Lost*. The *Talmud*, the ancient book of Jewish law, describes rue as a medicine so important to the people that no tithe was imposed on it. Rue was the main ingredient in Mithridates's famous poison antidotes. Mithradates (132 B.C.–A.D. 63) became ruler of Pontus in Asia Minor by poisoning his opposition. Fearful of revenge, he daily consumed minute doses of aconite, hellebore, opium, and other poisons to build up his immunity. Rue was included as an antidote. After he was killed (with a knife!) the secret formula was found on him. The famous antidote recipe eventually discarded the poisons, but always contained rue. It inspired (along with formulas that Galen copied from the Greeks) other secret and very expensive cure-alls such as "The Drink of the Apostles," the "Drink of Antioch," "Gratia Dei," and an assortment of "theriacas" that were sold throughout Europe until the mid-nineteenth century. Many contained over one hundred ingredients, including horehound, pennyroyal, lavender, saffron, fennel, and carrot seeds, that were mixed with honey or wine and said to cure almost every imaginable disease, including the plague, tuberculosis, and snakebite. The name therica came from snake—which often served as an ingredient! Later the potions were called "electuaries."

Rue and garlic were included in the "Vinegar of the Four Thieves" (see page 29) during the plague. Rue stems were tied into bouquets of rosemary and southernwood to protect judges from *gaol-fever* (typhoid). Charles Dickens (1812–1870) refers to these courtroom herbs in *A Tale of Two Cities*. It was called the "Herb of Grace" and the "Herb of Repentance," and the dew water that collects in the cuplike flowers was the original holy water used for high mass. The gardener in Shakespeare's Richard II noted rue when he said:

> Poor Queen,
> Here did she fall a tear; here in this place
> I'll set a bank of rue, sour herb of grace.
> Rue, even for Ruth, shall shortly here be seen,
> In the remembrance of a weeping queen.

CULINARY: As pungent as it is, rue is nevertheless added to Italian salads, but in very small amounts. Ethiopians prepare a sharp sauce of cayenne and rue, make rue cheese, and mix it with their coffee-leaf beverage. In the United States, the oil is a commercial flavoring in some baked goods, candies, and desserts. Rue is found in an Italian liqueur called *grappa con ruta,* which may have its origins in a rue-flavored honey mead mentioned by Pliny and later known as "sack."

MEDICINAL: Although once an officially recognized treatment for hypertension, diabetes, and allergic reactions, rue is no longer used much medicinally in the United States. It is a popular folk medicine in countries as diverse as Mexico, Lebanon, Iran, India, and China. In traditional Chinese medicine, the leaves are applied to reduce inflammation from snakebites, insect bites, strains, and sprains. The rutin it contains strengthens fragile blood vessels and helps alleviate varicose veins, although using the whole plant has been found to work better. Both an eyewash and a tea are suggested for soothing tired eyes and headaches from eyestrain, and the tea is also used to decrease the pain and inflammation of an earache. Rue increases blood flow to the digestive tract, relaxes muscles, and calms heart palpitations, nervous indigestion, and colic. The Unami medicine of India recommends rue not only to treat various physical conditions, but to improve mental clarity and as an *an*aphrodisiac—although the Polish consider it an aphrodisiac! Ruta is a well-known cold and menstrual cramp remedy in Latin America, where an ointment is also applied for gout and rheumatic pains, and strong tea compresses are placed on the chest for bronchitis. It is used to kill intestinal parasites, and Arabs add it to suspect water to counteract any ill effects.

CONSIDERATIONS: Some people experience dermatitis from touching rue, so the ancients rubbed olive oil on their arms before harvesting the herb. It should not be taken during pregnancy since it is a uterine stimulant. The coumarins may cause photosensitivity; large dosages can be poisonous.

OTHER: Rue's seedpods are used in dried wreaths. Rue water was once sprinkled around the house to repel insects, especially fleas. Rue is also used in homeopathy.

Ruta graveolens
Rue

Of use to sight, a noble plant is Rue;
O blear-eyed man, 'twill sharpen sight for you!
In men, it curbs love's strongest appetite,
In women, tends to amplify its might.
Yet rue to chastity inclines mankind,
Gives power to see and sharpens, too, the mind;
And instantly, when in decoction, frees
Your house for ever from tormenting fleas.
—"Of Rue," **Regimen Sanitatis Salerni, 10th-Century Italy**

Rue, myrrh, and cummin for the sphinx
Her muddy eye to clear.
—"The Sphinx," **Ralph Waldo Emerson (1803–1883), American**

Salvia officinalis
SAGE

Salvia clevelandii
CLEVELAND SAGE

Salvia purpurea
PURPLE SAGE

Salvia officinalis • Sage

FAMILY: Labiatae.

DESCRIPTION: Small, rounded shrub. Height: 2 feet (60 cm). Width: 2 feet (60 cm). Flowers: Violet-blue, pink, or white, to 1³/₈ inches (3.4 cm) long, small, tubelike, clustered together in whorls along the stem tops. Leaves: Woolly white, textured, elongated ovals, 1 to 2¹/₂ inches (2.5 to 6.25 cm). The drier the weather, the grayer the leaf color. Blooms: May to June.

HABITAT: North and central Spain to the west Balkans and Asia Minor.

CULTIVATION: Perennial. Zone: 4–5. Germination: 2 to 3 weeks. Space: 1¹/₂ to 2 feet (45 to 60 cm). Soil Temperature: 60° to 70° F (15° to 21° C). Soil: Well drained, sandy, fairly rich with some nitrogen. pH: 6 to 6.5. Sun: Full sun. Propagation: By seed, cuttings, or layering. Sow seeds 6 to 8 weeks before the first frost. Needs mulch when temperatures drop below 0° F (–18° C). Dry the leaves quickly so they don't blacken.

GARDEN DESIGN: The stately sage is a necessity for the herb garden. Its gray leaves contrast especially well with green herbs and pink flowers, such as those of wood betony, or blend with textures of other gray herbs. It can be used as a border, although severe trimming exposes hollow areas.

CONSTITUENTS: Essential oil (to 2.8%) includes thujone, cineole, borneol, linalool, camphor, salvene; estrogenlike substances, flavonoids; organic acids.

RELATED SPECIES: There are more than 750 *Salvias* throughout the world. Some garden favorites with the same flavor as *S. officinalis* are purple sage *(S. officinalis* 'Purpurascens' and 'Purpurea') and variegated sage *(S. officinalis* 'Tricolor') with green and white, sometimes purple and pink, mottled leaves. The more tender *S. officinalis* cv. 'Icterina' has yellow-edged leaves. All are edible. Two of my personal favorites, both from Mexico, are pineapple-scented sage *(S. elegans)* and Mexican sage *(S. leucantha)* with deep purple, woolly flowers. The most widely cultivated is the tender scarlet sage *(S. splendens),* which blooms all summer but must be treated as an annual in cold climates.

HISTORY: Sage was used in Crete in 1600 B.C. to clear throat inflammation—still one of its most popular uses today. Both the common and botanical names originate in the Latin *salvare*, "to save," perhaps referring to its ability to save health. Greeks called it *elifagus*, which became the Greek *sphakos* and later, *sawge* in Old English. To assure good health, the English toasted with, "He that would live for aye, Must eat Sage in May" as they drank an ale made of sage, betony, spikenard, squinnette, and fennel seed. The Chinese also valued sage *(Shu-wei-ts'ao)*, eagerly trading their black tea for it.

CULINARY: Sage is a strong antioxidant and antibacterial agent that was added to meat, especially sausage, not only for flavor but as a preservative. Sage pancakes maintained a long-standing popularity that lasted from the 5th century B.C. to the 18th century! Early Americans made sage breads and rolls and sage butter to top them. They also candied both flowers and leaves. Sage has long been added to improve the bouquet of poor wine. Sage wine was a favorite of England's King Henry III (ruled 1216–1272) and his son Edward I (ruled 1272–1307). Sage makes an excellent vinegar and is the main seasoning in most stuffings.

MEDICINAL: Sage leaves are a well-known cold germ and flu fighter. For centuries, sage has been gargled for laryngitis and tonsillitis and used as a mouthwash or swab for infected gums and sores in the mouth. It has been found to be very effective against staph infections.[1] Basically, sage reduces many physical emissions. Sweating is reduced by half about 2 hours after taking sage. The essential oil is used in some body deodorants. A German product, Salsat®, is marketed as an antiperspirant.[2] Sage's hormonal components are thought to be responsible for decreasing mother's milk and reducing painful menstruation or hot flashes during menopause.[3] The Greek philosopher Theophrastus (circa 372–287 B.C.) called sage an "excellent article for excessive desire or sexual debility." Sage also lessens saliva production, and the tea was proven to lower blood sugar in diabetics, especially when taken on an empty stomach.[4]

AROMATHERAPY: In France, the fragrance of sage was said to relieve mental grief and physical stress. Asthmatics used to smoke the dried leaves or inhale the fumes of burning sage.

COSMETIC: Sage is a hair and scalp conditioner that brings out dark highlights in the hair. Its astringent effect on the skin and scalp counters excessive oiliness, dandruff, and perspiration.

CONSIDERATIONS: Although sage contains very little thujone (also found in wormwood and a number of other herbs), it should not be taken in large amounts over a long period of time. The small amount used to flavor food is not a problem. It does cause indigestion in some people.

SAGE WALNUT STUFFING

Use as stuffing to fill cooked acorn squash halves.

2	**medium onions, chopped**
¹/₄	**cup (60 ml) oil or butter**
¹/₂	**teaspoon (2.5 ml) sage, ground**
¹/₈	**teaspoon (.6 ml) black pepper, ground**
¹/₈	**teaspoon (.6 ml) thyme, ground**
¹/₂	**teaspoon (2.5 ml) salt**
2	**tablespoons (30 ml) parsley flakes**
2	**cups (500 ml) dry bread crumbs**
1	**cup (240 ml) walnuts, chopped**
¹/₄	**cup (60 ml) celery, diced**
6	**ounces (180 g) mushrooms**

Sauté onions in oil or melted butter and add spices. Combine bread crumbs, walnuts, celery, and mushrooms. Stir onion blend into bread crumb mixture.

> *Why should he die, whose garden groweth sage?*
> *No other plant with death such stife can wage.*
> *Sage soothes the nerves, and stills a trembling hand,*
> *And sharpest fevers fly at his command.*
> *The beaver, sage, and lavender will bring,*
> *With tansy, and the cress, first gifts of spring.*
> —"OF SAGE." *REGIMEN SANITATIS SALERNI,* 10TH-CENTURY ITALY

Salvia sclarea
CLARY SAGE

Salvia sclarea • Clary Sage

FAMILY: Labiatae.

DESCRIPTION: Large leaves grow off a central stalk that bends with the weight of the flowers. Height: To 3 feet (90 cm). Width: 1 foot (30 cm). Flowers: Lilac or pale blue, pink or white, in whorls on top of the stems, with the upper lip curled up. Leaves: Broad oval or heart-shaped, in pairs, 6 to 9 inches (15 to 22.5 cm) long, covered with fine silver-white hairs, almost stalkless. Blooms: June to July.

HABITAT: Southern Europe and possibly Syria.

CULTIVATION: Biennial. Zone: 6. Germination: 12 to 15 days. Space: 2 to 3 feet (60 to 90 cm). Soil Temperature: 70° F (21° C). Soil: Well drained, fertile, moist preferred, but tolerates dry conditions. pH: 5.3 to 7.2. Sun: Full sun. Propagation: Seedlings started in spring will flower the following season. Plants self-sow.

GARDEN DESIGN: Very effective either in isolated groups or with other herbs in a mixed border. The flowers are very showy.

CONSTITUENTS: Essential oil (to 0.15%) includes linalol; saponine.

RELATED SPECIES: Related to common sage *(S. officinalis)* and about 500 other sage species. *S. sclarea* var. *turkestaniana,* from Turkestan, is similar but particularly striking with its pink-tinged white flowers. Wild clary *(S. verbenaca),* a medieval favorite, was called *Oculus Christi* because it served mainly as an eyewash.

HISTORY: The Romans called it *sclarea,* from *clarus,* or "clear," because they used it as an eyewash. A pun on its name, clary was also

known as "clear eye." The practice of German merchants of adding clary and elder flowers to Rhine wine to make it imitate a good Muscatel was so common that Germans still call the herb *Muskateller Salbei,* and the English know it as Muscatel Sage. The *Dictionnaire o Economique,* by Chomel (translated by R. Bradley in 1725), described the method: "Take some pounds of Clary-flowers and as much Lees of Wine as will wet the Flowers, which must be grossly pounded; suffer them to macerate for some days; then distil and rectify them thrice on other flowers, and so putting some drops of it into water, or some other liquor, it will make it taste like Muscadine." Clary sometimes replaced hops in beer to produce an enhanced state of intoxication and exhilaration, although this reportedly was often followed by a severe headache. This usage probably contributed to clary's being considered a 12th-century aphrodisiac.

CULINARY: Culpeper recommended a 17th-century sage dish: "The fresh leaves, fried in butter, first dipped in a batter of flour, eggs, and a little milk, serve as a dish to the table that is not unpleasant to fancy and exceedingly profitable."

MEDICINAL: Like its relative sage, clary tea, the leaf juice in ale or beer, was recommended for many types of women's problems, including delayed or painful menstruation. It was once used to stop night sweating in tuberculosis patients. An astringent is gargled, douched, and poured over skin wounds. It is combined with other herbs for kidney problems. The clary seeds form a thick mucilage when soaked for a few minutes, and placed in the eye, helps to remove small, irritating particles. A tea of the leaves is also used as an eyewash. Clary is used not only to improve eyesight, but to reduce muscle spasms.

AROMATHERAPY: Clary is strongly aromatic, with a fragrance sometimes compared to ambergris. According to William Turner, clary "comforts the vital spirits, and helps the memory, and quickens the senses." Aromatherapists use it to produce a state of relaxed euphoria and laboratory studies report it potentiates hypnotic drugs. As a massage oil, it is rubbed into muscle cramps and used to release mental tension. It is also a fixative in perfumes. Clary water (with cinnamon and a little ambergris dissolved into brandy and sugar) was used both to improve the complexion and to aid digestion.

COSMETIC: It is used to reduce excess oil or dandruff on the scalp and for excessively oily complexions.

CONSIDERATIONS: Large doses can produce headaches. And, unless you are interested in having a headache, avoid taking alcohol in conjunction with clary.

CLARY AMULET

Elizabeth Cleland included this recipe for a side dish in her 1755 book *Easy Method of Cookery.*

8	*eggs*
2	*gills (2¹/₂ cups or 600 ml) cream*
¹/₂	*teaspoon (3 ml) pepper*
¹/₂	*teaspoon (3 ml) salt*
	dash nutmeg
	handful clary, chopped fine
1	*tablespoon (15 ml) butter or oil*

Beat the eggs then beat in the other ingredients. Fry in butter or oil over low heat. Turn to brown slightly on both sides.

Serves 4.

Sambucus nigra
ELDER

Sambucus nigra • Elder

FAMILY: Caprifoliaceae.

DESCRIPTION: Small tree with many small trunks rising directly from the ground. Height: To 30 feet (9.1 m). Flowers: Tiny, ¹/₅ inch (5 mm), white, in large, saucerlike umbels, to 8 inches (20 cm). Leaves: Dull green, divided into slender leaflets to 3¹/₂ inches (8.75 cm). Fruit: Clusters of deep purple-black, round fruit that is juicy when ripe. Blooms: June.

HABITAT: Europe, North Africa, and western Asia. Introduced in other areas, and naturalized in cool parts of Australia. Usually found in woodlands in moist areas, by creeks, or high water tables.

CULTIVATION: Perennial. Zone: 5. Germination: 10 to 20 days —soak 2 months at 60° to 65° F (15° to 18° C), stratify then sprout at 40° F (4° C). Space: 10 feet (3 m) from each other, or grow smaller herbs beneath it. Soil Temperature: 65° to 70° F (18° to 21° C). Soil: Nitrogen-rich, moist, or with high water table. pH: 5.5. to 7.5. Sun: Partial shade preferred, or full sun. Propagation: Can be grown from seed, but is usually propagated by cuttings or sometimes root division of young plants.

GARDEN DESIGN: Elder is a small tree, so use it as a backing in a garden setting, or as a shaded, central focus for a bed in a large herb garden. It can be pruned and shaped if needed.

CONSTITUENTS: Flowers: essential oil, flavonoids (rutin, quercertin), alkaloids, anthocyanins, vitamin C. Berries: flavonoids, sugar, fruit acid, vitamin C.

RELATED SPECIES: There are about 20 species and many cultivars. Some cultivars grown for edible berries are sold in garden catalogs. The North American sweet elder *(S. canadensis)* and western elder *(S. caerulea)*, which grow in zone 4, can replace the European species. The American red elder *(S. pubens)* has poisonous red berries. Australian native elderberries are white elderberry *(S. Gaudichaudiana)* and yellow elderberry *(S. australasica).*

HISTORY: Elder has been used at least since the ancient Egyptians discovered that applying its flowers improved the complexion and healed burns. The ancient Romans also used elder, naming it *sambucus.* Called "the medicine chest of the country people" by Europeans, elder has a rich folklore. John Evelyn, the 17th-century botanist, reported that the "berries greatly assist longevity," and the British of his day sipped on elderberry cordials in their coffee houses and eating establishments. My favorite story is of a king whose party, lost in the woods, comes upon an elderly man sitting on his porch, crying because he had dropped his father while carrying him and had been scolded. In disbelief that such an old man could have a living father, the king entered the house and found it filled with extremely elderly people, quietly going about their work. When questioned, they attributed their good health to a simple diet and elderberries. In fact the root of the word *elder,* referring to both an elderly person and the tree, comes from the Anglo-Saxon word for old, *eald.* The 17th-century *The Anatomie of the Elder,* by Dr. Martin Blokwich, recorded over 70 diseases treatable with elderberries. It is the principal herb in the 1988 French film *The Sorceress,* a poignant story, based on fact, about a medieval herbalist who used elder to reduce the serious annual fevers that afflicted the townspeople.

CULINARY: The flowers are eaten raw or turned into fritters, and the young buds can be pickled. The flowers are attractive floating in a punch bowl. The berries can even provide the punch! The traditional elderberry and lemon drink is now sold as a carbonated beverage. The fruit is turned into a variety of jams, jellies, and conserves, as well as elderberry wine. It contains more vitamin C than any herb, except roseships and black currant. Australian Aborigines ate native elderberries.

MEDICINAL: A couple of cups of hot elder tea—made from equal parts of elder flowers, peppermint, and yarrow flowers—is an old and effective remedy for reducing a fever and treating colds, flus, hay fever, and sinus congestion. Elder flowers also make a soothing gargle that reduces the swelling and pain of a sore throat, and a strong tea (made from distilled water and carefully strained through a coffee filter) makes an excellent eyewash, even to treat severe infections like conjunctivitis. The constituent that reduces inflammation is thought to be ursolic acid.[1] Elder flower is a common ingredient in salves for burns, cuts, and swellings. In previous centuries, elderberries were used to treat rheumatism and gout. In 1899, one story goes, a sailor told a physician in Prague, Czechoslovakia, about a sure cure for rheumatic pains; he simply got drunk on port wine. It turned out it wasn't the wine, as the sailor suspected, but the elderberries used to darken and "age" the cheap port.

COSMETIC: Elder flowers in cosmetics and skin washes refine the complexion and help relieve eczema and psoriasis, especially when mixed with other skin-healing herbs.

CONSIDERATIONS: Eating the berries of any species raw can have a strong laxative effect and may cause indigestion. Always cook them to alter this property. The leaves, root, and bark have previously been used by herbalists, but all are too strong for internal use.

OTHER: The berries produce a deep blue dye. Native Americans used flexible, hollow elder stems in basketmaking. Along with the Europeans, they used the hollow stems to make wind instruments and blowguns.

ELDER FLOWER WATER

³/₄   cup (180 g) elder flowers
¹/₄   cup (60 ml) lavender flowers
1   pint (500 ml) distilled water
1   ounce (30 ml) vodka
1   ounce (30 ml) glycerin (optional)

Place elder and lavender flowers in a pan. Cover with boiling water, and let sit until cool. Add vodka. Add glycerin, if desired. Let stand for 12 hours, then strain and bottle. Use as a skin wash.

ELDER FLOWER FRITTERS

1   egg, separated
5   ounces (150 ml) water
1   cup (225 g) flour
2   tablespoons (30 ml) vegetable oil
      Elder flower heads, whole

Blend egg yolk and water into flour. Add oil, and fold in stiffly beaten egg whites. Dip the flower heads into the batter, and fry in hot oil. Drain on paper towels. Serve immediately, with elderberry jam, if you wish.

Sanguinaria canadensis • Bloodroot

FAMILY: Papaveraceae.

DESCRIPTION: Small with a single leaf and flower. Height: 8 inches (20 cm). Width: 8 inches (20 cm). Flower: White (sometimes tinged pink), 8 to 10 petals, 2 to 4 inches (5 to 10 cm) wide with golden stamens. Leaves: Single, 6 to 10 inches (15 to 25 cm), with 5 to 9 deep lobes, wraps around the flower. Size increases after the flower dies. Fruit: 1-inch- (2.5-cm-) long seedpods contain 25 or more seeds. Root: Deep red-orange, brittle, wiry. Blooms: March to May.

HABITAT: Shady woodlands of eastern North America.

CULTIVATION: Perennial. Zone: 3. Germination: 1 year if seeds dry out. Stratify. Space: 7 to 10 inches (17.5 to 25 cm). Soil Temperature: 60° to 70° F (15° to 21° C). Soil: Moist but not wet, sandy, well drained, and slightly rich. pH: 4.8 to 8.2. Sun: Shade. Propagation: By seed or root division. Seeds mature about 4 weeks after the flowers bloom. Plant them fresh for best results. Plants should have their roots laid horizontally.

GARDEN DESIGN: Bloodroot will grace your herb garden with its beautiful early spring flowers when most herbs are still coming up. Clusters of the flowers under the shade of a tree make a dramatic effect. They combine well with other early spring flowers like violets and trilliums.

CONSTITUENTS: Alkaloids (1%) include sanguinarine, protopine, sanguidimerine, cholerythrine, berberine; red resin; chelidone acid.

RELATED SPECIES: A cultivar with double flower petals (*S. canadensis* 'Multiplex') is available.

HISTORY: Bloodroot's name describes the deep orange-red juice of the root, which was used by Native American tribes as a stain and a dye. They also squeezed it on to maple sugar to make instant sore throat lozenges. Native Americans treated cancers of the breast, uterus, skin, nose, and ear with bloodroot and used it for treating various respiratory problems and rheumatism. It was an official medicine in the *U.S. Pharmacopoeia* from 1820 until 1926.

MEDICINAL: The Native Americans also used bloodroot to prevent tooth decay and mixed it with powdered bayberry as a snuff for nasal prolapse. Studies find that sanguinarine, a compound found in bloodroot, kills bacteria, stops them from converting carbohydrates into gum tissue–eating acid, and blocks enzymes that destroy collagen in gum tissue. Some studies have shown small amounts to be even more effective in reducing dental plaque than chlorhexidine, the active ingredient in mouthwashes commonly used by dentists, and the effects can last up to 4 hours. According to European patents, bloodroot makes gums less sensitive. At least 2 products sold in the United States, Viadent mouthwash and toothpaste, contain sanguinaria. Due to conflicting study results, Viadent has not yet received the American Dental Association's seal of approval. Nevertheless, two studies sponsored by the product's manufacturer, Vipont Pharmaceuticals, found that Viadent does decrease plaque buildup by about 30%. The studies suggested that best results could be achieved using the toothpaste and mouthwash together. Herbalist David Winston reports that the root in a vinegar extract makes a very good antifungal wash for athlete's foot.

CONSIDERATIONS: Bloodroot is a beautiful addition to the herb garden, but it is too poisonous for home use. An irritant to mucous membranes, it can cause burning in the stomach, vomiting, faintness, and restriction of eyesight. The root is caustic enough to help remove warts.

OTHER: Native Americans painted bloodroot on their bodies and dyed their clothes with the root. The root produces a red-orange dye.

Sanguinaria canadensis
BLOODROOT

Santolina chamaecyparissus
GRAY SANTOLINA

Santolina chamaecyparissus • Gray Santolina

FAMILY: Compositae.

DESCRIPTION: Grows in mounds, forming tall ground cover. Height: 2 feet (60 cm). Width: 2 feet (60 cm). Flowers: Numerous, bright yellow, buttonlike. Leaves: Long, to 1³/₄ inches (4.3 cm), divided into many tiny segments, gray, soft, strongly aromatic when crushed. Blooms: July to August.

HABITAT: Spain and North Africa to Dalmatia, Yugoslavia, and an escapee in parts of the United States.

CULTIVATION: Perennial. Zone: 6. Germination: 1 to 3 months. Space: 1 to 1¹/₂ feet (30 to 45 cm). Soil Temperature: 65° to 70° F (18° to 21° C). Soil: Well drained, sandy, dry or moist, poor soil fine. pH: 6.5 to 8. Sun: Full sun, or partial shade in hot climates. Propagation: Start by seed, cuttings, or layering; pruning in the autumn will encourage new spring growth.

GARDEN DESIGN: Santolina forms a low border or edging that can be trimmed and shaped—it was popular in Elizabethan knot gardens. An excellent, gently rolling groundcover, it is a common landscaping plant and is grown around homes as a firebreak on slopes in the dry southern California hills.

CONSTITUENTS: Essential oil, flavonoids.

RELATED SPECIES: Green santolina *(S. virens)* has green leaves. The cultivar 'Plumosus' has silver-gray, very feathery foliage. There is also dwarf santolina *(S. chamaecyparissus* 'Nana'), which forms a low-growing, tight groundcover.

HISTORY: The Greeks called santolina *abrotonon* and Romans knew it as *habrotanum* to describe the treelike branches. It was also called lavender cotton because, until it flowers, it resembles a fuzzy version of lavender. Santolina found its way into northern Europe in the 16th century and quickly gained popularity incorporated into formal knot gardens. Elizabethan-era gardeners entwined it with thyme and germander plants to create elaborate designs and mazes. In 1629, Parkinson wrote, "The rarity and novelty of this herb, being for the most part but in the gardens of great persons, doth cause it to be of great regard."

MEDICINAL: Santolina is rarely found in the modern medicine cabinet in the West, but Arabs value it as a skin antiseptic and an eyewash. Culpeper stated in the 17th century that it "resists poison" and kills intestinal worms. It also destroys bacterial and fungal infections. Santolina may be rubbed into muscles to prevent spasms. It is also a bitter digestive that improves digestion, but it *is* bitter.

AROMATHERAPY: A perfume oil is extracted from the leaves.

OTHER: Santolina repels wool moths. The leaves are used in wreath making but become brittle so are best added while still fresh.

Saponaria officinalis • Soapwort

FAMILY: Caryophyllaceae.

DESCRIPTION: Slightly branched. Height: 3 feet (90 cm). Width: 2 feet (60 cm). Flowers: White or pink petals, to 1 inch (2.5 cm) long, in loose clusters. Leaves: Elongated ovals to 4 inches (10 cm) long, with 3 obvious veins, smooth. Root: Pale brown on outside and yellow-white inside. Blooms: July to September.

HABITAT: Europe, Asia, naturalized elsewhere, including North America and Australia.

CULTIVATION: Perennial. Zone: 2. Germination: 10 to 15 days. Needs complete dark to germinate. Space: 1 foot (30 cm). Soil Temperature: 70° F (21° C). Soil: Well drained, can be poor. pH: 6 to 7.5. Sun: Full sun or partial shade. Propagation: Seeds, sow 2 months before last frost.

GARDEN DESIGN: The smooth green leaves and pale flowers blend well with other herbs. Soapwort has little definite form, but it can be clipped in midspring to shape.

CONSTITUENTS: Saponins (to 5%), gums, flavonoids, vitamin C, vitexin.

HISTORY: Dioscorides was probably describing soapwort when he discussed *struthion* in the 1st century. In the Middle Ages, it became known as *herba fullonis,* since fullers used the leaves to clean cloth. The suds it produces were even used in Europe to produce a foamy head on beer. William Turner in *The Names of Herbs* mentioned it as "soapwort" in 1548. Today, it is also called wild sweet william or bouncing bet.

MEDICINAL: Soapwort is used to treat skin irritations, including psoriasis, eczema, and acne. It is also effective when applied to poison ivy and poison oak, especially in combination with other herbs, such as mugwort. It was once taken internally to help eliminate toxins from the liver, and in India, a specially prepared root is used to increase mother's milk.

CONSIDERATIONS: Soapwort is poisonous if eaten due to the soaplike saponins it contains, and there are reports of it being fatal to both animals and people, so don't use it internally.

OTHER: The leaves and roots produce a soapy lather that can be used like soap. Today, it is still used in the Middle East for cleaning delicate tapestries. Museums clean and revitalize precious antique fabrics with it. Soapwort also temporarily stupefies fish so they can be collected from the water. It also makes a nice cut flower.

Saponaria officinalis
SOAPWORT

Sassafras albidum • Sassafras
(Previously *S. officinale, S. variifolium*)

FAMILY: Lauraceae.

DESCRIPTION: Deciduous tree. Height: Varies with climate, larger in the south where it grows from 60 to 125 feet (18.3 to 38 m). Width: To 6 feet (1.8 m). Flowers: Green-yellow, to 2 inches (5 cm) long. Leaves: Thin, with up to 3 lobes, resembling "mittens," to 5 inches (12.5 cm) long, green on top, pale beneath, turn color in late autumn. Root: Woody, with a red-brown bark that is intensely aromatic. Fruit: Dark blue-black, with fleshy red pedicel. Blooms: April to May.

HABITAT: Throughout United States, from Maine to Florida, Texas, and eastern Kansas.

CULTIVATION: Perennial. Zone: 4. Germination: 2 to 3 weeks. Stratify 4 months at 35° to 42° F (1.6° to 5.5° C). Seeds are viable about 2 years. Soil: Sandy, fairly rich, well drained. pH: 6 to 7. Sun: Full sun in cool regions, or partial shade in warm areas. Propagation: By seed or cuttings, but easier by root cuttings. Cut the seedling's roots from mother plant with a shovel, and wait until the roots are well established before transplanting. It doesn't produce flowers and fruit until about 10 years old.

GARDEN DESIGN: This is a tree that offers shade for a larger garden or can be kept small by growing in a pot in a small garden. Its attractive foliage turns yellow and orange with red streaks in the fall.

CONSTITUENTS: Essential oil (to 35%) includes safrole (to 80%); phellandrine; pinene.

RELATED SPECIES: The central Chinese *S. tzumu* is similar but has 8-inch (20-cm) leaves. The Australian black or southern sassafras *(Atherosperma moschatum)* and gray sassafras *(Doryphora aromatica)* and New South Wales sassafras *(D. sassafras)* are all aromatic and contain safrole. They are not related.

HISTORY: Sassafras was imported in the 16th century to Spain, where Seville physician Nicolas Monardes wrote 22 pages about this amazing New World herb in his 1574 *Historia Medicinal.* It is thought to be the first native American medicinal plant that found its way to Europe and became one of the earliest American export items. Many early American colonies selected locations near sassafras trees for a potentially marketable crop. Native Americans had long used the root bark for fevers. It was quickly adopted into the settler's medicinal repertoire. A 1734 cancer cure from Virginia stated, "Let him drink Sassafras Tea every Morning, live temperately, upon light and innocent Food; and abstain entirely from strong liquor." It was found in many patent medicines—the well-known Godfrey's Cordial combined sassafras with opium! Sassafras is still recognized in Ozark folk medicines as springtime blood "thinner" or purifier.

CULINARY: Filé powder, made with sassafras leaves, thickens the Creole gumbos for which New Orleans, Louisiana, is famous. The powder is added to a hot dish but not allowed to boil, or it will become stringy. In the southeastern United States, a sassafras and violet leaf soup is prepared. The spicy young tips and flowers of sassafras can also be eaten in salads. Sassafras is responsible for much of root beer's popular taste—now from a safrole-free extract.

MEDICINAL: The root bark of sassafras improves digestion and increases sweating during flus, fevers, and measles. It is diuretic, slightly laxative, and has been used to reduce high blood pressure and to decrease mother's milk. Externally, the oil of sassafras kills lice and is added to liniments to warm sore muscles. It is also a remedy for poison ivy and oak rash poison. Native Americans used a wash of the antiseptic bark to bathe infected sores and of the twigs as eyewash.

AROMATHERAPY: Oil used in perfumery.

CONSIDERATIONS: The FDA banned safrole (and sassafras itself) for use in human foods in 1960 after safrole root bark caused liver cancer in laboratory mice. Sassafras root bark now must be labeled "not for food use."[1] The results are controversial since the study was done on large quantities of safrole, not the whole bark. Also, when human subjects were given small doses of safrole, it did not turn into the cancer-producing substance as it did in rats, suggesting to the scientists that the toxic reaction of humans and rats is different.[2] Safrole may not be the only culprit since safrole-free derivatives produce cancer in rats.[3] Smaller amounts of safrole are found in black pepper, star anise, basil, cinnamon leaf, nutmeg, sage, and witch hazel.

OTHER: Sassafras is used to flavor tobacco, and the wood is used to make fencing, small boats, and barrels. The wood and bark make a yellow dye.

FILÉ

2	tablespoons (30 ml) young sassafras leaves, dried
1	tablespoon (15 ml) dried okra
1/2	teaspoon (2.5 ml) allspice
1/2	teaspoon (2.5 ml) coriander
1/4	teaspoon (1 ml) sage

Mix and powder ingredients. Store in a jar with a tight lid.

GUMBO

2	cups (500 ml) tomatoes
1/2	cup (120 ml) green corn
1	cup (240 ml) okra, sliced
1	pepper, green or red, chopped
1/2	teaspoon (2.5 ml) salt
1/4	onion, diced
1/4	cup (60 ml) rice, cooked
5	cups (1 l) water
2	teaspoons (10 ml) filé powder

Simmer vegetables and rice in water, uncovered, until tender. Moisten filé powder with a little water and add. Serve warm.

> *Fill me with sassafras, nurse,*
> *And juniper juice!*
> *Let me see if I'm still any use!*
> —"SPRING ODE," DON MARQUIS (1878–1937), AMERICAN

Sassafras albidum
SASSAFRAS

Satureja hortensis • Savory
(Previously *Calamintha hortensis*)

FAMILY: Labiatae.

DESCRIPTION: Small herb with sparse foliage. Height: 1 foot (30 cm). Width: 1½ feet (45 cm). Flowers: Pale lavender to white, sparse. Leaves: Dark green, on reddish stems, linear, to ⅞ inch (2.2 cm) long. Blooms: August to September.

HABITAT: The Mediterranean, introduced into southwest Asia and Africa.

Satureja hortensis
SAVORY

CULTIVATION: Annual. Germination: 2 to 3 weeks. Space: 1 foot (30 cm). Soil Temperature: 68° F (20° C) at night and 86° F (30° C) during the day. Soil: Well drained, moist underneath, but dry on surface. pH: 7 to 8. Sun: Full sun. Propagation: By seed. It can become top-heavy as it matures and may need bracing.

GARDEN DESIGN: Summer savory is not known for design qualities, but it has a wonderful aroma. It tends to look best planted in small patches. For low borders, plant winter savory.

CONSTITUENTS: Essential oil (1.5%) includes carvacrol, cymene.

RELATED SPECIES: Winter savory *(S. montana)* is a perennial that sometimes replaces summer savory, although it is more pungent and not quite so tasty. Yerba buena *(S. douglasii)* was used by California Indians to relieve colic, purify the blood, reduce fevers, alleviate arthritis, and as a general tonic.

HISTORY: Called summer savory to distinguish it from its winter cousin, this herb has probably been cultivated since very ancient times. The Romans enjoyed *satureja* vinegar, and Virgil suggested planting the herb near bee hives to improve the honey. Perhaps he also considered the instant relief if offers when placed on bee and wasp stings. Italians cultivated it in the 9th century and claimed it had aphrodisiac properties. The English took the name savory from the French *savoré.*

CULINARY: Savory is found so often in pea and bean dishes that the Germans call it *bohnenkraut,* or "bean herb." In recipes, it offers a lighter substitute for sage or a stronger version of mint. For a change of pace, substitute a savory garnish in place of parsley or chervil. The essential oil is used commercially as a flavoring in salami and other foods.

MEDICINAL: Savory has been found to destroy bacteria and to reduce muscle spasms.[1] It also kills intestinal worms. Like many culinary herbs, it improves digestion and also relieves intestinal gas, probably one reason it is so popular with bean dishes. It also helps to eliminate lung congestion.

MARINATED SAVORY BEANS

Other beans, such as garbanzos, may be substituted.

2	*cups (500 ml) green beans, cooked*
2	*tablespoons (30 ml) lemon juice*
½	*cup (120 ml) vinegar*
3 to 6	*garlic cloves, whole*
1	*teaspoon (5 ml) savory*

Combine ingredients and let sit at least 1 week. Drain and serve.

Satureja douglasii
YERBA BUENA

Scutellaria lateriflora • Skullcap

FAMILY: Labiatae.

DESCRIPTION: Height: 1 to 2 feet (30 to 60 cm). Width: 8 inches (20 cm). Flowers: Small, blue, in clusters on upper areas of stems, about ⅓ inch (8 mm) long. Leaves: Thin, almost oval coming to a sharp point, toothed around the edge. Blooms: July to September.

HABITAT: United States, Newfoundland to British Columbia and south to Georgia, and California, in wet places.

CULTIVATION: Perennial. Zone: 4 to 5. Germination: 3 to 4 weeks. Space: 6 to 10 inches (15 to 25 cm). Soil Temperature: 60° to 70° F (15° to 21° C). Soil: Moist. pH: 6 to 8. Sun: Partial shade. Propagation: By seed or by root division. It spreads on its own, but not too quickly and can be easily contained.

GARDEN DESIGN: A small plant that easily fades into the background, skullcap can be highlighted by growing it in a patch enclosed by stones or in a raised bed. It does well in a pot, provided the soil stays moist.

CONSTITUENTS: Flavonoid glycosides (scultellonin, scutellarinan), essential oil.

RELATED SPECIES: A number of species, including *S. galericulata* and *S. minor,* both native to Europe, have similar properties. In traditional Chinese medicine, *S. baicalensis* is a sedative that relieves muscle and rheumatism pains, lowers fever, expels tapeworms, and corrects some heart conditions. True skullcap is dried to very little weight and is often substituted in the United States with the heavier and more abundant germander (*Teucrium* species).

HISTORY: Skullcap was such a well-known remedy for rabies, it was once even called "mad-dog weed." This property was discovered by Dr. Lawrence Van Deveer in 1773, although his claim was never substantiated. Rafinesque, in his 1830 *Medical Flora,* said that his use of the herb "prevented 400 persons and 1,000 cattle from becoming hydrophobic." It found its way into many 19th century patent medicines as a nerve tonic, especially for "female weakness," and as an epilepsy "cure."

MEDICINAL: Skullcap leaves are used mostly for their actions on the nervous system: They help relieve anxiety, depression, insomnia, nervous headache, nervous twitches, muscle cramps, and convulsions. The Eclectic doctors of the nineteenth century found skullcap helpful in cases of nervousness due to emotional stress or physical exhaustion and used it as a bitter to stimulate digestion. Although few scientific studies have been performed on this species, it is likely that it possesses many of the medicinal properties found in similar species. Most of the research that has been done comes from Russia, where studies support many claims of skullcap's usefulness as a sedative and stabilizer of stress-related heart disease.[1] Those studies also discovered that it lowers blood pressure and cholesterol. Native Americans did use skullcap to treat heart disease, as well as to promote afterbirth and menstruation. Herbalist Michael Tierra has found skullcap helpful in combating drug and alcohol withdrawal symptoms. Clinical tests with *S. baicalensis* in China found it improved symptoms in over 70% of patients with chronic hepatitis, increasing appetite, improving liver function, and reducing swelling.[2] Other studies show it reduces inflammation and allergic reactions.

CONSIDERATIONS: Very large doses are said to cause dizziness, erratic pulse, and mental confusion.

OTHER: Skullcap is used in homeopathy.

Scutellaria lateriflora
SKULLCAP

Senecio cineraria • Dusty Miller
(Previously *Cineraria maritima* and *Centauréa maritima* 'Diamond')

FAMILY: Compositae.

DESCRIPTION: Silver, woolly white herb. Height: 2½ feet (75 cm). Width: 1 foot (30 cm). Flowers: Yellow or cream, ½ inch (1.25 cm) across, 12 to a bunch. Leaves: 6 inches (15 cm) long, thick, woolly with dense white hairs underneath, in 10 to 12 segments so divided, they appear to be individual leaves. Blooms: July to September.

HABITAT: The Mediterranean.

CULTIVATION: Perennial. Zone: 6. Germination: 10 to 15 days. Space: 8 to 10 inches (20 to 25 cm). Soil Temperature: 65° to 70° F (18° to 21° C). Soil: Light and well drained. pH: 7 to 8. Sun: Full sun. Propagation: By cuttings, layering, or seeds. Start seeds in early spring or 8 to 10 weeks before last frost.

GARDEN DESIGN: This silver-gray plant is very popular in herb gardens, where it stands out with its contrasting color and leaf texture. Keeping flowers cut off encourages more foliage and keeps the plant from looking leggy.

CONSTITUENTS: Pyrrolizidine alkaloids (jacobine, jacodine, senecionine).

RELATED SPECIES: The ornamental *S. vira-vira* has more finely cut foliage and no ray petals on the flowers. *S. cineraria* 'Dwarf Silver' is a short, 9-inch (22.5-cm) version with leaves even more divided. Life root *(S. aureus)* is still an ingredient in Lydia Pinkam's women's herbal formula for genitourinary problems.

HISTORY: Cineraria means "ashy gray," the coloring that also gives this herb the common name of "dusty." The color was also said to resemble the dusty white wings of the miller moth. (The miller moth itself was named after the dusty clothing worn by grain millers in previous centuries.)

MEDICINAL: Sterilized plant juice has been used for eye drops for capsular and lenticular cataracts.

CONSIDERATIONS: Dusty miller and the other species mentioned all contain pyrrolizidine alkaloids, which are presently under scientific scrutiny for safety.[1]

Senecio cineraria
DUSTY MILLER

Silybum marianum
MILK THISTLE

Silybum marianum • Milk Thistle
(Previously *Carduus marianus*)

FAMILY: Compositae.

DESCRIPTION: Wide, bristly plant—obviously a thistle. Height: To 4 feet (1.2 m). Width: 2 to 3 feet (60 to 90 cm). Flowers: Bristly tight cup, deep purple, 2 inches (5 cm) across. Leaves: Large, 2½ feet by 1 foot (75 cm by 30 cm), glossy, thick, marbled with white veinlike patterns, prickly edges. Fruit: Oval, smooth, mottled with brown. Blooms: June to September.

HABITAT: The Mediterranean, naturalized as a weed on the West Coast of the United States, in dry, rocky areas, wastelands, and fields. Naturalized in Australia and on various noxious weed lists.

CULTIVATION: Annual or biennial. Germination: 10 to 15 days. Space: 3 feet (90 cm). Soil Temperature: 65° to 75° F (18° to 24° C). Soil: Well drained, dry, very drought tolerant. pH: 6–8. Sun: Full sun. Propagation: By seed. Since it reproduces by seed, it is easy to keep under control in a garden setting.

GARDEN DESIGN: If you know this thistle as a weed, you may question putting it in your herb garden, yet its attractive, mottled leaves are very interesting and stand out beside other herbs.

CONSTITUENTS: Seeds: essential oil, flavolignans called silymarine, such as silybin.

RELATED SPECIES: Also known as variegated thistle and Our Lady's Thistle. Not closely related to holy or blessed thistle *(Cnicus benedictus)*, although they are often confused with each other.

HISTORY: Early Christian tradition dedicated milk thistle to Mary, calling it Marian thistle. It was considered interchangeable with blessed thistle *(Cnicus benedictus)*. Long before research was done on the herb, it was suggested as a bitter digestive, liver tonic, and poison antidote. German physician Rademacher reported success in giving it to his liver patients in the early 19th century.

CULINARY: Dioscorides suggested eating *silybon* "sodden with oil and salt," which would probably hide the taste of anything. Actually, the steamed leaves are quite tasty, providing the prickly edges have been cut off! The young stalks were once widely cultivated as a vegetable, and their taste was considered superior to that of cabbage in the 18th century. The seeds, with a slightly bitter nutty flavor, can be ground and sprinkled on food.

MEDICINAL: Milk thistle has been proven to protect the liver from damage—even against the deadly deathcap mushroom *(Amacita phalloides)*, which contains some of the most potent liver toxins known. When silybin, a constituent from milk thistle, was injected into human patients up to 48 hours after they accidentally ingested deathcap, it prevented the normally anticipated fatalities.[1] Many commercial preparations are manufactured in Germany from the seeds. An official *Tinctura Cardui Mariae Rademacher* is still listed in the pharmacopoeias of some countries. The latest research will probably reestablish milk thistle's place as a medicine, at least in some synthesized version. Clinical studies show that symptoms of acute hepatitis, especially digestive problems, improved within 2 weeks of taking milk thistle. Well-being and appetite also improved. It also has successfully treated patients with chronic hepatitis and cirrhosis of the liver.[2] The detrimental effects of jaundice, drugs, environmental toxins, and alcohol on the liver may be countered with milk thistle. More information can be found in *Milk Thistle: The Liver Herb* by Christopher Hobbs (Botanica Press, 1985).

Stachys byzantina
Lamb's Ears

Stachys officinalis
Wood Betony

Stachys byzantina • Lamb's Ears
(Previously *S. lanata, S. olympica*)

FAMILY: Labiatae.

DESCRIPTION: Erect, furry leaves. Height: To 3 feet (90 cm). Width: 1 foot (30 cm). Flowers: Purple or pink, to 1 inch (2.5 cm), running along furry, white, 12-inch (30-cm) stalks. Leaves: Thick, long, very soft and covered with woolly, white hairs. Blooms: May to June.

HABITAT: Turkey, southwest Asia.

CULTIVATION: Perennial. Zone: 2 to 3. Germination: 1 to 2 weeks. Space: 8 to 15 inches (20 to 38 cm). Soil Temperature: 70° F (21° C). Soil: Fairly rich, well drained, but tolerates poor conditions. pH: 7.5 to 8.5. Sun: Full sun, or partial shade. Propagation: By seed or divide root clumps. It spreads easily on its own.

GARDEN DESIGN: The soft, gray leaves of lamb's ears provide excellent contrasts in any garden. It is a favorite plant of children so be sure to place it where they can easily feel its furry leaves. It forms an ornamental groundcover that is ideal for lining the edges of pathways.

CONSTITUENTS: Essential oil, tannin.

RELATED SPECIES: Related to betony *(S. officinalis).*

HISTORY: The exceptionally fuzzy leaves gave it the names lamb's ears and woolly betony.

CULINARY: Lamb's ears make a light-tasting tea. The leaves can be steamed and eaten, although some people find their fuzziness unappealing.

MEDICINAL: Also called woundwort, lamb's ears makes a natural bandage and dressing to staunch bleeding.

Stachys officinalis • Wood Betony
(Previously *S. betonica, Betonica officinalis*)

FAMILY: Labiatae.

DESCRIPTION: Softly textured bush. Height: 2 to 3 feet (60 to 90 cm). Width: 2 feet (60 cm). Flowers: Bright blue, ¼ inch (6 mm), arranged in whorls on the top of the spikes. Leaves: A rosette of stiff, slightly hairy, pointed leaves, about 5 inches (12.5 cm) long. Blooms: July to August.

HABITAT: A European native that has naturalized itself in many parts of the world.

CULTIVATION: Perennial. Zone: 4. Germination: 15 to 20 days. Space: 14 to 18 inches (35 to 45 cm). Soil Temperature: 70° F (21° C). Soil: Well drained, dry. pH: 6.5 to 7.5. Sun: Full sun. Propagation: Easily grown from seed or divided by prying apart the thick clumps, or by cuttings.

GARDEN DESIGN: A well-contained herb that can be used as a high border or set near the back of the bed. It is most noticeable when flowering, since the vivid blue flowers are highlighted against pinks, grays, and greens.

CONSTITUENTS: Tannins (to 15%), saponines, glucosides, alkaloids (bettonicine, stachydrine, trigonelline).

RELATED SPECIES: Lamb's ears, or woolly betony *(S. byzantina),* a very attractive herb with furry white leaves, is a children's favorite. It is perfect for rock gardens or as a groundcover. A white betony *(S. officinalis* 'Alba'*)* has white instead of blue flowers. This betony is not related to the wood betonys *(Pedicularis* species) or lousewort *(P. sylvatica),* which is also a headache remedy.

HISTORY: An old Italian proverb indicated this herb's value when it declared, "Sell your coat and buy betony." The Spanish agreed, complimenting each other with the phrase, "He has as many virtues as betony." Betony was also appreciated by the ancient Greeks, the Romans, and the Anglo-Saxons, who discussed it in their 11th century *Lacnunga.* A treatise written by Antonius Musa, physician to Emperor Augustus, listed 47 diseases that could be helped by *betonica.* The name was derived from *vettonica,* from the Vettones, an ancient people inhabiting the Iberian peninsula.

MEDICINAL: Betony, which means "head herb," was a traditional remedy for problems associated with the head; the *Medicina Britannica* of 1666 states, "I have known obstinate headaches cured by daily breakfasting for a month or six weeks on a decoction of Betony." It was also used to treat giddiness, dizziness, and hearing difficulties. The British traditionally relieved headaches by snuffing or smoking betony leaves combined with eyebright and coltsfoot in the famous "Rowley's British Herb Snuff." The French recommended the leaves of *beteine* for lung, liver, gallbladder, and spleen problems. One of its constituents, trigonelline, also found in fenugreek, has been shown to lower blood sugar levels. Betony was appropriately known as woundwort, since applied externally it stops bleeding, promotes healing, and draws out boils and splinters.

OTHER: A dark yellow dye can be extracted from betony. It makes an attractive cut flower, as well.

Symphytum officinale • Comfrey

FAMILY: Boraginaceae.

DESCRIPTION: Densely growing patches of leaves. Height: 3 feet (90 cm). Width: 2 to 3 feet (60 to 90 cm). Flowers: Purple-pink, hanging in bell-like clusters from the tips of the stems. Leaves: Tall, rigid and very prickly to the touch, to 1 foot (30 cm) tall, 5 inches (12.5 cm) wide, on hollow, bristly stems. Roots: Thick, fleshy roots that can trail 6 feet (1.8 m). Blooms: April to September.

HABITAT: Most of the 25 or so species are native to Europe and Asia, but comfrey has naturalized itself elsewhere, including parts of the United States, mostly in rich, wet meadows and ditches.

CULTIVATION: Perennial. Zone: 3. Space: 2 feet (60 cm). Soil: Moist, fairly rich. Sun: Full sun to partial shade. Propagation: Comfrey propagates so readily from even the smallest piece of root, that it is rarely grown from seed, and often does not produce seed. Repeated cuttings can produce 4 to 10 harvests of comfrey in one season.

GARDEN DESIGN: Comfrey is difficult to eradicate once established. If you want to include comfrey in a small garden, plant it in a submerged barrel or pot with drainage holes in the bottom.

CONSTITUENTS: Mucilage, allantoin, protein (to 35%), alkaloids (including pyrrolizidine), sterols, zinc, tannic acid, asparagine, vitamin B_{12}.

RELATED SPECIES: Russian comfrey *(S.* x *uplandicum)* has been considered superior, but does contain more pyrrolizide alkaloids. It has been used very little in Russian folk medicine. *S. officinale* 'Variegatum' has white-rimmed leaves.

Symphytum officinale
COMFREY

plants, including comfrey. In one study, rats fed a comfrey diet (up to 33%) developed liver cancer. The isolated symphytine, one of 8 pyrrolizidine alkaloids identified, was also found to produce liver cell tumors in rats.[2] So far, only two cases of possible comfrey poisoning have been reported in people. One was a 13-year-old British boy who ate comfrey regularly for about 3 years, but the researchers admitted that he "may have been more susceptible . . . because of his underlying inflammatory bowel disease." They also stated, "These alkaloids are less toxic than those in other plants—for example *Senecios*—which may explain why only a few cases of hepatic veno-occlusive disease caused by ingestion of comfrey are known." Scientists assume that applying comfrey externally, as in poultices and salves, is perfectly safe. As far as internal use goes, the fresh root contains approximately 10 times more PA than fresh leaves.[3] Fresh, young, spring leaves average .22% PA, young fall leaves have .05% PA, mature leaves have only .003% PA, and two investigations did not detect PA at all in dried leaves.[4] It is interesting that water extracts of the whole leaves actually decreased tumor growth and increased survival time in cancer patients.[5] The Ames test for toxicity showed comfrey produced less mutants than the control, suggesting it may have anticancer activity. Some reports on comfrey's toxicity have resulted from a mistaken identification of the poisonous foxglove—the leaves of which resemble comfrey. A complete modern history is found in *Comfrey: Fodder, Food, and Remedy* by Lawrence D. Hills (New York: Universe Books, 1976).

OTHER: Comfrey is a rich addition to the compost pile.

Tagetes patula • French Marigold

FAMILY: Compositae.

DESCRIPTION: A densely compact annual producing many flowers. Height: 2 feet (60 cm). Width: 1 foot (30 cm). Flowers: Various combinations of orange, yellow, red-brown, 2½ inches (6.25 cm) across. Leaves: Divided with ragged edges. Blooms: July to August.

HABITAT: Mexico.

CULTIVATION: Annual. Germination: 5 to 7 days. Space: 6 to 12 inches (15 to 30 cm). Soil Temperature: 70° to 75° F (21° to 24° C). Soil: Dry, well drained, fair—too rich a soil produces more foliage and less flowers. pH: 4 to 6. Sun: Full sun, open location. Propagation: Very easy to cultivate by seed. In cold climates, start indoors 6 to 8 weeks before the last frost. In warmer areas, sow from midsummer through autumn to avoid hottest weather during flowering, or any frost. Picking the flowers increases the bloom.

GARDEN DESIGN: Single-petaled forms are the most popular. The abundant flowers and long blooming season make French marigolds perfect for filling in empty spots. They make a low, easily controlled, and colorful hedge.

CONSTITUENTS: Essential oil includes limonene, carvone, citral, camphene; valeric acids, salicylaldehyde, tagetones.

RELATED SPECIES: Many flower sizes and colors in various cultivars; most have an extended flowering season, and some resist heat better. They are often confused with pot marigold *(Calendula officinalis).* 'Tangerine gem' *(T. tenuifolia* cultivar) has distinctly lemon-scented leaves. There is also an orange-scented marigold *(T. tenuifolia* 'Pumila').

HISTORY: The name comfrey comes from the Latin *con firma,* "with strength," and *Symphytum* is derived from the Greek *symphytos,* "to unite." It is also popularly called knitbone. The gummy root, when spread on muslin and wrapped around a sprain, torn ligament, or broken bone that has been set, stiffens into a cast. Squires in *The Companion* to the 17th-century *British Pharmacopoeia,* 1916, describes a bonesetter who used comfrey in this manner. A few avid Englishmen began promoting comfrey as fodder in the late 19th century. Henry Doubleday first used comfrey to substitute for the difficult-to-obtain stamp glue known as gum arabic.

CULINARY: The leaves, steamed like a vegetable, lose their prickly texture and can be eaten, but read "Considerations" first.

MEDICINAL: Comfrey leaves and especially the root contain allantoin, a cell proliferant that increases the healing of wounds. It also stops bleeding, is soothing, and is certainly the most popular ingredient in herbal skin salves for wounds, inflammation, rashes, varicose veins, hemorrhoids, and just about any skin problem. Taken internally, comfrey repairs the digestive tract lining, helping to heal peptic and duodenal ulcers and colitis (inflammation of the colon). Studies show it inhibits prostaglandins, which cause inflammation of the stomach lining.[1] Comfrey has been used to treat a variety of respiratory diseases, and is a specific when these involve coughing of blood.

CONSIDERATIONS: Investigations on pyrrolizidine alkaloids (PA) have found over 200 types occurring in about 3% of the world's

Tagetes patula
FRENCH MARIGOLD

HISTORY: Early Mexicans fed marigold petals to chickens to color their skin and to brighten their eggs. For centuries, long before the term "companion planting" was coined, the South American Incas interplanted marigolds with their potatoes to reduce insect damage. According to Robert Sweet, in his *Hortus Britannicus* (1826), the marigold arrived in Europe in the 16th century. Thinking they came from India, the botanist Pierandrea Mattioli designated them *Caryophyllus indicus*, "a clove pink from India." They were in high fashion in both Europe and the United States throughout the 19th century and still find a place in flower, vegetable, and herb gardens. In Holland, they are still interplanted with roses as an insect repellent.

CULINARY: The oil is a food flavoring in frozen dairy desserts, baked goods, gelatins, puddings, relishes, and some alcoholic and nonalcoholic beverages.

MEDICINAL: Marigold flowers were an Aztec remedy for coughs and dysentery (probably *T. erecta*). Various species, especially *T. minuta*, have also been used to lower blood pressure, as a tranquilizer, to dilate the bronchials, and to reduce inflammation. The leaves were placed on skin sores and made into a wash for inflamed eyes. The Chinese find *T. erecta* useful in treating whooping cough, mumps, and colds. South Americans use various species to eliminate intestinal parasites and colic. The polyacetylenes in French marigolds have displayed some anticancer properties.

CONSIDERATIONS: Some people get a contact skin dermatitis from touching marigolds.

OTHER: Researchers at the University of British Columbia, Vancouver, found that French marigolds actually attack some insects. The polyacetylenes they contain excite surrounding oxygen when activated by light every time a munching insect breaks the leaf cells. Scars have actually been found on insects the plant has attacked. Marigolds also inhibit the ability of some insects to detect surrounding vegetables, and they deter white flies; *T. minuta* even kills surrounding weeds. Naturalized in Australia, this species is known as stinking Roger. In studies at the University of California, San Jose, French marigold greatly reduced cabbage worm eggs and larvae and worm damage, although 4 plants were required in every 14-square-inch (90-square-cm) plot! The only problem is that crop yields were also reduced. The roots exude a substance that deters nematodes, destructive microinsects found in soil. Scientists also found that a diluted tea of the flowers is lethal to mosquito larvae.[1] French marigold flowers look great and are long-lasting, although their strong smell has kept them from being placed in vases as often as other species. The rich marigold color also is used in potpourri and produces a yellow dye on silk and wool.

As for marigolds, poppies, hollyhocks, and valorous sunflowers, we shall never have a garden without them, both for their own sake, and for the sake of old-fashioned folks, who used to love them.

—"Star Papers," *A Discourse in Flowers*, Henry Ward Beecher (1813–1878), American

Tanacetum parthenium • Feverfew
(Although listed as *Chrysanthemum parthenium* in *Hortus Third*, the newest name is well established. Previously *Pyrethrum parthenium* and *Matricaria parthenoides*, *M. capensis*, *M. eximia*)

FAMILY: Compositae.

DESCRIPTION: Small, bushy herb, strongly scented. Height: To 4 feet (1.2 m). Width: 2 feet (60 cm). Flowers: Daisylike, with white petals and raised yellow centers, 1 inch (2.5 cm) in diameter, clustered together with up to 30 heads. Leaves: Yellow-green, divided, flexible, shaped like miniature oak leaves, 3 inches (7.5 cm). Blooms: June to August.

HABITAT: Native to southeast Europe; introduced elsewhere. Brought to America as an ornamental, it proceeded to make itself at home. Cultivated commercially in Japan, Kenya, South Africa, and parts of central Europe.

CULTIVATION: Perennial. Zone: 4. Germination: 10 to 14 days. Light improves germination. Space: 8 to 12 inches (20 to 30 cm). Soil Temperature: 70° F (21° C). Soil: Well drained, average. pH: 5 to 7.5. Sun: Full sun or partial shade. Propagation: By seed or by cuttings (taken with the heel of the plant intact).

GARDEN DESIGN: The small, white flowers show up especially well against dark green plants like betony or next to a fence.

CONSTITUENTS: Essential oil, sesquiterpene lactones (parthenolide, santamarine).

RELATED SPECIES: A golden-leaved feverfew *(T. parthenium* 'Aureum') is available.

HISTORY: Feverfew has experienced a botanical-name identity crisis. The Greeks called it *pyrethron*, probably from *pyro*, meaning "fire," descriptive of its taste. This became *pyrethrum* to the Romans. Feverfew was first designated botanically as *Matricaria* as a close relative of chamomile—an herb for which it is often mistaken. Since then, it has joined forces with the chrysanthemums and the pyrethrums and now shares the genus with tansy. Old England knew it as featherfew. While the common name feverfew, from the latin *febri*, or "fever," represents one of its possible uses, herbalists rarely use it to reduce fevers.

CULINARY: Feverfew has been added to food to cut the greasy taste but is extremely bitter and disagreeable to most palates.

MEDICINAL: Feverfew is gaining fame for its ability to alleviate migraine headaches. It is not a new idea. John Hill, in *The Family Herbal*, stated in 1772, "In the worst headache this herb exceeds whatever else is known." Clinical studies at the Department of Medicine and Haematology at City Hospital in Nottingham, England, had 20 headache patients eat fresh feverfew leaves (.9 grain, or 60 mg) daily for 3 months and stop using headache-related drugs during the last month. After they were given capsules of .37 grains (25 mg) of freeze-dried leaf every day, they experienced less severe headaches and fewer symptoms, including nausea and vomiting, than a placebo group. As an added benefit, their blood pressure went down from an average of $134/86$ to $125/82$ in six months. Some even described a renewed sense of well-being.[1] Perhaps Gerard was onto something in the 17th century when he suggested feverfew "for them that are giddie in the head . . . melancholike, sad, pensive." Another, double-blind study saw a reduction of migraine headaches, as well as nausea, by 24% in 72 volunteers.[2] E. S. John-

Tanacetum parthenium
FEVERFEW

son, a feverfew researcher and author of *Feverfew, A Traditional Herbal Remedy for Migraine and Arthritis* (Sheldon Press, 1984), speculates that feverfew can help not only migraine, but premenstrual and menstrual headaches, as well as diseases caused by chronic inflammation, such as arthritis. It is hypothesized that feverfew prevents blood vessel spasms in the head by inhibiting amines, including serotonin, certain prostaglandins, and histamine that create inflammation and constrict blood vessels, which may contribute to headaches. It may be more active than other nonsteroid, antiinflammatories, such as aspirin. For instance, it has not been shown to inhibit blood clotting.[3] While many herbalists feel the fresh leaves, or an extract made from them, are preferred, results have been seen with fresh, freeze-dried, and air-dried leaves, although boiling feverfew tea for 10 minutes instead of steeping it did reduce its activity in one study.

CONSIDERATIONS: Problems such as mouth ulcers and soreness and occasional digestive disturbances have been reported in about 18% of those using feverfew on a regular basis.[4]

OTHER: Feverfew is a moth repellent.

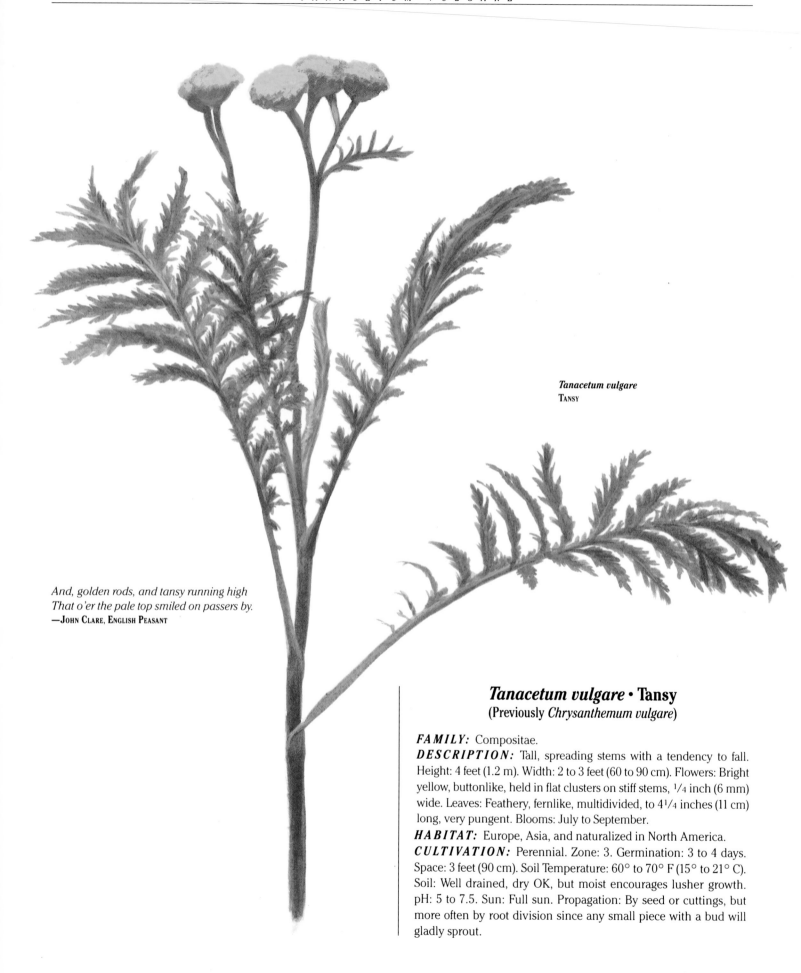

Tanacetum vulgare
TANSY

And, golden rods, and tansy running high
That o'er the pale top smiled on passers by.
—JOHN CLARE, ENGLISH PEASANT

Tanacetum vulgare • Tansy
(Previously *Chrysanthemum vulgare*)

FAMILY: Compositae.
DESCRIPTION: Tall, spreading stems with a tendency to fall. Height: 4 feet (1.2 m). Width: 2 to 3 feet (60 to 90 cm). Flowers: Bright yellow, buttonlike, held in flat clusters on stiff stems, $1/4$ inch (6 mm) wide. Leaves: Feathery, fernlike, multidivided, to $4^1/4$ inches (11 cm) long, very pungent. Blooms: July to September.
HABITAT: Europe, Asia, and naturalized in North America.
CULTIVATION: Perennial. Zone: 3. Germination: 3 to 4 days. Space: 3 feet (90 cm). Soil Temperature: 60° to 70° F (15° to 21° C). Soil: Well drained, dry OK, but moist encourages lusher growth. pH: 5 to 7.5. Sun: Full sun. Propagation: By seed or cuttings, but more often by root division since any small piece with a bud will gladly sprout.

GARDEN DESIGN: Gardeners who prefer a trim garden tend not to appreciate tansy's haphazard nature. It flops on plants next to it and spreads rapidly. It is helpful in restricted situations to keep the flower stalks under control by tying them together. I've found the best location is out of the main herb garden, as a border along a lawn, large path, or driveway, where it can be contained.

CONSTITUENTS: Essential oil (from .12% to .18%) includes thujone (to 70%), borneol; glycosides; sesquiterpene lactones; terpenoids (pyrethrins), vitamin C; citric and oxalic acids.

RELATED SPECIES: Curly leaf tansy *(T. vulgare* var. *crispum)* with its finely cut, luxuriant foliage is more ornamental and easier to contain, although some curly forms don't produce flowers. Botanists think that tansy has a number of subgroups, or races, distinguished by their different essential oil compositions. Tansy or common ragwort *(Senecio jacobaea)* is an unrelated European native with similar leaves that is considered a troublesome weed and poisonous to cattle in the United States, especially in Oregon, and in Australia, where it is considered a noxious weed.

HISTORY: A Greek legend tells of a beautiful young man, Ganymede, who was given a tansy drink to make him immortal, so he could serve Zeus. The Greeks called it *athanasia,* or "immortality," because, according to 16th-century herbalist Dodoen, the flower lasts so long. It became the Spanish *atanasia,* then the French *tanaisie,* and finally the English *tansie.* A favorite herb of Emperor Charlemagne, it was planted in all his monasteries. The monastery of St. Gall in Switzerland has grown it for over 1,000 years.

CULINARY: In 1677, John Evelyn described eating a hot dish of young tansy leaves stir-fried with orange juice and sugar as "most agreeable." Tansy was added to omelets and garnished other dishes. Elizabethan "tansies" were puddings flavored with the fresh herb that were purposely made with the bitter herb during Lent to offset the taste of salted fish. Chances are that tansy was eaten as a spring bitter long before Lent existed. William Coles, in 1656, wrote that it counteracted "the moist and cold constitution winter has made on people . . ." The Irish in County Cork sometimes still use tansy to flavor their drisheens. In Scotland, the roots have been preserved in honey or sugar and eaten for gout. Some alcoholic beverages are still flavored with tansy, including Chartreuse, although it must be with a thujone-free extract.

MEDICINAL: As Gerard said in the 16th century, tansy "be pleasant in taste and good for the stomache." The constituent thujone kills intestinal roundworms and threadworms, scabies, and heals other infected skin conditions. Very small doses have been used to treat epilepsy and to encourage menstruation.

CONSIDERATIONS: Tansy contains thujone, which is also found in wormwood. Potentially harmful to the central nervous system, an overdose can produce seizures. Don't eat much tansy, and none if pregnant.

OTHER: Tansy deters ants (which means they walk around it instead of over it), fleas, and moths. Thomas Tusser, in his 1557 *Strewing Herbs of All Sorts,* described it as one of the best flea repellents. It was also rubbed over meat to keep flies away. A strong tansy tea repels several beetles, including the Colorado potato beetle *(Leptinotarsa decemlineata),* according to studies for Lehigh University in Pennsylvania. The leaves dye wood green and the flowers are excellent in dried flower arrangements and wreaths.

Taraxacum officinale • Dandelion
(Previously *T. leontodon* and *L. taraxacum*)

FAMILY: Compositae.

DESCRIPTION: Compact, low-growing plant. Height: 1½ feet (45 cm). Width: 2 feet (60 cm). Flowers: 1 bright yellow, sun-ray flower on a hollow stem. Opens with morning sun and closes in the evening. Leaves: Long, to 1 foot (30 cm), pliable, deeply toothed, growing from a central rosette. Fruit: White tufted globes, which are easily blown by the wind or children. Root: Fleshy taproot, brown with a milky, sap-filled core. Often 1 foot (30 cm) long and ½ inch (1.25 cm) in diameter. Blooms: April to June.

HABITAT: A European and Asian native, dandelion has needed no encouragement to take up housekeeping elsewhere and has done so throughout North America and Australia.

CULTIVATION: Perennial. Zone: 3. Germination: Varies greatly. Space: 8 to 10 inches (20 to 25 cm). Soil Temperature: 55° to 60° F (13° to 15° C). Soil: Not fussy! Prefers nitrogen-rich, slightly damp. pH: 4.2 to 8.2. Sun: Full sun. Propagation: Most people are more concerned about getting rid of dandelions than planting them, but they do grow sweeter leaves and roots when cultivated, and there is a large-leafed form sold for eating. Seeds sown in the autumn provide early spring greens. When growing dandelion for fancy salads, protect the plant's leaves from sunlight so they blanch like chicory leaves, for a pale, less bitter flavor. Collect the roots in the autumn or early spring. Autumn-harvested roots have been the official herb used for medicine since they contain more bitters and inulin and have been considered more medicinal, although according to the *British Pharmacopoeia,* spring roots are less bitter and contain more taraxacin. The laevulose and sugar convert to inulin during the growing season, so fall extracts contain less sweetness and more sediment. Frost decreases the root's properties. Old roots become leathery, twisted, and very bitter.

GARDEN DESIGN: If there are dandelions in your garden, you might as well make them prominent so visitors won't think you simply forgot to weed. Just explain that weeds are defined as plants you *don't* want!

CONSTITUENTS: Roots: taraxacin, triterpenes (taraxerol, taraxasterol), inulin (about 25% in the autumn), sugars, glycosides, phenolic and citric acid, asparagine, vitamins A, C, B, potassium. Leaves: Carotenoids, vitamins A, B, C, D, minerals (potassium and iron).

RELATED SPECIES: The true dandelion is often confused with a few different branched and bristly plants known collectively as "false dandelion" (*Agoseris* species). In China, *T. monogolicum* is used to treat infections, especially mastitis.

HISTORY: Dandelion was probably introduced into European medicine by the Arabs, who were writing about its virtues in the 10th century. Medieval pharmacists named it *Taraxacum* from the Greek *taraxis,* "to move or disturb", but the name originally may have come from the Persian name for the herb, *tarashqūn.* Both the Persians and East Indians used it for liver complaints. Dandelion became an official European apothecary drug in the 16th century, and one of the products sold was fresh dandelion juice. The shape of the leaves gives dandelion the French name, *dents de lion,* or "teeth of the lion." Another French name, *pis en lit,* or "pee in bed," celebrates its diuretic effects.

Taraxacum officinale
DANDELION

CULINARY: The young leaves, which are richer in vitamin A than carrots, can be mixed in salads or steamed and topped with a dressing. While in Greece, I dined every night on *horta*—a side dish of dandelions or other bitter greens drenched in olive oil. The English, who are not inclined toward bitter foods, do indulge in young dandelion greens on sandwiches with butter and salt, sometimes sprinkling them with pepper or lemon juice. Older leaves can be eaten if the bitter center rib is removed. The Pennsylvania Dutch pour a dressing of hot cider vinegar and sugar over their dandelion salads—traditional fare for Maundy Thursday. The roasted root makes a coffeelike tea or is added to coffee as an extender. The taste of flower buds fried in butter somewhat resembles mushrooms, and the buds are added to eggs. The Arabians make a *yublo* cake of honey, olive oil, flour, rose petals, and dandelion buds. Dandelion flower wine and beer were originally tonics with less alcoholic and certainly more medicinal properties than commercial beer today. The English enjoyed dandelion, nettle, and yellow dock beer. Recipes are found in the booklet *On the Trail of the Yellow Flowered Earth Nail: A Dandelion Sampler* by Peter Gail (Goosefoot Acres Press, P.O. Box 18016, Cleveland Heights, OH 44118—it also sells canned dandelion greens and Amish Dandelion Flower Jelly).

MEDICINAL: Dandelion root is a "blood purifier" that helps both the kidneys and the liver to improve elimination. It helps clear up many eczema-like skin problems that result when the kidneys or liver don't remove impurities from the blood. Used over a period of time, the root has successfully treated liver diseases, such as jaundice and cirrhosis, as well as dyspepsia, gallbladder problems, and gallstones.[1] It also improves appetite and digestion and is a mild laxative that works well to resolve chronic constipation. Clinical studies have favorably compared it to the often-prescribed diuretic drug Furosemide™. Instead of pulling potassium out of the body like most diuretics, dandelion helps the body to replace it.[2] Most herbalists consider the root the diuretic of choice for treating rheumatism, gout, and heart disease. It is also suggested for women's hormonal imbalances, especially those relating to liver or kidney problems, and Lydia Pinkham (1819–1883) included it in her famous women's tonic. The leaves have some weak antibiotic action against candida.

CONSIDERATIONS: The fresh latex that appears as white, sticky liquid in the root, and especially in the stem, can be caustic and cause skin irritations. One advantage of this property, however, is that it removes warts if applied religiously a few times daily. Use the dried root to prepare tea.

OTHER: It is an important honey plant, but the bees aren't alone —about 93 species of insects visit dandelion for its nectar. During Word War II, a rubber latex was made from the Russian dandelion (*T. kok-saghyz*).

Star-disked Dandelion, just as we see them,
Lying in the grass, like sparks that have leapt
From kindling suns of fire.
—"DANDELION," *THE PROFESSOR AT THE BREAKFAST TABLE,*
OLIVER WENDELL HOLMES **(1809–1894)**, AMERICAN

Dear common flower that grow'st beside the way,
Fringing the dusty road with harmless gold
First pledge of blithesome May
Which children pluck, and, full of pride, uphold
High-hearted buccaneers, o'erjoyed that they
An Eldorado in the grass have found,
Which not the rich earth's ample round
May match in wealth, thou art more dear to me
Than all the prouder summer-blooms may be.
—"TO THE DANDELION," JAMES RUSSELL LOWELL **(1819–1891)**, AMERICAN

DANDELION WINE

4	quarts (4.5 l) water
3	quarts (3.5 l) dandelion blossoms, fully open and dry
3	pounds (1.35 kg) sugar
1	orange, sliced
2	lemons, sliced
1	yeast cake

Pour boiling water over the freshly picked blossoms. Let stand 3 hours. Strain the liquid into a large cooking pot and add sugar to the liquid. Cook over medium heat 15 minutes. Place orange and lemons in a 2-gallon (7.6-l) container. Pour the hot liquid over the fruit. When cooled to 100° F (37° C), remove 1 cup (240 ml) and dissolve the yeast in it, then add to the rest. Let sit 12 hours and strain. Return mixture to the container, cover with layers of cheesecloth and let stand at room temperature 2 months. Filter, bottle, cap, and store in a cool place. In 6 months, strain into bottles and sample.

GREEK HORTA

The traditional but less nutritious Greek method is to boil the greens. For other variations, serve this dish raw or combine the greens with other vegetables.

15	dandelion leaves
1	small onion, sliced
8	black olives
2	tablespoons (30 ml) olive oil
1	tablespoon (15 ml) cider vinegar or lemon juice
	Salt to taste

Steam dandelion leaves and onion until soft. Serve mixed with olives and topped with the oil and vinegar. Season with salt.

Teucrium chamaedrys • Germander

FAMILY: Labiatae.
DESCRIPTION: Low-growing, full shrub. Height: 1 foot (30 cm). Width: 1 foot (30 cm). Flowers: Purple, rose to whitish, small, growing among leaves on upright stems. Leaves: Stiff, small, gray-green, marked with purple. Oblong, somewhat oak-shaped, but toothed and slightly hairy, to 1/2 inch (1.25 cm) long, aromatic. Blooms: June to September.
HABITAT: A Mediterranean native that also grows in Europe and Syria, often around ruins where it was once cultivated.
CULTIVATION: Perennial. Zone: 5 to 6. Germination: 3 to 5 weeks. Space: 12 to 15 inches (30 to 37.5 cm). Soil Temperature: 70° F (21° C). Soil: Well drained, average, light, dry. pH: 7–8.5. Sun: Full sun. Propagation: Plant seeds, divide clumps, or take cuttings. May experience some winterkill in zones 5 to 6, but comes back if mulched during the winter.
GARDEN DESIGN: Germander is a popular edging plant because it has a compact growing style that is dense enough to be trimmed into a hedge and it puts on rapid growth after pruning, which quickly fills any gaps. It formed border designs in formal Elizabethan knot and maze gardens, often interwoven with thyme. The soft coloring of the leaves and flowers adds a nice contrast to herbs with deeper pink and purple flowers.

Teucrium chamaedrys
GERMANDER

CONSTITUENTS: Essential oil includes caryophyllene (60%), glycosides, tannins.
RELATED SPECIES: Cat thyme *(T. marum)* has a sharp smell that cats enjoy. It is 12 to 18 inches (30 to 45 cm) high, with soft fuzzy leaves. It won't tolerate winter temperatures below 20° F (–6.6° C). Dwarf germander (*T. chamaedrys* 'Prostratum') is a low-growing variety that forms a thick carpet. Wood sage, or garlic germander *(T. scorodonia),* with its green-yellow flowers and camphorlike fragrance, was used to bring on menstruation and as a treatment for skin- and blood-related diseases. The silver tree germander *(T. fruiticans)* is a large, 4-foot (1.2-m) silver-green plant. Australian native germanders *(T. racernosum* and *T. corymbosum)* are garden plants that are not used medicinally. *T. polium* treats digestive problems, including ulcers, in Arab countries.

HISTORY: Germander is botanically named after Teucer (half-brother of Ajax), who gave it to his father-in-law, King Dardands of Troy, probably for gout. The herb had its moment of historical glory when the 16th-century German Emperor Charles V was cured of gout after drinking germander tea for 60 days. It helped the Duke of Portland with the same malady in the 18th century and became the key ingredient in Europe's celebrated "Portland Powders." They were manufactured well into the 19th century. The 17th-century herbalist Culpeper suggested drinking germander tea as an antidote to poisons and applying it on snakebites. He also steeped the flowering tops in wine to kill intestinal worms.

CULINARY: Used in tonic wines and as a bitter flavoring in liqueurs and mixed drinks.

MEDICINAL: In addition to curing gout, germander is used to treat indigestion and to stimulate appetite and bile production. It was previously recommended to treat uterine obstructions and water retention and for reducing fevers. It was once considered horehound's equal in relieving colds, flus, and coughs, although it is seldom used for those maladies today.

Thalictrum aquilegifolium
MEADOW RUE

Thalictrum aquilegifolium • **Meadow Rue**

FAMILY: Ranunculaceae.

DESCRIPTION: Tall, graceful herb. Height: 3 to 6 feet (.9 to 1.8 m). Width: 2 feet (60 cm). Flowers: No petals, but with long pink or purple stamens that are very prominent, striking, in open clusters. Leaves: Blue-green, smooth, divided into 3 segments, often with rounded lobes, resembling columbine (*Aquilegia* species). Blooms: May to June.

HABITAT: Europe, Asia.

CULTIVATION: Perennial. Zone: 5. Germination: 15 to 30 days. Space: 1 to 2 feet (30 to 60 cm). Soil Temperature: 50° to 60° F (10 to 15° C). Soil: Well drained, loamy, moist. pH: 5.5 to 7.5. Sun: Partial shade or full sun with plenty of water; complete shade in warmer regions. Propagation: By seed or root division.

GARDEN DESIGN: Very ornamental. Flowers have an airy quality. Choose a somewhat protected place because high winds can bend it over.

CONSTITUENTS: Alkaloid.

RELATED SPECIES: The popular flower garden cultivars and Asian species are available with different colored stamens. Southern Europe's *T. angustifolium* was used in folk medicine to reduce fevers. In 1977, *T. dasycarpum* showed tumor-inhibiting properties, attributed to the alkaloid thalicarpine.

HISTORY: Dioscorides used the leaves of thalictrum (from *thalic,* "to bloom") to cure old wounds. Gerard, calling it "bastard rhubarb" (probably *T. minus*), noted that the leaves and especially the roots were laxative. Native Americans considered purple meadow rue *(T. dasycarpum)* a love potion that could reconcile quarreling lovers. The seeds were sometimes placed in a couple's food by relatives trying to restore peace in the home. Smoking the dried seeds was also said to bring luck in both hunting and courting. They used the stems for straws, and a few different tribes named it "hollow stem." The leaves and seeds were placed on muscle cramps, and the seeds were sprinkled on herbal poultices to increase their potency. Roots were sometimes used on snakebites or made into a tea to reduce a fever.

MEDICINAL: Meadow rue is a purgative and diuretic. The 1916 *U.S. Dispensatory* described it as "bitter and tonic, for vaginal infection." It is a bitter digestive tonic that contains berberine (also found in goldenseal) or a similar alkaloid. The leaves were sometimes added to spruce beer in the 19th century as a digestive tonic.

CONSIDERATIONS: Handling the plant causes itching or dermatitis in many people.

OTHER: The leaves produce a yellow wool dye. The cut flowers of meadow rue are quite lasting, and the cut foliage resembles a large version of maidenhair fern. It can also be dried for wreath making.

Thymus vulgaris • **Thyme**

FAMILY: Labiatae.

DESCRIPTION: Creeping groundcover. Height: 1 foot (30 cm). Width: 1 foot (30 cm). Flowers: Small, white to lilac, 3/4 inch (1.88 cm) long, densely cover plant. Leaves: Small, almost oval, coming to a point, very fragrant, 3/16 to 5/8 inch (5 mm to 16 mm) long. Blooms: May to August.

Thymus vulgaris
THYME

HABITAT: The west Mediterranean to southwest Italy, on dry, rocky soil. Cultivated commercially in Europe, especially Hungary and Germany.

CULTIVATION: Perennial. Zone: 4. Germination: 3 to 4 weeks. Space: 1 foot (30 cm). Soil Temperature: 55° F (13° C). Soil: Well drained, light, rather dry. pH: 6 to 8. Sun: Full sun. Propagation: By seed, cuttings, root division, or layering. The fine root system makes thyme more difficult than most herbs to move. Transplant it so it has plenty of time to establish its fine root system months before a hard freeze. Even established plants can be damaged if the soil freezes solid and heaves. A layer of sand on top of the soil helps prevent damage from freezes. Eventually the clumps die out in the center, but if this occurs after only 2 to 3 years, it can indicate poor growing conditions. Studies at the University of Granada, Spain, found that maximum essential oil potency occurs in the summer months of July and August.

GARDEN DESIGN: Thyme is suitable in rock gardens and borders, alongside pathways, and as a fragrant groundcover. It is used in Elizabethan-style, formal knot gardens because its dense growth allows trimming. Thyme looks particularly nice cascading over the side of a hanging pot or raised terrace. Different varieties planted together highlight each other's colors.

CONSTITUENTS: Essential oil (to 2.5%) includes phenol, thymol (to 40%), carvacrol; terpenes; flavonoids; saponins.

RELATED SPECIES: There are 200 to 400 species of thyme, including numerous cultivars. It is no surprise that there is confusion in proper identification, even in nurseries. All are suitable culinary herbs. "Flavors" include lemon thyme (*T.* x *citriodorus* [pers.]), caraway thyme *(T. herba-barona),* creeping thyme *(T. praecox* ssp. *arcticus),* a tight, 4-inch- (10-cm-) tall groundcover with rosy, purple flowers.

HISTORY: Sumerian cuneiform tablets in 2750 B.C. suggested that thyme be dried and pulverized with pears and figs and enough water to make a thick paste for a poultice. The Egyptians used *tham,* "thyme," for medicine and to embalm their dead. The Romans liberally strewed *thymum* on their floors, burned it to deter venomous creatures, and flavored their cheese with it. Ancient Greeks felt complimented when told they "smelled of *thymbra.*" Their name for the herb (probably *T. capitatus*) might be associated with *thymain,* "to burn as incense," and *thymelē* their word for altar, although most sources claim it came from *thumus,* meaning "energy." For centuries, the bees on Mount Hymettus near Athens have produced a famous wild thyme honey. St. Hildegard mentioned it as a treatment for leprosy, paralysis, and "excessive" body lice.

CULINARY: Benedictine monks added it to their famous elixir. Today it is found in chowders, sauces, tomatoes, gumbos, pickled beets, stews, stuffings, and many different vegetables. By the way, when cookbooks refer to a "sprig" of thyme, they usually mean a half teaspoon (2.5 ml).

MEDICINAL: Thyme's main medicinal role is in treating coughs (including whooping cough) and clearing congestion. It makes an excellent gargle or mouthwash for sore throats and infected gums. Many pharmaceutical gargles, cough drops, mouthwashes, and vapor rubs contain thyme's constituent thymol, which destroys bacteria, some fungus,[1] and the shingles virus (herpes zoster). Participants in a study who rinse twice daily with Listerine™, containing thymol (with eucalyptol and menthol), found they developed 34% less gum inflammation and new plaque formation. Thyme improves digestion, relaxing smooth muscles. It reduces the prostaglandins responsible for many menstrual cramps.[2] Thyme also helps destroy intestinal parasites (especially hookworms and roundworms).

AROMATHERAPY: Rudyard Kipling wrote of the "wind-bit thyme that smells like the perfume of the dawn in paradise." The fragrance of thyme is said to dispel melancholy and nightmares, at least according to 17th-century herbalist Culpeper. Both red thyme oil and the redistilled white thyme are available to use in baths for rheumatism, in liniments, and in massage oils. The term *thymiatechny,* from *thyme* and *technē,* or "art," was once used to describe the "art of using perfumes as medicine," or aromatherapy.

OTHER: Thyme is found in many antimildew preparations and has long been used in linens to deter bugs. Studies show it kills mosquito larvae.[3] Thyme is used occasionally in potpourris and soap making. In addition, it is reported to allow one to see fairies, who are said to dance in beds of wild thyme on Midsummer Eve (June 20–21).

> *Young fairies perched in Rosemary Branches,*
> *while their elders danced in the Thyme.*
> —*LEAVES,* VERNON QUINN, 19TH CENTURY, AMERICAN

NINON DE L'ENCLOS' HAIR RINSE

This recipe dates from circa 1630.

2	*tablespoons (30 ml) thyme, crushed*
1	*tablespoon (15 ml) mint, crushed*
1	*tablespoon (15 ml) rosemary, minced*
1	*pint (500 ml) white vinegar*

Combine ingredients and let sit in a warm place for 3 weeks, then strain.

> *I know a bank where the wild thyme blows*
> *Where ox-lips, and the nodding violet grows;*
> *Quite over-canopied with luscious woodbine,*
> *With sweet musk-roses, and with eglantine.*
> —*A MIDSUMMER NIGHT'S DREAM,* WILLIAM SHAKESPEARE (1564–1616), ENGLISH

> *Here of Sunday morning*
>   *My love and I would lie,*
> *and I would turn and answer*
>   *Among the springing thyme.*
> —"THE SHROPSHIRE LAD," A. E. HOUSMAN (1839–1936), ENGLISH

> *Now the summer's in prime*
>   *Wi' the flowers richly blooming,*
> *And the wild mountain thyme*
>   *A' the moorlands perfuming*
> "THE BRAES O' BALQUHITHER," ROBERT TANNAHILL (1774–1810), SCOTTISH

Tradescantia virginiana • Spiderwort

FAMILY: Commelinaceae.

DESCRIPTION: Spiderlike fronds. Height: 3 feet (90 cm). Width: 2 to 3 feet (60 to 90 cm). Flowers: Violet-purple, occasionally rose or white, 3 petals with 3 sepals and 6 stamens, 1 inch (2.5 cm) wide. Only last 1 day. Leaves: Thin and pointed, 1 foot (30 cm) long, 1 inch (2.5 cm) wide. Blooms: May to August, with a long flowering period.

HABITAT: From Connecticut to Georgia, west to Missouri.

CULTIVATION: Perennial. Zone: 4 to 5. Germination: 10 to 30 days. Space: 2 feet (60 cm). Soil Temperature: 70° F (21° C). Soil: Moist, well drained, fairly rich preferred, but poor conditions tolerated. pH: 5.5 to 7. Sun: Filtered shade or full sun. Propagation: By seed, cuttings, dividing root clumps, or cutting off side shoots from stolons (aboveground runners).

GARDEN DESIGN: Spiderwort is an attractive plant that is used in landscaping design. It is best shown off when placed individually or in a pot that emphasizes its graceful form. Since it can eventually overrun an area with good growing conditions, consider interplanting with butterfly weed or other aggressive herbs or containing the bed.

RELATED SPECIES: Most horticultural spiderworts are *T.* x *andersoniana.* The most popular relative is the common houseplant wandering jew *(T. albiflora),* a widespread weed in parts of Australia.

HISTORY: Spiderwort may refer to the plant's spiderlike appearance or its previous use to cure spider bites. Instead of falling off, an

Tradescantia virginiana
SPIDERWORT

enzymatic reaction causes the old blossoms to turn runny, earning it the name "widow's tears."

CULINARY: The young stems and leaves can be steamed and eaten; use the colorful flowers to top a salad.

OTHER: Spiderwort plants are helping scientists to detect small levels of radiation, chemical mutagens, auto exhaust, sulfur dioxides, and pesticides. The genetically dominant blue cells in the stamens turn pink 8 to 18 days after exposure to such substances and can be seen under an ordinary microscope. In 1977, the Environmental Protection Agency (EPA) placed spiderwort plants near high-risk areas to monitor air pollution. According to spiderwort tests, petroleum refineries and mixed chemical processing plants have the highest mutation rates. In 1980, the plants detected radiation at the Trojan Nuclear Power Plant in Prescott, Oregon, and at other reactors. Dr. Sadao Ichikawa of the Saitama University in Japan found that as little as 150 millirems of radiation produce mutations. (The U.S. federal maximum level for man-made radiation is 170 millirems a year.) These occurred mostly on the windward side, only when the reactor was on. National Aeronautic and Space Association (NASA) scientists found that spiderwort is also one of the most effective plants at absorbing formaldehyde caused by poor ventilation in buildings. But before you run out to the nursery, know that you will need 70 plants for every 2½ yards (2.3 m) of floor space!

Trigonella foenum-graecum • **Fenugreek**

FAMILY: Leguminosae.

DESCRIPTION: Shrubby. Height: 2 feet (60 cm). Width: 1 1/2 feet (45 cm). Flowers: Whitish, by themselves or in pairs. Leaves: Divided into 3 almost cloverlike shapes, 1 inch (2.5 cm) long, toothed around the edges. Fruit: Beaked pod, 1 1/2 to 2 inches (3.75 to 5 cm) long, containing 10 to 20 seeds. Blooms: June.

HABITAT: Southern Europe and Asia in open clearings. Cultivated commercially in Lebanon, Egypt, and Argentina.

CULTIVATION: Annual. Germination: 2 days. Space: 12 to 18 inches (30 to 45 cm). Soil Temperature: 70° to 75° F (21° to 24° C). Soil: Dry and warm, or will rot. pH: 5.5 to 8.2. Sun: Full sun. Propagation: Start from seed in spring. (The seed sold at natural food stores for sprouting is suitable.)

GARDEN DESIGN: The profusion of sweetpealike flowers makes fenugreek a good garden addition. It is a legume that adds nitrogen to the soil and can be used as a cover crop to decorate and prepare new garden areas at the same time.

CONSTITUENTS: Mucilage (to 30%), alkaloids (trigonelline, gentianine, carpaine), steroidal saponins (mainly diosgenin), flavonoids, fixed oil (8%), protein (25%), amino acids (lysine, tryptophan, leucine, histidine, arginine), lecithin, vitamins A, B_1, C, minerals (calcium, iron).

HISTORY: Egyptian papyri tell of fenugreek's use as a food and to reduce fevers, as well as an ingredient in *kuphi* smoke, used in fumigation and embalming. It was discovered in King Tut's tomb (1323 B.C.). Ancient Arabic physicians used it, and a Middle Eastern greeting speaks of fenugreek, or *helbah*: 'May you tread in peace on the soil where it gave new strength, and fearless mood, and gladiators, fierce and rude, helbah grows!'' Fenugreek is an abbreviation of the early Latin name, *foenum,* ''hay,'' *graecum,* ''from Greece.'' It was an early fodder crop that has improved the scent of poor hay since at least the 2nd century B.C. Charlemagne ordered it grown in the 9th century and it was spread throughout Europe by Benedictine monks.

CULINARY: The seeds themselves seem to have little odor, but it increases with drying, becoming quite strong when cooked. A fenugreek extract is sold in grocery stores to give confections a maple or butterscotchlike taste. Greeks eat the seeds boiled or raw with honey; East Indians add them to curries and chutneys; and Egyptians roast them for a coffee substitute or eat the sprouts as vegetables. It is a main flavoring in the Middle East confection halvah and in breads from Arabia, Ethiopia, and Egypt. In all of these countries, including East India, the leaves are served as a vegetable. For the Ethiopians, fenugreek, or *abish,* is a most important food, along with beans, peas, and lentils. In North Africa, and particularly in Tunisia, the flour is used for putting on weight:

Trigonella foenum-graecum
FENUGREEK

3.5 ounces (100 g) of fenugreek is 25% protein, and contains 335 calories and 18 ounces (5.2 g) fat. While this may be discouraging to some people, harem women purposely ate the seeds to make them fleshier and more attractive, an indication of how fashions change! Fenugreek not only increases body weight, but also helps improve protein utilization, inhibits phosphorus secretion, and increases erythrocyte count.[1]

MEDICINAL: Fenugreek seeds are used in Indian and Ethiopian medicine to treat indigestion and diarrhea. Egyptians soak the seeds to make them into a thick paste that they claim is equal to quinine in preventing fevers. It is a folk remedy for diabetes, and clinical studies are proposed to support the preliminary findings that it reduces both blood sugar and cholesterol levels and delays sugar glucose transfer from the stomach to blood in animals.[2] It has a stimulating and toning effect on the uterus, possibly due to its diosgenin, the same hormonelike substance found in wild yam that closely resembles the body's own sex hormones. Fenugreek is currently being cultivated for more investigations.[3] In China, it is given to men to correct impotence and to women to reduce menopausal sweating and depression and as a calcium source. Fenugreek is also used to increase male fertility, although one study shows that direct contact with it may be spermicidal.[4] The Latin Americans boil it in milk, then drink it to increase mother's milk. A poultice has been used for rheumatic pain, burns, to draw out boils, and to relieve sore breasts.

CONSIDERATIONS: Because it stimulates the uterus, restrict use during pregnancy. The straight essential oil, similar to that of dill and parsley, can be narcotic.

OTHER: Fenugreek is still used as a flavoring in veterinary medicines, in conditioning powders for horses and cattle, and as a fodder plant. The pharmaceutical and food industries use it as an emulsifying agent. It is used as a yellow dye in India. The seeds are also planted as an agricultural cover crop.

"MAPLE" PANCAKE SYRUP

¹/₂   cup (120 ml) fenugreek seeds
1   cup (240 ml) water
¹/₄   cup (60 ml) honey

Soak the seeds in the water for 8 hours. Add honey and blend until mixture reaches a smooth consistency.

Trillium erectum • Trillium
(Previously *T. flavum*)

FAMILY: Liliaceae.
DESCRIPTION: Height: 2 feet (60 cm). Width: 10 inches (25 cm). Flowers: Brown-purple, occasionally white, yellow, or green, to 2 inches (5 cm) long, almost erect on 4-inch (10-cm) stems, surrounded by leaves. Leaves: Broad, triangular. Rhizome: Dull brown, often ringed with lines, with wrinkled rootlets underneath, yellow to red-brown. Tastes sweet, then acrid. Blooms: May to June.
HABITAT: Canada, through the Midwest and east coast of the United States. Found on moist soils in shaded woods.

CULTIVATION: Perennial. Zone: 2 or 3 to 7. Requires a cold winter to go dormant. Germination: 1 month. Stratify fresh seed. Space: 1 foot (30 cm). Soil Temperature: 60° to 70° F (15° to 21° C). Soil: Moist, fertile, humus. pH: 4.5 to 6.5. Sun: Partial shade. Propagation: By seed or root division. The first year from seed produces only 1 leaf. It takes 3 to 4 years to produce flowers from seed. Very hardy once established, except in hot climates. Makes a suitable potted herb and can be forced for winter flowers indoors.

GARDEN DESIGN: Very striking, especially when in bloom. Plant where larger herbs won't overshadow it. It contrasts well with other spring wildflowers, such as bloodroot. Be forewarned; flies pollinate the rancid-smelling flowers, so you may not want a patch of trilliums under a window.

CONSTITUENTS: Steroidal saponins (diosgenin), essential oil.

RELATED SPECIES: There are other species of trillium, including the most popular, white-flowering trillium *(T. grandiflorum),* with fragrant, large flowers.

HISTORY: Trillium's name describes its 3 *(tri)* distinct petals, 3 sepals, and 3 leaves. When introduced in 1830 by Rafinesque, any species was used medicinally, although the Native Americans regarded the white-flowering trilliums most effective. Then, in 1892, Charles Millspaugh declared that only *T. erectum* should be used. Many species were actually grouped together and classified as *T. pendulum* (a name no longer used) by wildcrafters. Called wake-robin, it is said to wake the robins into song as it pushes through the last snowdrifts in early spring.

MEDICINAL: The trillium rhizome is used mostly for menstrual disorders, such as relieving cramps and excessive flow, and for vaginal infections. It was an ingredient in the Compound Elixir of Viburnum Opulus (cramp bark), which was used for similar women's complaints. Trillium is also used after childbirth to stop bleeding, which gave it the common name birth root, or beth root. The diosgenin it contains (which also occurs in wild yam root *[Dioscorea villosa]*) is related to human sex hormones and to cortisone. As an external astringent, it can be applied to wounds, ulcers, and sores and used to treat chronic skin infections. Taken internally, it stops digestive tract bleeding and is included in diarrhea and dysentery treatments. It is also used to relieve lung congestion.

Trillium erectum. **Trillium catches the eye with its significant three petals borne above three distinct leaves.**

Tropaeolum majus
NASTURTIUM

Tropaeolum majus • **Nasturtium**

FAMILY: Tropaeoliceae.

DESCRIPTION: Climbing or trailing vine. Length: 5 to 10 feet (1.5 to 3 m). Flowers: Broad petals, 2½ inches (6.25 cm) across, yellow, orange, or red and sometimes spotted, funnel-shaped, with long spur in back. Leaves: Almost round, slightly ruffled, 2 to 7 inches (5 to 17.5 cm) across, thin, slightly succulent. Fruit: Globe-like seedpods filled with many seeds. Blooms: Throughout the summer, most of the year in warm climates.

HABITAT: Native to the Andes in South America.

CULTIVATION: Annual. Germination: 7 to 10 days. Fresh seed is best. Needs darkness to germinate. Space: 1 foot (30 cm). Soil Temperature: 65° F (18° C). Soil: Well drained, slightly sandy, average—will produce less flowers if too moist or rich. pH: 7.5 to 8.5. Sun: Full sun in cool climate or partial shade in hot climate. Propagation: From seed. Flowers 8 weeks after germination. Best in cool conditions and will bloom in the winter in warm climates.

GARDEN DESIGN: The brightly colored flowers are a popular ornamental in flower gardens. They can climb up a wall or fence, hang from a pot, or become a rapid groundcover. Place them so they won't detract from small herbal flowers. Watch out! It may attract aphids during hot weather.

CONSTITUENTS: Glycoside (glucotrapaeoline), which hydrolyzes to antibiotic and antifungal sulfur compounds and an essential oil, isothiocyanate (or mustard oil); high vitamin C content in flowers and leaves.

RELATED SPECIES: The dwarf *(T. minus)* scrambles more than climbs. *T. tuberosum* is an important vegetable in its native Andes.

HISTORY: Introduced to Spain by conquistadores in the early 17th century, nasturtium was called Indian cress and promoted as a vegetable and medicine. It was originally placed in the same family as watercress. Calling it yellow lark's heel because of the flower's spur, in 1629 John Parkinson suggested that the fragrant nasturtium could be combined with carnations and clove pinks "to make a delicate tussie-mussie, . . . or nosegay, both for sight and sent."

CULINARY: The flowers and especially the buds are pickled as a caper substitute. The fresh leaves and flowers are eaten in salads and sandwiches, much like lettuce, but in smaller amounts. Any part of the plant can be whipped with warmed butter into a tasty "nasturtium butter" to spread on crackers or bread.

MEDICINAL: Nasturtium flowers and leaves contain a natural antibiotic that doesn't interfere with intestinal flora—it is even effective against some microorganisms that have built up resistance to common antibiotics. The leaves are eaten or made into tea for both the reproductive and genitourinary tract and respiratory infections. It is reputed to promote red blood cell production. The juice of the fresh plant has been rubbed on itching skin.

CONSIDERATIONS: Large amounts of the seeds are purgative.

OTHER: Has been fed to chickens to prevent and cure fowl pox.

NASTURTIUM CAPERS

This recipe was adapted from *The British Housewife*, written in 1770 by Martha Bradley. Of the initial cooking process of the buds, she wrote, "They will fade a little, and they will soon be as dry as when just gathered; and being thus faded they will take the vinegar better than if they had been quite fresh." If you are patient and let them sit 6 weeks, "In that Time the Vinegar will have penetrated them thoroughly and the Taste of the Spices will be got into their very Substance, so that they will be one of the finest Pickles in the World," promised Bradley.

Nasturtium buds to fill a 1-quart (1-l) jar
1   **quart (1 l) vinegar**
¹/₄   **teaspoon (1.25 ml) nutmeg**
¹/₂   **teaspoon (2.5 ml) black pepper, whole**
6   **cloves**

Stir buds in cold water, drain, and repeat, then lay on a sieve to dry. Loosely fill a well-washed quart (litre) jar with buds, sprinkling in spices as you go. Fill the jar with vinegar and put on a lid. Let sit 6 weeks before opening.

LATIN CHICHEGHI SALATASSI (NASTURTIUM SALAD)

Here is a recipe from the *Turkish Cookery Book* of 1862 by Turab Effendi.

Put a plate of flowers of the nasturtium in a salad-bowl, with a tablespoon of chopped chervil; sprinkle over with your fingers half a teaspoonful of salt, two or three tablespoons of olive oil, and the juice of a lemon; turn the salad in the bowl with a spoon and fork until well mixed, and serve.

> *The Indian cress our climate now do's bear,*
> *Call'd Larksheel 'cause he wears a horse-man's spur,*
> *This gilt-spun knight prepares his course to run*
> *Taking his signal from the rising sun,*
> *And stimulates his flow'r to meet the day*
> *So Castor mounted spurs his steed away*
> *This warrior sure has in some battle been*
> *For spots of blood upon his breast are seen.*
> —ABRAHAM COWLEY (1618–1667), ENGLISH

Tussilago farfara • Coltsfoot

FAMILY: Compositae.
DESCRIPTION: Low-growing and spreading. Height 4 to 8 inches (10 to 20 cm). Width: 6 inches (15 cm). Flowers: Bright yellow, 1 inch (2.5 cm), resemble dandelions, but held aloft on purplish, scaly, 8-inch (20-cm) stems. Turn into white tufted seed heads. Leaves: Slightly lobed and toothed around the edge. Dull green, flat with a downy white underside, 4 to 7 inches (10 to 17.5 cm) wide. They appear in late spring, long after the flowers. Mucilaginous and somewhat bitter-tasting. Blooms: March to April.
HABITAT: Native to Europe, northern and western Asia, northern Africa; naturalized in other areas, including the northeastern United States, in moist, loamy soils of wastelands.

CULTIVATION: Perennial. Zone: 2. Germination: 1 to 2 weeks. Space: 6 to 8 inches (15 to 20 cm). Soil Temperature: 60° to 70° F (15° to 21° C). Soil: Heavy, rich loam that holds moisture. Will grow in poor conditions, but develops more bitterness. pH: 4.5 to 7.5. Sun: Sun or partial shade. Propagation: Grow from seed or divisions. Once established, it will happily take over the garden if not restrained; 3 to 6 cuttings a year are possible.
CONSTITUENTS: Flavonoids (rutin, hyperoside, isoquercetin), polysaccharide mucilage (8%), pyrrolizidine alkaloids, sterols, essential oil, minerals (potassium, calcium salts), tannin, inulin.
RELATED SPECIES: Coltsfoot is often confused with western coltsfoot (*Petasites* spp.), a much larger herb used for lung congestion that grows wild in the northwest United States. They have similar medicinal uses.
HISTORY: The ancients imagined that the outline of coltsfoot leaves resembles a colt's footprint. The Romans called it *Filius ante patrem*, "the son before the father," because the flowers appear and wither in the spring before the leaves emerge. For the same reason, the Russians call it *mat i matcheha*, or "mother and stepmother." In Pliny's day (the 1st century A.D.), Romans inhaled smoke from coltsfoot leaves burnt on cypress charcoal through a reed, then sipped wine, to stop obstinate coughing. For centuries, it was a popular ingredient in herbal tobaccos and is still the main ingredient in "British Herb Tobacco" (with buckbean, eyebright, betony, rosemary, thyme, lavender, and chamomile). In the past, a picture of the coltsfoot flower painted on the doorpost identified French pharmacies.

Tussilago farfara
COLTSFOOT

Tussilago farfara. **The unusual characteristic of coltsfoot flowers is that they appear before the leaves, signaling the early days of spring.**

CULINARY: The leaves were eaten as a vegetable and the flowers were once used to flavor wine.

MEDICINAL: Herbalists, from Dioscorides in the 1st century to present-day practitioners, have recommended coltsfoot leaves for lung problems such as laryngitis, bronchitis, and asthma, and to control spastic coughing. It is a soothing expectorant, and the flavonoids it contains reduce inflammation, especially in the bronchials. Even its name *Tussilago* comes from *tussis*, Latin for "cough." Coltsfoot is also applied as a poultice to sores and ulcerations and as a cream for cold sores.

CONSIDERATIONS: Coltsfoot contains traces of pyrrolizidine alkaloids (PA) (similar but not identical to those in comfrey root), and the jury is still out concerning its safety. The alkaloids cause liver toxicity in rats fed high daily doses, although not those given low doses.[1] More encouraging studies show that the immune systems of mice were stimulated when the animals were given an extract made from the whole plant.[2] So far, the alkaloids have not been shown to cause any damage to human chromosomes in the test tube.[3] A 1987 case reported an infant born with severe liver injury after her mother had consumed coltsfoot tea daily for a lung problem, but the tea was later proven to be adulterated with *Petasites*, which contains much higher concentrations of PA. The early evidence in this case prompted Germany to ban 2,500 products containing herbs with PA in January 1989. They propose restricting coltsfoot to about 1 teaspoon of dried herb, 6 grams, or 1 microgram of PA daily for no more than 4 weeks.

OTHER: The feathery seed heads were once collected for pillow stuffing.

Coltsfoot's a classical fixture
In one old smoking mixture.
Some say after heating
The leaves fit for eating,
But that's a debatable issue.
— *"COLTSFOOT,"* **JAMES A. DUKE (b. 1929), AMERICAN**

Urtica dioica • Nettle

FAMILY: Urticaceae.

DESCRIPTION: Bristly herb with few branches. Height: 3 to 6 feet (.9 to 1.83 m). Width: 2 to 3 feet (60 to 90 cm). Flowers: Small, white, loosely clustered. Leaves: Oval, coming to a point, deeply serrated around edge, downy, covered with stinging hairs, to 6 inches (15 cm). Even slight pressure releases fluid from a capsule at the base of each hollow stinger hair. Blooms: June to September.

HABITAT: Eurasia, naturalized elsewhere, including Australia.

CULTIVATION: Perennial. Zone: 2. Germination: 10 to 14 days. Space: 1 to 2 feet (30 to 60 cm). Soil Temperature: 65° to 75° F (18° to 24° C). Soil: Damp, rich with nitrogen. pH: 6.5 to 7.5. Sun: Full sun or partial shade. Propagation: By seed, cuttings, or root division. Likes to grow by running water.

GARDEN DESIGN: It might be wise to place nettle beyond reach of visitors in the garden, who may injure themselves touching and smelling the herbs.

CONSTITUENTS: Formic acid, which causes the painful reaction, found in hairs; indoles (histamine, serotonin); acetylcholine; minerals (iron, silica, potassium, manganese, sulphur); vitamins A, C; especially high in chlorophyll.

HISTORY: Nettles have supplied fiber for cloth and paper from the Bronze Age (4,000–3,000 B.C.) into the 20th century. The name is derived from the Anglo-Saxon *netel,* which some authorities think originated from *noedl* (a needle) because of its stingers. More likely, it comes from *net,* akin to the Latin fishnet, *nassa,* which was made out of nettles. Roman soldiers in Britain planted *urtica,* from *urere,* meaning "to sting," to rub on their limbs so they could better tolerate the cold winter (probably *U. pilulifera).* Later, it was cultivated in Scotland, Denmark, and Norway to make fine linen, coarse sailcloth, and strong fishnets. Eventually, flax was preferred, but nettles were still used to weave coarse household cloths, called scotchcloth, from the 16th through the 19th centuries. Scottish poet Thomas Campbell (1777 to 1844) related,

> *In Scotland, I have eaten nettles, I have slept in nettle sheets, and I have dined off a nettle tablecloth. The young and tender nettle is an excellent potherb, . . . I have heard my mother say that she thought nettle cloth more durable than any other species of linen.*

To make cloth, the nettles were cut, dried, and steeped in water, then the fibers were separated and spun into yarn. In the Hans Christian Anderson (1805–1875) fairy tale *The Princess and the Eleven Swans,* the coats the princess made for her brothers were woven from nettle. In *Les Misèrables,* the character Monsieur Madeleine describes its virtues:

> *When the nettle is young, its leaf forms an excellent vegetable; when it matures, it has filaments and fibres like hemp and flax. Nettle fabric is as good as canvas. Chopped, the nettle is good for poultry; pounded it is good for cattle. The seed of the nettle mingled with fodder imparts a gloss to the coats of animals; its root mixed with salt produces a beautiful yellow color. It is besides excellent hay and can be cut twice. And what does the nettle require: Little earth, no attention, no cultivation. Only the seed falls as it ripens, and is difficult to gather. That is all. With a little trouble, the nettle would be useful; it is neglected, and becomes harmful.*
> —*LES MISÈRABLES,* **VICTOR HUGO (1802–1885), FRENCH**

Urtica dioica
NETTLE

MEDICINAL: Nettle leaves are a blood builder often used as a spring tonic and to treat anemia and poor circulation. They contain both iron and vitamin C, which aids iron absorption. In the past, nettle was eaten or sipped to reduce uric acid and to treat gout and arthritis. I've even observed arthritics directly hitting stinging nettles on joints to relieve their pain. They considered the sting minor compared to the temporary relief it provided. Nettle also encourages mother's milk, lowers blood sugar, and decreases profuse menstruation; it acts as a light laxative and diuretic. Both a tea and a poultice (of cooked nettles) are used to treat eczema and other skin conditions. An astringent that stops bleeding, the powder is snuffed to stop nosebleeds. Curled dock leaves *(Rumex crispus)*, another widespread weed, provide a remedy for nettle's sting. "Nettle in, dock out, dock rub nettle out!" goes an old rhyme. Interestingly, the fresh juice of nettles themselves relieves the sting. Australia's Aborigines are said to have used a nettle *(U. incisa)* lotion for sprains, and to have boiled leaves for a poultice.

COSMETIC: Nettles are found in hair conditioners and shampoos. They are said to promote hair growth when applied to the scalp, although they are probably more helpful when taken internally.

CONSIDERATIONS: Wear gloves when picking.

OTHER: Nettles are a source of commercial chlorophyll. Biodynamic gardeners use them as compost starter to activate the compost pile. The plants are also said to increase the essential oil content of nearby herb plants. Swedish studies at the University of Lund show that a strong water extract of either dried or fresh nettles (especially spring-harvested) poured on plants stimulates their growth. It makes a permanent green dye on wool or yellow with alum. Ukranians use nettles to dye Easter eggs with their elaborate batik designs and as a green confection dye. Nettles are also added to animal feed to increase the milk production and health of farm animals.

NETTLE PUDDING

1	*gallon (4.5 l) young nettle tops*
2	*leeks or onions*
2	*heads broccoli or small cabbage*
¹/₄	*pound (113 g) rice*
1	*teaspoon (5 ml) salt*

Combine ingredients. Boil or cook in a pressure cooker until rice is done. Serve with gravy or melted butter.

STCHI

The following was adapted from *The Epicure in Imperial Russia* written by Marie Alexandre Markevitch and published in 1941.

1	*pound (500 g) young, fresh nettle shoots*
¹/₂	*cup (120 ml) cream*
1	*quart (1 l) bouillon*

Steam or boil nettles, and chop finely. Let cool. Mix in cream and bouillon and bring to a boil.

> *If they would drink Nettles in March,*
> *And eat Mugwort in May,*
> *So many fine maidens*
> *Wouldn't go to the clay.*
> —"PROVERBS," MICHAEL DENHAM, ENGLISH

CULINARY: When cooked or dried for winter use, nettles lose their sting. The young, steamed tops taste somewhat like spinach. Nettle porridge was popular in the 17th century, and nettles were the Roman Pliny's favorite pudding. The Scots still make nettle pudding with leeks, broccoli, and rice. Italians make herb *knodel* by cooking nettles like dumplings. The Russians serve *stchi*, often called "green borscht," with stuffed eggs. Cheese makers use it as a rennet substitute. (One cup of strong tea is made and mixed with ¹/₃ cup [80 ml] salt, and 1 tablespoon [15 ml] is added to 2 pints [1 l] of milk.) I've found it doesn't coagulate milk as solidly, but does make a fine soft cheese. Australian Aborigines ate native nettle leaves after baking them between heated stones.

Vaccinium myrtillus
BILBERRY

Vaccinium myrtillus • Bilberry

FAMILY: Ericacea.

DESCRIPTION: Ornamental, deciduous shrub that turns yellow-green, then red in the fall. Height: 1 to 2 feet (30 to 60 cm). Width: 3 to 4 feet (90 to 120 cm). Flowers: Pale, green-pink, 1/4 inch (.63 cm), and solitary. Leaves: Shiny, leathery, bright green, finely dented around the edges, oval, 1 inch (2.5 cm) long. Fruit: Resembles currants, slightly acid, globe-shaped, 1/3 inch (8 mm) in diameter, purple. Root: Thin, creeping. Blooms: May to August.

HABITAT: Europe, northern Asia, and North America, from British Columbia south to New Mexico. Found mostly in damp woodlands and moorlands.

CULTIVATION: Perennial. Zone: 5. Space: 2 feet (60 cm). Soil Temperature: 65° to 75° F (18° to 23° C). Soil: Damp, peaty with humus, moist. Plenty of water but not standing. pH: 4 to 5. Sun: Filtered shade. Propagation: From rooted cuttings.

GARDEN DESIGN: The bilberry gives the garden height or defines the outlying edges. It adds a colorful touch to the autumn garden when many of the herbs have ceased flowering.

CONSTITUENTS: Fruit: anthocyanin, responsible for the fruit's blue color (at least 0.3%); alkaloids (myrtine, epimyrtine); glycosides (quercitrin); tannins (to 7%), organic acids; pectin; sugar; vitamins A and C. Leaves: glucoquinine.

HISTORY: The genus contains about 150 species with the common names interchanged so often, no one is sure which berries the older writings refer to when they mention *Vaccinum,* the name used by the Roman Pliny. We do know bilberry was a medicinal herb in the 16th century. It is a good chance that they are the "black whortles" Gerard described as eaten with cream by the people of Cheshire in the 17th century. The English are still calling them whortleberries—and eating them with cream. The Scots know them as blaeberries. The American name bilberry came from the Danish *bollebar,* or "dark berry." In the United States, they are also called huckleberries.

CULINARY: A favorite way to prepare bilberries has been to stew them with lemon and sugar. The small size of the seeds makes them ideal for jams, syrups, and conserves. They have been added to liqueurs and wines to make them seem richer and more aged.

MEDICINAL: A drink of the fruit and roots steeped in gin is an old remedy to stop diarrhea and relieve nausea and indigestion— although, as with blackberries, large amounts of the whole berries eaten with their pips (seeds) and skin provide a laxative bulk. They can decrease intestinal inflammation and help protect the digestive tract lining. The berries are also said to be a refrigerant that lowers body heat. Studies show an effect on heart contractions and blood vessels that is thought to be caused by the berries stimulating the production of prostaglandins.[1] There is evidence that they also help prevent blood clots. Bilberries are incorporated into European pharmaceuticals that are used to improve circulation and night vision. Several scientific studies support this use. In Russia, berries and leaves are used to treat colitis, stomach problems, and sugar diabetes. The leaves are also found, along with related species, in folk remedies of other countries to treat diabetes. The glucoquinine in the leaves does show a weak ability to lower blood sugar. Clinical studies have been proposed to back the hypoglycemic effects found in animals.[1] German researchers have also suggested that the quinic acid produced from a tea of dried bilberry leaves is a potential treatment for rheumatism and gout.

OTHER: The berries produce a blue-purple dye (with alum) and other colors. They were used in Norway to treat scurvy.

Valeriana officinalis • Valerian
(Previously *V. excelsa*)

FAMILY: Valerianaceae.
DESCRIPTION: Leafy herb with tall, hollow, flowering stalk. Height: 5 feet (1.5 m). Width: 1 foot (30 cm). Flowers: White, pink, or lavender; fragrant; to 3/16 inches (4 mm). Leaves: Very divided into 7 to 10 segments. Roots: Their smell has often been compared to dirty socks. Blooms: May to July.
HABITAT: Europe and western Asia. Naturalized in Canada and northern United States, in low meadows and wet woods.
CULTIVATION: Perennial. Zone: 4. Germination: To 3 weeks. Space: 1 foot (30 cm). Soil: Moist. pH: 6 to 7. Soil Temperature: 60° to 70° F (15° to 21° C). Sun: Full sun or partial shade. Propagation: By seed or root division. It is difficult to remove once established. The root can be harvested by the autumn of the second year. Some gardeners take the flowers off young plants to hasten root development.

GARDEN DESIGN: Valerian looks best when its flowers begin to gracefully sway on their tall stalks. It goes well towards the back of the garden, where it will happily grow in tight clumps.
CONSTITUENTS: Iridoids called valepotriates (to 2%); glycoside (valerosidatum); essential oil (to 2%) includes esters of acetic, butyric, and isovalerianic acids, which yield isovalerianic acid when dried, giving valerian its distinct aroma; sesquiterpene; alkaloids. In 1907, researcher Chevalier stated that fresh valerian is more active than the dried root.
RELATED SPECIES: Native American species have similar properties. Indian valerian *(V. wallichii)* contains four times the valepotriates (0.5%).[1] The sedative Himalayan valerian *(Nardostachys jatamansi,* formerly *V. Jatamansi)* is thought to be the fragrant spikenard, or "nard," of the Bible that is still used in East India to scent clothing and ointments. Red valerian, or Jupiter's beard, *(Centranthus ruber,* previously *V. coccinea)* is a very different plant. Valerian is sometimes called "garden heliotrope" because its flowers resemble the unrelated, sub-tropical *Heliotropium arborescens*.

Valeriana officinalis
VALERIAN

HISTORY: The Roman name *valere* was derived from *valor* for courage—which might describe the strength needed to drink the strong-tasting brew. Galen and Dioscorides called valerian *phu*—another descriptive response to its odor! (This species is designated *V. Phu.*) The 11th century Anglo-Saxon "leech" books describe it, as does Saladinus of Ascoli, founder of Salernum Medical School (c. 1450). In modern history, valerian was prescribed in England for enduring World War II air-raids.

CULINARY: As strong as it may be, valerian was used as a spice in the Middle Ages and the leaves were used as Anglo-Saxon salad herbs. Gerard mentioned the esteem in which the 16th century Scots held valerian, noting that "no broth or pottage…be worth anything if *setewale* be not there."

MEDICINAL: Valerian root is a general tranquilizer used for relieving nervous tension, insomnia, and headaches. Widely studied, it has been shown to sedate the central nervous system due to the valepotriates and other components found in the essential oil.[2] Valerian decreases muscle spasms, so is useful for cases of nervous digestion, irritable bowel syndrome, and stomach or menstrual cramps. It contains many types of valepotriates that have opposing effects, indicating that it has the ability to regulate many conditions. In one study, it sedated agitated patients, but stimulated those suffering from fatigue.[3] Valerian improved the quality of sleep in subjects in another study, as observed in their brain-wave patterns. It also reduced the time it took them to fall asleep, especially the elderly and the habitually poor sleepers, but did not affect their dream recall or ability to wake up in the morning.[4] In Germany, hyperactive children have been treated with valerian since the 1970s. After taking valerian for only a few weeks, 120 children diagnosed as hyperactive, anxious, or learning disabled had better muscle coordination and reaction time, and showed less aggression, restlessness, anxiety, and fear.[5] Valerian may also lower blood pressure and strengthen the optic nerve in the eye, although thus far, only animal studies have been done.[6]

AROMATHERAPY: The essential oil of valerian is closely related to whale and porpoise oil and oxidized animal fats and secretions. This may not make it seem a contender for aromatherapy, but very minute amounts actually produce pleasing scents for soap and after-shave fragrances. The roots were used in the 17th and 18th centuries to scent clothing.

CONSIDERATIONS: Valerian is reported to cause headaches, muscle spasms, and heart palpitations in very large or prolonged doses, although no other adverse effects in humans have been documented.[7] It can also increase certain effects of alcohol. Avoid during pregnancy.

OTHER: The root excites some animals, especially rats and cats, but they usually won't know it is in your garden unless it is uprooted. It is rumored that the famous Pied Piper of Hamelin owed his success in leading the rats out of the city to having had his pockets stuffed full of valerian rather than to his music! Valerian is still used by rat catchers.

Verbascum thapsus • Mullein

FAMILY: Scrophulariaceae.

DESCRIPTION: Height: To 6 feet (1.8 m). Width: 2 to 3 feet (60 to 90 cm). Flowers: Yellow, 1 inch (2.5 cm) across, 4 petals, clustered densely around single flower spike. Sometimes smaller side spikes. Leaves: Large ovals, to 2 feet (60 cm) long, thick, and covered with fine, somewhat prickly hairs. They form a rosette, from which flower stalk grows. Blooms: July to August, 2nd year.

HABITAT: Europe and Asia, and naturalized extensively in the United States and Australia, on stony wastelands and cleared areas.

CULTIVATION: Biennial. Zone: 3. Germination: 15 to 12 days. Space: 2 to 3 feet (60 to 90 cm). Soil Temperature: 60° to 70° F (15° to 21° C). Soil: Dry, well drained, slightly poor. pH: 5.5–7.5. Sun: Full sun. Propagation: By seed, self-sows easily, especially in good garden soil.

GARDEN DESIGN: Mullein stands out in the garden, especially when in bloom. Since only a single flower stalk gives it height, it is best suited in the middle among other low-growing herbs.

CONSTITUENTS: Saponins, essential oil, flavonoids, glycosides (acubin), mucilage.

RELATED SPECIES: *V. bombyciferum,* with its very white, fuzzy leaves and large flowers, is often grown as an ornamental herb. Various species are medicinal, especially *V. thapsiforme* and *V. phlomoides.* Saponins contained in their seeds stupefy fish and are used to catch them; they also eliminate tapeworms.

HISTORY: The Romans called mullein *verbascum,* probably from the Latin *barba,* or "beard," and the name mullein must have originated with the latin *mollis,* or "soft." Both describe its fuzzy leaves. Dr. Prior, in his *The Popular Names of British Plants,* thinks that mullein's name was derived from the Latin *malandrium,* or "malady." Whatever the case, it later became the Anglo-Saxon *molegn.* When in flower, it looks like a large candle; in fact, the flowers dipped into tallow and lit make a primitive torch, giving it the name *haege* or *hage* (hedge) taper, sometimes confusingly turned into "hag's" taper! Parkinson reports that such candles were called *Latines Candela Regia* and carried during ceremonies, especially funerals.

MEDICINAL: Mullein is one of the primary herbs for any lung problem, including whooping cough, asthma, bronchitis, and chest colds. It was traditionally smoked for lung conditions. It is also a diuretic used to relieve urinary tract inflammation, diarrhea, and inflammation, colitis, or other bleeding in the bowel. The flowers extracted into olive oil make a preparation that is well known to reduce the pain and inflammation of earache, insect bites, bruises, hemorrhoids, and sore joints. A distilled flower water or a poultice has been placed on burns, ringworm, boils, and sores.

CONSIDERATIONS: The fine hairs irritate some people's skin, producing rashes, a warning for those who wish to use the leaves as "natural toilet paper."

OTHER: The flowers make a pale yellow dye. Roman women took advantage of this to bring out light highlights in their hair. The ashes were once made into soap for a hair tonic.

Verbascum thapsus
MULLEIN

Verbena officinalis
VERVAIN

Verbena officinalis • **Vervain**

FAMILY: Verbenaceae.

DESCRIPTION: Erect, stiff herb. Height: 4 to 5 feet (1.2 to 1.5 m). Width: 2 feet (60 cm). Flowers: Small, vivid blue, rising on spikes. Leaves: Oblong, to 6 inches (15 cm), edges slightly serrated. Blooms: May to June.

HABITAT: Europe, naturalized in Australia.

CULTIVATION: Perennial. Zone: 4 to 5. Germination: 3 to 4 weeks. Needs dark to germinate. Space: 1 foot (30 cm). Soil Temperature: 70° to 75° F (21° to 23° C). Soil: Light, well-drained. Sun: Full sun. Propagation: By seed, cuttings, or root division.

GARDEN DESIGN: Vervain is a tall, stately herb that fits well in a mixed border of herbs, and forms a nice backdrop for other plants.

CONSTITUENTS: Glycosides (verbenalin, verbenin), alkaloid, bitter principle, essential oil.

RELATED SPECIES: Garden verbena *(V. × hybrida)* includes many fragrant and colorful cultivars. The older species were used in perfumery, but the scent has been hybridized out.

HISTORY: The name vervain is often said to have come from the Celtic *ferfaen*, or *fer*, meaning "to drive away," and *faen*, "a stone," from its function of eliminating bladder stones. More likely, it was derived from the Latin *verbena*, meaning "a shoot or green branch," also the Latin generic term for an altar plant. Romans not only adorned altars, but also decorated peace messengers with vervain, and they believed it could rekindle dying love. Vervain was also a magic plant in Celtic and Germanic cultures. It became known as *herba sacra* and *herba veneris* in the early church.

MEDICINAL: In previous centuries, vervain leaves were used to treat autumn fevers. They were found in formulas for liver and gall bladder problems and chronic skin conditions. Vervain leaves were a traditional remedy for uterine cramping, and the glycosides they contain do show evidence of promoting menstruation and increasing mother's milk.[1] Vervain is made into a mouthwash for infected gums and a poultice for hemorrhoids or wounds. A tea has been used as a nerve tonic, to treat insomnia, and as a digestive. Vervain is also used in home-made liqueurs. South American, Mexican, and Chinese folk medicines suggest vervain tea for treating various growths and cancers, particularly of the neck, spleen, and scrotum.

CONSIDERATIONS: Avoid during pregnancy.

Vetiveria zizanioides • **Vetiver**
(Previously *Andropogon zizaknioides*)

FAMILY: Gramineae

HABITAT: Found in tropical India, cultivated throughout the tropical world and in parts of Louisiana.

DESCRIPTION: Large, bushy grass. Height: 7 to 8 feet (2.1 to 2.4 m). Flowers: Only the northern "khus" type blooms, in pairs on 6 to 12 stems. Leaves: Long, thin, pointed with sharp edges, 5/16 inches (8 mm) wide. Roots: Thin, spindly, brown, richly scented when broken.

CULTIVATION: Perennial. Zone: 9. Space: 2 to 3 feet (60 to 90 cm). Soil: Dry, well-drained, fairly poor soil is suitable. Sun: Full sun. Propagation: By root division of clumps. Sufficient phosphorus and potash increase oil yield.

GARDEN DESIGN: Somewhat lacking in design qualities, vetiver is best as a thick backing or filler, or used as a hedge plant.

CONSTITUENTS: Essential oil includes at least 29 different compounds.

HISTORY: Vetiver has been used for centuries as incense and perfume. The name is derived from the Tamil *vetivern*. East Indians differentiate the cultivated "vetiver" from the wild "khus" of northern India, which flowers and has a slightly different chemistry.

MEDICINAL: Vetiver roots are occasionally taken as a stimulating tonic drink in India. They are used to improve digestion, encourage menstruation, and kill parasites. It is said to have a "cooling" effect on the body and to increase sweating. East Indians treat fevers, flus, and rheumatism with it.

AROMATHERAPY: Vetiver is one of India's main essential oil crops. The long roots are woven into fragrant window blinds and floor mats. On hot days, water is thrown on them so the wind releases their scent. According to Guenther, in *The Essential Oils*, the roots are at peak oil production when two years old, but tests at the Lemongrass Research Station on Odakkali, India, indicate that 18 months is the preferred age. Guenther also states that vetiver oil is "…one of the most valuable and most important perfumers' raw materials."

OTHER: Haitians make thatch from vetiver. Fans and baskets woven from the roots are sold in import stores.

Vetiveria zizanioides
VETIVER

© Steven Foster

Viburnum opulus • Cramp Bark

FAMILY: Caprifoliaceae.

DESCRIPTION: Large, deciduous bush with spreading branches. Height: To 12 feet (3.6 m). Width: 6 feet (1.8 m). Flowers: Small, white, form large semicircular balls 3 to 4 inches (7.5 to 10 cm) across. Leaves: Maplelike with 3 to 5 lobes, hairy underneath. Fruit: Scarlet, then purple, drooping. Blooms: May to July.

HABITAT: A native of Europe, northern Africa, and northern Asia, grown ornamentally in the United States, where it sometimes escapes from cultivation. Popular in Australian gardens.

CULTIVATION: Perennial. Zone: 3. Germination: 3 to 8 months. Space: 4 to 5 feet (1.2 to 1.5 m). Soil Temperature: 70° F (21° C). Stratify in refrigerator 3 months, then 70° F (21° C) for 1 to 2 months. Soil: Heavy, somewhat rich, loamy, moist. pH: 6 to 8. Sun: Full sun. Propagation: From seed, hardwood cuttings, or bareroot trees planted in the fall.

CONSTITUENTS: Tannins, isovalerianic acid, resin (iburnine), salicosides.

RELATED SPECIES: The American cranberry bush *(V. trilobum)* is almost identical. Other, similar species from the eastern United States are used medicinally, including: possum haw *(V. nudum),* southern black haw *(V. rufidulum),* and black haw *(V. prunifolium).* Nurseries most often sell the snowball bush *(V. opulus* 'Roseum'), which produces sterile seeds.

HISTORY: In Europe, cramp bark has been mostly a Polish and Romanian folk medicine, although Chaucer (1340–1400) did note that the "gaitre-beries shal be for your hele." The various American species were used by the natives and adapted into many patent remedies sold in 19th-century America. Cramp bark was first described by John King as a uterine tonic that prevented hemorrhaging. It remained official in the *U.S. Pharmacopoeia* from 1882 until 1926. It is often called "snowball tree" because of its round, white flower clusters. An older name, guelder rose or rose de Gueldre, probably came from its associations with the Dutch province Gulderland.

CULINARY: Yet another common name is cranberry tree, because the cooked fruits have been eaten, even though they are bitter. The Scandinavians and Siberians prepare a liqueur and a honey paste from the fruit.

MEDICINAL: Cramp bark's name well describes its uses. The bark lessens the chance of miscarriage and decreases muscle cramps, especially painful menstruation. It has been shown to be a uterine and nervous system tonic and relaxant.[1] Other effects include relieving asthma, hysteria, convulsions, heart palpitations, and rheumatism. In Russia, the berries are made into a brandy called *nastoika,* a peptic ulcer remedy. The Japanese make a vinegar extract from the berries for treating cirrhosis of the liver, and the Chinese use both the leaves and berries as an emetic and laxative.

CONSIDERATIONS: The uncooked berries are potentially poisonous and can cause indigestion even when taken in small amounts.

OTHER: The berries, which turn black when dried, are a fabric dye and were once used to make ink.

> Sweet is the air with budding haws, and the
>   valley stretching for miles below
> Is white with blossoming cherry trees, as if just
>   covered with the lightest snow.
> —GOLDEN LEGEND, HENRY WADSWORTH LONGFELLOW (1807–1882), AMERICAN

> What is sweeter, after all
> Than black haws, in early fall?
> —JAMES WHITCOMB RILEY (1849–1916), AMERICAN

Viola odorata • Violet

FAMILY: Violaceae.
HABITAT: Europe, Africa, and Asia.
DESCRIPTION: Low-growing groundcover, growing on a creeping rhizome. Height: 4 inches (10 cm). Flowers: 3/4-inch (2-cm) across, deep violet, occasionally rose or white, drooping, with a short spur in back, sweetly scented. These rarely set seed, but a second set of smaller, autumn flowers do. Leaves: Heart-shaped and slightly toothed around the edges. Roots: Thin, brown, in a creeping network. Blooms: February to April.
CULTIVATION: Perennial. Zone: 5 to 6. Germination: 10 to 20 days. Stratify. Needs dark to germinate. Space: 6 to 8 inches (15 to 20 cm). Soil Temperature: 70° F (21° C). Soil: Rich. pH: 7 to 8. Sun: Full sun. Partial shade in very hot climates. Propagation: By seed or root division. The easiest method is to remove off-shoots in late winter or early spring and root them in sand.
GARDEN DESIGN: Suitable for rock gardens or low borders, banks, or beneath deciduous trees.
CONSTITUENTS: Essential oil includes ionine; saponins; glycoside (violarutin); methyl salicylate; mucilage; vitamins A and C; alkaloid (odoratine).
RELATED SPECIES: There are many horticultural forms, some with double flowers, and many related species too numerous to mention.
HISTORY: Cultivated for over 2,000 years, violets have been well-loved in many cultures. The Romans scattered violet leaves and flowers in their banquet halls as they drank *viola* wine and adorned themselves with head garlands made of the flowers, which were thought to prevent headaches or dizziness from drinking. (In France today, violets are still used to treat hangovers.) After the festivities, violet liniments in vinegar relieved gout, and liver and spleen problems. Violets were an ancient symbol of fertility, depicted in the final love scenes in the medieval Cloisters tapestries (preserved at The Cloisters, Metropolitan Museum of Art, New York City). Lucky medieval patients were given violet water, then rubbed down with violet oil and wrapped in clean linen. The water was also a popular gift for birthdays and saint's days. "Violet Plate," really violet sugar, was sold in all 17th century apothecaries for consumption. Violet was the most popular English and French fragrance in the 19th century—although much of the violet scent really came from the less expensive orris root *(Iris × germanica).* Napoleon, who loved violets, was toasted as "Corporal Violette" and they became his party's emblem. His first wife, Josephine, carried violets in her locket and covered his grave with them.
CULINARY: Violet flowers are candied or eaten raw in salads and floated on soups. They import a delicate taste and flavor to white vinegar. The Roman gourmet Apicius made *Violetum* by soaking the leaves in wine. In the Middle Ages, a broth of violets, fennel, and savory was popular, and the flowers decorated all types of dishes. A quick way to make candied violets is to brush fresh flowers with egg white and sprinkle with granulated sugar.
MEDICINAL: Violet leaves and flowers were once made into a popular and tasty cough syrup and sore throat gargle, and were used to relieve sinus and lung congestion. Said to have a "cooling" nature, violets are slightly sedating and suggested for people suffering from anxiety, insomnia, and high blood pressure. Studies in Pakistan have shown that violets increase sweating, and a violet extract (more effective than a tea) is a safe and non-toxic way to reduce fever. Headaches can be relieved by drinking violet flower tea and placing a cool compress on the forehead. Traditional Chinese medicine places violet leaf and root poultices on hot swelling, inflammation, and mumps, while in the west, they traditionally have been used on swollen or tumorous breasts.
AROMATHERAPY: The Greeks called violets *ion agrion* and the aromatic principle responsible for the scent became known as "ionine." Concerning that scent, Francis Bacon said, "That which above all others yields the sweetest smell in the air, is the violet..." It is best described as fleeting, it has a soporific effect on the olfactory nerves and after a few sniffs, the scent can no longer be detected. Shakespeare noted this fact in *Hamlet,* when Laertes said:

> *A violet in the youth of primy nature,*
> *Forward, not permanent; sweet, not lasting.*
> *The perfume and suppliance of a minute. No more.*

COSMETIC: A Celtic poem recommends steeping the flowers in goat's milk to make a formula to improve the complexion.
CONSIDERATIONS: Watch out for the seeds and do not take large amounts of the leaves—they cause vomiting and diarrhea. (Violets have been used in place of ipecac syrup *(Cephaelis ipecacuanha)* to induce vomiting, although the effects are much less severe).
OTHER: Although not as popular as in bygone days, violets are still sold as cut flowers.

VIOLET ICE

1¹/₂ cups (360 g) sugar
¹/₂ cup (120 ml) water
¹/₂ cup (120 ml) grape juice
1 handful violet petals
3 lemons, juiced

Combine ingredients except lemon juice, and boil slowly for 10 minutes. Cool, strain, add lemon juice, and blend well. Freeze in ice-cube trays. Serve garnished with fresh violets and leaves. Serves 6. A whole violet flower can be frozen in each cube.

VIOLET MOUSSE

This recipe is adapted from *Cox Gelatine Cookery,* published in Edinburgh in 1909.

1 teaspoon (5 ml) gelatine, or agar
¹/₄ cup (60 ml) water
2 cups (500 ml) milk
whites of 3 eggs
1 cup (240 ml) whipping cream
2 tablespoons (30 ml) sugar
¹/₂ teaspoon (2.5 ml) violet tincture or extract
Candied or fresh violets

Put gelatin or agar and water into a saucepan and bring to a boil for a couple of minutes. Let cool slightly, add water and milk, stir over a fire until hot, then add sugar and stiffly beaten egg whites. Stir until thick, add cream and violet extract. Pour into a mold. Place in refrigerator until set. Garnish with violets and serve.

Viola odorata
VIOLET

A violet by a mossy stone
    Half hidden from the eye!
Fair as a star when only one
    Is shining in the sky.
—''SHE DWELT AMONG THE UNTRODDEN WAYS,'' WILLIAM WORDSWORTH
(1770–1850), ENGLISH

Vitex agnus-castus • Chaste Tree

FAMILY: Verbenaceae.

DESCRIPTION: Graceful aromatic shrub. Height: 10 to 20 feet (3 to 6.1 m). Flowers: Small, lavender to lilac, in dense clusters to 6 inches (15 cm). Leaves: Divided into 5 to 7 leaflets to 4 inches (10 cm), dark green with a gray underside. Blooms: July to August.

HABITAT: Southern Europe, naturalized in warm areas, including the United States.

CULTIVATION: Perennial. Zone: 6 (needs mulch in zone 5). Germination: Stratify. Space: 3 feet (90 cm) or more. Soil Temperature: 60° to 70° F (15° to 21° C). Soil: Average, well drained, dry. Very drought tolerant. pH: 5.5 to 8.5. Sun: Full sun or partial shade. Propagation: In spring, by seed, cutting, or layering from young, woody cuttings. Prune back old growth in the late winter since leaves will sprout on new growth. A nice deer-proof shrub.

GARDEN DESIGN: This small, graceful shrub is so attractive that a number of species are used as ornamentals in landscaping. It provides a lovely garden spot for shade-loving herbs or to shelter a seat for visitors.

CONSTITUENTS: Hormonal substances.

HISTORY: Both *agnus* and *castus* mean "chaste"—a condition chaste berries were said to promote. The 1st century A.D. Roman Pliny wrote that the seeds reduced "sexual desire" and the 4th century B.C. Greek physician Hippocrates suggested eating them for spleen problems. Athenian women placed the leaves in the beds of virgins during the feast of the harvest goddess, Ceres, and are reported to have sometimes put them in their husband's beds! The reputation for chastity continued into the Middle Ages when monks sprinkled the ground wild peppers, or *piper agreste,* liberally on their food to ensure continued chastity. It soon also became known as "monk's pepper." Italians still follow the old custom of strewing the flowers on the ground in front of novices as they enter the monastery or convent. In the 13th century, two Arabic medical formularies, one by Al-Samarquandi and the other by Al-Kindi, mention chaste tree to treat epilepsy and even insanity. The fruits (seeds) are still sold today in Egyptian bazaars to calm hysteria. An herbal now called *Agnus Castus* was first translated from the original Latin around the 14th century. It received this name because these were the first 2 words of a text containing 248 plants. It suggests, among other things, combining chaste berries with *fenkle* (fennel) seed to treat dropsy and placing the berries on the head to eliminate headaches.

CULINARY: Only by monks! (See "History".)

MEDICINAL: Back in the 17th century, herbalist Gerard accurately wrote that the seeds and leaves helped with pain and inflammation of the uterus. (He also used them to treat the liver and spleen.) The hormonelike substances found in the seeds help to correct female hormonal imbalances—such as those that can occur during menopause, premenstrual syndrome, or menstruation—and also help dissolve fibroids and cysts.[1] German researchers suggest the berries increase production of luteinizing hormone and prolactin.[2] Another study adds the increase of the hormone progesterone to the list.[3] The seeds do stimulate mother's milk flow, as shown in a clinical study when 100 nursing mothers taking chaste seeds were compared to those who were not. After reviewing German research, herbalist Christopher Hobbs suggests its use during the first 3 months only of pregnancy to help prevent miscarriage

Vitex agnus-castus
CHASTE TREE

and, with ginger, to allay morning sickness. Chaste berries can help regulate periods when there is excessive or too frequent bleeding.[4] It also reestablishes normal ovulation after contraceptive pills have been used. Most of the research has been done on a chaste berry extract called Agnolyt. When 53 women with excessive bleeding and short menstrual cycles were given this product, 65% showed improvement and about 47% were entirely cured! Those over age twenty experienced the most improvement.[5] Clinical studies with Agnolyt also found the chaste berry helps control acne in both young women and young men.[6] A booklet, *Vitex! The Woman's Herb* by Christopher Hobbs (Botanica Press, 1991), gives historic and medicinal information. An Asian and Australian native, *V. trifolia* is used medicinally in India, Malaysia, and Indonesia.

CONSIDERATIONS: According to information on Agnolyt, chaste berry may interfere with progesterone-containing medications. Also, it can delay the onset of menstruation a few days.

OTHER: The stems are used in basketweaving.

Zingiber officinale • Ginger

FAMILY: Zingiberaceae.

DESCRIPTION: Upright plant with stunning flowers. Height: 2 to 4 feet (.6 to 1.2 m). Width: 1 1/2 feet (45 cm). Flowers: Greenish flowers with cream blotches and purple edging, 3 inches (7.5 cm), growing on dense spikes. Leaves: Swordlike leaves that come to a sharp point, angling upwards, 1 foot (30 cm) by 1 inch (2.5 cm). Rhizome: Thick, tuberous, knotty, and sweetly fragrant. Blooms: Summer.

HABITAT: Originally from southeast Asia, ginger has been cultivated in many tropical countries for so long that it is no longer found wild.

CULTIVATION: Perennial. Zone: 10. Space: 1 foot (30 cm). Soil: Rich, moist but well drained. pH: 4.5 to 7.5. Sun: Filtered sun or partial shade. Propagation: Cut the eyes from the rhizomes and plant. Not frost-hardy, but may be grown as an indoor plant if given special care and plenty of warmth and light. Prefers a greenhouse temperature around 75° F (24° C). It likes warm weather and humidity.

GARDEN DESIGN: Place the pots in the summer garden or grow in the garden year-round in warm climates.

CONSTITUENTS: Essential oil (1% to 3%) includes zingiberone, bisabolenel, oleoresins (shogaols are produced from gingerol as the root dries, making it twice as pungent); fats, vitamins A, B, minerals.

RELATED SPECIES: Not to be confused with wild ginger (Asarum canadense), a North American native with a similar smell, but much stronger chemistry, that is used as a ginger substitute only in very small amounts. There are several Australian native gingers (Alpinia species).

HISTORY: Ginger appears in the Analects of Chinese philosopher Confucius (551–479 B.C.). East Indian Susruta the Older's Sanskrit text, Mushkakadigana (circa 4th century B.C.), called it sringavera, which described its shape as a "horn-root." This became the Latin zingiber, the Greek zigiberis, the Spanish gengibre, the French ginjgimbre, and the English "ginger." The Greeks were importing it from the East centuries before Dioscorides recorded its use in the 1st century A.D. In the early 16th century, the Spanish began cultivating and importing a superior-quality ginger from Jamaica. This is still preferred of the many grades, known as "races," from the Spanish-Portuguese raices, or "root." England's Henry VIII recommended ginger to fight the plague. Gingerbread was Queen Elizabeth I's favorite sweet, a passion shared by Shakespeare's Costard, who said "An I had but one penny in the world, thou shouldst have it to buy ginger-bread" (Love's Labour's Lost).

CULINARY: Ginger gives a "zing" to many Oriental main dishes and Indian chutneys (the Hindi word chatni means a "strong, spicy condiment"). Inspired by the Chinese, green ginger syrup became a delicacy in 15th-century Europe and is still produced in China today. Some New Englanders continue a custom borrowed centuries ago from England of passing around candied ginger after a meal. Eating gingerbread cookies at Christmas is another tradition borrowed from the English by Americans. The blue fruits of Australian native ginger were eaten by Aborigines.

MEDICINAL: The Chinese consider fresh gingerroot an important drug to treat colds and encourage sweating. They use dried ginger for respiratory and digestive disorders, such as gas and nausea. Its digestive enzyme, zingibain, is even more effective than papain from papaya.[1] Pregnant women also found that ginger relieved their morning sickness when they took 3 to 8 capsules first thing in the morning, before they got out of bed, and then 3 to 5 capsules at the first hint of nausea during the day. Ginger can prevent motion sickness better than even the popular drug, Dramamine.® One study noted that 90% of those who took 2 to 4 capsules prior to traveling, with 2 more every hour if needed, experienced no nausea at all. It even helped people who usually got so sick, they rarely ventured from their houses. Dizziness and vertigo were reduced in 40% to 50% of the cases.[2]

Ginger stimulates circulation, warming cold hands and feet. A ginger tea encourages delayed menstruation, especially when the delay is due to cold or overexertion. East Africans use it to reduce headaches and kill parasites. As a vermifuge, scientists showed that all 42 components found in ginger oil effectively kill intestinal roundworms. Some of these worked better than the commonly prescribed piperazine citrate preparations.[3] Ginger increases the availability of drugs and herbs by promoting absorption and protecting their destruction as they pass through the liver.[4]

AROMATHERAPY: Ginger liniments heat and relax sore muscles, ease menstrual cramps, and alleviate painful arthritic joints. It is a pick-me-up fragrance that combines especially well with citrus, as in lemon-ginger.

OTHER: A ginger suppository encourages showhorses to keep their tails up!

CRYSTALLIZED GINGER

The best ginger for this recipe is the tender, juicy, young "stem ginger" found in Oriental markets in summer, but any fresh ginger will work.

1	**pound (500 g) ginger**
	Water to cover
3	**cups (720 ml) sugar**
2	**tablespoons (30 ml) light corn syrup**
3	**cups (720 ml) water**

Scrape off the thin skin of the ginger and trim off leaf bases. Slice into 1/4-inch (6-mm) pieces. In a saucepan, place the ginger in enough water to cover by 2 inches (5 cm) and bring to a boil. Lower the heat, cover the pot, and simmer very low for about 3 hours, adding more water if needed. (A crock pot is ideal.)

Combine the sugar, syrup, and remaining water, and bring to a boil over medium heat for 2 minutes.

Add the ginger to the sugar mixture and heat to boiling again for 1 minute. Remove from heat and let stand until cool.

Return to heat and boil again, then turn down and simmer 1 to 3 hours, until the pieces are translucent and very tender. Add hot water if the syrup becomes too thick and starts to stick. Stir occasionally, cooking down to a spoonful of syrup. Fork the pieces onto a wire rack and let dry for a couple hours, then roll in granulated sugar. Store in a covered container.

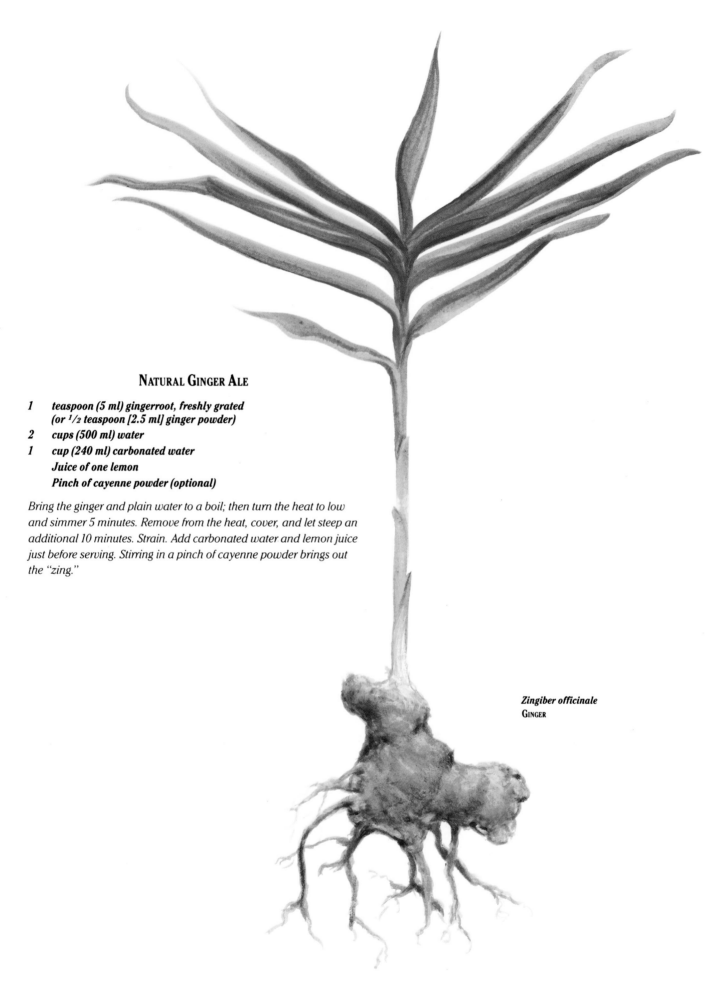

NATURAL GINGER ALE

1   **teaspoon (5 ml) gingerroot, freshly grated**
      (or *1/2* teaspoon [2.5 ml] ginger powder)

2   **cups (500 ml) water**

1   **cup (240 ml) carbonated water**
      Juice of one lemon
      Pinch of cayenne powder (optional)

*Bring the ginger and plain water to a boil; then turn the heat to low
and simmer 5 minutes. Remove from the heat, cover, and let steep an
additional 10 minutes. Strain. Add carbonated water and lemon juice
just before serving. Stirring in a pinch of cayenne powder brings out
the "zing."*

Zingiber officinale
GINGER

TYPES OF HERB GARDENS

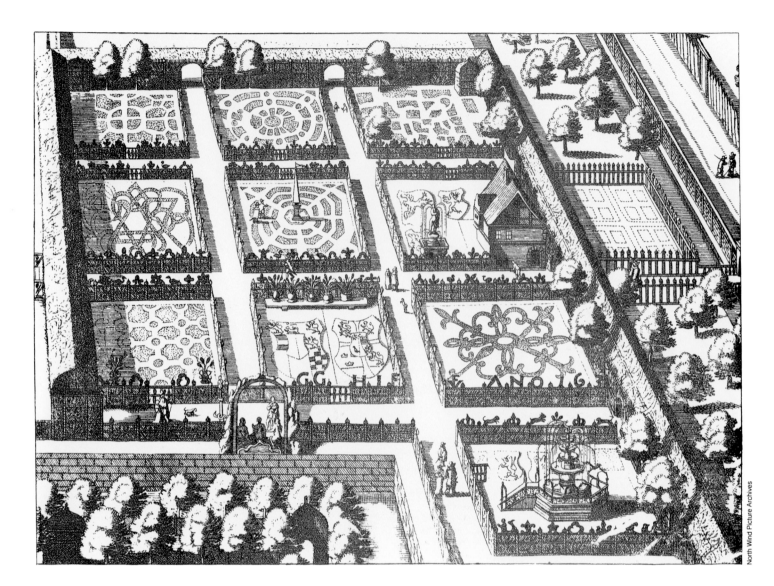

There are many kinds and styles of herb gardens to fit your design needs. Your herb garden can be as simple or as elaborate as you wish. Even the simplest herb garden will provide fragrance, colors, and textures, as well as tasty treats and natural medicines.

THE KITCHEN GARDEN The emphasis here is, of course, culinary herbs. Preferably, the garden should be located as near as possible to the kitchen door so fresh herbs are within reach. Paths in the garden are important for easy access, with the herbs most often used, such as parsley, planted along borders.

THE WILD GARDEN A wild garden allows the herbs to grow in natural patterns and to intermingle as they spread. Low-growing flowers can be set in informal patches. This doesn't mean you can't provide a few guidelines on where each one should grow. The wild garden isn't a no-work garden, but it is certainly one of the easier ones to maintain.

THE TERRACED GARDEN Steep slopes may seem to be the last place you would want to plant an herb garden, but such a loca-

tion gives you an opportunity to create terraces that can be filled with trailing rosemary, fragrant geraniums, and colorful thymes hanging gracefully over the sides. The terraces can be tall to accommodate even large herbs or as shallow as a set of stairs. If you have the time or money, consider building stone walls.

THE GROUNDCOVER HERB GARDEN Groundcovers provide an excellent way to fill in more space with herbs. Some herbs, like the low-growing Roman chamomile and pennyroyal, can actually be walked upon. Such herbs are perfect where lawn grass grows thin, such as under trees. They can also cover a sloped bank with color.

THE PATH GARDEN This is a strolling garden composed of the same low-growing herbs that are suitable for groundcovers. The plants themselves make wonderful, fragrant paths that fill the air

Your herb garden plan can be simple—or as elaborate as this extensive 17th century maze garden.

with fragrance every time someone walks on them. Use herbs for the path itself, or create a path by scraping an area flat, then placing flagstones, bricks, wood rounds, or other suitable material in it, then filling in between the materials with some topsoil and herbs.

THE STRIP GARDEN If lack of yard space for your herb garden is a problem, plant a strip of herbs along a backfence or next to a walk. Although not the ideal placement for edible herbs, this garden looks attractive placed next to a driveway or along a road. It can either be a high hedge of trimmed herbs, like lavender and rosemary, or a more free-wheeling type such as tansy.

THE PLANTER BOX GARDEN An herb garden in planter boxes can solve many problems for gardeners who are restricted by lack of space or poor soil or for those who have a difficult time bending over. And, of course, the boxes are also portable, in case you are planning to move but can't wait to begin your herb garden. Planter boxes can be made as tall as you need or desire. They have an advantage over pots in that the herbs don't get rootbound or dry out so easily. Planter boxes are usually constructed out of wood, but more permanent ones can be constructed from cement. Small ones can be used as windowboxes. A small planter box of herbs makes a thoughtful gift.

THE POTTED HERB GARDEN If you live in an apartment, or just want to bring part of your herb garden closer to home, plant your herbs in pots. Many will grow nicely even on a windowsill or the railing of a porch. If they are inside, make sure they also get plenty of light, either through a window or under a grow light. Just be sure to choose a large enough pot so the herbs will have enough root space. Clay pots are attractive, but they need to be monitored closely since the soil can dry out quickly. If you don't have time for constant watering or if you are going out of town, a saucer filled with water and placed under the pot allows water to "wick up" as needed. Still at a loss where to put your herb garden? You can always plant one in a large strawberry pot, with a different herb in each section. You'll be restricted to the smaller varieties, but many herbs will adapt well.

THE FORMAL GARDEN A formal effect can be achieved by keeping herbs well trimmed and by leaving large spaces between them to make each one distinct. Separate them with grass, herbal groundcovers or crushed rock. Paths are often symmetrical, with low borders of well-trimmed herbs edging them. A bird bath, fountain, or sundial completes the effect.

A KNOT GARDEN The knot garden intertwines herbs like santolina, thyme, and germander into elaborate and symmetrical patterns. Gray santolina is a favorite because it can be trimmed, and also contrasts nicely with greener plants.

THE ROCK GARDEN These gardens are highlighted by rocks as well as by plants. They usually include many herbs, such as thyme and other plants that accent the shapes and textures of the stones.

THE HANGING GARDEN Hanging gardens aren't a new idea, but they are rarely seen. The hanging garden is really a gar-

den in pots, except that the pots are suspended. It is not only a great space saver, but it is also an attractive way to show off cascading herbs. Hang them outside windows, along the edge of a porch or inside the house, especially above stairs or from a loft.

THE ARBOR GARDEN This is an overhead garden supported by an arbor, trellis, or gazebo. Quick-growing herbs such as hops, passionflower, and honeysuckle are excellent choices; or you may wish to grow climbing roses. The arbor garden can be accented with hanging pots or an herb-lined path.

THE POND GARDEN If you are lucky enough to have a pond —even a small one—try planting a garden around it. Mints will grow into the water and tall plants will tower above, lending their reflections to the water.

THE PERENNIAL FLOWER GARDEN Color is the main attraction of any flower garden. Here large, flowering herbs such as echinacea and butterfly weed provide stunning colors. This garden is not strictly an herb garden, and it can include perennial flowers whose only purpose is to provide colorful accents. If you already have a perennial flower garden, consider adding a few herbal flowers to it.

DRIED-FLOWER GARDEN If you are interested in making dried herbal wreaths and arrangements, a dried-flower garden will provide you with supplies for your craft. This is also by far the most colorful garden, even when fresh. Include easy access paths since most flowers must be picked continuously during the growing season, and so you'll want room for you and your basket to move in between the plants.

THE EDIBLE GARDEN Granted, it is difficult to make an herb garden inedible, but if you want to *emphasize* the edible, stick to french sorrel, the bulbous fennel, and other herbs that can be eaten as vegetables; of course, add a few seasoning herbs too.

THE HERB AND VEGETABLE GARDEN Combining herbs with vegetables offers the benefits of natural insect repellents for your vegetables. Use annuals that can be turned under with the vegetables at the end of the season, or incorporate perennials and move them. Some gardeners choose to make islands within the vegetable garden where perennial herbs can live permanently.

THE "INSTANT" GARDEN If you have a greenhouse, you can keep your herbs in pots for an early spring start. When the weather warms, move the pots outside and sink them into the ground. Some herbs won't reach full size, but you'll have an orderly, quick-growing garden. In the fall, simply pop the pots out and turn under any weeds.

A THEME GARDEN If you want to be very creative with garden design, try different themes in sections of your garden, or make use of a single theme for the whole garden. A few ideas might include a fragrance garden, a garden of silver herbs of *Artemisia*, or a garden that attracts butterflies, including, of course, butterfly weed. Other possibilities are a medicinal garden or a natural dye garden. Herbs can also be divided by their uses or by the parts of the world from which they originate.

RESOURCES

Periodicals

American Herb Association
PO Box 1673
Nevada City, CA 95959
Membership in the AHA includes the newsletter,
AHA Quarterly Newsletter, which is packed with
current information, written and produced by
herbalists. It includes scientific studies, book
reviews, dialogs between herbalists, reports on
controversies, environmental updates, legal issues,
and more. Send SASE for brochure.

Foster's Botanical & Herb Reviews
PO Box 106
Eureka Springs, AR 72632
Quarterly review of books, periodicals, and
computer resources.

Herbal Gram
PO Box 201660
Austin, TX 78720
Published by the American Botanical Council
and written by researchers and scientists with
information on herbs, news items, scientific
conferences, herbal texts, and studies.

Medical Herbalism
PO Box 33080
Portland, OR 99723
Bi-monthly newsletter of clinical herb studies for
practitioners.

Ontario Herbalists Association Newsletter
Box 253, Station J
Toronto, ON M4T 4Y1

Mail-Order Herbs, Plants, and Seeds

Abundant Life Seed Foundation
PO Box 772
Port Townsend, WA 98368
Seeds.

Goodwin Creek Gardens
Box 83
Williams, OR 97544
Plants and seeds.

Gardens of the Blue Ridge
PO Box 10
Pineola, NC 28862
Plants.

The Herb Farm
RR#4
Norton, NB E0G 2N0
Produce list $3.
Catalog $5.

Herbal Touch
30 Dover Street
Otterville, ON N0J 1R0

Otto Richter & Sons, Ltd.
357 Hwy 47
Goodwood, ON L0C 1A0
Seeds.

Roses of Yesterday and Today
802 Brown's Valley Rd.
Watsonville, CA 95076
Rose plants.

Tansy Farms
RR#1 5888 Else Rd.
Aggasiz, BC V0M 1A4
Catalog $1.50.

Taylor's Herb Garden
1535 Lone Oak Rd.
Vista, CA 92084
Plants.

Thompson & Morgan, Inc.
Box 1308
Jackson, NJ 08527
Seeds.

Well-Sweep Herb Farm
317 Mt. Bethel Rd.
Port Murray, NJ 07865
Plants.

West Kootenay Herb Nursery
RR#2 Bedford Rd.
Nelson, BC V1L 5P5
Plants.

Herb Schools

A current descriptive listing of herb schools and
herbal correspondence courses is available from
the American Herb Association for $3.50. The
organization also offers extensive, up-to-date listings
of mail-order herbal products for $4.

AHA
PO Box 1673
Nevada City, CA 95959

Associations

American Herb Association
PO Box 1673
Nevada City, CA 95959
The AHA is an excellent source of herbal
information.

American Herbalist Guild
Box 1683
Soquel, CA 95073
This is a group of professional herbalists.

Ontario Herbalists Association
Box 253, Station J
Toronto, ON M4T 4Y1

The Herb Society of America, Inc.
2 Independence Court
Concord, MA 01742
Concerning many aspects of herbalism, except
the medicinal.

The Botanic Medicine Society
Box 103
Normal, ON L0P 1K0

REFERENCES

Acorus Americanus L. **CALAMUS**
[1] Chan, H. ed., and P. But. 1986. *Pharmacology and
Applications of Chinese Materia Medica,* Vol. 1
[2] Keller, K. *et. al.* 1985. *Planta Med.* 51 (1), 6.
[3] Taylor, J.M., *et. al.* 1967. *Toxicology and Applied
Pharmacology* 10:405.
[4] Mathur, A.C., and B.P. Saxema. 1975. *Natur
wissenschaften* 62/12.

Agrimonia eupatoria L. **AGRIMONY**
[1] Bensky, D. and A. Camble. 1986. *Chinese Herbal
Medicine: Materia Medica* Washington: Eastland
Press.
[2] Drozd, G.A., *et. al.* 1983. *Khim. Prir. Soed.* 1:106.

Allium sativum **GARLIC**
[1] Chan, H. and P. But. eds. 1986. *Pharmacology and
Applications of Chinese Materia Medica. vol 1.*
Singapore: World Scientific.
[2] Petkov, W. *Arneim.-Forsch.* 11–3:288.
[3] Bordia, A. 1981. *Am. Clinical. Journ. Nutr.* 33(10)
2100–03.
[4] Brahmachari, M.D. and K.T. Augusti. 1962. *J.
Pharm. Pharmacol.* 14:254:617. Jain, R.C. and
Vyas, C.R. 1974. *Brit. Med. J.* 2:730.
[5] Jerry Lutomski. 1987. *Components and Biological
Properties of Some Allium Species,* Poland:
Institute of Medicinal Plants (27 Libelta St. 61-707
Poznan).

Aloe barbadensis Mill. **ALOE VERA**
[1] Blitz, J.J., *et. al.* 1963. *Journ. Amer. Osteo. Assoc.,*
62:731.
[2] El Zawahry, M., *et. al.* 1973. *Intern. Journ. Dermat.*
12(1):68–74.
[3] Heggers, J.P., *et. al.* 1979. *Journ. Amer. Med. Tech.*
41:293.
[4] Benenson, V. *Extract of Aloe, Supplement to
Clinical Data* USSR, Moscow: Medexport:
Moscow Stomatological Inst.
[5] 1986. *Harm. Research* 24(4):288–294.

Althea officinalis L. **MARSHMALLOW**
[1] Tomoda, M. *et. al.* 1980. *Chem. Pharm. Bull.*
28:823.

Angelica archangelica L. **ANGELICA**
[1] Chang, H.M., *et. al.* Eds. 1985. *Advances in Chinese Medicinal Materials Research.* Singapore: Pub. World Scientific Pub. Co.

Anethum graveolens L. **DILL**
[1] Debelmas, A.M. and J. Rochat. *Plant. Med. Phytother.* 1:23.

Arctium lappa L. **BURDOCK**
[1] Scuttle, K., *et. al.* 1967. *Arneim.-Forsch.* 17:828.
[2] Hartwell, J.L. 1968. *Lloydia* 31:71.

Armoracia rusticana P. Gaertn., B. Mey. & Scherb **HORSERADISH**
[1] Kienholz, M. 1962. *Allergy Therapeutik* 6;145.

Arnica montana L. **ARNICA**
[1] Werner, W. 1980. *Deutsche Apotheker Zeitung.* 121: 199.

Artemesia abrortanum L. **SOUTHERNWOOD**
[1] Nieschultz, O. and P. Schmersal. 1968. *Arneim.-Forsch.* 18;1330.

Artemisia absinthium **WORMWOOD**
[1] Klayman, D.L. 1985. *Science* 5–31,228:1049–55.
[2] Baumann, I.C., *et. al.* 1975. Z. *Allg. Med.* 51(17);784.
[3] Del Castillo, J., *et. al.* 1975. *Nature,* 253;365.
[4] Kinloch, J.D. 1971. *Practitioner* 206,44.

Asclepias tuberosa L. **BUTTERFLY WEED**
[1] Brower, *et. al.* 1972. *Science* 177:426–429.

Baptisia tinctoria (L.) Venten. **FALSE INDIGO**
[1] Markham, K.R., *et. al. 1970. Phytochem.* 9:1359.

Calendula officinalis L. **CALENDULA**
[1] Samochowiec, E. *et. al.* 1979. *Wiad. Parazytol.* 25 (1):77.
[2] Manolov, *et al.* 1964. *Eksp. Med. Morfol.* 3, 41.

Capsicum **CAYENNE**
[1] Glatzel, H. *Munch. Med. Wschr.* 107/7:332, 1965.
[2] *Lawrence Review* Vol. 6 (4) 4/85.
[3] Monsereenusorn, Y., *et. al.* 1982. *Crit. Rev. Toxicol.* 10:321.

Centella asiatica L. Urban. **GOTA KOLA**
[1] Satyavati, G.V., *et. al.* 1976. *Medicinal Plants of India,* Vol. I, ICMR, New Delhi, India. 217–19.
[2] Karawya, M.S., *et. al.* 1981. *Fitoterapia* 4,175.
[3] Allegra, G., *et. al.* 1981. *Clin. Terap.* 99:507.
[4] Vecchaio, A.D., *et. al.* 1984. *Farm. Ed. Prat.* 39(10):355.

Cichorium intybus L. **CHICORY**
[1] Forst, A.W. 1940. *Naunyn-Schmiedebergs Archiv für experimentelle pathologie und Pharkmakologie* 195. 1–250.
[2] Balboa, *et, al.* 1973. *Planta medica* 24:133.
[3] *Chem. Abstr.* 1963. 59.5535c.

Cimifuga racemosa (L.) Nutt. **COHOSH, BLACK**
[1] Benoit, P.S., *et. al.* 1976. *Lloydia,* 39(2–3);160–161.
[2] Genazzani, E. and L. Sorrentino. 1962. *Nature.* 194(48280):544–45.

Citrus limon (L.) Burm. f. **LEMON**
[1] Morel, A., and A. Rochaix. *Bulletin Sc. Pharmacol. et C. R. Soc. Biol.,* 192228.

Cnicus benedictus L. **BLESSED THISTLE**
[1] Vanhaelen-Fasté, R. 1973. *Planta Med.* 24:165–175.

Crataegus laevigata L. **HAWTHORN**
[1] Kandziora, J. 1969. *Muench. Med. Wochen.* 6, 295–298.
[2] Echte, W. 1960. *Arztliche Forsch.* 14(11), 1/560–566.
[3] Boehm, K. 1955. *Arztliche Forsch.* 9,442–442.
[4] Bersin T., *et. al.* 1955. *Arneim.-Forsch.* 5:490–491.
[5] Costa, *et. al.* 1986. *Plantes Med. Phytother.* 20:115–28.
[6] Bersin T., *et. al.* 1955. *Arneim.-Forsch.* 5:490–491.

Cymbopogon citratus (DC ex Nees) Stapf. **LEMON GRASS**
[1] Grane, D.O. 1976. *Drug. Cos. Ind.* 118(5):36.
[2] Carlini, E.A., *et. al.* 1986. *Journ. of Ethnopharm.* 17(1):37.

Echinacea purpurea (L.) Moench. **ECHINACEA**
[1] Becker, H. 1982. *Deutsche Apoth. Ztg.* 122:45,2320.
[2] Kleinschmidt, H. 1965. *Ther. d. Gegen.* 1258.

Eupatorium purpureum L. **JOE PYE WEED**
[1] Gassinger, C.A., *et. al. Arzneimit.-Forsch.* 31:732.
[2] Midge, M.D. and A.V. Rao. 1975. *Indian Journ. Chemistry,* 13:541.
[3] 1986. *Phytochemistry* V. 25(2).3777–3781.

Euphorbia lathyris L. **GOPHER PURGE, CAPER SPURGE**
[1] Calvin, M. 1976. *Science* 194:46,1976.

Filipendula ulmaria (L.) Maxim **MEADOWSWEET**
[1] Decaux, F. 1942. *Rev. Phytotherap.* 6:125.

Foeniculum vulgare Mill. **FENNEL**
[1] Albert-Puleo, M. 1980. *Journ. Ethnopharm.* 2:237–344.

Gentiana lutea L. **GENTIAN**
[1] Glatzel, H. 1969. *Hippokrates,* 40(23):916–919.

Ginkgo biloba L. **GINKGO**
[1] Hindmarch, I. and Z. Subhan. 1984. *Int. Journ. Clinical Pharm. Res.* 4:889–93.
[2] Vorgberg, G. 1985. *Clinical Trails Journ.* 22:149–157.
[3] Meyer, B. 1988. *In* Funfgeld, E.W., ed. 1988. *Rokan (Ginkgo biloba), Recent Results in Pharmacology, and Clinic.* Berlin: Springer-Verlag.
[4] Chung, K., *et. al.* 1987. *Lancet* i:248.
[5] Reuse-Bourgain, M. June 1986. *6th Int. Conf. Prostaglandins and Related Comp.* Florence, Italy. Pub. Fondzione Giovanni Lorenzini.

Glycyrrhiza glabra L. **LICORICE**
[1] Finney, S.H. and G.F. Somers. 1958. *Journ. Pharmacology and Pharmacodynamics,* 10(10),613–620.
[2] Cheng-chia, L. and T. Ching-ch'u. 1973. *Chinese Med. Journ.* 11,156.
[3] Yaginuma, T., *et. al.* 1982. *Nippon Sanka Fujinka Gakkai Zasshi,* 34(7):939–944.
[4] Wilson, J.A.C. 1972. *Brit. Journ. Clin. Practice,* 26:563–566.
[5] Hayashi, Y., *et. al.* 1979. *Yakuri to Chiryo* 7:3861.
[6] Epatein, N.M.T., *et. al.* 1977. Brit. Med. Journ. 1:488–490.

Hamamelis virginiana L. **WITCH HAZEL**
[1] Mockle, J.A. *Contributions a l'etude des plante Medicinales du Canada.* Paris ed. Jouve, p.63.
[2] List, P.H. and L. Hormammer. *Hager's Handbuch der Pharmazeutischen.* vol. 2–6. Berlin: Springer-Verlag.

Humulus Lupulus L. **HOPS**
[1] Wohlfart, R., *et. al. Planta Med.* 48:120–123, 1983. and *Ibid.* 1982. 45:224.
[2] Hansel, R. and H.H. Wagner. 1967. *Arneim.-Forsch.* 17:79.

Hydrastis canadensis L. **GOLDENSEAL**
[1] Genest, K. and D.W. Hughs. 1969. *Can. Journ. Pharm. Sci.* 4,41.
[2] Lahiri, S.C. and N.K. Cutta. *Journ. Indian Medical Assoc.* 53(1):22–24, 1970.
[3] Gupta, S. 1975. *Amer. Journ. Diseases of Childhood* 129:866.

Hypericum perforatum L. **SAINT JOHNSWORT**
[1] Kolesnikkova, A.S. 1986. *ZH Mikrobial Epidemiol. Immunobiol.* 3:75–76.
[2] Muldner, H. and M. Zoller. 1984. *Arneim.-Forsch.* 34 II(8):918.
[3] Suzuki, O., *et. al.* 1984. *Planta Med.* 3:272.

Hyssopus officinalis L. **HYSSOP**
[1] Harrmann, E.C. and L.S. Kucera. 1967. *Proc. Soc. Exp. Biol. Med.* 124:874.

Inula helenium L. **ELECAMPANE**
[1] *Chem. Ab.* 1977. 87, 162117.

Lavendula angustifolia Mill. **LAVENDER**
[1] *Chem. Ab.* 1972. 77,84292x.

Leonurus cardiaca L. **MOTHERWORT**
[1] Bensky, D. and A. Camble. 1986. *Chinese Herbal Medicine: Materia Medica.* Washington: Eastland Press.
[2] 1989. *Amer. Journ. Chin. Med.* XVII;65–70.
[3] Peng, Y. 1983. *Bull. Chin. Mat. Med.* 8:41.
[4] Xia, X.X. 1983. *Journ. Trad. Chin. Med.* 3:185.

Marrubium vulgare L. **HOREHOUND**
[1] Karryev, M.O., *et. al.* 1976. *Seriya Biologicheskikh Nauk.* 3:86–88.

Matricaria recutita **CHAMOMILE**
[1] Gould, L., *et. al.* 1973. *Journ. Clinical Pharm.* 13:475–479.
[2] (Kamillosan). *Kamillosan Scientific Information,* 12 p.
[3] Stern, P. and R. Milin. 1956. *Arneim.-Forsch.* 6:445–450.
[4] Aggag, M.E. and R.T. Yousef. 1972. *Planta Med.* 22:140–44.
[5] Wagner, H., *et. al.* 1984. *Arneim.-Forsch.* 34:659.
[6] Hegyi, E. 1979. *Allergi. Immunology* 25,104–115.
[7] Hausen, B.M. 1979. *Dermatologica.* 159:1–11.

Melissa officinalis L. **LEMON BALM**
[1] Kucera, L.S. and E.C. Herrmann. 1967. *Proc. Soc. Exp. Biol. Med.,* 124,865.
[2] Ozarowski, A. 1982. *Wiad, Ziel.* 4,7.
[3] DeLong, C.A.G. 1978. *Ned. Tijdschr. Geneeskd.* 112(3);82.
[4] Auf'mkolk, M. 1985. *Endocrinology* 116(5);1687.

Mentha × *piperita* L. **PEPPERMINT**
[1] Taylor, B.D., *et. al.* 1983. *Gut.* 24:992.
[2] Leicester, R.J. and R.H. Hunt. 1982. *The Lancet.* 10–30:989.
[3] Rees, W.D.W, *et. al.* 1979. *British Med. Journal.* 10-6:835–36.
[4] *Chem. Ab.* 1965. 62,3285c.
[5] Kucera, L.S., and E.C. Hermann. 1967. *Proc. Soc. Exp. Biol. Med.* 124:865, 874.
[6] Leung, A.Y. 1980. *Encyclopedia of Common Natural Ingredients Used in Food, Drugs and Cosmetics.* New York: Wiley-Interscience.

Mentha pulegium L. **PENNYROYAL**
[1] Sullivan, J.B., *et. al.* 1979. *Journ. Amer. Med. Assoc.* 242:2873–2879.

Nepeta cateraria **CATNIP**
[1] Kuklinski, M. 1969. *Deutsche Apotheker-Zeitung* 109:1144.

Ocimum basilicum L. **BASIL**
[1] Bepha Bull. 1988. (King George's Medical College, India). 31:414.
[2] Jain, M.L. and S.R. Jain. 1972. *Planta Med.* 22:66.

Oenothera biennis L. **EVENING PRIMROSE**
[1] Sim, A.K. and A.P. McCraw. 1977. *Thrombosis Research,* 10:385–97.
[2] Wright, S. and J. Burton. Nov. 1982. *Lancet.* 20.
[3] Cambell, A.C. and G.C. MacEwan. 1984. *British Journ. Cermatology.*

Origanum majorana L. **MARJORAM**
[1] Kucera, L.S. and K. Hermann, Ed. 1967. *Proc. Soc. Exp. Biol. Med.* 124:865 and 874.
[2] Herrmann, K. 1962. *Unters. Forsch.* 116:224.

Panax quinquifolius L. **GINSENG**
[1] Brekhman, II, 1957. *Zhen-shen,* Leningrad: State Publishing House for Medical Literature.
[2] Institute of Materia Medica at Chinese Academy of Medical Science. 1988. *Yaoxue Xuebao* 23(1):12026.
[3] Schimert, G. 1976. *Furtschr. Med.* 88:491.
[4] Laboratory of Pharmacology at Korea Ginseng and Tobacco Research Institute. 1987. *Clinical and Exper. Pharm. and Phys.* 14:543–546.
[5] Siegel, R.K. 1979. *Journ. Amer. Med. Assoc.* 241(15).

Passiflora incarnata L. **PASSION FLOWER**
[1] Lutomski, J.H., *et. al.* 1975. *Planta Med.* 27;112.

Pelargonium graveolens L'Her. ex Ait. **GERANIUM, ROSE**
[1] Vetrano, S. 1962. *Presse Medicle.*

Petroselinum crispum **PARSLEY**
[1] Merck and Co. 1968. *The Merck Index.* eighth ed.
[2] Middleton, E. and G. Drzewiecki. 1985. *Biochem. Pharmacol.* 33:3333. and Busse, W.W., *et. al.* 1984. *Journ. All. Clin. Immunol.* 73:801.

Phytolacca americana L. **POKE WEED**
[1] Ussberg, M.A., *et. al.* 1977. *Ann. NY Acad. Sci.,* 284:431.
[2] Hardin, J.W. and J.M. Arena. 1974. *Human Poisoning from Native and Cultivated Plants.* Duke University Press.

Pimpinella anisum L. **ANISE**
[1] Muller-Limmtroth, W. and H.H. Froehlich. 1980. *Fortschr. Med.* 98(3):95.

Plantago lanceolata L. **PLANTAIN**
[1] Duckett, S. 1980. *Lancet* 303(10):583.
[2] Matev, M., *et. al.* 1982. *Vutreshni bolesti* (Sophia) 21(2):133–137.

Podophyllum peltatum L. **MAY APPLE**
[1] (Pidofilox). 1989. Lancet 4–15;831.
[2] Zheng, Q.Y., *et. al.* 1987. *Int. Journ. Immunopharm.* 9(5):539–549.
[3] Jardine, I. 1980. *Anticancer Agents Based on Natural Product Models.* Cassady, J.M., and J.D. Douros, eds. Academic Press.

Poterium sanguisorba L. **BURNET, SALAD**
[1] Chan, H. and P. But, eds. 1986. *Pharmacology and Applications of Chinese Materia Medica.* vol. 1. Singapore: World Scientific.

Rosemarinus officinalis L. **ROSEMARY**
[1] Rao, B.G. and S.S. Nigam. 1970. *Indian Journ. Med. Res.* 58:627.
[2] Tattjke, D.H.E. *Pharm. Week.* 105;1241.
[3] Kovar, K.A., *et. al.* 1987. *Planta Med.* 53(4):315.

Salvia officinalis L. **SAGE**
[1] *Chem. Abstr.* 1977. 86,117603r.
[2] (Salsat). 1981. *Rote Liste.* Aulendorf/Wüftt 31;287.
[3] Bourret, J.C. 1981. *Les Nouveaux Succes de la Medicine par les Plantes;* 281, Paris.
[4] Berger, F. 1950. *Handbuch der Drogenkunde,* V.2, Verlag Wilhelm Maudrich, Vienna. 292–305.

Sambucus nigra L. **ELDER**
[1] Mascolo, N., *et. al.* 1987. *Phytother. Res.* 1(1):28.

Sassafra albidum (Nutt.) Nees. **SASSAFRASS**
[1] Borchet, P., *et. al.* 1973. *Cancer Res.* 33,575.
[2] Benedettis, M.S., *et. al.* 1977. *Toxicology* 7;69–83.
[3] Kapadia, E.B., *et. al.* 1978. *Jour. Nat. Can. Inst.* 60;633–686.

Satureja hortensis L. **SAVORY**
[1] Opdyke, D.L.J. 1976. *Food Cosmet. Toxicology* 14.

Scutellaria laterifolia **SCULLCAP**
[1] Usow, T., 1958. *Framakologiia i Toxikologiis,* 21(2);31–34.
[2] Chang, *et. al.* ed. 1985. *Advances in Chinese Medicinal Materials Research.* Singapore: World Scientific Pub. Co.

Senecio cineraria DC. **DUSTY MILLER**
[1] Willaman, J.J. and L. Hui-Li. 1970. *Lloydia* 33(3A):1.

Silybum marianum L. Gaertn. **MILK THISTLE**
[1] Vogel, G., *et. al.* 1984. *Toxicol. Appl. Pharmacol.* 51:265.
[2] Poser, G. 1971. *Arneim.-Forsch.* 21:1209.

Symphytum officinale L. **COMFREY**
[1] Furuya, T. and K. Asaki. 1968. *Chem. Pharm. Bull.* 16(12):2512–6.
[2] Hirono, I., *et. al.* 1979. *Journ. Nat. Cancer Inst.* 62:467–471.
[3] Tittel, G., *et. al.,* 1979. *Planta Med.* 37:1–8.
[4] Roitman, J.N. 1981. *Lancet* i;944.
[5] Taylor, A. and N.C. Taylor. 1965. *Proc, Soc. Exp. Biol, Med.* 114.

Tagetes patula L. **MARIGOLD, FRENCH**
[1] Maracutus, A.. *et. al.* 1978. *Lloydia* 41:181.

Tanacetum parthenium (L.) Schultz Bip. **FEVERFEW**
[1] Johnson, E.A., *et. al.* 1985. *British Medical Journal.* 291:569.
[2] Murphy, J., *et. al.* 1988. *Lancet.* 7–23:189–192.
[3] Heptinstall, S., *et. al.* 1985. *Lancet* i;1071.
[4] Johnson, E.A., *et. al.* 1985. *British Medical Journal.* 291, 569.

Taraxacum officinale Wiggers **DANDELION**
[1] Kroeber, L., 1950. *Pharmazie,* 5, 122–127.
[2] Racz-Kotilla, *et. al.* 1974. *Planta Med.* 26,212.

Thymus vulgaris L. **THYME**
[1] *Chem. Ab.* 1977. 86, 11760r.
[2] *Planta Med.* 1984. (4).
[3] *Chem. Ab.* 1969. 71,58264w.

Trigonella foenum-graecum L. **FENUGREEK**
[1] List, P.H., and L. Hormammer. *Hager's Handbuch der Pharmazeutischen* vol. 2–6. Berlin: Springer-Verlag.
[2] Beveer, B.O., and G.R. Zahand. 1979. *Quarterly Journ. Crude Drug Res.* 17:39.
[3] Arbo, M.S. and A.A. Al-Kafawi. 1969. *Planta Med.* 17:14.
[4] Setty, B.S., *et. al.* 1977. *Indian Journ. Exper. Biology* 15:231.

Tussilago farfara L. **COLTSFOOT**
[1] Hirono, I., *et. al.* 1976. *Gann* 67(1):125.
[2] Delaveau, P., *et. al. 1980 Planta Med.* 40–49.
[3] Kraus, C., *et. al.* 1985. *Planta Med.* 51(2):89.

Vaccinium myrtillus L. **BILBERRY**
[1] Bettini, V., *et. al.* 1985. *Fitoterapia* 56(1):3.

Valeriana officinalis L. **VALERIAN**
[1] Atal, C.K., and B.M. Kapur. 1982. *Cultivation and Utilization of Medicinal Plants.* Regional Research Lab., India. p. 27.
[2] Kreglstein, J. and D. Grusla. 1988. *Deut. Apoth Zeit.* 128:2071–76.
[3] Cionga, E. 1961. *Pharmazie,* 16:43.
[4] Leathwood, P. D., *et. al.* 1982. *Pharmacol. Biochem. Behav.* 17:65.
[5] Klich, R. 1975. *Medizinische Welt,* 26(25):1251–1254.
[6] Leung, A.Y. 1980 *Encyclopedia of Common Natural Ingredients Used in Food, Drugs and Cosmetics.* New York: Wiley-Interscience.
[7] Braun, R., *et. al.* 1982. *Deutsche Apoth. Ztg.* 122, 1109.

Verbena officinalis L. **VERVAIN**
[1] Gessner, Otto. 1974. *Diegilt und Pflanzen von Mittele Europa.*

Viburnum opulus L. **CRAMP BARK**
[1] Horhammer, L., *et. al.* 1966. *Botanical Magazine* (Tokyo) 79:510–525.

Vitex agnus-castus L. **CHASTE BERRY**
[1] Hahn, G., *et. al.* 1986. *Notabene Medici* 16:233–6, 297–301.
[2] Kayser, H.W. and S. Instanbulluoglu. 1954. *Hippokrates,* 25:717.
[3] Amann, W. 1977. *Selecta* XIX, 3688.
[4] Attelmann, H., *et. al.* 1972. *Geriatrie* 2:239.
[5] Kayser, H.W. and S. Istanbulluoglu. 1954. *Hippokrates,* 25:717.
[6] Amann, W. 1967. *Ther. d. Gegenw.* 106:124–126.

Zingiber officinale Roscoe. **GINGER**
[1] Thompson, E.H., *et. al.* 1973. *Journ. Food Science.* 38(4):652–655.
[2] Mowrey, D.B. and D.E. Clayson. 1982. *The Lancet.* 3–20:655–657.
[3] 1989. *Planta Med.* 55:105.
[4] Atal, C.K., *et. al. Journ. Ethnopharm.* 4(81):229–232.

INDEX OF COMMON AND BOTANICAL NAMES

Botanical—Common

A *Achillea millefolium* L.
Yarrow   Thousand-seal
Milfoil   Nose-bleed
Sanguinary
Acorus americanus L.
Calamus   Myrtle Flag
Sweet Flag   Flagroot
Agastache foeniculum (Pursh) O. Kuntze
[*A. anethiodora* Nutt. ex Britt.; *Lophanthus anisatus* (Nutt.) Benth.]
Anise Hyssop   Giant Hyssop
Agrimonia eupatoria L.
Agrimony   Harvest-lice
Cocklebur
Alchemilla vulgaris L.
Lady's Mantle
Allium sativum L. [*A. controversum* Schrad.]
Garlic
Allium schoenoprasum L.
Chive   Schnittlaugh
Cive
Aloe barbadensis Mill. [*A. perfoliata* L. var *vera* L.; *A. vera* (L.) Webb & Berth.]
Aloe Vera   Unguentine Cactus
Barbados Aloe
Aloysia triphylla (L'Hér.) Britt. [*A. citriodora* (Cav.) Ort.; *Lippia citriodora* (Ort.) HBK; *Verbena citriodora* Cav.; *V. triphylla* l'Hér.]
Lemon Verbena
Althaea officinalis L. [*A. kragujerancensis* Panc.; *A. taurinensis* DC. not C. A. Mey.]
Marshmallow   White Mallow
Anethum graveolens L. [*Peucedanum graveolens* (L.) C. B. Clarke.]
Dill
Angelica archangelica L. [*A. officinalis* Moench; *Archangelica officinalis* (Moench) Hoffm.]
Angelica   Archangel
Anthriscus cerefolium (L.) Hoffm.
Chervil   Salad
Aralia racemosa L.
Spikenard   Petty Morel
American Spikenard   Life-of-man
Arctium lappa L.
Burdock   Cuckold
Beggar's-buttons   Harlock
Clotbur
Armoracia rusticana P. Gaertn., B. Mey & Scherb.
Horseradish
Arnica montana L.
Arnica
Artemisia abrotanum L. [*A. procera* Willd.]
Southernwood   Old-man
Artemisia absinthium L.
Wormwood   Absinthe
Sagebrush
Artemisia dracunculus L. [*A. Redowski* Ledeb.]
Tarragon   Estragon
Artemisia vulgaris L.
Mugwort   Felon Herb
Asclepias tuberosa L.
Butterfly Weed   Tuberroot
Milkweed   Pleurisy Root
Silkweed   Chigger Flower

Atropa belladonna L.
Belladonna   Deadly Nightshade

B *Baptisia tinctoria* (L.) Venten.
False Indigo   Horsefly
Wild Indigo   Rattleweed
Borago officinalis L.
Borage   Cool-tankard
Talewort

C *Calendula officinalis* L.
Calendula   Marigold
Caltha palustris L. [*C. parnassifolia* Raf.]
Marsh marigold   Meadow-bright
Cowslip
Capsicum annuum L.
Cayenne
Carthamus tinctorius L.
Safflower   False Saffron
Carum carvi L.
Caraway
Caulophyllum thalictroides (L.) Michx.
Blue Cohosh   Papoose root
Centella asiatica
Gota Kola
Chrysanthemum balsamita L. [*C. majus* (Desf.) Asch.; *Tanacetum Balsamita* L.]
Costmary   Alecost
Chrysanthemum cinerariifolium (Trevir.) Vis. [*Pyrethrum cinerariifolium* Trevir.]
Pyrethrum   Dalmatia Pyrethrum
Cichorium intybus L.
Chicory   Witloof
Blue-sailors   Barbe-de-capuchin
Succory
Cimicifuga racemosa L.
Black Cohosh   Rattletop
Bugbane   Black Snakeroot
Citrus limon (L.) Burm.f.
Lemon
Cnicus benedictus L.
Blessed Thistle
Collinsonia canadensis L.
Stoneroot   Citronella
Coriandrum sativum L.
Coriander   Chinese Parsley
Crataegus laevigata (Poir.) DC.
Hawthorn
Crocus sativus L.
Saffron
Cuminum cyminum L. [*C. odorum* Salisb.]
Cumin
Cymbopogon citratus (DC. ex Nees) Stapf.
Lemon Grass   Oil Grass
Cypripedium calceolus L.
Lady's Slipper   Whippoorwill-shoe
Moccasin Flower   Nerveroot
Golden-slipper

D *Dianthus caryophyllus* L.
Clove Pink   Divine Flower
Digitalis purpurea L.
Foxglove

E *Echinacea purpurea* (L.) Moench [*Brauneria purpurea* (L.) Britt.; *Rudbeckia purpurea* L.]
Purple Coneflower   Echinacea
Eucalpytus globulus Labill.
Blue Gum
Eupatorium purpureum L.
Joe-Pye Weed   Boneset
Euphorbia lathyris [*Galarhoeus Lathyris* (L.) Haw.; *Tithymalus Lathyris* (L.) J. Hill]
Gopher Purge   Myrtle Spurge
Spurge   Mole Plant
Caper Spurge

F *Filipendula ulmaria* Mill.
Meadowsweet   Queen-of-the-meadow
Foeniculum vulgare Mill. [*F. officinale* All.]
Fennel

G *Galium odoratum* (L.) Scop. [*Asperula odorata* L.]
Woodruff   Bedstraw
Gaultheria procumbens L. [*G. repens* Raf.]
Wintergreen   Teaberry
Checkerberry
Gentiana lutea L.
Gentian
Ginkgo biloba L. [*Salisburia adiantifolia* Sm.]
Ginkgo   Maidenhair Tree
Glycyrrhiza glabra L.
Licorice   Sweetwood

H *Hamamaelis virginiana* L.
Witch Hazel
Hepatica americana
Liverwort
Humulus lupulus L.
Hops
Hydrangea arborescens L.
Hydrangea
Hydrastis canadensis L.
Orangeroot   Goldenseal
Yellow Puccoon
Hypericum perforatum L.
St.-John's-Wort
Hyssopus officinalis L. [*H. aristata* Godr.; *H. vulgaris* Bubani.]
Hyssop

I *Impatiens capensis* Meerb. not Thunb. [*I. biflora* Walt.]
Jewelweed   Snapweed
Balsam   Touch-me-not
Inula helenium L.
Elecampane
Iris × germanica L. [*I. violacea* Savi, not (Ker-Gawl.) Sweet, or Klatt.]
Orris   Fleur-de-lis
Flag
Isatis tinctoria L.
Woad   Asp-of-Jerusalem
Dyer's Woad

J *Jasminum officinale* L.
Jasmine   Jessamine

L *Laurus nobilis* L.
Bay   Laurel
Lavandula angustifolia Mill.
Lavender
Leonurus cardiaca L.
Motherwort
Levisticum officinale W. D. J. Koch
Lovage
Lobelia inflata L.
Lobelia   Indian Tobacco
Lonicera caprifolium L. [*L. verna* Hort. ex Lavall.]
Honeysuckle

M *Marrubium vulgare* L.
Horehound
Matricaria recutita L. [*M. chamomilla* of auth. not L.]
Chamomile   Matricary
Melissa officinalis L.
Lemon Balm   Bee Balm
Mentha × *piperita* L.: *M. aquatica* × *M. spicata.*
Peppermint
Mentha pulegium L.
Pennyroyal
Mentha spicata L. [*M. longifolia* of auth. not (L.) Huds.; *M. niliaca* of auth. not Juss. ex Jacq.; *M. viridis* L.]
Spearmint
Mitchella repens L.
Partridgeberry   Two-eyed Berry
Monarda didyma L. [*M. coccinea* Michx.]
Bergamot   Bee Balm
Horsemint   Oswego Tea

N *Nepeta cataria* L.
Catnip

O *Ocimum basilicum* L. [*O. bullatum* Lam.]
Basil
Oenothera biennis L. [*O. muricata* L.]
Evening Primrose   Sundrops
Origanum majorana L. [*Majorana hortensis* Moench]
Marjoram
Origanum vulgare L.
Oregano   Organy

P *Panax quinquefolius* L.
Ginseng
Passiflora incarnata L.
Passionflower   Apricot Vine
Maypop
Pelargonium graveolens L'Hér. ex Ait. [*P. terebinthinacum* Cav.]
Geranium
Petroselinum crispum (Mill.) Nyman ex A. W. Hill [*P. hortense* Hoffm.; *P. sativum* Hoffm.; *Carum petroselineum* (L.) Berth. & Hook.f.]
Parsley
Phytolacca americana L. [*P. decandra* L.]
Pokeweed   Pocan
Pokeberry   Garget
Scoke   Pigeon Berry
Pimpinella anisum L.
Anise

Plantago lanceolata L.
Plantain   Ripple-grass
Ribwort   Buckhorn
Ribgrass
Podophyllum peltatum L.
Mayapple   Raccoon Berry
Mandrake   Wild Jalap
Wild Lemon
Portulaca aleracea L.
Purslane   Moss Rose
Potentilla anserina var. sericea L.
Cinquefoil   Silverweed
Five-finger   Goose Grass
Poterium sanguisorba L. [*Sanguisorba minor* Scop.]
Burnet
Prunella vulgaris L. [*P. incisa* Link]
Self-heal   Heal-all
Pulmonaria officinalis L. [*P. maculata* F. Dietr.]
Lungwort

R *Rosa damascena* Mill.
Rose   Damask Rose
Brier
Rosmarinus officinalis L.
Rosemary
Rubia tinctoria L.
Madder
Rubus ursinus Cham. & Schlectend.
Blackberry   Pacific Dewberry
Bramble
Rumex scutatus L.
French Sorrel
Ruta graveolens L.
Rue   Herb-of-grace

S *Salvia officinalis* L.
Sage   Ramona
Salvia sclarea L.
Clary Sage   Ramona
Sambucus nigra L.
Elder   Elderberry
Sanguinaria canadensis L.
Bloodroot   Red Puccoon
Santolina chamaecyparissus L. [*S. incana* Lam.; *S. tomentosa* Pers.]
Santolina Gray   Lavender Cotton
Saponaria officinalis L.
Soapwort   Bouncing Bet
Sassafras albidum (Nutt.) Nees [*S. officinale* Ness & Ebermo.; *S. variifolium* (Salisb.) O. Kuntze]
Sassafras
Satureja hortensis L.
Summer Savory   Savory
Scutellaria laterifolia L.
Skullcap
Senecio Cineraria DC. [*Centauria maritima* 'Diamond'; *Cineraria maritima* L.]
Dusty Miller   Groundsel
Silybum marianum (L.) Gaertn. [*Carduus marianus* L.]
Milk Thistle   St. Mary's Thistle
Stachys byzantina C. Koch [*S. lanata* Jacq. not Crantz; *S. olympica* of auth. not Poir.]
Betony   Wooly Woundwort
Lamb's Ears

Stachys officinalis (L.) Trevisan [*S. betonica* Benth.; *Betonica officinalis* L.]
Wood Betony   Woundwort
Hedge Nettle
Symphytum officinale L.
Comfrey   Boneset
Healing Herb

T *Tagetes patula* L.
French Marigold
Tanacetum parthenium [*Chrysanthemum parthenium* (L.) Bernh.; *Matricaria capensis* Hort. not L.; *M. eximia* Hort.; *M. parthenoides* Hort.]
Feverfew   Golden-feather
Tanacetum vulgare L. [*Chrysanthemum vulgare* (L.) Bernh.]
Tansy   Golden-buttons
Taraxacum officinale Wiggers [*T. leontodon* Gueldenst.; *Leontodon taraxacum* L.]
Dandelion   Blowballs
Teucrium chamaedrys L.
Germander
Thalictrum aquilegifolium L.
Meadow Rue
Thymus vulgaris L.
Thyme
Tradescantia virginiana L.
Spiderwort   Widow's-tears
Trigonella foenum-graecum L.
Fenugreek
Trillium erectum L. [*T. flavum* Raf.]
Trillium   Stinking Benjamin
Wake-robin   Purple Trillium
Birthroot   Brown Beth
Tropaeolum majus L.
Nasturtium   Indian Cress
Bitter Indian
Tussilago farfara L.
Coltsfoot

U *Urtica dioica* L.
Nettle

V *Vaccinium myrtillus* L.
Bilberry   Whortleberry
Whinberry
Valeriana officinalis L. [*V. excelsa* Poir.]
Valerian
Verbascum thapsus L.
Mullein   Velvet Plant
Flannel Plant
Verbene officinalis L.
Vervain
Vetiveria zizanoides (L.) Nash
Vetiver   Khus-khus
Virburnum opulus L.
Cramp Bark   Guelder Rose
Arrowwood   Whitten Tree
Cranberry Bush
Viola odorata L.
Violet   English Violet
Sweet Violet
Vitex Agnus-castus L.
Chaste Tree   Sage Tree
Hemp Tree   Indian-spice
Monk's Pepper Tree   Wild Pepper

Z *Zingiber officinale* Roscoe.
Ginger

Common—Botanical

A Absinthe *Artemisia absinthium*
Agrimony *Agrimonia eupatoria*
Alecost *Chrysanthemum balsamita*
Aloe Vera *Aloe barbadensis*
American Spikenard *Aralia racemosa*
Angelica *Angelica archangelica*
Anise *Pimpinella anisum*
Anise Hyssop *Agastache foeniculum*
Apricot Vine *Passiflora incarnata*
Archangel *Angelica archangelica*
Arnica *Arnica montana*
Arrowwood *Viburnum opulus*
Asp-of-Jerusalem *Isatis tinctoria*

B Balsam *Impatiens capensis*
Barbados Aloe *Aloe barbadensis*
Barbe-de-capuchin *Cichorium intybus*
Basil *Ocimum basilicum*
Bay *Laurus nobilis*
Bedstraw *Galium odoratum*
Bee Balm *Monarda didyma*
Bee Balm *Melissa officinalis*
Beggar's-buttons *Arctium lappa*
Belladonna *Atropa belladonna*
Bergamot *Monarda didyma*
Betony *Stachys officinalis*
Bilberry *Vaccinium myrtillus*
Birthroot *Trillium erectum*
Bitter Indian *Tropaeolum majus*
Black Cohosh *Cimicifuga racemosa*
Black Snakeroot *Cimicifuga racemosa*
Blackberry *Rubus ursinus*
Blessed Thistle *Silybum marianum*
Bloodroot *Sanguinaria canadensis*
Blowballs *Taraxacum officinale*
Blue Cohosh *Caulophyllum thalictroides*
Blue Gum *Eucalyptus globulus*
Blue-sailors *Cichorium intybus*
Blueberry *Vaccinium myrtillus*
Boneset *Symphytum officinale*
Boneset *Eupatorium purpureum*
Borage *Borago officinalis*
Bouncing Bet *Saponaria officinalis*
Bramble *Rubus ursinus*
Brier *Rosa damascena*
Brown Beth *Trillium erectum*
Buckhorn *Plantago lanceolata*
Bugbane *Cimicifuga racemosa*
Burdock *Arctium lappa*
Burnet *Poterium sanguisorba*
Butterfly Weed *Asclepias tuberosa*

C Calamint *Satureja hortensis*
Calamus *Acorus americanus*
Calendula *Calendula officinalis*
Caper Spurge *Euphorbia lathyris*
Caraway *Carum carvi*
Catnip *Nepeta cataria*
Cayenne *Capsicum annuum*
Chamomile *Matricaria recutita*
Chaste Tree *Vitex Agnus-castus*
Checkerberry *Gaultheria procumbens*
Chervil *Anthriscus cerefolium*
Chicory *Cichorium intybus*
Chigger Flower *Asclepias tuberosa*

Chinese Parsley *Coriandrum sativum*
Chive *Allium schoenoprasum*
Cinquefoil *Potentilla anserina var. sericea*
Citronella *Collinsonia canadensis*
Cive *Allium schoenoprasum*
Clary Sage *Salvia sclarea*
Clotbur *Arctium lappa*
Clove Pink *Dianthus caryophyllus*
Cocklebur *Agrimonia eupatoria*
Coltsfoot *Tussilago farfara*
Comfrey *Symphytum officinale*
Cool-tankard *Borago officinalis*
Coriander *Coriandrum sativum*
Costmary *Chrysanthemum balsamita*
Cowslip *Caltha palustris*
Cramp Bark *Viburnum opulus*
Cranberry Bush *Viburnum opulus*
Cuckold *Arctium lappa*
Cumin *Cuminum cyminum*

D Dalmatia Pyrethrum *Chrysanthemum cinerariifolium*
Damask rose *Rosa damascena*
Dandelion *Taraxacum officinale*
Deadly Nightshade *Atropa belladonna*
Dill *Anethum graveolens*
Divine Flower *Dianthus caryophyllus*
Dusty Miller *Senecio Cineraria*
Dyer's Woad *Isatis tinctoria*

E Echinacea *Echinacea purpurea*
Elder *Sambucus nigra*
Elderberry *Sambucus nigra*
Elecampane *Inula helenium*
English Violet *Viola odorata*
Estragon *Artemisia dracunculus*
Evening Primrose *Oenothera biennis*

F False Indigo *Baptisia tinctoria*
False Saffron *Carthamus tinctorius*
Felon Herb *Artemisia vulgaris*
Fennel *Foeniculum vulgare*
Fenugreek *Trigonella foenum-graecum*
Feverfew *Tanacetum parthenium*
Five-finger *Potentilla anserina var. sericea*
Flag *Iris × germanica*
Flagroot *Acorus americanus*
Flannel Plant *Verbascum thapsus*
Fleur-de-lis *Iris × germanica*
Foxglove *Digitalis purpurea*
French Marigold *Tagetes patula*

G Garget *Phytolacca americana*
Garlic *Allium sativum*
Gentian *Gentiana lutea*
Geranium *Pelargonium graveolens*
Germander *Teucrium chamaedrys*
Giant Hyssop *Agastache foeniculum*
Ginger *Zingiber officinale*
Ginkgo *Ginkgo biloba*
Ginseng *Panax quinquefolius*
Golden-buttons *Tanacetum vulgare*
Golden-feather *Tanacetum parthenium*
Golden-slipper *Cypripedium calceolus*
Goldenseal *Hydrastis canadensis*

Goose Grass *Potentilla anserina var. sericea*
Gopher Purge *Euphorbia lathyris*
Gota Kola *Centella asiatica*
Goundsel *Senecio Cineraria*
Guelder Rose *Viburnum opulus*

H Harlock *Arctium lappa*
Harvest-lice *Agrimonia eupatoria*
Hawthorn *Crataegus laevigata*
Heal-all *Prunella vulgaris*
Healing Herb *Symphytum officinale*
Hedge Nettle *Stachys officinalis*
Hemp Tree *Vitex Agnus-castus*
Herb-of-grace *Ruta graveolens*
Honeysuckle *Lonicera caprifolium*
Hops *Humulus lupulus*
Horehound *Marrubium vulgare*
Horsefly *Baptisia tinctoria*
Horsemint *Monarda didyma*
Horseradish *Armoracia rusticana*
Hydrangea *Hydrangea arborescens*
Hyssop *Hyssopus officinalis*

I Indian Tobacco *Lobelia inflata*
Indian Cress *Tropaeolum majus*
Indian-spice *Vitex Agnus-castus*

J Jasmine *Jasminum officinale*
Jessamine *Jasminum officinale*
Jewelweed *Impatiens capensis*
Joe-Pye Weed *Eupatorium purpureum*

K Khus-khus *Vetiveria zizanoides*

L Lady's Slipper *Cypripedium calceolus*
Lady's Mantle *Alchemilla vulgaris*
Lamb's Ears *Stachys byzantina*
Laurel *Laurus nobilis*
Lavender *Lavandula angustifolia*
Lavender Cotton *Santolina chamaecyparissus*
Lemon Grass *Cymbopogon citratus*
Lemon Balm *Melissa officinalis*
Lemon *Citrus limon*
Lemon Verbena *Aloysia triphylla*
Licorice *Glycyrrhiza glabra*
Life-of-man *Aralia racemosa*
Lobelia *Lobelia inflata*
Lovage *Levisticum officinale*
Lungwort *Pulmonaria officinalis*

M Madder *Rubia tinctoria*
Maidenhair Tree *Ginkgo biloba*
Mandrake *Podophyllum peltatum*
Marigold *Calendula officinalis*
Marjoram *Origanum majorana*
Marsh marigold *Caltha palustris*
Marshmallow *Althaea officinalis*
Matricary *Matricaria recutita*
Mayapple *Podophyllum peltatum*
Maypop *Passiflora incarnata*
Meadow Rue *Thalictrum aquilegifolium*
Meadow-bright *Caltha palustris*
Meadowsweet *Filipendula ulmaria*
Milfoil *Achillea millefolium*

Milk Thistle *Silybum marianum*
Milkweed *Asclepias tuberosa*
Moccasin Flower *Cypripedium calceolus*
Mole Plant *Euphorbia lathyris*
Monk's Pepper Tree *Vitex Agnus-castus*
Moss Rose *Portulaca aleracea*
Motherwort *Leonurus cardiaca*
Mugwort *Artemisia vulgaris*
Mullein *Verbascum thapsus*
Myrtle Spurge *Euphorbia lathyris*
Myrtle Flag *Acorus americanus*

N Nasturtium *Tropaeolum majus*
Nerveroot *Cypripedium calceolus*
Nettle *Urtica dioica*
Nose-bleed *Achillea millefolium*

O Oil Grass *Cymbopogon citratus*
Old-man *Artemisia abrotanum*
Orangeroot *Hydrastis canadensis*
Oregano *Origanum vulgare*
Organy *Origanum vulgare*
Orris *Iris × germanica*
Oswego Tea *Monarda didyma*

P Pacific Dewberry *Rubus ursinus*
Papoose root *Caulophyllum thalictroides*
Parsley *Petroselinum crispum*
Partridgeberry *Mitchella repens*
Passionflower *Passiflora incarnata*
Pennyroyal *Mentha pulegium*
Peppermint *Mentha × piperita*
Petty Morel *Aralia racemosa*
Pigeon Berry *Phytolacca americana*
Plantain *Plantago lanceolata*
Pleurisy Root *Asclepias tuberosa*
Pocan *Phytolacca americana*
Pokeberry *Phytolacca americana*
Pokeweed *Phytolacca americana*
Purple Trillium *Trillium erectum*
Purple Coneflower *Echinacea purpurea*
Purslane *Portulaca aleracea*
Pyrethrum *Chrysanthemum cinerariifolium*

Q Queen-of-the meadow *Filipendula ulmaria*

R Raccoon Berry *Podophyllum peltatum*
Ramona *Salvia sclarea*
Ramona *Salvia officinalis*
Rattletop *Cimicifuga racemosa*
Rattleweed *Baptisia tinctoria*
Red Puccoon *Sanguinaria canadensis*
Ribgrass *Plantago lanceolata*
Ribwort *Plantago lanceolata*
Ripple-grass *Plantago lanceolata*
Rose *Rosa damascena*
Rosemary *Rosmarinus officinalis*
Rue *Ruta graveolens*

S Safflower *Carthamus tinctorius*
Saffron *Crocus sativus*
Sage *Salvia officinalis*
Sage Tree *Vitex Agnus-castus*
Sagebrush *Artemisia absinthium*
Salad *Anthriscus cerefolium*
Sanguinary *Achillea millefolium*
Santolina Gray *Santolina chamaecyparissus*
Sassafras *Sassafras albidum*
Savory *Satureja hortensis*
Schnittlaugh *Allium schoenoprasum*
Scoke *Phytolacca americana*
Self-heal *Prunella vulgaris*
Silkweed *Asclepias tuberosa*
Silverweed *Potentilla anserina var. sericea*
Skullcap *Scutellaria laterifolia*
Snapweed *Impatiens capensis*
Soapwort *Saponaria officinalis*
Southernwood *Artemisia abrotanum*
Spearmint *Mentha spicata*
Spiderwort *Tradescantia virginiana*
Spikenard *Aralia racemosa*
Spurge *Euphorbia lathyris*
St. Mary's Thistle *Silybum marianum*
St. John's Wort *Hypericum perforatum*
Stinking Benjamin *Trillium erectum*
Stoneroot *Collinsonia canadensis*
Succory *Cichorium intybus*
Summer Savory *Satureja hortensis*
Sundrops *Oenothera biennis*
Sweet Flag *Acorus americanus*

Sweet Violet *Viola odorata*
Sweetwood *Glycyrrhiza glabra*

T Talewort *Borago officinalis*
Tansy *Tanacetum vulgare*
Tarragon *Artemisia dracunculus*
Teaberry *Gaultheria procumbens*
Thousand-seal *Thymus vulgaris*
Touch-me-not *Impatiens capensis*
Trillium *Trillium erectum*
Tuberroot *Asclepias tuberosa*
Two-eyed Berry *Mitchella repens*

U Unguentine Cactus *Aloe barbadensis*

V Valerian *Valeriana officinalis*
Velvet Plant *Verbascum thapsus*
Verrain *Verbena officinalis*
Vetiver *Vetiveria zizanoides*
Violet *Viola odorata*

W Wake-robin *Trillium erectum*
Whinberry *Vaccinium myrtillus*
Whippoorwill-shoe *Cypripedium calceolus*
White Mallow *Althaea officinalis*
Whitten Tree *Viburnum opulus*
Whortleberry *Vaccinium myrtillus*
Widow's-tears *Tradescantia virginiana*
Wild Indigo *Baptisia tinctoria*
Wild Jalap *Podophyllum peltatum*
Wild Lemon *Podophyllum peltatum*
Wild Pepper *Vitex Agnus-castus*
Wintergreen *Gaultheria procumbens*
Witch Hazel *Hamamaelis virginiana*
Witloof *Cichorium intybus*
Woad *Isatis tinctoria*
Wood Betony *Stachys byzantina*
Woodruff *Galium odoratum*
Woolly Woundwort *Stachys byzantina*
Wormwood *Artemisia absinthium*
Woundwort *Stachys officinalis*

Y Yarrow *Achillea millefolium*
Yellow Puccoon *Hydrastis canadensis*